Freedom of Speech in the Western World

Freedom of Speech in the Western World

Comparison and Critique

Anthony Gray

LEXINGTON BOOKS
Lanham • Boulder • New York • London

Published by Lexington Books
An imprint of The Rowman & Littlefield Publishing Group, Inc.
4501 Forbes Boulevard, Suite 200, Lanham, Maryland 20706
www.rowman.com

6 Tinworth Street, London SE11 5AL

British Library Cataloguing in Publication Information Available

Library of Congress Cataloging-in-Publication Data

ISBN 9781498581981 (cloth)
ISBN 9781498581998 (electronic)

Contents

Acknowledgments

Thank you to Lexington for their commitment to academic scholarship and for providing me with one contract, and then two, towards my writing on free speech. I thank my University, the University of Southern Queensland, for granting me sabbatical leave so that I could devote significant time to this project. I would like to acknowledge the enormous contribution of the drafters of the United States *Bill of Rights*, justices of the Supreme Court of that country, and scholarship emanating from that country in particular. We owe a debt of gratitude for the intellectual leadership that these individuals have provided to the world, in the free speech space and more broadly. I have greatly benefited from this outstanding scholarship. Good scholarship is of course everywhere, but I am consistently impressed with the quality of American scholarship in academic journals and books, and with the sophistication of that nation's jurisprudence. Thanks to Professor Pauline Collins for her friendship and support over a long period of time. And thanks to my mother, Madison, Lockie, and Tom for always being there.

Introduction

A comparison of the way in which freedom of speech is protected in a range of jurisdictions is a mammoth task. It is such because of the very large volume of cases in which freedom of speech has been litigated. It is complicated by the different constitutional and human rights structures pursuant to which these cases have been decided, and the different culture and backgrounds which to some extent have led to particular outcomes. While for the most part, the Western jurisdictions chosen have a shared legal tradition, making comparison somewhat easier, this is mitigated by the different paths they have chosen to protect fundamental human rights, and the different time periods over which this occurred.

It was considered essential to understand the depth of the right to free speech. Thus Chapter 1 traces the right to early democracies. The clash between the will of an individual to speak their mind, and the will of those in power to try to suppress dissenting or critical views, is evidently as old as democracy itself. I trace the slow movement towards recognition of freedom of speech in England, particularly relevant in terms of subsequent development of the law in all of the jurisdictions studied, given they share this common law tradition. The chapter then discusses the various theories said to support freedom of speech. It is considered to be very important to understand these theories, in case they explain existing case law in a particular jurisdiction, or they help to decide a difficult case. There has been an impressive range of theories offered, though there is frustration that the cases often do not follow one particular theory, and that no theory devised to date can accurately or adequately explain the case decisions to date, or provide the elusive guidepost for the future. As will be seen, some jurisdictions specifically adopt these theories in determining how they approach the question of whether an infringement on free speech is valid.

I believe that before any meaningful comparison of legal principle among and between jurisdictions can occur, there must be a reasonable level of understanding of the existing precedent in each of the jurisdictions chosen. Prior knowledge of the law of any of the jurisdictions studied cannot be assumed. Thus, Chapters 2–5 are devoted to a description of the state of the case law in each of the chosen jurisdictions, the United States, Australia, Canada and Europe, discussing both United Kingdom and European Court decisions. A critique is offered with respect to the jurisprudence in each jurisdiction. They are appropriate comparator jurisdictions given their common law basis (with the partial exception of "Europe"), and their shared legal history and traditions. They share a basis in common culture, though as will be seen differences in culture may explain the current different state of the law of free speech in each jurisdiction studied. Though this takes up a significant portion of the book, the breadth of the factual circumstances in which these types of arguments are made necessitates a significant discussion of the case law.

In Chapter 6 there is a comparison of the similarities and differences that have been observed across the case law. This chapter includes a discussion of the cultural and historical differences between the jurisdictions that might help to explain some of the differences in approach. Specifically, there is a distinction between the use of proportionality in some jurisdictions and a category-based approach in others. The merits of each, the reasons why each jurisdiction have chosen each method, and an assessment of the likelihood of convergence is made.

There are a range of topics within freedom of speech that are thought to merit specific treatment on their own. They include regulation of so-called hate speech, speech by public servants, free speech within universities, and the challenges posed by technology. Originally they were to be included in this volume. However, the sheer breadth and depth of material has made two books inevitable. These specific issues will be the subject of a subsequent book *Freedom of Speech in Practice: Controversial Applications of Law and Theory*. Obviously, the books are designed to be read together, the first more descriptive, the second more critical and argumentative.

The most important things I have taken from my research to date, and on which I hope the book will provide stimulus for the work of others, includes the very long timeframe over which attempts by those in power to suppress speech have occurred, the philosophical importance of freedom of speech, and the way in which different histories and cultures of different jurisdictions have led to differences in approach and outcome. While it is believed that, in very broad terms, the differences between the United States on the one hand, and the other jurisdictions on the other, mean that neither will likely adopt the approach of the other, it is believed that each jurisdiction studied can learn from the approach and practice of the other jurisdictions studied. This, after all, is the main point of a comparative analysis, to understand the ways in which we are similar, why we are different, and what we can learn from one another. I hope the book and its companion will make a contribution to this venture.

Chapter One

History of the Freedom of Speech

SOME ANCIENT HISTORY

Arguments regarding the balance between the right of an individual to freedom of speech, and the right of a government to control information or curtail criticism or arguably dangerous speech or agitation, have been going on for millennia. In classical Greek times, Socrates was put to death for allegedly corrupting the minds of the young, and heresy. He was seen as a threat to established order. In this way, he has become a martyr for the cause of freedom of speech and its central importance in a "democracy."

While it is tempting to trace discussion of freedom of speech today back to the commencement of democratic governance in Greece, as scholars have, at least two points should be borne in mind when doing so. Firstly, one must overcome the tendency to see ancient debates through modern eyes. Specifically, while discussion of principles such as freedom of speech is in current debates referred to as an individual human right, designed to assist in an individual's self-actualization, development, or happiness, it would be a mistake to consider Greek practice through that lens.[1] Further, democracy as it was practiced in ancient Greece was of a direct kind, where individuals actually participated in the deliberations and made the decision, rather than of the more indirect kind of representative government with which we are now very familiar. These important differences must be borne in mind when any resort is had to historical Greek materials to better understand or articulate the metes and bounds of freedom of speech today.

So the early form of Greek democracy was characterized by the *demos* (the people) as the government. Individual citizens (unless excluded due to various deemed moral vices, the fact they were women, or were slaves) would turn up to the meeting place, and debate what the laws should be by which that society should be governed. This was a society that valued egalitarianism, or *isonomia*. In this light, it is not surprising that it would emphasize that any of the decision makers that turned up to the meeting would have the opportunity to express their views (*isegoria*). No-one was more entitled than another to speak. No topic was off-limits, although it should be acknowledged that ostracism was practiced for up to ten years of a person whose ideas were adjudged to be dangerous, and under the principle of *graphe paranomon*, a person could be indicted for making "illegal proposals."[2] As originally conceived, freedom of speech was not designed as a panacea to the evils of tyranny, or to limit the power of government. It was gifted to members of that government, in the form of the people. The Greek word for this was *parrhesia*, which some scholars translate as "free speech," but which others translate as "frank speech." It was the ability of a person to honestly express their views, without fear of reprisal.

Socrates lauded what Saxonhouse called "democratic amnesia," namely that the essence of democracy involved a society forgetting, and not being shackled by, what had happened in the past. This was important, because Greece's past had involved aristocracy and hierarchy. Socrates would emphasize the egalitarian nature of democracy, where hierarchy was unimportant, and each person's ability to contribute to governance the equal of others. Free speech (*parrhesia*) was essential to the kind of democratic government he described. It would allow society at any given time to decide on what its laws, procedures, and policies should be, rather than just apply inherited laws from a prior time.

While Plato strongly connected Greek democracy with freedom of speech, he also advocated censorship. He espoused the state having a role in censorship: "the first thing will be to establish a censorship of the writers of fiction and . . . reject the bad." He rejected publication of material that created fear of death; he disfavored humor. He was no fan of the arts, criticizing the showing of vulnerability by actors. He sought to limit the kinds of music to which individuals would have access. While he generally frowned upon lying, he created an exception for rulers. He sought to ensure that the young would be compliant and temperate, and be controlled in their sexual behaviors. He frowned upon publication of negative material about the Gods. This system was necessary, in the view of Plato, to achieve a good functional society.[3]

Further evidence of how free speech was lauded in this period is provided in the Aristotle work *Constitution of Athens*. Aristotle includes within this work a parable of 6th century BC ruler Peisistratus. Peisistratus was touring the countryside, and happened to meet a farmer. The farmer was digging rocks. The ruler, through his servant, asked the farmer what he was growing. The farmer, unaware that he was in the presence of Peisistratus himself, lamented that the ruler took 10 percent of the proceeds of his labors. Aristotle records that Peisistratus was pleased with the man's candor and free speech, and absolved him of an obligation to pay taxes. Aristotle uses the example to demonstrate the importance that Greek society traditionally placed on freedom of speech. Links between freedom of speech and truth were also emphasized.[4]

Scholars ponder how it was that a society which apparently prided itself on freedom of speech would execute a leading scholar precisely because of the things that he had been saying. Saxonhouse essentially finds that Socrates went "too far"; his ideas of democratic amnesia and admonition to question everything, and to encourage others to do the same, were considered dangerous by current decision makers. They were contrary to the polity's need for *aidos*, or hierarchy and structure in decision making.[5]

Cramer documents developments in this regard in the Roman Empire.[6] He speaks of a time during the reign of Julius Caesar when both official reports of senate proceedings were produced (*acta senatus*), as well as a *populi acts diurna*, which was effectively an early newspaper for the public, involving discussion, including critique, of the subject matter of such proceedings. It is important not to misinterpret such "freedom."[7] When Augustus took power following Caesar's death, the material included in the *populi acts diurna* became subject to government control.

Cramer records that initially in his reign Augustus largely respected freedom of speech, for instance, permitting the reading of wills in public, although they may have contained material critical of the government. However, his regime began to notice those who publicly criticized the government. Initially they would be subject to relatively mild sanctions, such as fines or exile. In what is believed to be the year 12 BC Augustus ordered that particular books be burned. These books might contain material critical of the government. Augustus, pushed on by his advisers, began to regulate and deal with unwelcome speech even more directly. His regime began to enforce an old Twelve Table law prohibiting defamation. It also began to enforce an old law prohibiting violated majesty. This law would find later parallels in what we would know as sedition and/or treason. Professors who presented two sides of an official Augustus policy were questioned. Material that was deemed to be treasonous and/or seditious would be burned. Later it would become a crime to possess writings deemed to be treasonous or seditious. Augustus also criminalized astrologists or other seers from prophesying the future.

When Tiberius took over after the death of Augustus, proceedings for "literary treason" increased, and the consequences for a breach of the law made more severe. A poet, Clutorius, was executed after he wrote an ill-advised poem mocking the grave sickness of an apparent heir to the reins of government, and lauding a political opponent. He was sentenced to the death penalty after being convicted of treason.

FREEDOM OF SPEECH IN ENGLAND

There were three main ways in England in which laws impacted upon freedom of speech: the crime of treason, seditious libels, and prior restraint laws. There were other ways, including the *Scandalum Magmatum* (1275 and later) dealing with the spreading of "fake news" in relation to the king.[8] The number of prosecutions under this legislation had petered out by the 16th century.[9]

The ecclesiastical courts were a further source of restrictions on free speech, through the ill-defined offense of heresy in relation to religious speech, which I will not dwell upon in detail. However, Anabaptists were burned during the reign of Elizabeth I, with the last reported burning for heresy in 1612.[10] Blasphemy was also dangerous.[11] Publications deemed to be obscene were also considered harshly in the ecclesiastical courts. This continued well after the end of the ecclesiastical courts, featuring in the successful prosecution of Wilkes in 1765 for his "Essay on Woman" for breach of a common law offense.

From early times, criticism of courts, decisions of courts, and judges could be punished by contempt. In a 1344 decision, De Northampton was found guilty of the offense of "scandalizing the court" for writing a letter which was critical of members of the King's Bench.[12]

On treason, the *Statute of Treasons* was enacted in 1352. The monarch clarified that the crime mainly involved three types of wrongdoing—levying war against the monarch, "adhering" to the king's enemies, and compassing or imagining the death of the king.[13] Speech by itself could not amount to treason at this time, because it was thought that the offense required an overt act. The reigns of Richard III and Henry VIII featured relaxations of this overt act requirement. Henry VIII created a type of treason offense where the defendant had slandered or maliciously published by express writing or words criticism of the monarch, or words that undermined the king's dignity, or which threatened the quiet enjoyment of his crown. Generally, the law was used with restraint. One court candidly admitted that the purpose of the law was not to punish subjects; rather, to regulate their behavior, by having the threat of prosecution hanging over them.[14] However, there were exceptions. One victim of this law was Twyn, who had apparently printed a book which maintained that the king should be accountable to his subjects. He was convicted and executed for his troubles.[15] Similarly Anderson was successfully prosecuted for treason for publishing a book entitled *Remarks on the Present Confederacy, and Late Revolution in England and a French Conquest Neither Desirable Nor Practicable*. His book was deemed to be a call in aid of the Jacobite rebellion, and he was executed. He did not have access to legal representation in court.

Treason proceedings often involved matters of religion. This was perhaps inevitable following the reformation, and the establishment of the monarch as the head of the established church. Religion and politics mixed. Thus, religious speech could be argued to be treasonous and/or seditious.[16] In the 1570s it became treasonable to call the monarch a heretic, or to publish a papal bull, or to "reconcile the Queen's subjects to the See of Rome."[17] In 1580 it became a crime to celebrate and/or hear mass. Jesuits and seminary priests were prosecuted for treason. James I insisted that anyone who refused to recognize him as the monarch or that the Pope had no power to depose him was guilty of treason.

In the late 18th century actions were taken against bodies agitating for universal suffrage and an annual parliament.[18]

However, prosecution of anti-government sentiment on the basis of the crime of treason remained difficult for the government. It was necessary for them to obtain evidence that the material had in fact been published, and amounted to treason. This could take time. Further, they needed to obtain a warrant to search premises which were thought to obtain questionable material, and these were sometimes not easily obtained. Most anti-government expressed sentiment was relatively mild in nature, and would probably not amount to treason.[19] The *Treason Trials Act* of 1696 accorded those accused with treason some due process protections, including a requirement that they be given a copy of the indictment, given the right to legal representation, the right to produce witnesses in their defense, and the need for the prosecution to have at least two witnesses to support the allegation. The accused was now given the names of potential jurors shortly before the trial. Obviously, this made prosecution for treason more difficult.

It is sometimes said that the Court of Star Chamber created the offense of seditious libel in the 1606 decision in *De Libellis Famosis*.[20] The defendants admitted publicly ridiculing senior members of the clergy. In convicting the defendants, the Star Chamber spoke more expansively about the general perils of public criticism of government and public persons, on the basis that it would inevitably invite disrespect. The criticism could be indirectly linked with criticism of the monarch, who had appointed the public official.[21] Truth was no defense.[22] The offense required that the material be seditious,[23] that the author had a seditious intent in writing the material (which could be implied), and that the content have been published. Levy notes the inherent subjectivity involved in the concept of "sedition," leaving it wide open to abuse.[24] It was typically used to oppress dissent from the government of the day: "everyone was a libeler who outraged the sentiments of the dominant party."[25] In 1629 a merchant was convicted of sedition for criticizing government policies towards businesspeople.[26]

It is said that the offense of seditious libel was created because the Star Chamber, with its use of secret, inquisitorial proceedings, was considered best suited for such a crime, and the crime of treason was charged in the common law courts.[27] The common law courts would insist upon use of a jury, and the indictment procedure. Members of the Star Chamber often belonged to the King's Council and served at the pleasure of the king. More generally, judicial independence and something approaching tenure would not be secured until after the events of the Glorious Revolution in 1688.[28]

Yet the dangers of punishing seditious libels were also presciently observed. Francis Bacon in his *History of the Reign of Henry VII* reflects on the punishment of Stanley for uttering a seditious libel, writing that his punishment

> Was a matter of great terror among all the King's servants and subjects; insomuch as no man almost thought himself secure, and men durst scarce commune or talk one with another, but there was a special diffidence everywhere, which nevertheless made the King rather more absolute than more safe. For bleeding inwards and shut vapors strangle soonest, and oppress most. Hereupon presently came forth swarms and vollies of libels (which are the gusts of liberty of speech restrained and the females of sedition) containing bitter invectives and slanders against the King and some of the council.[29]

The abolition of the Star Chamber led to a sharp increase in publications, with one estimate that in the year 1640, 22 pamphlets were published, while in 1641, 1,966 were published.[30] The hearing of allegations of seditious libels was transferred to the common law courts. Their existence would also survive the lapsing of the prior restraint laws, finally in 1694. This was explained by Blackstone:

> Where blasphemous, immoral, treasonable, schismatical, seditious or scandalous libels are punished by the English law . . . the liberty of the press, properly understood, is by no means infringed or violated . . . (it) consists in laying no previous restraint upon publications, and not in freedom from censure for criminal matter when published.[31]

Regarding the "prior restraint" of printed works, it is said that the Catholic Church in England in the early 15th century asserted a right to license books.[32]

It should be borne in mind that ideas about government were very different in those days. There was a view, not surprisingly taken by some monarchs, including most especially James I, that the monarch was not subject to law, and governed by divine right.[33] This may be reflected in the comment of Lord Coke in the *Magdalen College Case* that the "King cannot do a wrong,"[34] though the comment is clearly ambiguous. It is reasonably possible to interpret it to mean that the monarch must comply with the laws that apply to everyone else; alternatively, it can mean that the law should not be interpreted in such a way as to find that the monarch has committed a legal wrong.[35] General Crown immunity from suit has continued since that time, at least in modified form.[36] Further in 1607's *Case of Prohibitions* the court found that an individual claimant could have no remedy against a monarch.[37] It was left to statute to eventually reform this position.[38] Thus, in an era where the monarch claimed to govern by divine right and considered themselves to be above the law, it is not surprising that public statements against the monarch or their government would not be tolerated. As Shientag observes, in an era where "the King can do no wrong," "for a subject to suggest otherwise was a serious criminal offense."[39]

The story of freedom of speech in England, restrictions on it and its protection, assumed more prominence after 1476 when William Caxton introduced the concept of printing in that jurisdiction. As Bogen describes, at that time, the number of printers was small, and the material they printed relatively uncontroversial. In the next century the number of printers would grow exponentially. The Crown argued that its prerogative included control over printing. Initially, the monarch would order copyright in a work to be printed, which in some way reflected the monarch's permission to publish the material. However, this seemed to morph into a censorship regime.[40] After the reformation, the monarch moved that books be submitted to religious bodies before they could be published. Regulation became increasingly restrictive, and in the time of Elizabeth I, the Star Chamber expressly limited the number of printers that could continue in business, and required that every publication had to be approved by either the Archbishop of Canterbury or the Archbishop of London before it could be published.[41] This licensing system continued until the abolition of the Star Chamber in 1641.

However, censorship did not end there. In 1643 a Board of Licensors was established, and control over publications shifted from the monarch to parliamentary control. There it remained despite re-establishment of the monarchy in 1660; the *Printing Act* of 1662 continued with a licensing system. The licensor had a broad and vague power to censor publications. Not surprisingly, the power was exercised in an arbitrary, unprincipled manner.[42] As a result, monopolies were established and entrenched, and intellectual property was in some cases destroyed. One example involved Carr, who published a book entitled *The Weekly Packet of Advice from Rome* without a license. He was convicted.[43] This system in turn petered out in 1694, when the legislation was permitted to lapse. The number of printers had grown significantly, and there was a significant demand for anti-government literature.

The demise of this "prior restraint" policy, requiring that all intended publications be submitted for approval to government censors prior to publication, did not mean that the country adopted freedom of speech, at least as we would understand it today. Sir William Blackstone alluded to this position:

> The liberty of the press is indeed essential to the nature of a free state: but this consists in laying no previous restraints upon publications, and not in freedom from censure for criminal matter when published. Every free man has an undoubted right to lay what sentiments he pleases before the public; to forbid this is to destroy the freedom of the press; but if he publishes what is improper, mischievous or illegal, he must take the consequences of his own temerity . . . to punish . . . any dangerous or offensive writings which (are) . . . of a pernicious tendency is necessary for the preservation of peace and good order. . . .[44]

It should be noted that this position of Blackstone, that freedom of speech simply meant a lack of prior restraint, and was consistent with other forms of government restriction and control of speech, has been the subject of significant recent criticism. This is on the basis that Blackstone did not accurately capture the law of the times, which was more defensive of free speech according to these critics than Blackstone's position would suggest.[45]

At this time, significant restrictions on freedom of speech continued to exist in the law. The government reverted to other measures to restrain unwelcome speech, including pre-trial imprisonment and imposition of fines upon printers and publishers. They would sometimes use the *Scandalum Magnatum* statutes. However, they primarily re-engaged with the idea of prosecutions for seditious libel.[46]

The pivotal role of parliament in the development of freedom of speech principles should be acknowledged.[47] As parliament became more responsible for drafting laws for the consideration of the monarch, its members saw the benefit in having debate and discussion about proposals. It must be admitted that Parliament was a very different body than how we conceive of it today. It was not truly a "representative" chamber, with large swathes of the population lacking the franchise, and the "rotten borough" system effectively marginalizing the importance of the votes of many. However, despite these limitations, the role of parliament as a forum for public debate and dissent became established. Prosecutions for breach of parliamentary privilege grew. Inevitably, tensions built between the parliament and the monarch over speech in parliament. Coke, for instance, argued that free speech in parliament was a customary right; James I argued it was a privilege that existed only at his discretion. Dispute arose as to whether it was parliament or the monarch that had the power to punish for breach of parliamentary privilege or other breach of rules, part of a much bigger conflict between parliament and the monarch in the 16th and 17th centuries.[48]

History records a request by then Speaker Thomas More to the monarch in 1523 requesting that members of parliament have freedom of speech in their debates.[49] Maitland reports that in 1541, for the first time the Speaker announced that freedom of speech was one of the ancient and undoubted privileges which the Commons claimed of the king, and subsequent Speakers would also announce this, albeit couched in submissive terms, requesting the monarch's forbearance and consent. The practice was that the monarch would generally accept the request. As a result of the movement of this practice into orthodoxy, historians conclude that freedom of speech was "a recognized right" with the "status of an ancient liberty" by the mid-16th century.[50]

Elizabeth I would make some attempts to limit speech in the Commons, particular around issues of the royal succession, and around religious matters. She had mixed success. With the accession of James I to the throne, relationships between the monarch and the parliament deteriorated further. He committed four members of the parliament to the Tower. James I told the parliament that all of their powers and privileges were derived from him, and subject to alteration by him. He banned a book which apparently criticized parliament, the common law and the monarch's prerogative.

Relations between the monarch and the Commons continued to deteriorate. James I apparently had the view that parliament could discuss only what he wished to discuss, and was there to enable him to spend money as he wished. He believed that discussion of some matters, including church or state matters, the waging of war and other crown prerogatives, and complaints about the monarch, were beyond the wit of parliament.

In 1621 members of the House of Commons declared that by "ancient and undoubted birthright as English subjects" they could speak about any subject, and had freedom of speech. Crew had argued that if their freedom of speech was limited to what the monarch permitted them to discuss, this would be contrary to Magna Carta. Coke expressed a rudimentary view of representative government, that parliamentarians spoke of behalf of the people they represented. Rich argued forcefully in parliament that freedom of speech of parliamentarians must be maintained.[51] These remarks were recorded in official proceedings, before being shown to the monarch. Maitland notes that James I tore out the page of the parliamentary journal which contained this declaration, and proceeded to dissolve parliament once again.[52] He imprisoned several politicians he regarded as disloyal, including Coke, Pym, and Hakewill.[53] Civil war in England was nigh. Freedom of speech for parliamentarians was seen in some ways as a proxy for freedom of speech for the individual in society.[54]

The Glorious Revolution would finally establish the supremacy of the parliament over the monarch. Not surprisingly then, the *Bill of Rights 1689* (Eng) around that time would become the first written British constitutional document to enshrine the importance of freedom of speech, albeit limited to the parliamentary sphere.[55] However, the debate about limitations on speech that took place outside parliament was far from over.

The law of seditious libel had been shackled by limitations in its earlier iterations, limiting its usefulness to prosecutors. In particular, requirements that the material be seditious, that it shall have been written with seditious intent, and that it shall have been published. It bore some analogies to what to current eyes would seem to be the law of defamation, being based on criticism of individual government or public officers. However, as other forms of censorship waned, new attention was paid to these limitations, and judges began to relax them. So, for instance, in the case of *R v Bear*[56] the court convicted the accused of seditious libel for poems he had written and collected. There was no evidence the accused had published the allegedly libelous poems, or intended to do so. In the past, both the fact of publication and intention would need to be established in order to successfully prosecute for seditious libel. However, in *R v Bear* Holt CJ decided that neither publication nor intention was necessary, and the hapless poet Bear was convicted of seditious libel. Holt CJ briefly explained his position on the basis of the

> principle of the preservation of all government, and safety of all civil society: and if it should be no crime to write libels, the government and the magistrates must be exposed to the malice and discontents of disaffected persons.[57]

General warrants were issued, permitting authorities to conduct wide searches of an individual and their premises, with little evidence of justified suspicion needed. The search and seizure process itself was used by the government to threaten, bully and harass those whom the authorities suspected of libelous publication.

Holt CJ continued to expand the reach of the seditious libel principle by applying it not merely to statements about individuals, but general criticism of the government.[58] This occurred, for example, in a prosecution against Tutchin for publishing in his newspaper *The Observators* criticism of the then government. Finding Tutchin guilty of seditious libel for such publication, Holt CJ explained that:

> But this is a very strange doctrine, to say, it is not a libel, reflecting on the government . . . if men should not be called to account for possessing the people with an ill opinion of the government, no government can subsist, for it is very necessary for every government, that the people should have a good opinion of it. And nothing can be worse to any government than to endeavor to procure animosities as to the management of it. This has been always looked upon a s crime, and no government can be safe unless it be punished.[59]

Further, judges moved to assert their power over trials for seditious libels, by determining that they were entitled to decide whether or not the material in dispute was in fact libelous, the jury's role being limited to determining whether or not publication had occurred. In an era where the judiciary was clearly not independent of government, this had the effect of increasing the likelihood that a prosecution for seditious libel would be successful.

We see in these cases the significant expansion of the crime of seditious libel beyond its initial similarity to a defamation action, and towards a more general crime of speaking against the government.[60] Some courts took the word "libel" to be derived from the Latin "libelous," meaning little book, which emphasized the publication, rather than any kind of defamation.[61] It is perhaps not surprising in an era of turbulence for British government, including the threatened Jacobite rebellion, that judges, lacking the kind of independence from the government of the day that characterizes our current model of government, might be wanting to "shore up" the government by cracking down on published dissent.

Uncertainty persisted regarding the full extent of the offense of sedition. Specifically, it was not entirely clear whether it was necessary that the material of which complaint was being made had to be of a nature such as to incite those subject to it to unlawful action, particularly against the government, in order to secure some change, or whether mere criticism of the government was sufficient in order to commit the offense. Some cases proceeded on the belief that it was sufficient in order to commit sedition that the accused publish something intending to bring into hatred or contempt the government, including its members, the monarch and the courts.[62] Other cases seemed to proceed on the basis it would be necessary to show the offending words had incited or would be likely to incite violence.[63] Stephen suggested five different examples of what could amount to the offense of sedition.[64] There is evidence that Stephen tended to believe that sedition required proof of violence.[65]

At the request of Queen Anne in 1712, Parliament enacted a tax on all newspapers and ads. The United States Supreme Court noted that the prime objective of this tax was to suppress criticism of the government.[66]

Even libertarian voices at this time indicated significant limits on freedom of speech. Influenced as they were by a command theory of law, where a strong sovereign was necessary to curb the otherwise potentially violent excesses of individuals, even libertarians at the time agreed that limits on freedom of speech, such as sedition laws, were important. Examples here include Spinoza, the Levellers, John Lilburne, Roger Williams, and John Milton, and even to some extent John Locke. While the latter two in particular are lauded for their devotion to free speech, Milton's views and to some extent Locke's reflect a strong anti-Catholicism. He did not support the right of a person of the Catholic faith to express "Popish" views.[67] That was not the only exception to freedom of speech, in Milton's view.[68] Levy notes that Milton acted as one of Cromwell's censors.[69] Similarly Locke expressed anti-Catholic views, his idea of religious toleration being limited.[70] All agreed with the need for laws against sedition.[71] Other thinkers limited freedom of speech to the educated or the divine.[72]

Hamburger notes the extent to which politics played a part in prosecutions for seditious libel. He concludes that while conservative governments were minded to strongly enforce seditious libel laws, at least some Whigs were in favor of a broader protection of freedom of speech. He concludes that:

> In 1710 the idea of vigorous criticism of authority was as disturbing to most Tories as it may have been congenial to a small number of radical Whigs. Among Tories, Grub Street's pamphlet and newspaper onslaught elicited deep ideological as well as practical concern. Committed to a vision of hierarchical society established by divine authority and therefore unimprovable, unchanging and uniform, Tory ideologues in the excited atmosphere of 1710 perceived no alternative to the received religious and political establishment except complete moral and social disintegration. In church and state, according to extreme Tories, the slightest dissent posed a danger, and printed criticism of the government was no exception. In their second administration under Anne, as in their first, the Tories prosecuted printers and publishers for seditious libel, relying, where need arose, upon the judges to interpret the law in a way that would not be prejudicial to the requirements of the government.[73]

Hamburger notes that, by 1720, the populace seemed less anxious about the instability of their system of government, so popular support for prosecutions for seditious libels waned:

> By 1720 many men began to realize that ministers and factions, with all their petty squabbles and scurrilous printed attacks on one another, would come and go, but the English Establishment, a Protestant, parliamentary monarchy, would be secure in spite of all the liberties taken by the press. Accordingly although the Whig government continued to prosecute printers for seditious libel after 1714, it did so without expecting to bring the press to complete submission.[74]

Courts continued to punish speech about their activities that was deemed to be contemptuous. For example, in *R v Almon* the court emphatically denounced such speech on the basis it was an impeachment of the (monarch's) wisdom and goodness in the choice of his judges, and excites in the minds of the people a general dissatisfaction with all judicial determinations, and indisposes their minds to obey them; whenever men's allegiances to the laws is so fundamentally shaken, it is the most fatal and most dangerous obstruction of justice.[75]

In this early to mid-18th century period documents known as "Cato's Letters" became critical. These letters drew from the philosophical structure of Locke, and started advocating the importance of freedom of speech,[76] and connecting it with requirements of democracy. Specifically, the letters argued that it was essential in a democracy that individuals should have the right to publicly criticize government policies and government officials. They referred to the purpose of government.[77]

The letters were careful not to advocate unbridled freedom of speech, however:

> A libel is not the less a libel for being true. This may seem a contradiction, but it is neither one in law, or in common sense: there are some truths not fit to be told; where, for example, the discovery of a small fault may do great mischief; or where the discovery of a great fault can do no good, there ought to be no discovery at all; and to make faults where there are none, is still worse. But this doctrine only holds true as to private and personal failings, and it is quite otherwise when the crimes of men come to affect the public . . . the exposing of public wickedness, as it is a duty which every man owes to truth and his country, can never be a libel in the nature of things.[78]

Trenchard and Gordon spoke of the fact that a free people

> will be sh(o)wing that they are so, by their freedom of speech . . . it is the interest, and ought to be the ambition, of all honest magistrates, to have their deeds openly examined, and publicly scanned . . . freedom of speech is the great bulwark of liberty; they prosper and die together.[79]

Trenchard and Gordon stated that something like libels were a "necessary evil arising out of a much greater good."[80] They went further than previous libertarians, in attacking the existing law of sedition.

These slowly evolving attitudes towards free speech were a symptom of a change in how people saw their leaders in government, and the relation between the people and government. One favored more of a command style view of government, where the sovereign was all powerful, and subjects unquestioningly obeyed the sovereign. At this time ruling was precarious, and the structure of government unsteady.[81] Thomas Hobbes's *Leviathan* is an example of such a view of government, favoring an absolutist view of sovereign power.[82] Free speech was not strongly valued in such a system.[83] The other favored a more equal relationship, viewing the parliament as merely representatives of the people, and thus accountable to them.[84] This view appears not long after Leviathan in the late 17th century, for instance, in the writings of John Locke.[85] He rejected an absolutist view of power[86] just at the time of the Glorious Revolution when the supremacy of parliament over the monarch was established. In that type of light, criticism of government action became more acceptable.

Stephen notes this:

> Two different views may be taken of the relation between rulers and their subjects. If the ruler is regarded as the superior of the subject, as being by the nature of his position presumably wise and good, the rightful ruler and guide

> of the whole population, it must necessarily follow that it is wrong to censure him openly, that even if he is mistaken, his mistakes should be pointed out with the utmost respect, and that whether mistaken or not no censure should be cast upon him likely or designed to diminish his authority. If on the other hand the ruler is regarded as the agent and servant, and the subject of the wise and good master who is obliged to delegate his power to the so-called ruler because being a multitude he cannot use it himself, it is obvious that this sentiment must be reversed. Every member of the public who censures the ruler for the time being exercises in his own person the right which belongs to the whole of which he forms a part . . . to those who hold this view fully and carry it out to all its consequences there can be no such offence as sedition.[87]

Though public sentiment had clearly changed in favor of free speech, not for the first time the judges were slow to pick up on this change in community sentiment. Here, Lord Mansfield, a luminary in the field of commercial law, comes in for special criticism, on the basis that his achievements in reforming commercial law were not matched in reforming the law of libel, for instance, to provide more protection for freedom of speech.[88] In the famous case against John Wilkes, Lord Mansfield passionately defended the independence of the judiciary from public demonstrations and media pressure in favor of the defendant Wilkes.[89] Wilkes was arrested for making anti-government statements which he published in his newspaper the *North Briton*.

Yet others are critical of Lord Mansfield's position in *Wilkes*:

> Lord Mansfield made a great mistake. He failed entirely to distinguish between what he called 'public clamor' and a deep-seated public opinion that believed in the right to discuss governmental affairs and in good faith to find fault with public men. He failed to discern the birth of a new era. Unlike the critical scrutiny, the prescience and the liberal viewpoint with which he approached many problems of private law Lord Mansfield failed to appreciate that conditions had changed and that his countrymen had become politically minded.[90]

The treatment of Wilkes, who was jailed for nearly two years, and of others was pivotal in rousing public sentiment against how the law was being applied against those raising dissenting views and voices.[91] Walker writes of growing political sophistication of Englishmen throughout the second half of the 18th century (causing) a growing sense of discontent with the heavy-handed and transparently partisan use of prosecutions for seditious libel.[92]

He says that English people of the 18th century had grown to have strong belief in aspects of English constitutionalism, including freedom of speech and thought.[93]

Eventually the law was reformed to more closely align with changed community attitudes and values around freedom of speech. This reform came from parliament in the form of Fox's *Libel Act* of 1792. This Act re-balanced the respective roles of judge and jury in seditious libel cases. Earlier it had been pointed out that judges had arrogated for themselves the responsibility for determining whether or not impugned material was in fact libelous. This was particularly dangerous, coupled with the fact judges were not completely independent of the other arms of government until after 1688.[94] The 1792 Act established the power of juries to determine for itself all matters in dispute, including whether or not material was in fact libelous.[95] On the other hand, members of the existing political establishment remained anxious about threats, real or perceived, to the established system of government. Their anxieties had been heightened by the events of the French Revolution in 1789.

The Fox legislation had little impact in the prosecution of Thomas Paine in late 1792 for publishing *The Rights of Man*. He was convicted of seditious libel.[96] Palmer was convicted in 1793 for daring to advocate universal suffrage. Judges at his trial asked whether Palmer's comments amounted to a "total subversion of the constitution." He was sentenced to transportation to Australia for seven years. An emboldened government then legislated the *Seditious Meetings Act* of 1795. In 1811, John Drakard was convicted for publishing an article condemning flogging within military ranks. At his trial it was suggested by the judge that Napoleon was trying to influence the affairs of other nations through means of publications to the people. He suggested that Drakard's article might have the effect of reducing the number of men who would otherwise enlist in the British army, or encourage desertion. He denied that a person had the right to "make the people dissatisfied with the government . . . this is not to be permitted to any man—it is unconstitutional and seditious."[97]

Stephen says that prosecutions for seditious libel had "practically ceased" by 1832.[98] A further law reform occurred in 1843 with the passage of *Lord Campbell's Act*, finally making truth a defense to a libel action,[99] at least in connection with a public benefit argument. By 1868 the English Courts had adopted a very different position regarding importance of freedom of speech:

> Our law of libel has, in many respects, only gradually developed itself into anything like a satisfactory and settled form. The full liberty of public writers to comment on the conduct and motives of public men has only in very recent times been recognized. Comments on government, on ministers and officers of state, on members of both houses of parliament, on judges and other public functionaries, are now made every day, which half a century ago would have been the subject of actions or ex officio informations, and would have brought down fine and imprisonment on publishers and authors. Yet who can doubt that the public are gainers by the change, and that though injustice may often be done, and though public men may often have to smart under the keen sense

> of wrong inflicted by hostile criticism, the nation profits by public opinion being thus freely brought to bear on the discharge of public duties?[100]

Eventually the United Kingdom courts came to realize the importance of freedom of speech. Lord Keith for the House of Lords stated that it was "of the highest public importance that a democratically elected governmental body, or indeed any governmental body, should be open to uninhibited public criticism."[101] While in the past individuals had been prosecuted for criticizing judges, a much different view is evident in the early to mid-20th century. Lord Atkin noted in *Ambard v Attorney General for Trinidad and Tobago* that:

> The path of criticism is a public way; the wrong-headed are permitted to err therein: provided that members of the public abstain from imputing improper motives to those taking part in the administration of justice, and are genuinely exercising a right of criticism, and are not acting in malice or attempting to impair the administration of justice, they are immune. Justice is not a cloistered virtue: she must be allowed to suffer the scrutiny and respectful, even though outspoken, comments of ordinary men.[102]

On the other hand, what some might view as over-tenderness and concern for the message conveyed, rather than the right to convey it, appears in the judgment of Lord Scarman in the *Gay News* case, involving allegations of blasphemy. Lord Scarman there stated that it is not blasphemous to speak or publish opinions hostile to the Christian religion, or to deny the existence of God, if the publication is couched in decent and temperate language. The test to be applied is the manner in which the doctrines are advocated, and not as to the substance of the doctrines themselves.[103]

Section 1 of the *Racial and Religious Hatred Act 2006* (UK) amended the *Public Order Act 1986* (UK) so that s29B of the latter now prohibits the use of threatening words or behavior, or displays threatening written material intending to stir up racial hatred. Section 26 of the *Equality Act 2010* (UK) prohibits a person from engaging in unwanted conduct in relation to a protected characteristic[104] which has the purpose or effect of violating the victim's dignity, or creating an intimidating, hostile, degrading, humiliating, or offensive environment.

The English history is valuable in showing us the serious deficiencies in the common law dealing with freedom of speech. Eventually the system of licensing was abandoned. However, freedom of speech was not protected by the *Magna Carta* (1215) or *Petition of Right* (1628). Its protection in the *Bill of Rights* (Eng) (1689) was piecemeal. That Act did not have the status of a guarantee against future legislative incursion as the same-named document would have in the United States. The belief of the English in notions of parliamentary sovereignty ensured that. It shows that the tendency of those in power to seek to retain it by suppressing dissent or those who might be thought to threaten it is a venerable one. The fight for freedom of speech was a long one, with some martyrs paying with their lives or with lengthy jail terms, simply for expressing unwelcome views. While United Kingdom judges could resort to techniques of statutory interpretation to limit the impact of a law which apparently abrogated fundamental common law rights like freedom of speech, this technique for preserving fundamental freedoms obviously has its limits. Substantive protection of freedom of speech would have to await the implementation in the United Kingdom of the *European Convention on Human Rights* at the very end of the 20th century.

CLASSIC FREE SPEECH THEORISTS

John Locke was highly influential in the late 17th and 18th centuries in terms of a social contract view of government. As indicated above, this conception of the relation between a government and its people stood in marked contrast to the type of ruler-ruled relationship presaged earlier in the 17th century by Hobbes. It is likely that Locke's writing was heavily influenced by the Glorious Revolution of 1688. The idea of government radically changed, from a system based on divine rule by monarchy, to a parliamentary system voted upon by some of the people. A theoretical framework was necessary to explain this system. Locke's social contract theory, involving a starting point of individuals endowed with natural freedoms and rights, and agreeing to cede a limited number for the mutual benefit of those individuals, gained prominence. Social contract theory can be used to buttress an argument about free speech, on the basis that the contract requires a free flow of information so that citizens can give "informed" consent to the government.[105]

Locke lauded the "liberty and opportunities of a fair inquiry" and said that the freest part of individuals should be their understandings. He condemned the narrowness of thought of those who were "forced" to be of the religion of their country, to accept opinions without relevant background, or the ability to question them.[106]

Locke also advocated strong religious freedom in his *Letter Concerning Toleration*, a landmark document at the time, given ongoing overt discrimination at the time against religious minorities. He argued that government had no business interfering with a person's religious views, or their expression of same. He connected this with notions of truth, though in a different manner to how Mill would use it.[107] In this he was similar to Milton, who connected freedom of speech with truth in the religious context. For Locke, it was because religious truth *was* known that religious freedom was essential. Though his views were in the religious sphere, and he was wedded to a strict separation between that sphere and the public sphere, what he said about freedom of thought and speech in the religious context had obvious implications for freedom of speech at a more general level of abstraction. He likely influenced the confluence of freedom of speech and religious freedom protection in the *First Amendment* of the *United States Constitution.*

In modern times, the philosophical case for freedom of speech is most commonly sourced to the writings of John Stuart Mill in his classic *On Liberty*. He first notes that no defense is today needed in favor of the liberty of the press, given its role in preventing corrupt or tyrannical government. He similarly rails against attempts by governments to control what individuals should believe, or opinions they should be permitted to hear.[108] He says that even if the people agreed that their government should suppress a particular view, and the government purported to do so, it would be invalid: "the power itself is illegitimate."[109] This is because:

> The peculiar evil of silencing the expression of an opinion is that it is robbing the human race, posterity as well as the existing generation, those who dissent from the opinion, still more than those who hold it. If the opinion is right, they are deprived of the opportunity of exchanging error for truth; if wrong, they lose, what is almost as great a benefit, the clearer perception and livelier impression of truth, produced by its collision with error . . . we can never be sure that the opinion we are endeavoring to stifle is a false opinion, and if we were sure, stifling it would be an evil still.[110]

In other words, freedom of speech is pivotal in establishing "truth," or at least getting closer to "truth."[111] In this respect, he took a similar position to Milton.[112] It was a typical sentiment of the era.[113] Mill does not demonstrate how freedom of speech increases the likelihood that the "truth" will be determined; he merely asserts that freedom of speech will achieve this, or is likely to do so. Others have challenged this.[114] Mill's thesis has subsequently been adapted and applied by courts on the basis of the "marketplace of ideas" thesis, which will be discussed further later in the chapter.

Mill states that any attempt to stifle the expression of the views of another is an assumption of infallibility.[115] He points out that throughout history societies have held opinions which were subsequently proven to be false.

Mill also lauds the role of free speech in developing human beings. He asks why it is that, on the whole, human beings act rationally and hold rational opinions. He says that humans learn from their mistakes. This requires not just experience, but discussion, which interprets experience. He asks how a person acquires a status such that their judgment is deserving of confidence. He says that such a person

> Has kept (their) mind open to criticism of (their) opinions and conduct. Because it has been (their) practice to listen to all that could be said against (them); to profit by as much of it as was just, and expound to (themselves), and

> upon occasion to others, the fallacy of what was fallacious . . . the only way in which a human being can make some approach to knowing the whole of a subject is by hearing what can be said about it by persons of every variety of opinion, and studying all modes in which it can be looked at by every character of mind. No wise (person) ever acquired (their) wisdom in any mode but this; nor is it in the nature of human intellect to become wise in any other manner. The steady habit of correcting and completing (their) own opinion by collating it with those of others, so far from causing doubt and hesitation in carrying it into practice, is the only stable foundation for a just reliance on it.[116]

Referring to past scholars who apparently accepted limits to the right of some individuals in a society to speak, perhaps, for instance, Milton or Locke, Mill said it was "strange" that those who see the merit in freedom of speech agree to limits on speech at the "extremes," not realizing that the principle of free speech applies, or should apply, equally to those at the center of current political thought or orthodoxy, and those at the margins.[117] He espouses the evils of censorship:

> It is not the minds of heretics that are deteriorated most by the ban placed on all inquiry which does not end in the orthodox conclusions. The greatest harm done is to those who are not heretics, and whose whole mental development is cramped, and their reason cowed, by the fear of heresy. Who can compute what the world loses in the multitude of promising intellects combined with timid characters, who dare not follow out any bold, vigorous, independent train of thought, lest it should land them in something which would admit of being considered irreligious or immoral?[118]

Mill also refutes any suggestion that freedom of speech be permitted on the condition that it is exercised in a "temperate" manner. He refers to the practical impossibility of policing these, and the tendency of those whose arguments have been defeated to complain that the other party has expressed their views in an intemperate manner.[119]

As valuable as Mill's conception of freedom of speech was, his theories, perhaps counterintuitively, did not translate to him supporting broad participation of people in government. One might have thought that his lauding of the values of free speech in terms of self-actualization might also have called for broad participation of the people in processes of government, so that a particular society might advance through the freedom of speech it enshrines, just as an individual might so advance. However, Mill would have limited the franchise to the educated and the skilled.[120]

Mill also espoused the well-known harm principle, that the scope of government regulation of an individual's behavior was largely based on the question of harm. A government was only justified in regulating the actions of an individual where they caused "harm" to another individual.[121] He did not specifically reconcile what could be competing notions—that of the benefit to an individual, and thus by implication, broader society, in having a free flow of information in terms of their development, with the fact that the dissemination of some of that information might harm another. This might be, for example, because the individual to which the information relates might wish it to remain private, or the relevant speech involved is "hate speech." Specifically, it may be legitimately wondered what Mill's position might be on laws that prohibit whatever might be considered to be "hate speech." Would Mill disagree with such laws, because they inhibit the free flow of information that is critical to self-development and broader societal progress? Or would he permit them, on the basis that "hate speech" may harm the target?[122] It is not entirely clear to me, from a reading of Mill's work, what the answer would be for Mill. It is suggested that given his devotion to freedom of speech, he would likely have favored it, even in relation to what some might call "hate speech." Some say that the harm principle justifies greater restrictions in action than mere speech, on the basis that actions are more likely to harm others than speech would.[123]

One of the problems with the harm principle is the extent to which it might be utilized to justify interference with freedom of speech. As Helle points out, anything a person does potentially has some effect on others which might be labeled by some as "harm."[124] Bogen states that the harm principle was utilized by drafters of the *Alien and Sedition Act 1798* (US) to justify criminalizing criticism of members of the government:

> The drafters of the (Act) adopted one logically justifiable method of interpreting the guarantee of freedom of speech and of the press. The Federalists read freedom of speech to be a category distinct from abuses of speech. They then confined the category of freedom to those situations where a majority of those who participated in the adoption of the *First Amendment* would have agreed it was applicable. Substantively, under their views freedom encompasses truthful, respectful criticism of government measures. The guarantee would also apply to expression that could be demonstrated to cause no harm of any kind to any person. Procedurally, freedom would be inconsistent with a universal system of prior censorship or the determination of the criminality of utterances other than by a jury. Intemperate language, personal remarks that harm others, discussion of sexual matters, incorrect statements attacking the government, and advocacy of any harmful activity could all be condemned as abuses of speech and punished if within the purview of matters confided to government.[125]

Wolfson is similarly unimpressed and wary of any limitation of free speech based on notions of harm. Conceding that racist and sexist insults do cause harm to the targets, he concludes that "if harm to the listener is the measure by which we regulate speech, there will be nothing left of the *First Amendment*."[126] Moon criticizes the willingness of the Canadian Supreme

Court to abandon protection of freedom of expression as soon as the "victim" of such speech can point to any harm.[127]

Mill's liberal political philosophy envisages a relatively small role for the state. It is necessary to accord individuals maximum freedom to allow them to grow and develop their potential as individuals. Disciples of the Mill approach have elaborated upon this idea at length, typically emphasizing the benefits to individuals from freedom of speech, including such concepts as "self-fulfilment"[128] or "individual self-realization."[129] These are not precise connections. So, for instance, the "truth" concept may be narrower than "self-actualization." For example, it is difficult for the truth principle to justify the protection of pornography as part of freedom of speech; on the other hand, some may argue that access to such material assists in terms of their individual development.[130] These self-development concepts have clear links with Aristotle's view of individual happiness based on fulfilment of personal potential. Freedom of speech is a necessary tool in achieving such potential. It is what we would in modern days refer to as a "Socratic" method of learning, applied to the broad scale of society, as opposed to an individual. Similar sentiments might also be expressed through references to individual autonomy.[131]

For these scholars, democracy is not an end in itself, but lauded for what it does for individuals living within it. Through its participatory aspects, it encourages development of the individual.[132] Obviously, this theory provides protection to a very broad range of speech and communication. Individuals require access to a free flow of information on basically anything in which they are interested, to assist them in making life decisions, and to improve themselves as individuals.

It should also be acknowledged that there is broad disagreement about what a democratic form of government means. As with most concepts, broad and narrow conceptions are possible. For example, what Craig calls a "top-down" view of democracy might view it as only requiring the population to express a view at election time. In contrast, a more republican (or participatory) view of democracy might require more frequent involvement of the people in governance. It would tend to support a broader self-fulfilment view of freedom of speech, as opposed to a functionalist approach which focuses mainly or exclusively on what happens at election time.[133]

Others have suggested three different models of representative democracy: (a) protective theory, emphasizing the accountability of the politicians to the people, thus requiring free and fair elections, a universal franchise, and freedom of speech and association; (b) participatory theory, maximizing the extent to which individuals participate in political processes; and (c) elite theory, limiting democracy to the choice of decision makers.[134] Clearly options (a) and (b) provide stronger and broader protection of freedom of speech than a view of representative democracy like (c).

A natural progeny of Mill's free speech rationale is the so-called theory of marketplace of ideas espoused by Holmes on the United States Supreme Court. Classically Holmes in *Abrams v United States*[135] stated that:

> When men have realized that time has upset many fighting faiths, they may come to believe even more than they believe the very foundations of their own conduct that the ultimate good desired is better reached by free trade in ideas—that the best test of truth is the power of the thought to get itself accepted in the competition of the market and that truth is the only ground upon which their wishes safely can be carried out. That at any rate is the theory of our Constitution.[136]

It is not surprising that a country built on capitalism, and with an affection for principles of laissez-faire economics evident in the famous *Lochner* case of a decade prior,[137] would seek to link freedom of speech with an economic concept. However, events would subsequently show the folly of a totally market dependent model in economics. Most interestingly for current purposes, economic theory came to accept the notion of "market failure," and it became accepted that there was a role for government regulation of the market, to deal with cases of "market failure," however conceived. In the realm of economics, market failure might look like sub-optimal economic outcomes, lack of competition, high barriers to entry, incomplete information, irrational participants, etc. Economists also developed the idea of "transaction costs" that might otherwise inhibit the efficient production and exchange of resources. These are costs associated with parties to a transaction acquiring the kind of knowledge that the market model might assume to exist.[138] Holmes did not extend his market analogy to instances of market failure.[139]

The interesting question for current purposes is, if we persist with the economic analogy in the realm of freedom of speech,[140] what "market failure" might look like in the freedom of speech space, in the sense that actual or perceived or threatened market failure justifies regulation of what would otherwise be free reign.[141] For instance, would speech that threatened the continued existence of a government be the kind of market failure which would justify a curb on free speech?[142] Would speech that was offensive so represent? What about obscenity? What about factually false statements? Would it apply when there was a monopoly or oligopoly regarding access to speech outlets? What if some voices were magnified over others? Does it occur in times of emergency, because the market does not have time to work properly? Does this represent market failure, permitting and justifying the legislature in censoring speech during some temporary emergency? Is this why the judges recognized a clear and present danger exception, justifying censorship of speech in cases of immediate danger, because in such cases there was not time for the "market" to work as it usually did, and (presumably) for the erroneous speech to be rebutted.[143]

The market failure principle may be of some use, but in some ways it merely shifts the goal posts onto another field about which there are strong competing arguments, rather than provide a solution to the arguments about the boundaries of free speech.[144] And of course there may be transaction costs associated with digesting information provided by others, or in assembling information we would like to present to the world.

Another challenge in viewing free speech through an economic lens is the question of externalities. Economists generally like to allocate costs to the person or organization that created it. In that way, behavior can be priced accurately. However, this is difficult to apply in a free speech setting. For example, a person may say nasty things about a public figure. The person saying the nasty things does not "wear" all of the costs of doing so; at least some of the "cost" will be imposed on the person about whom things are said. Similarly with hate speech, it is likely that some of the "cost" of that speech will be borne on those at whom the hate is directed.[145] At this point we have exceeded that ability of conventional economic theory to explain or articulate the proper boundaries of free speech. No-one suggests that we can impose all of the externalities on the speaker within a free speech society, yet economics would require that we did.

On the other side, there is an argument that with speech, the positive externalities create issues. Much of the benefit of free speech is not captured by the individual who exercises it, but accrues to listeners. While the speakers gains some benefit in terms of expressing themselves, more of the benefit is reposed in the listeners. Thus, positive externalities are generated. An orthodox economic view would suggest that, as such, the speaker will have less incentive to create such speech, because they do not capture all of the benefits. Thus, it may be that such speech should be "subsidized" by the state in order to ensure it occurs at optimal levels. Such a subsidy could take the form of constitutional protection of free speech. While this clearly exists, it is doubtful that the founding fathers had this in mind in drafting the *First Amendment*, and it is extremely rare to find this sort of argument in any actual free speech decision.

The other advantage of this notion of free speech is that it permits change in society. It acknowledges that democracies are dynamic, rather than static, in nature.[146] Scholars have pointed out that a broad freedom of speech can bring out dissatisfaction with the status quo, and create momentum for change. These scholars point out that societies are constantly changing, in terms of their needs, wishes, thoughts, and values. The legal system needs to accommodate this restlessness. If it strongly protects freedom of speech, it can foster the expression of dissatisfaction with the status quo. In some cases this will lead to legal change, for instance, this has occurred in terms of the freeing up of laws around morality over the years. In other cases, it will not lead to change. However, even those who unsuccessfully sought change will at least have had the satisfaction of having their grievances heard. They may be more likely to accept a society that has considered, but rejected, their views, as opposed to a society that has actively suppressed their expression.[147] It is to be hoped that the angst that such a person feels about an issue may be assuaged by the fact they have been able to have their views heard, reducing the likelihood they will resort to more anti-social, even violent, means to have their views heard, or take out their anger in an inappropriate way.

Notions of "truth" are challenging to apply to some types of speech. It is difficult to say that arts and literature should be protected on this basis. It is difficult to say that pornography should be protected on this basis. Further, it is difficult in the realm of opinion—so, for instance, a person who advocates the overthrow of capitalism, and the adoption of socialism, because this would create a better society. Can this speech be defended on the basis of "truth"? Is there any truth to the question of whether capitalism or socialism is "better," or is it essentially just a matter of opinion? The truth rationale thus can struggle to justify and explain all aspects of free speech doctrine.

Of course, there are also those who doubt the power of free speech to advance us towards "truth." They argue it has not been shown that more speech will inevitably inch a society towards discovery of truth, that a society might equally well land upon a false position as a result of speech, than it might arrive at truth.[148] There is also much conjecture about what truth is, and whether things can ever be completely known.[149]

Many lament the power of the powerful to get themselves heard in a free market world, and the effective silencing of the dissent.[150] They might argue that one of the reasons the so-called marketplace of ideas theory is deficient is that the market is not a level playing field. This is the idea that the rich and powerful have the "megaphones" in this market, such that it is a skewed and cornered market, rather than one providing a fair opportunity for all to have their voices heard. This is part of a broader critique of liberal philosophy more generally, that it preserves the status quo, protects those with existing power, and does nothing to assist the marginalized in society.[151] On the other hand, others suggest that the explosive growth of the Internet has naturally levelled the playing field.[152] It is no longer the case that significant resources are needed in order to have voices heard. All one needs is access to a computer or mobile phone, and anyone can amplify their voice and be heard by many, in an increasingly connected global world. This might dampen criticisms of the notion of the marketplace of ideas, and the claim it favors big players.

A more nuanced version of the truth rationale is suggested by Schauer, who lauds free speech because of his skepticism of the motives of those seeking to regulate or censor speech, and the ability of censors to objectively determine which speech should be permitted and which speech should be banned. They may be corrupt; they may be incompetent; they may act for reasons other than the public interest. Thus free speech is not by any means perfect, but it is better than a regime under which a totalitarian government is able to regulate what can be said and what cannot be said.[153] This may be seen as a negative conception of freedom of speech.[154]

This type of articulation of the rationale for and limits on freedom of speech is typically referred to as the *deontological* approach, given its basis in rights.

There was an intellectual move away from a rights-based perspective of freedom of speech. This may be explained by acceptance of utilitarian ideas about the happiness of the greatest number, over the rights of the few. Holmes was clearly a leading utilitarian who favored the right of the government to protect the needs of the many over individual rights. He eschewed natural rights theory in favor of legal positivism.[155] This philosophy was a rejection of what was seen as the excesses of individual rights theory espoused by the Supreme Court in *Lochner v New York*.[156] Pound from the legal academy was another who favored this view of societal interests overriding individual interests.[157] This philosophical shift led others to re-think the foundations of free speech, seeking to move it away from an individual rights perspective, in favor of an acknowledgment of its communal benefit. Such an idea appealed to Meiklejohn.

Alexander Meiklejohn had a narrower conception of freedom of speech. Writing of the United States *First Amendment* in the mid-20th century, he saw it mainly as a practical consequence of the system of self-government for which that country's *Constitution* provides. Its raison d'etre and boundaries are explained by the system of self-government:

> When (individuals) govern themselves it is they—and no-one else—who must pass judgment upon unwisdom and unfairness and danger. And that means that unwise ideas must have a hearing as well as wise ones, unfair as well as fair, dangerous as well as safe, un-American as well as American . . . the principle of the freedom of speech springs from the necessities of the program of self-government. It is not a law of nature or of reason in the abstract. It is a deduction from the basic American agreement that public issues shall be decided by universal suffrage.[158]

He acknowledged that one purpose of free speech was to test the truth of ideas, through the "marketplace of ideas" rationale championed by Oliver Wendel Holmes and others. However, Meiklejohn said that more important in a system of self-government was the notion that whatever truth that was known was made available to citizens. This counted against censorship: "no idea, no opinion, no doubt, no belief, no counter-belief, no relevant information, may be kept from them."[159]

There is a division among scholars who advocate the self-government rationale for freedom of speech, between those who emphasize the social benefits of such a model, and those who emphasize the individual benefits of such a model. Those who advocate the *social benefits* of such a model point out that the best decisions are made when the public is informed and educated, and has had access to a full range of views before making their decision. Those who advocate the *individual benefits* of such a model point to the necessity of equal access to participate in decision making. This does not necessarily mean that these decisions are "best"; rather, simply that each member of society has had an equal opportunity to participate in the decision, legitimizing the decision actually made.[160]

Meiklejohn's conception of free speech as relating to self-government dictated limits to the freedom, at least as enshrined in the *Constitution*:

> The guarantee given by the *First Amendment* is not, then, assured to all speaking. It is assured only to speech which bears, directly or indirectly, upon issues with which voters have to deal—only, therefore, to the consideration of matters of public interest. Private speech, or private interest in speech, on the other hand, has no claim whatever to the protection of the *First Amendment.* If (individuals) are engaged . . . in argument or inquiry or advocacy or incitement which is directed towards our private interest . . . the *First Amendment* has not concern over such protection.[161]

Meiklejohn expressed the idea of tolerance towards views, although extreme or unpopular, on any political topic. This was an expression of society's culture, and its confidence in its own values and ideas, that it would tolerate the expression of views wholly antithetical to those values and ideas. Yet Meiklejohn's "tolerance" apparently has limits. He denounces commercial radio, denying that its content is entitled to *First Amendment* freedoms, because

> It is not cultivating those qualities of taste, of reasoned judgment, of integrity, of loyalty, of mutual understanding upon which the enterprise of self-government depends . . . on the contrary, it . . . corrupts both our morals and our intelligence.[162]

This type of articulation of the rationale for and limits on freedom of speech is said to be *consequentialist* in nature, because it is based on the public or social benefits of free speech. One of the reasons for Meiklejohn's limited conception of free speech is that he seems to believe that the same protections afforded to members of Congress to speak, protected by Article I s6 of the United States Constitution, ought to be afforded to private citizens.[163]

Subsequently several scholars have supported the position of Meiklejohn that freedom of speech protection in the *First Amendment* is limited to what may be characterized as "political speech."[164] At one point the United States Supreme Court embraced it.[165] It may be linked to notions of the social contract espoused by Locke and others. Specifically, in order for the social contract to work effectively and as intended, people must have free access to information to allow them to assess the government, before they can consent to its governing.

Others have been critical. Bork, for instance, disagrees with Meiklejohn's apparently very broad view, at least eventually, as to what "political speech" was, including arts and literature. He seeks to confine narrowly the scope to which *First Amendment* protection is given to speech about government, including evaluation, criticism, and electioneering, but not scientific, literary, commercial, or educational expression.[166]

Others make a different criticism, that to limit free speech rights to political speech, is too narrow. Some have acknowledged the practical difficulty, even if otherwise the task were a worthy one, in drawing a neat dividing line between speech that is political in nature, and speech that is non-political in nature.[167] Bollinger says Meiklejohn's theory faces a logical circuity: "it appears anomalous to restrict limitations on speech in the name of preserving self-government when the self-governing process has generated those very limitations."[168] Meiklejohn's theory is criticized as overly narrow.[169] Others say that involvement in the political process is not an end in itself, but merely a step towards individual self-realization, so it is Mill's theory of freedom of speech that is correct, rather than Meiklejohn's narrower approach.[170] It is argued to be illogical that the right of citizens to free flow of information is, according to Meiklejohn and others, guaranteed in cases where individuals only have an indirect say in decision making (through legislatures), but not in cases where individuals directly make decisions (all other decisions they make). Others deny that the link between free speech and self-government is axiomatic or automatic.[171] They may utilize arguments that not every country that protects free speech could be counted as a democracy.[172] Theories that defend freedom of speech on the basis that they are a check on government abuse of power fit with this conception of freedom of speech.

It should be noted that Meiklejohn seemed to canvas a broader scope for freedom of speech in his later writings than what would be deemed purely "political speech." Specifically, for instance, he said that arts and literature was protected by the *First Amendment* because of their social importance.[173] It would be difficult to say that arts and literature was always "political speech," so he clearly expanded his view of the scope of the *First Amendment* over time.

Bollinger attempts a reconciliation of these two competing views of freedom of speech as follows:

> The writings of Holmes and Meiklejohn are representative of an extremely important but generally unnoticed shift in perspective on the meaning and function of the free speech principle. No longer is the premise of our discussion about free speech the assumed need to secure 'our' liberty to speak freely against some 'other' antagonistic political body or power. The center of focus has shifted away from the purpose of establishing an unrestrained zone of liberty in which we can fulfil 'our' interests to speak and to hear the information and ideas we value (or negative liberty)—towards the purpose of creating a zone of unregulated behavior against which 'we' can test and develop a general character of mind through confrontation with that behavior—what may be thought of as the goal of exploring the virtues of tolerance . . . (or positive liberty), that is the wish on the part of the individual to be his own master.[174]

Tsesis posits that freedom of speech should not be seen solely either in a purely democratic self-government role, or in a personal freedom light. Others have made the related point that freedom of speech cannot be justified according to any one theory.[175] In contrast, freedom of speech is capable of contributing to the attainment of both such goals. In this sense they are complementary, rather than conflicting goals:

> The range of matters involving speech are all connected to a grand principle of representative democracy with the essential features of general welfare, such as self-government, self-fulfillment, the quest for knowledge and entertainment. The political self is inexorably linked to the private individual. Manifestation of the people's will in their written and implied forms are beneficial to the polity as a whole and the citizens who compose it.[176]

Tsesis says that the role of government is to further the interests of members of society. Because members of society benefit when they can freely express and hear a range of views, there is no inconsistency between freedom of speech as grounded on an individual rights basis, and based on self-government. They are congruent, because the role of government is to provide for protection and enforcement of rights of individuals.[177]

Sadurski suggests that special protection of freedom of speech, as opposed to other rights, is justified on the basis of the peculiar weakness of the legislature in relation to regulating that right. In a way that is not applicable to other fundamental human rights, the exercise of free speech rights can cause significant harm to a government. As a result, government has a natural inclination to suppress or limit particular kinds of speech. For Sadurski, this justifies placing free speech on a higher plane than other fundamental human rights and, arguably, not subjecting it to the same kind of "harm" analysis that might justify legislative incursion on other rights.[178]

OTHER THEORIES

This chapter has discussed at length the leading philosopher on freedom of speech, John Stuart Mill, as well as the writings of John Locke in terms of social contract theory. Obviously the views of Mill and Locke provide a robust defense to freedom of speech rights.

It should be noted for the sake of completeness that other legal theorists would be much less defensive of fundamental human rights like freedom of speech. It was pointed out earlier that those who viewed law on the basis of the command theory, like Hobbes and Austin, would believe that a strong sovereign had every right to create limits on the right of an individual to speak. No legal remedy would be called for in such a situation, according to such theorists. In terms of discussion of free speech, Blackstone should be bracketed here,[179] since the only limit he placed on the right of the parliament to censor speech was to not permit prior restraint policy. This left parliament free to punish whatever speech it wished, and individuals charged with such offenses would have no ability to argue the validity of the law, under the system of parliamentary supremacy favored by the British. Clearly Blackstone rejected the writings of John Locke in relation to social contract theory, preferring a more Hobbesian-like model. This had significant implications for his view of freedom of speech.

Further, a utilitarian, for example, Jeremy Bentham, would generally permit the legislature to abrogate fundamental legal rights for the sake of the broader wellbeing of society, on the basis of the greater good for the greatest number. However even Bentham was critical of prosecutions for seditious libel, and Blackstone's apparent acceptance of broad limits on freedom of speech.[180] We see strong evidence of this utilitarian approach in some of the United States cases decided in the late 19th and early 20th centuries, permitting broad legislative freedom to suppress or censor speech that was supposedly dangerous to the common good. This is a classic utilitarian approach, in sharp contrast to a natural rights or social contract infused view of the (legal) world.

CONCLUSION

Societies through the ages have sought to reconcile the wish to maintain existing government structures, with the wish to involve citizens in decision making, either directly, as in early times, or in more recent iterations, through the principle of representative government. Initially the focus was on protecting those in power from criticism, through prosecutions of dissenters and critics, the threat of same, and controls over media. This suited a Hobbesian view of Leviathan government. However, as security and confidence in government structures grew, and the threat of revolution and rebellion dissipated, ideas of government evolved. Ideas of the social contract and representative government developed. The law responded with stronger protection of free speech, in the knowledge that such was essential in a representative democracy system of government.

Through history, the leading philosophies said to underpin and explain free speech doctrine have been the "search for truth," often coupled with the marketplace of ideas argument, typically associated with Mill, the democratic self-government argument, championed especially by Meiklejohn, and the self-actualization argument, favored by Mill and many other scholars. There is a sense that given the vastness of the case law on freedom of speech, particularly in the United States, that none of the theories in themselves suffices to explain all of the decisions made and, perhaps more importantly, that it is in vain to seek to develop an all-encompassing theory to guide the development of future case law.[181] Perhaps we are setting the bar too high in expecting that a theory can so explain all of the cases, given the extent of them. That fact does not necessarily mean we should discard them as being unhelpful.

More positively, at least such theories might provide guidance to judges asked to make difficult decisions regarding the extent to which free speech should be protected. If a particular regulation could conceivably impinge upon at least one of the theories justifying freedom of speech, this might be at least an indicia of unconstitutionality. As we will see later, of all of the jurisdictions studied, Canada makes most consistent use of the theories today in determining whether or not an infringement of free speech is valid.

NOTES

1. Arlene Saxonhouse, *Free Speech and Democracy in Ancient Athens* (Cambridge University Press, New York, 2006), 96.

2. Moses Finley, *Democracy Ancient and Modern* (Rutgers University Press, New Jersey, 1985), 26. He explains that "every social organism considers itself legitimate and assumes the right to defend itself both internally and externally; it therefore seeks to weaken or eliminate opposition, or at least some forms of opposition. The Athenians of the fifth century did not often kill critics of the system, as did the Roman emperors, but they sometimes ostracised them . . . (sending them into exile) and both methods were effective forms of censorship" (145–146).

3. Plato, *The Republic* (Benjamin Jowett trans, The Modern Library, New York, 1941), discussed in Nicholas Wolfson, "Free Speech Theory and Hateful Words," *University of Cincinnati Law Review* 60 (1991): 8–9.

4. Demosthens, *Funeral Speech*: "democracies have many other beautiful and just things to which those who think rightly ought to hold fast, and especially parrhesia from which it is impossible that the truth not be safe and sound, that the truth not be made clear": 60.26; Arlene

Saxonhouse, *Free Speech and Democracy in Ancient Athens* (Cambridge University Press, New York, 2006), 93.

5. Arlene Saxonhouse, *Free Speech and Democracy in Ancient Athens* (Cambridge University Press, New York, 2006), 117: "Socrates is educating/corrupting the young not so much by introducing new gods into the city, but by teaching the shamelessness that questions the reverence due to 'beautiful things discovered long ago,' due to the values of the city, to the hierarchy of age, and to the gods. When shame serves as the glue of a community, the educator in shamelessness such as Socrates dissolves the glue."

6. I am indebted for my summary of the developments in Roman times to the article by Frederick Cramer, "Bookburning and Censorship in Ancient Rome: A Chapter from the History of Freedom of Speech," *Journal of the History of Ideas* 6(2) (1945): 157.

7. As Finley points out, it is not correct to assume from this that the Romans believed in an inalienable right of an individual to speak their mind. It is more accurate to deduce from the lack of sanction that the offensive material was not deemed to be dangerous to the existing state of affairs: Moses Finley, *Democracy Ancient and Modern* (Rutgers University Press, New Jersey, 1985), 170.

8. "From henceforth none be so hardy to tell or publish any false news or tales, whereby discord, or occasion of discord or slander may grow between the king and his people, or the great men of the realm": *Scanadalis Magnatum* or *Scandalum Magnatum 1275* (Eng).

9. William Holdsworth, *A History of English Law* (Methuen, London, 5th ed, 1922), 409. It was eventually repealed in 1887 (c. 59 *Statute Law Revision Act 1887* (UK)).

10. Frederic W Maitland, *A Constitutional History of England* (Cambridge University Press, Cambridge, 1908), 516.

11. "To say that religion is a cheat is to dissolve all those obligations whereby civil societies are preserved": *R v Taylor* (1687) 1 Ventris 293 (Hale J). The offense of blasphemy only disappeared from the statute books in 2008: *Criminal Justice and Immigration Act 2008* (UK) s79.

12. David Norris, "Scandalising the Court," *The Judicial Review* 5 (2001): 67; Patricia Londono, ATH Smith and Hon Justice Eady, *Arlidge, Eady and Smith on Contempt* (Sweet and Maxwell, London, 5th ed 2017), 1–5.

13. Charles Montesquieu: "there was a law passed in England under Henry VIII, by which whoever predicted the king's death was declared guilty of high treason. This law was extremely vague; the terror of despotic power is to great that it recoils upon those who exercise it. In the king's last illness, the physicians would not venture to say he was in danger; and surely they acted very right. . . . Marsyas dreamed that he had cut Dionysius's throat. Dionysius put him to death, pretending that he would never have dreamed of such a thing by night if he had not thought of it by day. This was a most tyrannical action, for those it had been the subject of his thoughts, yet he had made no attempt towards it. The laws do not take upon them to punish any other than overt acts": 1 *The Spirit of Laws* (Duncan, Robertson and Shaw, Glasgow, 1793), 192–193.

14. *A Complete Collection of State Trials* 564 (1816) (the relevant trial was in 1663).

15. *Rex v Twyn* 84 ER 1064 (K.B. 1663); 6 *Cobbett's Collection of State Trials* (1810) 513. Leonard Levy reports the manner of Twyn's death was typically brutal for one convicted of treason—he was hanged, cut down while alive, emasculated, disembowelled, quartered, before being beheaded: *Legacy of Suppression* (Harvard University Press, Cambridge, 1960), 11.

16. Willis R Vance, "Freedom of Speech and of the Press," *Minnesota Law Review* 2 (1918): 245; William Mayton, "Seditious Libel and the Lost Guarantee of a Freedom of Expression," *Columbia Law Review* 84 (1984): 120.

17. Frederic W Maitland *A Constitutional History of England* (Cambridge University Press, Cambridge, 1908), 514.

18. William Mayton, "Seditious Libel and the Lost Guarantee of a Freedom of Expression," *Columbia Law Review* 84 (1984): 102.

19. Philip Hamburger, "The Development of the Law of Seditious Libel and the Control of the Press," *Stanford Law Review* 37 (1985): 719–721.

20. (1606) 5 Co. Rep. 125a; 77 ER 250.

21. "If (a libel) be against a magistrate, or other public person, it is a greater offence (than if against a private man): for it concerns not only the breach of the peace, but also the scandal of government; for what greater scandal of government can there be than to have corrupt or wicked magistrates to be appointed and constituted by the King to govern his subjects under him, and greater imputation to the state cannot be, than to suffer such corrupt men to sit in the sacred seat of justice, or to have any meddling in or concerning the administration of justice" (Coke).

22. *Beauharnais v Illinois* 343 US 250, 254 (1952) (Justice Frankfurter for the Court).

23. This was notoriously difficult to define. Blackstone defined it as "dangerous or offensive writings which, when published, shall on a fair and impartial trial be adjudged of a pernicious tendency": *Commentaries on the Laws of England 1765–1769* (Clarendon Press, Oxford, 1769), 152.

24. Leonard Levy, *A Legacy of Suppression* (Harvard University Press, Cambridge, 1960), 10: "any comment about the government which could be construed to have the bad tendency of lowering it in the public's esteem or of disturbing the peace was seditious libel, subjecting the speaker or writer to criminal prosecution."

25. Irving Brant, "Seditious Libel: Myth and Reality," *New York University Law Review* 39 (1964): 18–19.

26. *Rex v Chambers* (1629) 3 St. Tr. 373.

27. William Mayton, "Seditious Libel and the Lost Guarantee of a Freedom of Expression," *Columbia Law Review* 84 (1984): 104.

28. *Boucher v The King* [1951] SCR 265, 319 (Locke J).

29. (1622) (Brian Vickers ed, Cambridge University Press, 1918), 115.

30. Vincent Blasi, *Milton's Areopagitica and the Modern First Amendment* (Yale Law School Occasional Papers, Paper No. 6, 1995), 2–3.

31. William Blackstone, *Commentaries on the Laws of England 1765–1769* (Clarendon Press, Oxford, 1769), 151–152.

32. Philip Hamburger, "The Development of the Law of Seditious Libel and the Control of the Press," *Stanford Law Review* 37 (1985): 671–672.

33. James I, Speech in the Star Chamber, 20 June 1616; John Kenyon *The Stuart Constitution 1603–1688: Documents and Commentary* (Cambridge University Press, Cambridge, 1986), 84–86.

34. (1615) 11 Co Rep 66, 72a; 77 ER 1235, 1243

35. Anthony Gray, "Crown Immunity from Suit and Statute," *Canberra Law Review* [2010]: 1.

36. *Province of Bombay v Municipal Corporation of the City of Bombay and Another* [1947] AC 58.

37. [1607] EWHC KB J23.

38. *Petition of Rights Act 1860* (UK).

39. Bernard Shientag, "From Seditious Libel to Freedom of the Press," *Brooklyn Law Review* 11 (1942): 129.

40. Willis R Vance, "Freedom of Speech and of the Press," *Minnesota Law Review* 2 (1918): 244.

41. Philip Hamburger, "The Development of the Law of Seditious Libel and the Control of the Press," *Stanford Law Review* 37 (1985): 672.

42. William Mayton, "Toward a Theory of First Amendment Process: Injunctions of Speech Subsequent Punishment and the Costs of the Prior Restraint Doctrine," *Cornell Law Review* 67 (1982): 248.

43. Trial of Henry Carr 7, *A Complete Collection of State Trials* (1816) 187 (trial was in 1680): "to print or publish any newsbooks or pamphlets of news whatsoever is illegal . . . (this is) a public notice to all people, and especially printers and booksellers that they ought to print no book or pamphlet of news without authority" (Scroggs J).

44. *Commentaries on the Laws of England 1765–1769* (Clarendon Press, Oxford, 1769), 152. Blackstone did not apparently accept Locke's social contract theory involving individuals ceding limited rights to a collective legislature; he favored a more authoritarian view of rulers along the lines of Hobbes.

45. Wendell Bird, "Liberties of Press and Speech: 'Evidence Does Not Exist to Contradict the . . . Blackstonian Sense' in Late 18th Century England?" *Oxford Journal of Legal Studies* 36(1) (2016): 23: "what became the narrow Blackstone definition of liberties of press and speech receded from primary to secondary position in English (publications), even before Blackstone published it in 1769 and before the courts adopted it in 1770. By 1770 most English essays addressing the issue generally did not identify those liberties as mere freedom from prior restraint (licensing), to the exclusion of freedom from subsequent punishment; only a receding minority advocated the narrow meaning. And seditious libel receded from being generally viewed as not inconsistent with liberty of press to being more often criticised as violating that liberty . . . many English writers protested that freedoms of press and speech were endangered or unsecured . . . the narrow Blackstone approach to liberties of press and speech was not an ancient rule of English law. It was only adopted by the Crown judges in 1770, after Blackstone so summarised English law."

46. Philip Hamburger, "The Development of the Law of Seditious Libel and the Control of the Press," *Stanford Law Review* 37 (1985): 725: "following 1696, the law of seditious libel shed its seventeenth century obscurity. It had become the sole surviving instrument of prosecution in the government's arsenal of antipress weapons."

47. It must also be acknowledged that on occasion parliament (mis)used its power to punish for contempt to suppress unwelcome speech. The United States Supreme Court in *Watkins v United States* 354 US 178, 189 (1957) recount the case of Floyd, a Catholic who expressed pleasure about a bad situation affecting the King's Protestant son in law and his wife in the early 17th century. Floyd was not a member of parliament and none of the other parties involved were either; notwithstanding this, the House of Commons found that he was in contempt of parliament, and he was given a harsh sentence.

48. Examples include the imprisonment by a court of Strode, a member of the House of Commons, for having introduced contentious bills. Parliament responded with a statute declaring that parliament had the sole power to discipline members for actions, including speech, in parliament. Later the King successfully argued in court that this statute applied only to Strode, and did not establish a general principle: Frederic W Maitland *The Constitutional History of England* (Cambridge University Press, Cambridge, 1908), 242.

49. David Colclough, *Freedom of Speech in Early Stuart England* (Cambridge University Press, Cambridge, 2005), 131.

50. David Colclough, *Freedom of Speech in Early Stuart England* (Cambridge University Press, Cambridge, 2005), 137.

51. "Let us first recollect what liberties have bene impeached and then to provide the remedy. Concerning freedom of speech, that hath bene impeached in matter and manner. Meddle not with this business, goes to this business first (by which we are restrained from the choice of our business). When I speak of freedom of speech, I mean not Licentiousness and exorbitance, but speech without servile fear or, as it were, under the rode": Sir Nathaniel Riche (Commons Debates 1621, v, 242–243).

52. Frederic W Maitland, *The Constitutional History of England* (Cambridge University Press, Cambridge, 1908), 242–243.

53. David Colclough, *Freedom of Speech in Early Stuart England* (Cambridge University Press, Cambridge, 2005), 184.

54. David Colclough, *Freedom of Speech in Early Stuart England* (Cambridge University Press, Cambridge, 2005), 195; Tindal *Reasons Against Restraining the Press* (1704) 9–10: "if the Honourable House of Commons have upon a solemn Debate thought fit to publish their proceedings to prevent being misrepresented, why should they deny those they Represent the same Liberty?"

55. David Bogen, "The Origins of Freedom of Speech and Press," *Maryland Law Review* 42 (1983): 431–433.

56. (1698) 2 Salkeld 417; 90 ER 1132, 91 ER 1175 (K.B).

57. *R v Bear*, Hardwicke Papers, British Library, Add. M.S. 35981, 8 (quoted in Philip Hamburger, "The Development of the Law of Seditious Libel and the Control of the Press," *Stanford Law Review* 37 (1985): 732).

58. "For more than a century prior to the adoption of the (First) Amendment–and indeed for many years thereafter–history discloses a persistent effort on the part of the British government to prevent or abridge the free expression of any opinion which seemed to criticize or exhibit in an unfavourable light, however truly, the agencies and operations of the government": *Grosjean v American Press Co* 297 US 233, 245 (1936) (Justice Sutherland, for the Court).

59. (1704) R v *Tutchin* Holt, K.B. 424, 424–425; 90 ER 1133, 1133–1134 (Q.B).

60. Philip Hamburger, "The Development of the Law of Seditious Libel and the Control of the Press," *Stanford Law Review* 37 (1985): 740.

61. *Curll* (1727) 2 Str. 788; this is discussed in Colin Manchester, "A History of the Crime of Obscene Libel," *Journal of Legal History* 12 (1991): 46.

62. *O'Connell v Reg* (1844) 11 Cl. & F. 155; *R v Hart and White* (1808) 30 St. Tr. 1131; *Rex v Corbett* (1804) 29 St. Tr. 1, 50: "it is no new doctrine that if a publication be calculated to alienate the affections of the people by bringing the government into disesteem, whether the expedient be by ridicule or obloquy, the person so conducting himself is exposed to the inflictions of the law" (Lord Ellenborough); *Halsbury's Laws of England* (2nd ed) Vol 9: "a seditious intention is an intention (1) to bring into hatred or contempt, or to excite disaffection against the king or the government or the constitution of the United Kingdom, of either House of Parliament, or the administration of justice" (302).

63. *Rex v Neale* (1839) 9 C & P. 431.

64. These were summarized by Rand J in *Boucher v The King* [1951] SCR 265, 287 as: (a) to bring into hatred or contempt, or to excite disaffection against the monarch, government, or constitution of the United Kingdom; (b) to excite the monarch's subjects to attempt, by unlawful means, to alter state law; (c) to incite others to commit crime in breach of the peace; (d) to raise discontent or disaffection among the monarch's subjects; or (e) to promote feelings of ill-will and hostility between different classes of subjects.

65. James Fitzjames Stephen, *A Digest of the Criminal Law* (Macmillan, London, 1904), 375 ("nothing short of a direct incitement to disorder and violence is a seditious libel"), and 381 ("the question would be whether the writer's object was to procure a remedy by peaceable means, or to promote disaffection and bring about riots"); see also Lord Cockburn, *Examination of Trials for Sedition in Scotland*: "the guilt of sedition is often described as consisting of its tendency to produce public mischief—and so it is. But it is not every sort of mischief that will exhaust the description of the offence. It must be that sort of mischief that consists in, and arises out of directly and materially obstructing public authority" (8).

66. *Grosjean v American Press Co* 297 US 223, 246 (1936) (Justice Sutherland, for the Court).

67. John Milton, *A Treatise of Civil Power in Ecclesiastical Causes* (London, 1659); John Milton, *True Religion, Heresie, Schism and Toleration* (London, 1673); Willis R Vance, "Freedom of Speech and of the Press," *Minnesota Law Review* 2 (1918): 239, 244.

68. "I mean not tolerated popery and open superstition, which, as it extirpates all religions and civil supremacies, so itself should be extirpate . . . that also which is impious or evil absolutely, either against faith or manners, no law can possibly permit, that intends not to unlaw itself": John Milton, *Areopagitica* (Holland and Co, London, 1906), 747.

69. *Legacy of Suppression* (Harvard University Press, Cambridge, 1960), 97.

70. Carolyn Maree Evans *Legal Protection of Religious Freedom in Australia* (Federation Press, Sydney, 2012), 8.

71. Leonard Levy *Legacy of Suppression* (Harvard University Press, Cambridge, 1960), 104: "(Locke and Milton) were of their time, and one of its a priori premises, unthinkable for anyone to attack, was the state's incontestable right to prescribe sedition, a commodious concept encompassing everything from mild criticism of public policy to attempted overthrow of the government. Neither Locke, Milton nor their contemporaries ever indicated disagreement with the common law's spacious definition of unlawful discourse nor sought to limit its application."

72. Anthony Collins, *Discourse of Free Thinking* (Garland Publishing, New York, 1713).

73. Philip Hamburger, "The Development of the Law of Seditious Libel and the Control of the Press," *Stanford Law Review* 37 (1985): 748.

74. Philip Hamburger, "The Development of the Law of Seditious Libel and the Control of the Press," *Stanford Law Review* 37 (1985): 752.

75. (1765) 97 ER 94 (Wilmot J); see David Hay, "Contempt by Scandalising the Court: A Political History of the First Hundred Years," *Osgoode Hall Law Journal* 25 (1987): 431. Explaining the case, Londono Smith and Eady note it was decided in "an age when judges were much less used to vigorous public debate. In the eighteenth century, the judiciary were much exercised by the proper controls that should be set upon the newly established press, and the tradition of the virulent seventeenth century pamphleteers was by no means dead": *Arlidge, Eady and Smith on Contempt* (Sweet and Maxwell, London, 2017), 5–233. That branch of contempt known as "scandalising the court" was finally abolished in the United Kingdom in 2013: *Crimes and Courts Act 2013* (United Kingdom) s33.

76. "Without freedom of thought there can be no such thing as wisdom, and no such thing as public liberty, without freedom of speech," "whosoever would overthrow the Liberty of the Nation, must begin by subduing the Freedom of Speech," "Freedom of Speech is the great bulwark of Liberty; they prosper and die together": John Trenchard and Thomas Gordon, *Cato's Letters: Essays on Liberty, Civil and Religious* (Wilkins et al., London, 1733), 96–103. Trenchard and Gordon were Whigs who strongly supported freedom of expression, and the right to question and criticize government action.

77. "Let it be remembered for whose sake government is, or could be, appointed; then let it be considered, who are more to be regarded, the governors or the governed."

78. 246–247.

79. 111, 114.

80. 252.

81. Leonard Levy, *A Legacy of Suppression* (Harvard University Press, Cambridge, 1960), 7: "the danger was particularly great for several centuries after the emergence of the national state, when the life of the monarch was in jeopardy and the peace and security of the state were precarious. Freedom of religion and political expression was feared as a means of triggering conspiracies, internal disorders, wars, revolutions, or some other disastrous chain of events that might pull down church and state."

82. *Leviathan* (Broadview Press, Ontario, 2005).

83. James Fitzjames Stephen, *A History of the Criminal Law of England* (Macmillan, London, 1904), 299: "the ruler is regarded as the superior of the subject . . . (and) it must necessarily follow that it is wrong to censure him openly." Stephen says this view prevailed until the 18th century.

84. John Locke, *Two Treatises of Government* (Peter Laslett ed., Cambridge University Press, Cambridge, 1960): "the community perpetually retains a supreme power of saving themselves from the attempts and designs of any body, even of their legislators, whenever they shall be so foolish, or so wicked, as to lay and carry on designs against the liberties and properties of the subject": [150](Second Treatise).

85. *Two Treatises of Government* (Peter Laslett ed., Cambridge University Press, Cambridge, 1960).

86. "He that thinks absolute power purifies mens' bloods, and corrects the baseness of his human nature, need read but the history of this, or any other age, to be convinced of the contrary": *Second Treatise of Government*, [92]; "as if men when quitting the state of nature entered into society, they agreed that all of them, but one, should be under the restraint of laws, but that he should still retain all the liberty of the state of nature, increased with power, and made licentious by impunity. This is to think that men are so foolish that they take care to avoid what mischiefs may be done them by pole-cats or foxes, but are content, nay think it safety, to be devoured by lions": [93].

87. James Fitzjames Stephen, *A History of the Criminal Law of England* (Macmillan, London, 1904), 299–300. He adds that "the practical enforcement of this doctrine (of sedition) was wholly inconsistent with any serious public discussion of political affairs is obvious" (348); see also Zechariah Chafee, "Freedom of Speech in War Time," *Harvard Law Review* 32 (1919): 945–947.

88. Wendell Bird, "Liberties of Press and Speech: 'Evidence Does Not Exist to Contradict the . . . Blackstonian Sense' in Late 18th Century England?" *Oxford Journal of Legal Studies*

36(1) (2016): 3 accused Lord Mansfield of "rewriting" the history of seditious libel by falsely asserting that the liberty of the press was simply a lack of prior restraint and falsely asserting that no-one had complained about the narrowing of the issues which the jury, rather than the judge, was to determine in seditious libel cases, and of using a "misleading" starting point in his discussions of the relevant law. John Wilkes was, not surprisingly, scathing in his assessment: "Lord Mansfield has succeeded so far in his vile, his infamous design of destroying the liberty of the press" (The Scourges, London, 23 January 1771), and newspaper essays at the time accused him of using principles derived from the despised Star Chamber, mocking the jury and common sense, and attacking free speech via "chicanery, circumvention and sophistry." Various newspaper essay quotes appears in Bird's article, 10–11.

89. *R v Wilkes* (1770) 4 Burr. 2527, 2561; 98 ER 327, 346.

90. Bernard Shientag, "From Seditious Libel to Freedom of the Press," *Brooklyn Law Review* 11 (1942): 125, 133.

91. "Wilkes became a symbol (and an immensely popular and powerful demagogue) of both middle-class demands for parliamentary reform and radical dedication to press freedoms. The issue of the 'Wilkes affair' and the slogan 'Wilkes and Liberty' became for nearly a dozen years the rally cry of city merchants, London's labourers and craftsmen, and the freeholders and householders of Middlesex, Westminster and Surrey": George Rude, *Paris and London in the Eighteenth Century* (Viking Press, New York, 1970), 325.

92. Jeffrey Walker, "A Poisen in Ye Commonwealth: Seditious Libel in Hanoverian London," (1996) 25 *Anglo-American Law Review* 25 (1996): 358.

93. 366.

94. Specifically, for example, two judges who found the monarch had not been libelled in a given case were shortly thereafter removed from the bench: *The Seven Bishops* (1688) 12 St. Tr. 183 (Holloway and Powell JJ were removed after the decision), noted by Locke J in *Boucher v The King* [1951] SCR 265, 318–319.

95. *Beauharnais v Illinois* 343 US 250, 295 (1952) (Jackson J, dissenting).

96. *R v Paine* (1792) 22 How. St. Tr. 357.

97. 31 How. St. Tr. 495, 535 (Baron Wood) (1811).

98. James Fitzjames Stephen, *A History of the Criminal Law of England* (Macmillan, London, 1904) 373; similarly Zechariah Chafee, "Freedom of Speech in War Time," *Harvard Law Review* 32 (1919): 951: "liberalism triumphed in 1832."

99. *Beauharnais v Illinois* 343 US 250, 295 (1952) (Jackson J, dissenting).

100. (1868) *Wason v Walter* LR 4 QB 73, 93 (Cockburn CJ).

101. *Derbyshire County Council v Times Newspapers Ltd* [1993] AC 534, 547; *Hector v Attorney-General of Antigua and Barbuda* [1990] 2 AC 312, 318: "in a free democratic society it is almost too obvious to need stating that those who hold office in government and who are responsible for public administration must always be open to criticism. Any attempt to stifle or fetter such criticism amounts to political censorship of the most insidious and objectionable kind" (Lord Bridge).

102. [1936] AC 322, 335; see also *R v Gray* [1900] 2 QB 36, 40: "judges and courts are alike open to criticism and if reasonable argument or expostulation is offered against any judicial act as contrary to law or the public good, no court could or would treat that as contempt of court" (Lord Russell CJ); *Attorney-General v Times Newspapers Ltd* [1974] AC 273, 315: "the first public interest involved is that of freedom of discussion in democratic society. People cannot adequately influence the decisions which affect their lives unless they can be adequately informed on facts and arguments relevant to the decisions. Much of such fact-finding and argumentation necessarily has to be conducted vicariously, the public press being a necessary instrument" (Lord Simon); *Reg v Commissioner of Police of the Metropolis; Ex Parte Blackburn* (No2)[1968] 2 QB 150, 155 (Lord Denning MR).

103. *Gay News* [1979] AC 617, 665.

104. These are defined in s4 to include age, race, religion or belief, gender reassignment, gender, sexual orientation, pregnancy or marriage.

105. Kent Greenawalt, "Free Speech Justifications," *Columbia Law Review* 89 (1989): 148–149.

106. *An Essay Concerning Human Understanding* (Dent, London, 1959), 593.

107. Steven Smith, "Scepticism, Tolerance, and Truth in the Theory of Free Expression," *Southern California Law Review* 60 (1987): 701–703.

108. John Stuart Mill, *Utilitarianism, On Liberty, Considerations on Representative Government* (Geraint Williams ed., Everyman, London, 1910), 83.

109. 84.

110. 85; to like affect Thomas Emerson, "Towards a General Theory of the *First Amendment*," *Yale Law Journal* 72 (1963): 881–882: "many of the most widely acknowledged truths have turned out to be erroneous. Many of the most significant advances in human knowledge–from Copernicus to Einstein–have resulted from challenging hitherto unquestioned assumptions. No opinion can be immune from challenge . . . there is no way of suppressing the false without suppressing the true."

111. The truth rationale for freedom of speech has often been critiqued: see, for example, Kent Greenawalt, "Free Speech Justifications," *Columbia Law Review* 89 (1989): 119, 131–138; Alexander Meiklejohn, "The *First Amendment* is an Absolute," *Supreme Court Review* (1961): 263: "I have never been able to share the Miltonian faith that in a fair fight between truth and error, truth is sure to win"; Harry Wellington, "On Freedom of Expression," *Yale Law Journal* 88 (1979): 1130: "it is naïve to think that truth will always prevail over falsehood in a free and open encounter, for too many false ideas have captured the imagination of man"; Stanley Ingber, "The Marketplace of Ideas: A Legitimizing Myth," *Duke Law Journal* (1984): 1.

112. *Areopagitica* (Holland and Co, London, 1906): "and though all the winds of doctrine were let loose play upon the earth, so truth be in the field, we do injuriously by licencing and prohibiting to misdoubt her strength. Let her and falsehood grapple; who ever knew truth put to the worst in a free and open encounter."

113. Karl Popper, *Conjectures and Refutations: The Growth of Scientific Knowledge* (Routledge, London, 1989), 5: "the great movement of liberation, which started in the Renaissance and led through the many vicissitudes of the reformation and the religious and the revolutionary wars to the free societies in which the English-speaking peoples are privileged to live, this movement was inspired throughout by an unparalleled epistemological optimism: by a most optimistic view of man's power to discern truth and to acquire knowledge."

114. See, for example, Edwin Baker, "Freedom of Speech," *UCLA Law Review* 25 (1978): 965: "because of monopoly of control of the media, lack of access of disfavoured or impoverished groups, techniques of behaviour manipulation, irrational response to propaganda, and the non-existence of value-free, objective truth, the marketplace of ideas fails to achieve the desired results"; Benjamin DuVal, "Free Communication of Ideas and the Quest for Truth: Towards a Teleological Approach to *First Amendment* Adjudication," *George Washington Law Review* 41 (1972): 188–194; Lawrence Solum, "Freedom of Communicative Action: A Theory of the First Amendment Freedom of Speech," *Northwestern University Law Review* 83 (1989): 70; Stanley Ingber, "The Marketplace of Ideas: A Legitimizing Myth," *Duke Law Journal* (1984): 27: "conflicts in the marketplace . . . are not likely to lead to conclusive agreement on what is 'true' or 'best' . . . it is difficult to treat free speech as uniquely essential to the discovery of truth or to the encouragement of informed choice. Experience more likely provides the information needed to confront life's exigencies than does speech"; Dean Wellington, "On Freedom of Expression" (1979) 88 *Yale Law Journal* 1105, 1130: "it is naïve to think that truth will always prevail over falsehood in a free and open encounter, for too many false ideas have captured the imagination of man"; Eric Barendt, *Freedom of Speech* (Clarendon Press, Oxford, 2nd ed 2005), 9–11.

115. 85.

116. 88.

117. 89.

118. 101.

119. 121.

120. Jeremy Kirk, "Constitutional Implications from Representative Democracy," *Federal Law Review* 23 (1995): 46.

121. 143; other scholars have adapted the "harm principle" to one of "harming autonomy of consciousness." A legislature is justified in regulating speech that would otherwise harm the

autonomy of consciousness of others: O Lee Reed, "A Free Speech Metavalue for the Next Millennium: Autonomy of Consciousness in First Amendment Theory and Practice," *American Business Law Journal* 35 (1997): 1.

122. Mari Matsuda, "Public Response to Racist Speech: Considering the Victim's Story," *Michigan Law Review* 87 (1989): 2378–2379.

123. Martin Redish, "Value of Free Speech," *University of Pennsylvania Law Review* 130 (1982): 601.

124. Steven Helle, "Whither the Public's Right (Not) to Know—Milton, Malls and Multicultural Speech," *University of Illinois Law Review* (1991): 1096.

125. David Bogen, "The Origins of Freedom of Speech and Press," *Maryland Law Review* 42 (1983): 463–464.

126. Nicholas Wolfson, "Free Speech Theory and Hateful Words," *University of Cincinnati Law Review* 60 (1991): 21.

127. Richard Moon, *The Constitutional Protection of Freedom of Expression* (University of Toronto Press, Buffalo, 2000), 60–62.

128. Thomas Emerson, "Towards a General Theory of the *First Amendment*," *Yale Law Journal* 72 (1963): 879.

129. Martin Redish, "The Value of Free Speech," *University of Pennsylvania Law Review* 130 (1982): 593. Redish says that self-realization encompasses both self-governance and development of an individual's potential (627); O Lee Reed, "A Free Speech Metavalue for the Next Millennium: Autonomy of Consciousness in First Amendment Theory and Practice," *American Business Law Journal* 35 (1997): 25: "free speech is anterior to self-realization. Before we can have equal and fully realized 'selves,' we must have the social freedom of speech to conceive, to express, and more basically to realize, these notions"; Thomas Emerson, "Towards a General Theory of the First Amendment," *Yale Law Journal* 72 (1963): 879; O Lee Reed, "A Free Speech Metavalue for the Next Millennium: Autonomy of Consciousness in *First Amendment* Theory and Practice," *American Business Law Journal* 35 (1997): 19: "before there is the self, there must be speech/language."

130. Others may have a different view based on their notion of "harm" in this context.

131. C Edwin Baker, "Autonomy and Free Speech," *Constitutional Commentary* 27 (2011): 259; Thomas Scanlon, "A Theory of Freedom of Expression," *Philosophy and Public Affairs* 1 (1972): 204; Robert Post, "Meiklejohn's Mistake: Individual Autonomy and the Reform of Public Discourse," *University of Colorado Law Review* 64 (1993): 1109.

132. C Macpherson, *The Life and Times of Liberal Democracy* (Oxford University Press, Oxford, 1977), 51: "democracy drew the people into the operations of government by giving them all a practical interest, an interest which could bring down a government. Democracy would thus make people more active, more energetic; it would advance them in intellect, in virtue, and in practical activity and efficiency"; Jack Walker, "A Critique of the Elitist Theory of Democracy," *American Political Science Review* 60 (1966): 288: "the most distinctive feature . . . of classic democratic theory was its emphasis on individual participation in the development of public policy . . . the classical theorists accepted the basic framework of Lockean democracy with its emphasis on limited government (but) they were not primarily concerned with the policies which might be produced in a democracy . . . they were concerned with human development, the opportunities which existed in political activity to realize the untapped potentials of men"; Alexander Tsesis, "Free Speech Constitutionalism," *University of Illinois Law Review* (2015): 1043: "the purpose of representative governance is the protection of individual rights for the common good."

133. Paul Craig, *Public Law and Democracy in the United Kingdom and the USA* (Clarendon Press, Oxford, 1990), 197.

134. Glen Patmore, "Making Sense of Representative Democracy and the Implied Freedom of Political Communication in the High Court of Australia," *Griffith Law Review* 7 (1998): 97; David Held, *Models of Democracy* (Stanford University Press, Stanford, 3rd edition 2006).

135. 250 US 616 (1919).

136. 630 (Holmes J dissenting).

137. *Lochner v United States* 198 US 45 (1905).

138. Ronald Coase, "The Nature of the Firm," *Economica* 4 (1937): 386.

139. Stewart Jay, "The Creation of the *First Amendment* Right to Free Expression: From the Eighteenth Century to the Mid-Twentieth Century," *William Mitchell Law Review* 34 (2008): 876: "Holmes did not consider that the market in ideas, like the financial market, is fraught with imperfections that hinder it from even approximating the truth at times . . . if, as is well known, markets in stocks and commodities were in need of regulation, why wouldn't it follow that the market in expression needed government oversight?"

140. Some deny the utility of doing so: "free speech, free press, free exercise of religion are placed separate and apart; they are above and beyond the police power; they are not subject to regulation in the manner of factories, slums, apartment houses, production of oil, and the like": *Beauharnais v Illinois* 343 US 250, 286 (1952) (Douglas J, dissenting); Laurence Tribe, "Towards a Metatheory of Free Speech," *Southwestern University Law Review* 10 (1978): 240: "a theory of free speech should not be too confined by the assumptions of any particular form of economic life . . . any theory built exclusively on the assumptions of capitalism—or any other economic system–must therefore be rejected as too narrow."

141. Joseph Blocher, "Institutions in the Marketplace of Ideas," *Duke Law Journal* 57 (2008): 821.

142. Blocher says that the "clear and present danger" test was a response to market failure in freedom of speech, where the imminence and seriousness of danger prevents the market from working normally, and not permitting a range of voices to be heard, and (presumably) rationality to win out: "Institutions in the Marketplace of Ideas," *Duke Law Journal* 57 (2008): 833–834.

143. Stewart Jay, "The Creation of the *First Amendment* Right to Free Expression: From the Eighteenth Century to the Mid-Twentieth Century," *William Mitchell Law Review* 34 (2008): 876.

144. For example, some have argued that "fighting words doctrine and hate speech also find themselves grouped into the 'market failure' category; they arguably cause harms that cannot be remedied by more speech. Because hate speech disempowers those at whom it is directed, the argument goes, anti-hate and anti-fighting speech has no real chance to 'compete'": Joseph Blocher, "Institutions in the Marketplace of Ideas," *Duke Law Journal* 57 (2008): 835.

145. Frederick Schauer, "Uncoupling Free Speech," *Columbia Law Review* 92 (1992): 1321–1324.

146. Jeremy Kirk, "Constitutional Implications from Representative Democracy," *Federal Law Review* 23 (1995): 50.

147. Thomas Emerson, "Towards a General Theory of the *First Amendment*," *Yale Law Journal* 72 (1963): 884–885; Nicholas Wolfson, "Free Speech Theory and Hateful Words," *University of Cincinnati Law Review* 60 (1991): 40.

148. Frederick Schauer, "Free Speech in a World of Private Power," in Tom Campbell and Wojciech Sadurski ed., *Freedom of Communication* (Aldershot, England, 1994), 6–7; Tom Campbell, "Rationales for Freedom of Communication," in Tom Campbell and Wojciech Sadurski ed., *Freedom of Communication* (Aldershot, England, 1994), 26; Edwin Baker, "Scope of the *First Amendment* and Free Speech," *UCLA Law Review* 25 (1977): 966; Noah Chomsky, *Necessary Illusions: Thought Control in Democratic Societies* (CBC Enterprises, Montreal, 1989), 5–6.

149. Tom Campbell, "Rationales for Freedom of Communication," in Tom Campbell and Wojciech Sadurski ed., *Freedom of Communication* (Aldershot, England, 1994), 23.

150. Eric Barendt, *Freedom of Speech* (Clarendon Press, Oxford, 2nd edition 2005), 12.

151. Noam Chomsky, *Necessary Illusions: Thought Control in Democratic Societies* (CBC Enterprises, Montreal, 1989), 5–7; Deborah Cass, "Through the Looking Glass: The High Court and the Right to Speech," *Public Law Review* 4 (1993): 241.

152. Michael Chesterman, *Freedom of Speech: A Delicate Plant* (Aldershot, Ashgate, 2000), 316; *Reno v American Civil Liberties Union* 521 US 844 (1997).

153. Frederick Schauer, *Free Speech: A Philosophical Enquiry* (Cambridge University Press, Cambridge, 1981), 33–34; Vincent Blasi, "Reading Abrams Through the Lens of Schauer," *Notre Dame Law Review* 72 (1997): 1343; *New York Times v Sullivan* 376 US 254, 270 (1964) where the Supreme Court noted that the *First Amendment* "presupposes that right conclusions

are more likely to be gathered out of a multitude of tongues, than through any kind of authoritative selection."

154. Somewhat analogously, Elena Kegan posited a theory of free speech that suggested improper legislative motive was the touchstone for *First Amendment* invalidity: "Private Speech, Public Purpose: The Role of Government Motive in *First Amendment* Doctrine," *University of Chicago Law Review* 63 (1996): 413.

155. Oliver Wendel Holmes Jr., "The Path of the Law," *Harvard Law Review* 10 (1897): 460 rejecting "rights of man in a moral sense" as a constitutional brake. Holmes denied that rights had an independent existence; instead he claimed they were conferred and limited by positive law: 457–461.

156. 198 US 45 (1905).

157. Roscoe Pound, "Interests of Personality Parts I and II," *Harvard Law Review* 28 (1915): 355, 457 (explaining that the law, for example, sought to prevent violence, but that was not primarily to protect a victim's right to bodily integrity, but rather to preserve the peace for everyone).

158. Alexander Meiklejohn, *Political Freedom: The Constitutional Powers of the People* (Oxford University Press, New York, 1960), 27. Book 1 of this book, entitled *Free Speech*, was written in 1948.

159. 75.

160. Stanley Ingber, "The Marketplace of Ideas: A Legitimizing Myth," *Duke Law Journal* (1984): 8–12.

161. 79–80.

162. Alexander Meiklejohn, *Free Speech and its Relation to Self-Government* (Harper Bros, New York, 1948), 104.

163. This assumption is criticized: "it would hardly seem self-evident that the framers believed that the scope of protected debate on the floor of the Congress would be precisely coextensive with that throughout the country at large": Lee Bollinger, "Free Speech and Intellectual Values," *Yale Law Journal* 92 (1983): 450.

164. For example, Lillian BeVier, "The *First Amendment* and Political Speech: An Inquiry Into the Substance and Limits of Principle," *Stanford Law Review* 30 (1978): 299; Robert Bork, "Neutral Principles and Some First Amendment Problems," *Indiana Law Journal* 47 (1971): 20: "constitutional protection should be accorded only to speech that is explicitly political. There is no basis for judicial intervention to protect any other form of expression, be it scientific, literary or that variety of expression we call obscene or pornographic"; Alexander Bickel, *The Morality of Consent* (Yale University Press, New Haven, 1975), 62; Robert Post, "Reconciling Theory and Doctrine in *First Amendment* Jurisprudence," *California Law Review* 88 (2000): 2362.

165. *Richmond Newspapers v Virginia* 448 US 555, 575 (1980) where Burger CJ for White and Stevens JJ noted of the *First Amendment* that "these expressly guaranteed freedoms share a common core purpose of assuring freedom of communication on matters relating to the functioning of government" (Brennan Marshall Stewart and Blackmun JJ concurring in the judgment).

166. Robert Bork, "Neutral Principles and Some *First Amendment* Problems," (1971) 47 *Indiana Law Journal* 47 (1971): 28. Though he criticizes other *First Amendment* jurisprudence on the basis of arbitrary line drawing (e.g., in relation to pornography being that which "appeals to a prurient interest in sex"), his distinction between speech that is political and speech which is not is arguably no different in principle.

167. Lillian BeVier, "The *First Amendment* and Political Speech: An Inquiry Into the Substance and Limits of Principle," *Stanford Law Review* 30 (1978): 344–345; Harry Wellington, "On Freedom of Expression," *Yale Law Journal* 88 (1979): 1111; Lee Bollinger, "Free Speech and Intellectual Values," *Yale Law Journal* 92 (1983): 448–449; Andrew Koppelman, "Veil of Ignorance: Tunnel Constructivism in Free Speech Theory," *Northwestern University Law Review* 107 (2013): 678–679; Alexander Tsesis, "Free Speech Constitutionalism," *University of Illinois Law Review* (2015): 1036; Robert Bork, "Neutral Principles and Some *First Amendment* Problems," *Indiana Law Journal* (1971): 27.

168. Lee Bollinger, "Free Speech and Intellectual Values," *Yale Law Journal* 92 (1983): 451–452; to like effect Wojciech Sadurski, *Freedom of Speech and its Limits* (Kluwer International Publishers, Boston, 1999), 25; Eric Barendt, *Freedom of Speech* (Clarendon Press, Oxford, second edition 2005), 19.

169. "Free speech is not just a practical tool for making systemic repairs, but an affirmation or statement of what we value as a people. To define ourselves exclusively in terms of our political functions . . . is too limited a self-conception": Lee Bolinger, "Free Speech and Intellectual Values," *Yale Law Journal* 92 (1983): 444.

170. Martin Redish, "Value of Free Speech," *University of Pennsylvania Law Review* 130 (1982): 601: "political democracy is merely a means to -, or in another sense, a logical outgrowth of—the much broader value of individual self-realization"; Jack Walker, "A Critique of the Elitist Theory of Democracy," *American Political Science Review* 60 (1966): 288: "the most distinctive feature, and the principal orienting value, of classic democratic theory was its emphasis on individual participation in the development of public policy. . . . Although the classical theorists accepted the basic framework of Lockean democracy, with its emphasis on limited government, they were not primarily concerned with the policies which might be produced in a democracy; above all else they were concerned with human development, the opportunities which existed in political activity to realise the untapped potentials of men."

171. Benjamin DuVal, "Free Communication of Ideas and the Quest for Truth: Towards a Teleological Approach to *First Amendment* Adjudication," *George Washington Law Review* 41 (1972): 194–198.

172. Dieter Grimm, "Freedom of Speech in a Globalized World," in Ivan Hare and James Weinstein, *Extreme Speech and Democracy* (Oxford University Press, New York, 2009), 12: "we know of countries that recognize and respect a fundamental right to free speech without being democracies. Historically constitutionalism is not necessarily linked with democracy. Germany before the Weimar Constitution is an example . . . it shows that freedom of speech does not derive its raison d'etre from democracy. Before being a necessary element of self-government and personal dignity, which is at the centre of the idea of individual fundamental rights."

173. Alexander Meikeljohn, "The *First Amendment* is an Absolute," *Supreme Court Review* [1961]: 262–263: "people do need novels and dramas and paintings and poems because they will be called upon to vote."

174. Lee Bollinger, "Free Speech and Intellectual Values," *Yale Law Journal* 92 (1983): 472.

175. Lawrence Tribe, *American Constitutional Law* (Foundation Press, New York, 1988), 789; Lawrence Alexander and Paul Horton, "The Impossibility of a Free Speech Principle," *Northwestern University Law Review* 78 (1984): 1319.

176. Alexander Tsesis, "Free Speech Constitutionalism," *University of Illinois Law Review* (2015): 1021.

177. 1042–1043: "a theoretically satisfying explanation of free speech should discount neither its public nor private components; the two go hand in hand because representative democracy legitimizes governmental authority insofar as it furthers the interests of individuals . . . the *First Amendment* . . . is not exclusively concerned with self-expression nor self-government but a combination of the two."

178. Wojciech Sadurski, *Freedom of Speech and its Limits* (Kluwer International Publishers, Boston, 1999), 28.

179. Blackstone described law as a "rule of action, which is prescribed by some superior, and which the inferior is bound to obey." Citizens must pay "due respect and obedience" to what is "set over them" by their superiors: 1 William Blackstone, *Commentaries on the Laws of England 1765–1769* (Clarendon Press, Oxford, 1768), 38 and 271.

180. *A Fragment on Government* (Cambridge University Press, Cambridge, 1988), 153–154.

181. Stewart Jay, "The Creation of the *First Amendment* Right to Free Expression: From the Eighteenth Century to the Mid-Twentieth Century," *William Mitchell Law Review* 34 (2008): 780; Kent Greenawalt, *Speech, Crime and the Uses of Language* (Oxford University Press, New York, 1989), 340; Larry Alexander and Paul Horton, "The Impossibility of a Free Speech Principle," *Northwestern University Law Review* 78 (1983): 1319.

Chapter Two

United States Case Law

The United States has amassed a very substantial jurisprudence of case law and secondary literature considering many aspects of the *First Amendment* protection of free speech. Its jurisprudence is sophisticated compared with the other jurisdictions studied in this book, because it has provided constitutional level protection for freedom of speech much longer than the others, allowing a mass of case law and secondary material to develop. Further, its society has demonstrated concern for and practical support for free speech protections virtually since its inception, in contrast with the other jurisdictions studied. The United Kingdom is a special case. Although of course historically it long pre-dates the United States, it long permitted the kind of restrictions on freedom of speech which are completely unpalatable by today's standards.

Further, the secondary material discussing all aspects of freedom of speech is also very voluminous (and very impressive), compared with the secondary writing available on such matters in each of the other jurisdictions studied. American scholars have as a rule considered these issues much more deeply than scholars elsewhere. There is much to learn from the American jurisprudence. This does not, of course, mean the American position is perfect or that the other jurisdictions should necessarily adopt all or some of it. The position of jurisdictions on freedom of speech is to some extent a product of their history, culture and values, so that it is dangerous to simplistically advocate for the adoption of one system's principles or approaches to another, without careful consideration.

The sheer volume of material means it can be challenging to present this material in a coherent and succinct manner. This chapter is structured as follows. Firstly, I will present a succinct summary of the history of freedom of speech in the United States, including a discussion of pre-revolutionary days, adoption of the *First Amendment* and the possible intention behind it, and pivotal developments post-independence. Secondly, I will make some preliminary comments about the approach to various principles that have been utilized in the *First Amendment* case law. Thirdly, I will discuss the categories of free speech case identified in the United States law, because different rules are applied to different categories. Finally, I will make some critical observations about the development of *First Amendment* jurisprudence in the United States.

HISTORY OF FREE SPEECH IN THE UNITED STATES

It is fair to say that rebellion against effective restrictions on freedom of speech was, at least indirectly, one of the causes of the independence movement in the United States.[1] Obviously, one of the concerns of the revolutionaries was the taxation imposed upon them by the British government. They sought to petition the king to at least have their grievances considered. Most significantly, this included the *Stamp Act*, which was imposed on newspapers.[2] As applied, the provisions effectively acted as a form of censorship, discouraging the publication of views disfavored by the then British monarch.

This led the United States Supreme Court to note in *Grosjean v American Press Co*[3] that the English stamp legislation

> constituted one of the factors that aroused the American colonists to protest against taxation for the purposes of the home government, and that the revolution really began when, in 1765, that government sent stamps for newspaper duties to the American colonies.[4]

Justice Sutherland further noted that the fact that the stamp legislation raised revenue was of minor concern; rather the real concern was to exert control and influence over what was published, and to limit the awareness of citizens of the activities of their government. Historians have noted the close link between the revolutionary movement and concerns over freedom of speech.[5] The framers of the *Constitution* insisted upon a narrow definition of the offense of "treason" being included within it, which required that the accused commit an overt act.[6] Mere speech in itself could not amount to treason, in a marked departure from past British practice.[7] Recall from Chapter 1 that at the time of revolution, protection of freedom of speech in United Kingdom law was relatively weak. The various bitter conflicts had eventually led to a dropping of the licensing system and notions of prior restraint. However, parliament's ability to legislate for various offenses to deal with dissidents, including seditious libel, was undeniable in a jurisdiction which celebrated the doctrine of parliamentary sovereignty.

The question was the approach the new American colonies were going to take to speech. How far would they depart from the English law that pertained in the last quarter of the 18th century? Would they have a grand conception of freedom of speech rights, or would they be hemmed in by the position then arrived at in the United Kingdom? Erskine, in his defense of Thomas Paine, had opined that "the liberty of opinion keeps governments themselves in due subjection to their duties."[8] Others would take a narrower view. Positive signs for free speech advocates included acquittal of New York printer Zenger in 1735 on a charge of seditious libel for daring to criticize the royal governor's conduct. A brave jury ignored the judge's instructions that their brief was confined to assessing whether or not the accused was the publisher, which was conceded. Nevertheless, the jury acquitted him. There were no further convictions for seditious libel per se subsequently.[9]

The Court noted in *Grosjean* that the framers of the *Bill of Rights*, specifically the *First Amendment*, must be taken to have been aware of, and responsive to, past practices of the British government in seeking to curb the publication of opinions unfavorable to them. For instance, given the British had abandoned notions of prior restraint of publication, the *First Amendment* could clearly not countenance a government system of approval of publications prior to their being made public.[10] This does not mean that the *First Amendment* was intended to be limited to prohibiting prior restraints on speech.[11] Further extrapolation from the British experience might be difficult, however, since the law in that country continued to develop after 1789, as seen in Chapter 1.

James Madison reflected upon other reasons for the disparate treatment of freedom of speech in American, as opposed to British law, noting that a doctrine of seditious libel might be accommodated in a country governed by a hereditary monarchy, and a legislature which was at least partly hereditary (House of Lords). He contrasted that with the system of government in the United States, where "the executive magistrates are not held to be infallible, nor the legislatures to be omnipotent; and both, being elective are both responsible."[12] This made it "both natural and necessary . . . that a different degree of freedom in the use of the press should (here) be contemplated."[13]

Scholars such as Stephen and Chafee have also noted that evolving ideas about the nature of government naturally impact on attitudes towards free speech. One who believes in government as Leviathan as a strong controlling body with complete power over individuals would not see free speech as necessarily important in preserving that system. The needs and rights of individuals would be completely subjugated to the will and power of the all-powerful sovereign body. Chafee says that this describes the United Kingdom until the late 18th century.

The view of the founding fathers of the United States of the people as sovereign, who consent to being governed by representatives in an accountable democratic body, was much different. In order for that kind of government to function, free speech was absolutely critical.[14] More generally, it has been observed that the Americans' experience with autocratic rule made them suspicious of government, and that this attitude of distrust and suspicion is deeply ingrained in American culture in a way that is not apparent in the other countries which are featured in this book.[15] Further, American culture reflects very much a focus on the individual, and their rights, as opposed to the collective, a concern with making one's own way, as opposed to reliance on government, and a market-oriented, lightly regulated economy, in comparison with other economies. It is not really surprising in that light that the marketplace of ideas notion of free speech first gained prominence in the United States, that *First Amendment* jurisprudence should not reflect a strong concern that not all voices might have access to that market on equal terms.

The founding fathers were aware of continuing English prosecutions and convictions for seditious libel well into the late 18th century, and must be taken to have been aware of attempts to prosecute printers in the original thirteen colonies prior to the revolution, including against Zenger, a New York printer.

Clearly also, those who framed the *First Amendment* were aware of limitations on the free exercise of religion, having experienced firsthand the fact of religious-based persecution, and knowing that the Pilgrims had sailed to Plymouth in order to escape such persecution. It would be a surprise if these great upheavals did not sharpen the concern of the framers of the *Bill of Rights* that freedom of speech and of the press, and freedom of religion, were both fundamental to the kind of society they wished to create, and that the two great freedoms would sometimes overlap.

Having said that, others deny that the framers of the *Bill of Rights* had a collective idea as to the purposes of the *First Amendment*.[16] Some say the founding fathers simply meant to prevent systems of prior licensing; others say that was the "chief purpose" of the provision[17]; others say they intended much stronger protection of free speech than that.[18] It is also a mistake to over-read the intention of the founding fathers. Some have pointed out that the original target of the *First Amendment* was federal law, not state law.[19] It is thus historically inaccurate to paint those why drafted the *Bill of Rights* as being committed to a nation free of censorship and government control over communication, when the original scope of the *First Amendment* was so limited.[20] Many legal scholars view the *Bill of Rights* as more of an attempt to limit the powers of the new central government, rather than a grand vision of human rights protections.[21]

They would deny that the section was intended to prevent the criminalization of sedition.[22] Others have noted that in the early 19th century, states used criminal libel statutes to imprison government critics.[23] States, particularly in the south, banned the publication of literature seen to be anti-slavery and abolitionist in nature. It was only in the 20th century, post the reconstruction era and the passage of the *Fourteenth Amendment*, that it was determined that the *First Amendment* applied to the States, as well as the federal government.[24] Obviously, the events leading up to the civil war had shown that the state governments were just as capable and likely of infringing fundamental human rights as the central government was, and the need for protection of human rights against state government intrusion was painfully evident.

It should also be acknowledged that in the early years of the independence of the United States, Congress passed the *Alien and Sedition Acts* of 1798, under which those critical of the government could, and did, face trial and punishment.[25] The Act contained classic viewpoint discrimination, only prohibiting critical comments about the government. Ten individuals were convicted under the legislation, largely for criticizing the Adams Presidency. Truth was a defense, but this did not prevent successful prosecutions. While the constitutionality of the legislation was never tested in the Supreme Court, some members dismissed constitutional challenges to the legislation while acting as circuit court judges.[26] That Court has latterly suggested that the legislation would have been struck out due to its incompatibility with the *First Amendment*.[27]

Argument over the *Alien and Sedition Act*, with Federalists arguing it was necessary to suppress lies about government in order to permit it to function, and Madison and Jefferson denying the power of Congress to make unlawful pure speech,[28] was a throwback to original debate in Greece about the balancing of free speech with the right of a society to make rules by which it can be effectively governed, and would present a preview for much of the underlying dispute involved in many future *First Amendment* cases, many of which are discussed below. It is said that Jefferson himself, once he gained the Presidency, used seditious libel charges against the Federalists.[29] He used the same law against which he so strongly railed when he was not the president.

Still, after the civil war, reconstruction and the passage of the *Fourteenth Amendment*, censorship continued. An 1891 prosecution against William Lamb for libel was successful. Lamb had criticized a local politician in his newspaper. In 1918 Eugene Debs was jailed for ten years for speaking against American involvement in World War I. The Supreme Court upheld the sentence.[30]

Now that some of the important historical development in the United States has been identified, I will now identify some general principles and approaches that are evident in the United States case law. These principles and approaches transcend the categories into which *First Amendment* case law has morphed, so need to be outlined first.

Preliminary Comments on the United States Case Law

Nearly Absolute Principle of Freedom of Speech

The first is the transcendent idea of "near absolute" liberty in relation to freedom of speech. The phrase "near absolute" implies some limits, and much of the discussion around freedom of speech has been around where the boundary between speech that should be legally permitted, and speech that should be regulated or banned, should be drawn. These limits were acknowledged:

> The rights of free speech and assembly, while fundamental in our democratic society, still do not mean that everyone with opinions or beliefs to express may address a group at any public place and at any time. The constitutional guarantee of liberty implies the existence of an organized society maintaining public order, without which liberty itself would be lost in the excesses of anarchy.[31]

An equivalent view was expressed by Goldberg J for the Court in *Cox v Louisiana*:[32]

> The rights of free speech and assembly, while fundamental in our democratic society, still do not mean that everyone with opinions or beliefs to express may address a group at any public place and at any time. The constitutional guarantee of liberty implies the existence of an organized society maintaining public order, without which liberty itself would be lost in the excesses of anarchy.[33]

Implicitly, courts have an important role in preserving free speech principles, because it is natural for those in power, including governments, to seek to sideline those who challenge that power by criticizing its use.[34] History has taught us about the tendency of governments to do this. Part of the checks and balances in the *Constitution* include the role of the court in preserving fundamental rights, as against attempts by other arms of government to interfere with such rights. The role of courts in interpreting and defending rights as against a powerful legislature and executive is of course contentious, and questions are sometimes raised about the "democracy" aspect of a non-elected arm of government sitting in judgment on the validity of legislative and executive measures. It is not necessary to engage in that rich debate here. However, these concerns tend to be more muted when the rights at issue directly concern aspects of the democratic process, as freedom of speech surely does.[35]

The "near absolute" idea also counters suggestions that some justices have made, to be considered below but often associated with Black and Douglas JJ, that freedom of speech is "absolute," although it is often noted that Black and Douglas JJ were not complete absolutists, and supported some restrictions on freedom of speech. If freedom of speech is not absolute, it becomes important to articulate what limits are constitutionally acceptable. The answer may depend on whether one advocates the truth, marketplace of ideas, democratic self-government, distrust of government or human dignity justifications for freedom of speech, or some combination of some or all of them. Sometimes, more than one of these justifications for freedom of speech is contained within the one judgment.[36]

As will be seen, the United States Supreme Court has broadly passed through several phases in its *First Amendment* articulations in expressing what limits there are on the (otherwise) absoluteness of the right. Given that most judges have accepted that the right is not absolute, the inevitable task was to articulate what such limits were, and what approach to take in identifying them. In terms of limits and approach, the court accepted that speech creating a "clear and present danger" could be regulated. Then it accepted that speech that had a "bad tendency" could be proscribed. Then it adopted an approach known as ad hoc balancing, where freedom of speech is merely one right or interest, to be "balanced" by the court with other rights and interests. Balancing is described in the following passage from *Douds*.

> When particular conduct is regulated in the interests of public order, and the regulation results in an . . . abridgement of speech, the duty of the courts is to determine which of these two conflicting interests demands the greater protection . . . in essence the problem is one of weighing the probable effects of the statute upon the free exercise of the right to speech and assembly against the congressional determination that political strikes are evils of conduct which cause substantial harm . . . we must undertake the "delicate and difficult task . . . to weigh the circumstances and to appraise the substantiality of the reasons advanced in support of the regulation of the free enjoyment of the rights" (quoting the case *Schneider v State* 308 US 147, 161 (1939)).[37]

Obviously a system of balancing can be criticized in terms of its inherent uncertainty and subjectivity:

> In the area of public speech, the result of this 'balancing' has often been tragic. Merely human judges, while extolling the right to speak, have sacrificed it to fear, to the passion of majorities, and to base, self-serving politics. More mundanely, they have compromised speech because of their own bad guesses about the public interest.[38]

There is also disagreement about whether balancing is even appropriate in the case of free speech. Some would accord it special status in the pantheon of rights, it being necessary before other rights can be enjoyed, and thus immune to the kind of balancing that characterizes consideration of other rights.[39]

Perhaps for these reasons, the court moved from an ad hoc balancing approach,[40] in favor of a category-based system.[41] Here, different rules applied to different types of speech. For instance, greater protection of freedom of speech would apply in relation to discussion of public figures than protection afforded to commercial speech. Effectively, this remains the process today for determining *First Amendment* cases.

Occasionally, it is suggested that the federal government lacks constitutional power at all to regulate speech.[42] This would have the same effect as an absolutist position on free speech, at least partly. However, it would leave free speech in a precarious position, since many of the laws which have been challenged on the basis of the *First Amendment* have been state laws. Perhaps not surprisingly, this idea has not gained significant traction in arguments as to how to best protect freedom of speech rights in the United States.

First Amendment and Political Theory

Freedom of speech is fundamental to the framers' concept of the social contract underlying the American *Constitution*, by which the people as sovereign agree to cede certain of their powers to the legislature. It is a system of self-government. The legislature governs as representative of, and with the consent of, the people.[43] Connected with this is an abhorrence of the idea that the government should have a role in controlling what individuals think, believe or communicate. It is considered the essence of self-government that individuals have a right to speak about public affairs,[44] as do corporations.[45] As the Court emphatically put it in *West Virginia Board of Education v Barnette*:

> If there is any fixed star in our constitutional constellation, it is that no official, high or petty, can prescribe what shall be orthodox in politics, nationalism, religion or other matters of opinion or force citizens to confess by word or act their faith therein. If there are any circumstances which permit an exception, they do not now occur to us.[46]

That Court placed the *First Amendment* in the context of liberalism, including prime focus on the individual as the center of society, an emphasis on maximum liberty to a person, and a belief that this was best obtained through small government.[47] There has been recognition that freedom of speech is in a sense foundational to the enjoyment of all other human rights.[48]

The Court also acknowledged the practical challenges in applying the principle to the very different political environment of today.[49] Obviously, the size and role of government has increased substantially today compared with earlier times. This debate is important in assessing the extent of the right to freedom of speech. It is entangled with a broader argument over the political philosophy of liberalism, favoring small government, on the assumption that this is the best choice in order to maximize individual freedom. Under this theory, individuals enjoy maximum choice over their own affairs. Specifically in relation to freedom of speech, liberalism would suggest a very broad ability for an individual to speak their mind, and to access the views of others. It would favor very few restrictions on freedom of speech. Liberalism generally as a political philosophy rose in the 18th and 19th centuries, and peaked early in the 20th century. Obviously it can be seen in evidence in a range of legal principles, including laissez-faire economic theory, contractual and property rights, tort law, as well as constitutional law, and interpretation of the bill of rights.

Liberalism came to be challenged in the 20th century. Calls increased for government regulation of industry practices, and government management and control over the economy. In the United States, this fed the birth of antitrust laws of the early 20th century, and the New Deal of the 1930s. Discussion of rights was not immune from this debate.

Utilitarianism, championed by philosophers such as Bentham, appealed to United States scholars like Oliver Wendel Holmes Jr. and others. Notions of the "greater good" could support and justify what liberals in the classic tradition might view as egregious breaches of individual rights. In the second half of the 20th century, critical legal scholars and others could lament that freedom of speech reinforced existing power structures in society, including patriarchy and racism, and the idea that freedom of speech did not actually deliver on its promises, because those with the power had the microphone, with minority interests sidelined from debates.

Inevitably, those who believed this would reject "truth" and "marketplace of ideas" rationales for protecting speech, on the basis that there were high barriers to entry to the market, and that only certain voices, typically the powerful, were being heard.[50] At the extreme, they might argue there was no such thing as objective truth. Those arguments made it easier to argue for a greater government role in regulating speech. The argument might be that government regulation of speech was necessary to create some kind of "equality." Obviously, such adherents could point to the Greek traditions of freedom of speech, particularly *isonomos*, in this regard. They would argue that government regulation of speech was necessary in order to create the kind of equality of participation that democracy demanded.[51]

To take an example like regulation of so-called hate speech, a classic liberal would likely reject such regulation, on the basis of the individual's right to express their view, as distasteful as it might be to others. This is subject to the possible rider that Mill thought that freedom of speech was subject to the "harm" principle, and some argue that hate speech does harm others, and so should not be protected by freedom of speech principles. However, most free speech advocates would tolerate such speech on the basis of marketplace of ideas philosophy, and the deep antipathy towards regulation of speech based on content and/or viewpoint. In contrast, a critical legal scholar might argue that the fact that the person making the hate speech is able to do so is reflective of power and race structures in our community, which the law should not perpetuate by failing to respond to such speech. On this argument, that speech should not be protected by the law, because it does not address, but perpetuates, lack of equality among members of society.[52] Others argued hate speech should only be permitted if it is made by the oppressed minority.[53] Some have argued that by failing to condone such speech, the government is in effect actively supporting it.[54] This argument about the limits of freedom of speech is really part of a much broader debate between adherents of classic liberalism, favoring small government on the basis that it maximizes personal freedom and liberty, and post-modernist thought, favoring a larger, interventionary government, on the basis that laissez-faire is inequitable, and reflects entrenched power based on patriarchy, race, or other features.[55]

Further, the focus of rights had moved from the individual to embrace notions of "social interests" and "public interests."[56] Pound and others suggested that the law did and should protect individual rights not for the sake of the individual per se, but for, and to the extent of, protection of important social and public interests.[57] This brought out the tension between notions of individual rights and notions of communal rights.

This shift in philosophical sentiment explains how in the 20th century there has been greater judicial acceptance of the legitimacy of the government regulating speech. There are quite broad articulations of the scope of government power to legislate in a manner invasive of *First Amendment* rights. So, for instance, in *United States v O'Brien*,[58] Warren CJ for the Court suggested four elements should be applied in determining whether or not a law infringed the *First Amendment*: (a) whether it was within the constitutional power of the government; (b) whether it furthered an important or substantial governmental interest; (c) whether the governmental interest was unrelated to the suppression of free speech; and (d) whether the incidental restriction on alleged *First Amendment* freedoms was no greater than necessary to further that interest.[59] On this basis, the Court justified the conviction of a person who willfully burned their draft card. The Court has insisted on evidence that the government's claims that the challenged legislation is needed to further a legitimate government interests, rather than simply accept the government's claims on face value.[60] It should be acknowledged that this finding occurred in the context of a burden on expression that was incidental in terms of an intention to proscribe particular conduct.

Purpose and Objective of Free Speech Protection in the First Amendment

Another theme that can be seen across the case law is difference of opinion as to the actual purpose of the *First Amendment*. While some courts clearly favor the marketplace of ideas/discovery of truth rationale,[61] others clearly favor the role of free speech in developing an individual and permitting them to reach their full potential.[62] Others tie free speech very closely to notions of self-government; in other words that the need for freedom of speech flows from the notion of self-government.[63] Laurence Tribe has set out what he considers to be essential components of a satisfactory doctrine of free speech,[64] but it is not clear that any of the above approaches meets the criteria that the learned professor has set.

It has been observed by other scholars in the field that we must be careful not to conceive of free speech as mere protection from an authoritarian government. While this is an important aspect of freedom of speech rights, scholars have noted that it is relatively common that interferences with freedom of speech are in fact a reflection of democracy, in the sense of a government acting with the likely consent of a majority of people, against a minority. Those scholars who believe this are naturally not going to be supportive of freedom of speech as confined by Meiklejohn in terms of self-government, and what is needed for such a system of government to function.[65] As discussed, Meiklejohn was primarily concerned that individuals have all of the required information to make informed decisions, rather than government efforts at suppression of speech. Similarly, Isaiah Berlin speaks of concepts of "negative liberty," under which individuals have a right to speak and to hear information, towards a concept of "positive liberty," linked to self-development.[66]

Whether the Type of Speech Matters

The next question is whether the tone of the speech matters, in determining the extent to which it is constitutionally protected. A recurring theme is that the *First Amendment* applies to speech, although it is expressed caustically.[67] It is not confined to civilized discourse.[68]

The second question is whether the fact that comments are controversial matters, in determining the extent to which it is constitutionally protected. *First Amendment* rights extend to inappropriate and controversial comments.[69] The Court has found that, in fact, speech may best achieve its purpose when it induces unrest, discontent and anger.[70] It includes the expression of views that most members of society would disagree with and/or find morally objectionable.[71]

There can be a fine line, though, between speech that is merely controversial and/or unpopular, and thus protected by the *First Amendment*, and speech which the Court has permitted the legislature to regulate, on the basis that it is so controversial that it is likely to provoke unrest. It should be conceded that the cases are not all able to be reconciled, and that at some times on the free speech versus public order continuum, the Court has landed in different places over time. Obviously, changes in court personnel over time go some way to explaining this. And, of course, the Court is not immune from changes in society and community sentiment. It may not be a surprise that during wartime and times of great uncertainty, for instance, in the immediate aftermath of World War I, or the start of the Cold War, the Court's tolerance for government censorship of speech was greater.[72]

The Court has acknowledged, though, that some types of speech have such little value that they should be accorded bare *First Amendment* protection. These categories of non-protected speech include so-called fighting words,[73] libelous speech,[74] obscenity,[75] and child pornography.[76] The Court rejected an opportunity to add depiction of animal cruelty to this list,[77] as well as violent video games aimed at youth.[78] The Court's current attitude appears to tolerate these historical exceptions to free speech principles, but to interpret the existing ones narrowly, and not to add new categories.

Different views have been expressed regarding whether the value of the particular speech, or its contribution to the purposes of free speech, is relevant in determining its constitutionality. Here note a sharp contrast in sentiments expressed by Murphy J for the Court in *Chaplinsky v New Hampshire* in 1942,[79] and Roberts CJ for Stevens Scalia Kennedy Thomas Ginsburg Breyer and Sotomayor JJ in *United States v Stevens*.[80] In *Chaplinsky* Murphy J explained why certain categories of speech, including at that time obscenity, libel, fighting words and speech tending to a breach of the peace, enjoyed no *First Amendment* protection. He said this was because

> such utterances are no essential part of any exposition of ideas and are of such slight social value as a step to truth that any benefit that may be derived from them is clearly outweighed by the social interest in order and morality.[81]

In other words, the view at this time was that speech should be categorized into particular kinds, with *First Amendment* protection extending to some categories and not others, and some categories enjoying stronger protection than others. This category-based approach to free speech contrasts with the approach in other jurisdictions, which typically adopt a proportionality approach.[82] This distinction will be further considered in Chapter 6. The other idea contained in the *Chaplinsky* dicta above was that particular speech enjoys protection based on its connection with the purposes of free speech. This view remains contentious. It tends to be reflected more in the Canadian court's approach to free speech, as we will see in Chapter 4.

In terms of recognizing that some kinds of speech are more valuable than others, there is evidence that the Court believes that speech about so-called public issues, however defined,[83] is sometimes entitled to the strongest protection under the *First Amendment*.[84] Something like commercial speech would attract some, but not full-throated, protection. Of course, this does not mean that the right to free speech is limited to the political context. Indeed, the court has pointedly denied that it is so limited:

> Freedom of discussion, if it would fulfil its historic function in this nation, must embrace all issues about which information is needed or appropriate to enable the members of society to cope with the exigencies of their period.[85]

There is often strong disagreement as to whether a topic is one of "public concern" and thus entitled to the highest level of *First Amendment* freedom. freedom. So, for example, the Court split 5:4 on the question of whether information about the solvency of a business was considered to be of "public concern."[86]

This does not mean that other kinds of speech are completely unprotected: "our cases have never suggested that expression about philosophical, social, economic, literary or ethical matters—to take a nonexhaustive list of labels—is not entitled to full *First Amendment* protection."[87] In contrast, some other types of speech is entitled only to marginal protection, for example, swearing[88] and/or personal invective or abuse.[89] Not all justices accept this.[90] Speech that may not be protected when made available to all members of the public, including minors, may be protected if it is only available to adults.[91]

Recently the Court has spoken against trying to place a presume value on particular kinds of speech, reifying some speech over others. This was the position of eight justices in *Stevens*:

> most of what we say to one another lacks religious, political, scientific, educational, journalistic, historical or artistic value (let alone serious value), but it is still sheltered from Government regulation.[92]

Perhaps the best way to reconcile all of these comments is to state that the *First Amendment* applies to speech on all topics, apart from the categories of non-protected speech noted earlier. The Court will not engage in the business of trying to identify whether speech is "valuable," given the inevitable difficulties involved in doing so. However, the extent of its protection does seem to vary according to the nature of the speech in terms of topic, for instance, that speech on public issues will be given greater protection than commercial speech. But both types of speech enjoy protection.

The third question is whether the fact the material is demonstrably true or false is relevant, in determining the extent to which it is constitutionally protected. The general position is that it is not necessary that material be true, or that it presents a nuanced or balanced view, to be accorded *First Amend-*

ment protection.[93] These are often today referred to as "fake news," and it is clear that the exponential growth of technology has permitted vast quantities of "fake news" to be distributed among members of the community. Demonstrably, like the categories noted in *Chaplinsky*, untruths or fake news might be considered of "little social value as a step to truth," and given their tendency to be believed and to mislead, may actively take individuals a few steps along a path away from truth. For a while, the Court suggested that deliberate untruths were outside *First Amendment* protection. In *Garrison v Louisiana* it said that

> calculated falsehood falls into that class of utterances which "are no essential part of any exposition of ideas and . . . of slight social value as a step to truth" (citing *Chaplinsky*) . . . hence the knowingly false statement and the false statement made with reckless disregard of truth do not enjoy constitutional protection.[94]

However, eventually the Court would turn against this notion. They would be aware that in the past, innocuous sounding legislation seeking to criminalize the spreading of "false news" was used ruthlessly to silence political opponents. By 2012, a majority had turned away from the idea that demonstrably false speech could be outside the realm of *First Amendment* protection, invalidating a statute that made it a crime for a person to falsely claim they had received military medals. The accused admitted they had made these false claims, but the Court found that generally the *First Amendment* did not permit governments to criminalize the spreading of false news, unless there was evidence it was done for material gain.[95]

The fourth question is whether the identity of the speaker is relevant in determining the extent to which the *First Amendment* protect speech. Specifically, some special rules may be applied to public officers. Speech by public officers on matters of public interest may be especially valuable in terms of their contribution to important public policy debate, given the expertise and insights that a public officer may have, that other members of the community may not.[96] This is particularly appropriate when they are speaking as a private citizen, rather than as an employee of the organization.[97] These matters will be elaborated upon further in a subsequent book: Anthony Gray, *Freedom of Speech in Practice: Controversial Applications of Law and Theory* (Lexington Books, Maryland, 2019). The Court has found that other groups, for example, military personnel, may also have more limited *First Amendment* rights than those in the civilian realm.[98]

Discrimination Based on Content or Viewpoint

Somewhat confusingly and inconsistently, though I have just acknowledged that the court appears to value speech of a certain kind (on public issues) more than it does commercial speech, at the same time the court has decried legislation that discriminates on the basis of content. Even worse is legislation that discriminates on the basis of viewpoint.[99] Thus, although the court itself discriminates on the basis of content in determining the extent of *First Amendment* protection to be accorded speech, it frowns upon legislatures that do so.[100]

Not all content-based restrictions are invalid.[101] Those relating to "low-value" speech are more likely to be validated.[102] However, content-based restrictions must be justified by a compelling state interest, and narrowly drawn to achieve that end.[103] In other words, they are subject to a strict scrutiny test. The state will have to lead evidence as to this, and the court will carefully consider whether the state has made its case with strong evidence.[104] It is rare that legislation passes a strict scrutiny test, but possible.[105]

Some cases have found that regulation is content-neutral where it is passed in order to achieve an objective other than that of censoring speech,[106] although this is disputed.[107] Clearly the concern with content and viewpoint-based discrimination is that it is effectively censorship; the perception arises that the government regulator is seeking to prevent the dissemination of an idea or viewpoint with which it disagrees. Obviously, this raises very serious *First Amendment* questions, given the role of free speech in the marketplace of ideas, truth-seeking, self-actualization theory, and/or self-government. The idea that a government could censor an idea with which it disagrees is very difficult to accept, regardless of which *First Amendment* theory is chosen. Where restrictions on speech are content and viewpoint neutral, they will be subject to what some call "intermediate scrutiny" rather than strict scrutiny.[108] Under a system of intermediate scrutiny, the government must show that its regulation is narrowly tailored to a significant government interest, and that alternative avenues remain available for communication. It need not be the least restrictive means available.[109] Where regulation is content-neutral, an intermediate level of scrutiny, rather than strict scrutiny, is applied. However, it is dangerous for the government when a substantial portion of its legislation does not link with its supposed goals.[110]

Thus, reasonable "time, place and manner" restrictions may be valid,[111] where they serve a legitimate government interest, where they are narrowly tailored to meeting that interest, and whether other channels of communication are readily available.[112]

The Importance of Classifying the Forum

If the challenged legislation applies in particular government-owned or government-controlled spaces only, the court will have to consider its existing jurisprudence in relation to space-based restrictions. The extent of the state's constitutional power to regulate speech or communication depends on whether the relevant "forum" in which the speech or communication has or would take place is public in nature.[113] Speech made in a traditional public forum or designated public forum is treated more deferentially than speech in a non-public forum, and laws impinging upon it will be subject to strict scrutiny, requiring compelling justification and narrowly drawn to serve that justification.[114] Traditionally a public place would include parks, streets and sidewalks. Recently the Court suggested cyberspace would now qualify as a public forum.[115] A University room commonly made available for the holding of public meetings is a public forum.[116] A designated public forum is one which is not traditionally used for exchanges, but one which the government has opened for the purposes of discussion.[117]

Sometimes universities are classified as limited public fora. In a limited public forum, restrictions on speech are generally permissible, if they are reasonable in light of the purpose/s of the forum.[118] Restrictions based on content, but not viewpoint, may be permitted, but only if the reasons for regulation are compelling, and the restrictions are narrowly tailored.[119] An interschool mail system and teacher inboxes have been treated as being equivalent to a (limited) public forum.[120] So have a range of student groups recognized within a school environment and permitted to meet on school premises outside hours of tuition.[121] A student-run newspaper has been treated as effectively a non-public forum, in circumstances where the school principal had to approve the content of the newspaper prior to its release.[122]

If the legislature seeks to regulate speech within a forum designated as public, it must meet a heavy burden. In most cases regulation will be content-neutral. In such cases, reasonable "time, place, and manner" restrictions will be acceptable, if they are narrowly tailored to meet a significant government interest or objective, and there are sufficient alternative channels of communication.[123] Viewpoint-based restrictions will generally not be acceptable.[124] Content-based restrictions might be justified, but would be subject to strict scrutiny. The legislature would need to show a compelling state interest in regulating speech in a public forum, and that the legislation was no more invasive than necessary in order to achieve that interest (strict scrutiny). These are not easy tests to satisfy.

Of course, the fact that a University hosts a group holding a meeting does not imply that the University agrees with, endorses or condones any of the views that might be aired at the meeting.[125] Universities also occupy a somewhat privileged position given their important role in public debate.[126] Of course, classifying the University as a public forum or limited public forum does not deny the University's protected right to make academic judgments about how it will allocate its resources, whom to employ, what to teach and how, and whom to enroll.[127]

Legislatures are much more free to regulate speech in areas that are not public fora. They could regulate speech in a non-public forum provided the restrictions are reasonable and non-viewpoint based.[128] In other words, content-based restrictions are acceptable in the case of a non-public fora, if they meet the tests of reasonableness. School classrooms are an example of a non-public forum, as are election polling stations.

Sometimes there can be conjecture as to how to classify a particular space as a public forum or non-public forum. This is not surprising, since such a determination can have a significant impact on the resolution of the *First Amendment* question. So, for example, protesters who protested in the grounds of the state capitol building were within their *First Amendment* rights, partly because the grounds had traditionally been open to and used by the public.[129] In contrast, a closely divided court found that protesters engaged in a peaceful protested conducted on jail grounds not typically used by the public were not within their *First Amendment* rights.[130]

Prior Restraints

The Court has repeatedly expressed concern with any system under which an individual is required to obtain a license or permit or other type of permission before they can communicate. This type of regime has obvious parallels with the kind of prior restraint system used for many years in England prior to independence, and which would have been uppermost in the minds of those who drafted the *Bill of Rights*. A system of prior restraint is not per se invalid,[131] but where it is coupled with broad, unbridled discretion in a public official as to whether or not such license or permit should be granted, it is likely to be unconstitutional due to its breach of *First Amendment* rights.[132]

The Court accepted in *Near v Minnesota* that the prohibition on prior restraint provisions was not absolute.[133] It nominated three situations where it might consider a prior restraint regime. The first was a time of war, where restrictions that may not be acceptable in peace time may be acceptable, the second related to the government's right to enforce standards of decency, and the third permitted the state to take measures to protect the security of the community.[134]

It would interpret these exceptions narrowly. It cited a "heavy burden of showing justification for the imposition of such a restraint."[135] It rejected the United States President's attempt to enjoin the publication of sensitive government material that had fallen into the hands of the press, including material on the controversial Vietnam war, though members of the court acknowledged that publication of the material would seriously damage public interests.[136]

The Court also began to turn against measures providing for prior government approval prior to distribution, such as movies.[137]

Right to be Left Alone

It should also be conceded that the Court has recognized the right of an individual to be left alone.[138] Thus, where a person has indicated they do not wish to receive particular communications, it is not offensive to the *First Amendment* for legislation prohibiting the further distribution of that kind of communication to that individual.[139] Somewhat analogously, the Court has frowned upon what it regards as "compelled speech"; in other words, provisions which in effect force a person to support speech which they do not favor. For this reason, the Supreme Court recently invalidated on *First Amendment* grounds a provision which required non-union members to be represented by a union, whether or not the individual agreed to it, and required them to pay "agency fees" to the union.[140]

Applicability of General Constitutional Doctrines

General principles of constitutional due process, including the void for vagueness principle and the restriction on laws based on "overbreadth," are also regularly applied in the context of laws limiting speech. Examples of laws that have been declared invalid due to the void for vagueness principle in the speech area include a law that made it unlawful to "treat contemptuously the flag of the United States,"[141] a law prohibiting the display of a red flag in a public or meeting place as a symbol of opposition to organized government,[142] a law prohibiting three or more individuals from congregating on a sidewalk and conducting themselves in a manner that is "annoying" to passers-by,[143] a law attempting to define a "gangster" as someone who was in the company of at least one another, not engaged in lawful employment, and with prior convictions for disorderly conduct,[144] and a law prohibiting the knowing transmission of "obscene or indecent" or "patently offensive" messages to minors.[145] The concern here is with the possibility of arbitrary and/or discriminatory application of the relevant laws. Concerns arise when intelligent people are required to guess at the meaning of the provision.[146] The Court has said it will apply the void for vagueness doctrine more stringently when the relevant law impacts *First Amendment* freedoms.[147]

A law might be overbroad because its scope is larger than can be justified. So, for example, a law prohibiting association might be overbroad where it is liable to ensnare innocent associations.[148] A law might be overbroad because it is overly prescriptive, in terms of time, place or manner of expressive conduct,[149] or because it requires administrative approval based on broad or non-existent criteria prior to *First Amendment* rights being exercised.[150] It might be overbroad because its reach is larger, or substantially larger, than required by the legitimate interests said to animate its enactment.[151] A law regulating conduct and not speech may also be found to be overbroad, although in such cases the Court has insisted the overbreadth be substantial.[152]

Conduct Versus Speech

Finally, the *First Amendment* does not preclude the state from legislating to make a course of conduct illegal, as opposed to speech. A feature of *First Amendment* doctrine is a sharp division between freedom of speech, for which substantial protection will be accorded, and activity, which legislatures are much more free to regulate.[153] For example, a state can make it unlawful for an individual to target a business because they will not agree to anti-competitive practices. Although this might violate the individual's freedom of speech, a law of that nature will not infringe the *First Amendment*.[154] The right to freedom of speech extends to expressive conduct[155]; again, the fact the idea expressed may be offensive to some or many is irrelevant.[156]

Having said that, it should not be thought that the line between speech, on the one hand, and conduct, on the other, is always clear. The Court has acknowledged the fact that conduct can be highly expressive in nature. One notorious example is the burning of a cross, particularly in the south of the United States. Some doubt whether the distinction can or should be made.[157]

At a more general level, at times the United States Supreme Court has distinguished between mere speech, and actions that may be related to speech, for example, that speech has motivated or induced action. Specifically, it has sometimes been said that while the *First Amendment* protects virtually all speech, it has less to say regarding the regulation of conduct.[158] However, the Court came to doubt the notion that a neat division could be made between speech, on the one hand, and action on the other.[159]

Injunctions

Some difference of opinion is evident on the question of whether the *First Amendment* is applied in the same way in the context of an injunction that affects free speech compared with a statute which does so. A majority of the Court said that in the case of an injunction, the question was whether it burdened no more speech than was necessary to serve a significant governmental interest; a minority said that in such cases strict scrutiny was required, and the injunction would only survive *First Amendment* scrutiny if it was shown to serve a compelling government interest and narrowly tailored to meet that objective.[160]

Categories of Case

I will now consider in more detail the categories of case in which free speech issues have been discussed in the United States.

Cases Involving Sedition Type Legislation

The main periods during which this kind of legislation flourished in the United States were the late 18th and early 20th centuries, though some might add the start of the Cold War period as a further example. With the benefit of hindsight, Emerson draws several conclusions about the sedition-type legislation crafted in these eras. Firstly, he states the need for restrictions on speech were overstated; that restrictions on free speech were hastily crafted and regulated speech extremely tightly; that the legislation suffered from vagueness in its language; truth was not a defense; proof of intent was not required; the administration of the provisions included practices antithetical to a free society, including lack of due process; the legislation was used to achieve objectives quite distinct from its purported objectives; the social gains attributable to the restrictions used proved to be minimal; but the social cost of such legislation were very heavy, in terms of those prosecuted. He concluded the lesson of history was that limitations imposed on discussion tended to quickly destroy the structure of free speech, and were very difficult to keep within manageable boundaries.[161]

It was pointed out above that there were numerous convictions of individuals under the *Alien and Sedition Act* 1798. The constitutionality of that legislation was never considered by the Supreme Court, but individual members of the Court on circuit dismissed *First Amendment* challenges to it. A sequel to that legislation was the *Espionage Act* 1917, the same year in which the United States joined World War I. The Act created offenses of making false statements or reports intending to interfere with the war effort, including promoting enemy successes, causing insubordination, disloyalty or mutiny among members of the armed forces, and obstruction of enlistment and recruitment. It was amended in the following year to prohibit disloyal, profane, scurrilous or abusive language about the United States form of government, and to urge curtailment of manufacture of items used in the war effort.

Chafee notes that in various state decisions made pursuant to the Act, individuals were jailed for lengthy periods merely for making anti-war statements. He noted a case where the defendant's statement in a newspaper that she was for the people, and the government was for profiteers, attracted a 10 year jail term. Others who compared the plight of American troops with Hessian troopers were jailed for 20 years. He noted that the results were similar to those under the 1798 legislation, concluding that:

> The courts have treated opinions as statements of fact and then condemned them as false because they differed from the President's speech or the resolution of Congress declaring war. They have made it impossible for an opponent of the war to write an article or even a letter in a newspaper of general circulation because it will be read in some training camp where it might cause insubordination or interfere with military success.[162]

It was said that more than 2,000 individuals were charged with offenses under the legislation, with about half convicted.[163] Proof that the charged individuals had in fact compromised America's war effort was unnecessary.

In the shadows of World War I, a defendant was convicted after distributing leaflets that opposed the military draft, and urged others not to submit to it.[164] His appeal on the basis that the relevant espionage legislation infringed his *First Amendment* rights was unsuccessful. Again, this was despite there being no evidence that the defendant's actions in any way actually disrupted America's war efforts. This era presented the first opportunities for the Court to indicate how it would reconcile the needs of national security with the ideals of free speech. Was free speech to be absolute in nature? If it were not absolute, how would the court articulate the acceptable parameters for suppression of speech, for the greater good of national security?

It was here in *Schenck* that Holmes J for the Court rejected an argument that freedom of speech was absolute. Further, he attempted to articulate the test to be utilized in determining the validity of legislation which impacted speech. He would utter the famous *First Amendment* dictum that speech might be outside its protections when it created a "clear and present danger" of the bringing about of substantive evils that governments had a right to prevent.[165] And further, that based on this reasoning, the act of a person shouting "fire" in a theatre, thereby causing panic, would not be accorded *First Amendment* protection. Similar sentiments were evident in *Abrams v United States*.[166]

These formulations were clearly a narrower description of the circumstances in which state regulation of speech was constitutionally acceptable, compared with the state decisions pre-dating *Schenck* and *Abrams*.[167] However, many scholars were critical of the compromise articulated by Justice Holmes on the basis that it did not accord sufficient weight to freedom of speech values.[168] Holmes also insisted on proof of actual intention to subvert America's war effort, rather than surmise based on an idea that an accused could be expected to have intended the reasonable consequences of their behavior.[169]

Many states followed the lead of the federal government. By 1920, 32 states had anti-sedition legislation outlawing the making of statements deemed seditious and displaying of the "red flag," which was interpreted to mean support for anarchy.

In one leading case, *Gitlow v New York*,[170] the appellant was charged with an offense against New York criminal law. The offense was criminal anarchy, defined as a doctrine advocating the overthrow of government by force or violence, by assassination of relevant government officers, or other unlawful means. The New York law made it an offense to advocate what amounted to criminal anarchy. Gitlow was charged with the offense after circulating a pamphlet that suggested the overthrow of organized government by force, violence, and unlawful means.

The Supreme Court rejected a constitutional challenge to the provision. In so doing, it found that the *First Amendment* did not contain an absolute right to speak or publish anything one wished. It found that the state in the exercise of its police power could punish individuals who abused the freedom "by utterances inimical to the public welfare, tending to corrupt public morals, incite to crime, or disturb the public peace."[171] This seemed to be a broader formulation of the ability of legislatures to restrict speech notwithstanding the *First Amendment* than what the Court had articulated just a few years earlier. The Court added that a state was entitled to punish utterances endangering the foundations of organized government. It concluded the state could punish conduct considered to imperil or subvert the government, and "impede or hinder it in the performance of its governmental duties."[172] A state had a right, indeed a duty, to self-preserve. This became known as the "bad tendency" doctrine, permitting speech to be regulated given its possible or likely negative impacts on listeners. The dangers it posed to free speech have been noted.[173]

The Court reached a similar conclusion with respect to criminal syndicate legislation outlawing the advocacy, teaching or aiding and abetting of the commission of crime as a method of seeking change in industrial ownership or control, or effecting political change. The legislation survived constitutional challenge.[174] Again, the Court was asked to articulate how free speech rights could be reconciled with the responsibility of the state to provide a safe and secure community.

Justice Brandeis, concurring, sought to limit restrictions on freedom of speech in terms of "fear and imminent danger of some substantive evil." He balanced this with strong freedom of speech protections in this way:

> Those who won our independence believed that the final end of the state was to make men free to develop their faculties; and that in its government the deliberative forces should prevail over the arbitrary. They valued liberty both as an end and a means. They believed liberty to be the secret of happiness and courage to be the secret of liberty They believed that freedom to think as you will and to speak as you think are means indispensable to the discovery and spread of political truth; that without free speech and assembly discussion would be futile; that with them, discussion affords ordinarily adequate protection against the dissemination of noxious doctrine; that the greatest menace to freedom is an inert people; that public discussion is a political duty; and that this should be a fundamental principle of the American government. They recognized the risks to which all human institutions are subject. But they knew that order cannot be secured merely through fear of punishment for its infraction; that it is hazardous to discourage thought, hope and imagination; that fear breeds repression; that repression breeds hate; that hate menaces stable government; that the path of safety lies in the opportunity to discuss freely

supposed grievances and proposed remedies; and that the fitting remedy for evil counsels is good ones. Believing in the power of reason as applied through public discussion, they eschewed silence coerced by law . . . recognizing the occasional tyrannies of governing majorities, they amended the *Constitution* so that free speech and assembly should be guaranteed.

Fear of serious injury cannot alone justify suppression of free speech and assembly. Men feared witches and burnt women. It is the function of speech to free men from the bondage of irrational fears. To justify suppression of free speech there must be reasonable ground to fear that serious evil will result if free speech is practiced. There must be reasonable ground to believe that the danger apprehended is imminent (and serious) . . . even advocacy of violation . . . is not a justification for denying free speech where the advocacy falls short of incitement and there is nothing to indicate that the advocacy would be immediately acted on. The wide difference between advocacy and incitement, between preparation and attempt, between assembling and conspiracy, must be borne in mind. In order to support a finding of clear and present danger it must be shown either the immediate serious violence was to be expected or was advocated, or that the past conduct furnished reason to believe that such advocacy was then contemplated.

Those who won our independence were not cowards. They did not fear political change. They did not exalt order at the cost of liberty. To courageous, self-reliant men, with confidence in the power of free and fearless reasoning applied through the processes of popular government, no danger flowing from speech can be deemed clear and present, unless the incidence of the evil apprehended is so imminent that it may befall before there is opportunity for full discussion. If there was time to expose through discussion the falsehood and fallacies, to avert the evil by the processes of education, the remedy to be applied is more speech, not enforced silence. Only an emergency can justify repression . . . (but) even imminent danger cannot justify resort to prohibition of these functions essential to effective democracy, unless the evil apprehended is relatively serious . . . the fact that speech is likely to result in some violence or in destruction of property is not enough to justify its suppression. There must be the probability of serious injury to the state. Among free men, the deterrents ordinarily to be applied to prevent crime are education and punishment for violations of the law, not abridgment of the rights of free speech and assembly.[175]

On the other hand, the Court struck out criminal syndicalism legislation in *De Jonge v Oregon.*[176] The petitioner had been charged with such an offense. The evidence suggested he had assisted in the conduct of a meeting of the Communist Party. No unlawful conduct was advocated, encouraged, or discussed at the meeting. The Court found the legislation was invalid due to its free speech implications. It conceded that free speech rights

May be abused by using speech or press or assembly in order to incite to violence and crime. The people through their legislatures may protect themselves against that abuse. But the legislative intervention can find constitution-

> al justification only by dealing with the abuse. The rights themselves must not be curtailed. The greater the importance of curtailing the community from incitements to the overthrow of our institutions by force and violence, the more imperative is the need to preserve inviolate the constitutional rights of free speech, free press and free assembly in order to maintain the opportunity for free political discussion, to the end that government may be responsible to the will of the people and that changes, if desired, may be obtained be peaceful means. Therein lies the security of the republic, the very foundation of constitutional government.[177]

The legislation was invalid because it sought to make peaceful assembly a crime.[178]

At the start of the Cold War, legislation making it unlawful to advocate, abet, or advise the propriety of overthrowing any government in the United States, to publish, distribute, or teach the necessity of overthrowing or destroying any government in the United States, or to organize any group or assembly who teach, advocate, or encourage the overthrow of any such government was held valid, despite a *First Amendment* challenge.[179] The accused were leaders of the Communist Party in the United States. The majority asserted the right of government to limit speech, where such speech was of the kind considered here, threatening the very structure of government. This was an occasion where the "clear and present danger" exception to freedom of speech applied. Governments were not helpless "in the face of preparation for revolution."[180] Relevant factors would include whether the relevant group was of sufficient size so as to be dangerous, whether it was sufficiently oriented towards action, and other facts suggesting the practical threat of imminent attack.

A few years later the Court distinguished between mere advocacy of "abstract doctrine," though it may be communist in nature and antithetical to American culture, and the advocacy of action. It was the distinction between urging someone to believe something, and urging someone to do something. Essentially, the *First Amendment* protected the former, but not the latter.[181]

Somewhat analogously, the Court upheld statutes requiring as a condition of employment in the public sector that would-be employees swear allegiance to the United States government, and were not members of an organization with an objective of overthrowing the established government through violence or other unlawful means. However, the Court conditioned the validity of such measures on a finding that the relevant person who joined the organization was aware of the organization's unlawful objectives; mere association or membership of the group was not sufficient in order for them to be denied employment on that basis.[182] This spelled invalidity for a state statute conditioning employment at a state university on the basis that the employee expressed an oath confirming their support for the United States system of government, and requiring them to declare they had not been a member of a communist organization within the past five years.[183]

The actions of the House of Representatives Committee on Un-American Activities were unsuccessfully challenged in *Barenblatt v United States.*[184] There the petitioner was called to testify before the committee, based on the suspicion that he was a communist working in an American University. When the Committee asked him whether he was or had been a member of the Communist Party, he refused to answer. He was convicted of failing to answer questions put to him by the committee, and sentenced to a six month jail term. His argument that the legislation, by in effect forcing him to answer questions, was offensive to the protection of free speech in the *First Amendment* was rejected by a majority of the Court.[185] The Court noted earlier cases had recognized a close connection between Communist Party activity, and attempts to overthrow the government.

Again a prosecution against a member of the Communist Party was upheld in 1961 in *Scales v United States.*[186] The statute made it an offense to knowingly be a member of an organization that advocated the overthrow of the government by violence or force. In validating the provision, the majority of the Court confined it to "active" members who performed actions for the benefit of the proscribed organization. Black and Douglas JJ (dissenting) maintained their argument in favor of an absolutist position on freedom of speech, as opposed to a balancing approach, and noted that *Scales* had committed no actions that were in themselves criminal; thus in effect he had been jailed for what he believed in, a situation which the *Constitution* itself did not portend, defining treason in such a way as to require overt acts, rather than mere beliefs.

While at one time the Supreme Court accepted the constitutional validity of loyalty oath requirements,[187] legislation conditioning a tax exemption upon the taxpayer signing a pledge of loyalty to the United States was struck out on due process and *First Amendment* grounds.[188] Black and Douglas JJ articulated their absolutist, or near absolutist, position on freedom of speech.[189] They maintained that the rights protected by the *First Amendment* were absolutely indispensable for the American system of government based on the consent of informed citizens and on the basis of an agreement to respect the rights of all, including unpopular minorities. They called attempts to penalize individuals because of their political views "hopelessly repugnant" to freedom of speech principles.[190]

Subsequently a broader view would be taken of the extent of *First Amendment* protection in relation to such statutes in *Brandenburg*. Thus, there was a successful challenge to a statute creating a criminal offense to advocate "the duty, necessity, or propriety of crime, sabotage, violence, or unlawful methods of terrorism as a means of accomplishing industrial or political reform," and for creating an association to further such ends.[191] The person convicted was a leader of the Ku Klux Klan. He was a member of a group which burned a cross, and made derogatory comments about African-American people and Jewish people. During a speech, he referred to the possibility that if the President continued, in his view, to "suppress the white, Caucasian race," there might have to be "revengeance."

The Supreme Court overturned his conviction. The majority found that the state could not criminalize the advocacy of force or law violation, unless such advocacy was directed to inciting or producing imminent lawless action, and was likely to do so. This was a refinement to the "clear and present danger" test of earlier decisions. This should be distinguished from mere abstract teaching that might include references to the use of force or violence.[192] By not distinguishing between the two, the statute was overbroad, and infringed the appellant's *First Amendment* rights. The majority also overturned the earlier decision in *Whitney v California* and its "bad tendency" approach to *First Amendment* questions. The protection of free speech contemplated by the *First Amendment* was much broader.

Concurring, a broader conception of the protections to speech encompassed in the *First Amendment* was articulated by Douglas J, with whom Black J agreed. Douglas J rejected the "clear and present danger" limit on speech, articulated in *Schenck* and other cases.[193] It could easily be manipulated to destroy important aspects of the *First Amendment*. Douglas J agreed with the majority's overrule of *Whitney*, on the basis that it could be argued that the expression of every idea was an incitement. Douglas J emphasized that action was entitled to just as much *First Amendment* protection as pure speech.[194]

At one time governments were able to demand details of the membership lists and oath requirements of particular associations. Such a law was considered by the Supreme Court in 1928 in *New York ex rel Bryant v Zimmermann*.[195] The measure was held valid. No member of the court raised any *First Amendment* objection on free speech or free association grounds to a requirement that details of membership of an organization be disclosed to the government. However, by the 1950s the Court's position had substantially altered, striking down a law that would have required the NAACP to disclose its list of members to the state.[196] In fairness, this decision was made in the tumultuous days after *Brown v Board of Education*,[197] where African-American activists sought to make sure the Supreme Court's word was enforced, while some of those in government sought to thwart the impact of the ruling.

Finally, despite the general development of the precedents in this area, the Court accepted the constitutional validity of jailing members of the military for things they said in 1974 in *Parker v Levy*.[198] There an army officer, who was a physician, was court-martialed for refusing to obey an instruction of a superior officer, and for public comments he made. He said that:

> The United States is wrong in being involved in the Vietnam War. I would refuse to go to Vietnam if ordered to do so. I don't see why any colored soldier would go to Vietnam; they should refuse to go to Vietnam and if sent should refuse to fight because they are discriminated against and denied their freedom in the United States, and they are sacrificed and discriminated against in Vietnam by being given all the hazardous duty and they are suffering the majority of casualties. . . . Special Forces personnel are liars and thieves and killers of peasants and murderers of women and children.

He was convicted by court-martial of disobeying an order of a superior officer, of conduct unbecoming of an officer and a gentleman, and conduct to the prejudice of good order and discipline, and bringing discredit to, the armed forces. He was dismissed from the service and ordered to confinement for three years with hard labor. A majority of the Court found no constitutional objection to this outcome. It reasoned that the rights of members of the military to freedom of speech were more circumscribed than for civilians. There were legitimate reasons for strict imposition of military discipline in terms of obeying orders and of limiting public comments by members of the military. The concepts of conduct unbecoming of an officer and prejudice to good order and discipline were historically well understood.[199] Stewart J, with whom Douglas and Brennan JJ joined (dissenting), would have voided the provisions regarding unbecoming conduct and conduct bringing discredit to the armed forces on the basis of vagueness.[200]

Breaches of the Peace

In an early case, the Supreme Court placed some parameters around the constitutional power of the state to regulate breaches of the peace, given the *First Amendment*. In *Cantwell v Connecticut*, it indicated that laws which sought to prevent or punish conduct amounting to clear and present danger of riot, incitement to violence, disorder, interference with traffic on public streets, or other immediate threat to peace, order or safety might withstand a *First Amendment* challenge.[201] Similarly, the state could punish epithets or personal abuse. The court emphasized the role of the *First Amendment* in terms of an individual's personal development.[202]

The Supreme Court upheld a statute forbidding the uttering of any "offensive, derisive or annoying word" in a public place, or to call a person an offensive name.[203] The appellant was arrested after he publicly denounced another as a "damned Fascist" and "damned racketeer." His argument that the statute as applied to him was a breach of his *First Amendment* speech rights was rejected.

Justice Murphy for the Court noted that

> There are certain well-defined and narrowly limited classes of speech, the prevention and punishment of which have never been thought to raise any

> constitutional problem. These include the lewd and obscene, the profane, the libelous, and the insulting or 'fighting' words—those which by their very utterance inflict injury or tend to incite an immediate breach of the peace. It has been well observed that such utterances are no essential part of any exposition of ideas, and are of such slight social value as a step to truth that any benefit that may be derived from them is clearly outweighed by the social interest in order and morality. Resort to epithets or personal abuse is not in any proper sense communication of information or opinion safeguarded by the *Constitution*, and its punishment as a criminal act would raise no question under that instrument.[204]

The difference between the outcomes in *Cantwell* and *Chaplinsky* might be argued to be that in the latter case, the words used were likely to provoke a violent response and a breach of the peace, whereas this was unlikely in the case of Cantwell's proselytizing.

A closely divided court reached a similar conclusion with respect to an Illinois statute forbidding the showing of materials in public which exposes members of any race, color, creed, or religion to contempt or derision such as could produce breach of the peace or riots.[205] The law was deemed a criminal libel law. The petitioner was charged with a breach of the statute for displaying photographs said to cast African-American people in a negative light, together with a call for governments to take action to halt the supposed negative impacts on society of the growing African-American population.

A bare majority validated the legislation in the face of a *First Amendment* challenge. Justice Frankfurter for the majority stated that the state had a right to seek ways of curbing false or malicious defamation of racial and religious groups. The behavior of the petitioner could well induce a breach of the peace, a danger the state was entitled to seek to prevent through legislative means. The majority dismissed the argument that such a state power could be abused; any power could be abused; this was not reason to deny it, according to the majority.

Strong dissents were authored by Black J, with whom Douglas J agreed, and Reed J, with whom Douglas J agreed, and Douglas and Jackson JJ in separate opinions. Justice Black espoused essentially an absolutist position on freedom of speech.[206] Black J cast doubt on the limits to free speech articulated in *Chaplinsky*, but in any event distinguished this case on the facts—here nothing had been said about an individual. Black J denounced the legislation as effectively an attempt at state censorship fundamentally at odds with the kind of free government intended by the founding fathers.[207] It represented a continuing, overhanging threat to freedom of speech, press and religion. Governments could simply not prohibit those who wished to petition the government for the address of grievances from doing so. The founding fathers decided that the danger possibly posed by extreme speech during public discussions was outweighed by the danger of the stifling of speech and expression.[208] Douglas J likewise was concerned about the creeping influence of state censorship.[209]

The tide began to turn against breach of the peace legislation, in tune with the civil rights revolution in the United States of the 1960s and 1970s. Key here was *Brown v Louisiana*,[210] where a majority of the Court overturned state legislation prohibiting congregating in a public building or failing to disperse or move on when ordered to do so, where the accused intended to provoke a breach of the peace or where a breach of the peace might be occasioned. The factual context was a peaceful, quiet sit-in at a Louisiana public library, where a form of segregation was being applied in relation to service to library users. The sit-in was a form of protest against it. Brown and others were arrested when they refused to leave the area where white customers would be served. As well as deciding the case on statutory interpretation grounds, a majority of the Supreme Court found that a peaceful protest in a public library about segregation practices was speech protected by the *First Amendment*.

Like in the context of sedition-type laws, laws which prohibit breaches of the peace or disorderly conduct are likely to be vulnerable to a *First Amendment* challenge where the nature of what the petitioner said is not directed to cause imminent lawless action or is not likely to actually do so.[211] Legislation proscribing conduct which is said to "tend" to a breach of the peace or be "calculated" to do so, or which uses other vague language,[212] will be highly vulnerable to challenge due to the vagueness of the concepts used in infringing the fundamental constitutional right.[213] A University campus speech code prohibiting the use of speech which "stigmatizes or victimizes" groups on the basis of race, ethnicity, religion, gender, sexual orientation, nationality, ethnicity, ancestry, age, marital status, disability, or veteran status was struck out on the basis of vagueness, as well as overbreadth.[214] The Court has articulated why the fact that legislation is vague can lead to unconstitutionality.[215] Bans on a newspaper which contained anti-Jewish sentiment were thrown out on free speech grounds in *Near v Minnesota*.[216]

The state may not criminalize the act of failing to disperse upon police order, in circumstances where protesters are engaged in a peaceful demonstration.[217] Systems requiring would-be public speakers to obtain a license or permit prior to doing so are likely to be struck down as prior restraints on speech contrary to the *First Amendment*.[218] They are even more egregious when the power to award a license or permit is reposed in an administrative official who must apply vague and uncertain criteria as the basis for considering an application.

Legislation which sought to prevent the formation of a picket line outside a business was successfully challenged on constitutional grounds.[219] The Supreme Court extended *First Amendment* protections to a very broad range of topics:

> freedom of discussion, if it would fulfil its historic function in this nation, must embrace all issues about which information is needed or appropriate to enable the members of society to cope with the exigencies of their period.[220]

Here the Court also emphasized the value of free speech in terms of truth discovery, the weeding out of "noxious" doctrines, and public education.[221] A picket near a funeral was also accorded *First Amendment* protection.[222] This was partly due to the "political" nature of some of the messages displayed at the picket, distasteful as the views expressed may have been to many.

The Court has noted that legislatures have more discretion to regulate expressive conduct than they do the spoken or written word. Even so, convictions for burning the American flag were overturned, on the basis that the regulation as applied to the defendant was contrary to the *First Amendment.*[223]

The potential of the *First Amendment* to effectively protect highly offensive speech is evident in decisions such as *RAV, Petitioner v City of St Paul, Minnesota*[224] and *Skokie v National Socialist Party of America et al.*[225] The former case dealt with the constitutionality of a statute which made it unlawful to place "a symbol, object, appellation, characterization, or graffiti—including a burning cross—which one knows or has reasonable grounds to know arouses anger, alarm or resentment in others on the basis of race, color, creed, religion or gender." All members of the Supreme Court found the legislation was constitutionally invalid.[226]

The main reasons pointed out that some content-based discrimination might be permissible consistently with the *First Amendment.*[227] For instance, so-called fighting words could be regulated. However, it could not be such as to suggest that official suppression of ideas was being practiced.[228] Here, the legislation was unconstitutional, because it singled out speech that was offensive based on particular features, that is, the discussion of race, color, creed, religion, or gender. This was impermissible. It did not fit within any of the exceptions to the general rule, in that it was not confined to so-called fighting words, or words that were threatening.[229] Nor could it be justified for reasons based other than on the content of the speech.[230] The county failed to show that their content-discriminatory law was *necessary* in order to serve what it argued was a compelling state interest of protecting those who have historically been subject to discrimination, supporting the right of those individuals to live in peace.[231] There were legitimate alternative legislative measures, not involving content discrimination, that could work to achieve the laudable objective. Further, it was discriminatory in terms of viewpoint, because it was only negative views regarding one of the above categories that was prohibited.[232]

In *Skokie* the right of individuals to peacefully assemble while displaying a Nazi swastika armband was upheld. The Court re-affirmed the right of individuals to convey ideas which many, or most, would find distasteful or offensive. The so-called fighting words exception in *Chaplinsky* was held not to apply.[233]

"Obscenity"

Not surprisingly the issue of allegedly "obscene" material and the *First Amendment* has given rise to sharp differences of opinion on the Court. In the early cases the Court seemed more prepared to accept the criminalization of activity associated with "obscene" material.[234] So, for instance, it validated a statute which made it an offense to mail material that was "obscene, lewd, lascivious or filthy." The majority applied the view expressed in *Chaplinsky* regarding speech that was regarded as having no redeeming social importance, which was stated to include the lewd and the obscene. The Court in *Chaplinsky* indicated such speech was not entitled to *First Amendment* protection, a position which the majority accepted and applied in *Roth.*[235]

This position could obviously conflict with another of the *First Amendment* doctrines, under which the court would generally frown on systems of prior restraint. Sometimes, a legislative measure might require prior permission before a particular communication, such as a book or publication, or movie, could occur. The court was clearly ambivalent about such systems, torn between their recognition of the historic evil of prior restraint, but in some cases recognizing a legitimate government interest in protecting the public from material thought to be obscene. The ambivalence is clear from a couple of cases in the 1950s, both involving systems or prior restraint. In one of them, a majority validated a measure under which a public official could order the confiscation of material intended for public distribution if they believed it was obscene.[236] In the other, a majority struck out a measure under which a public body could refuse permission for a movie to be shown to the public on the basis of its supposed obscenity.[237]

Attempts to regulate obscenity could also founder upon another fundamental constitutional principle, that of void for vagueness. An individual is entitled to be able to reasonably determine the scope and reach of legislative measures in order to be able to determine their application to her or his activity. Measures that prohibit obscene material, or equivalent measures, are risky in the sense that it may be difficult to adequately define obscenity with an acceptable degree of accuracy.[238] Sometimes, legislation attempting to criminalize obscenity were struck out on the basis that they were criminal in nature yet did not apparently include a scienter requirement, that is, they imposed a system of strict liability.[239]

This argument explains the Court's attempts, regardless of what might think of their success, to define what obscenity is. In *Roth*, it defined "obscenity" as material which "deals with sex in a manner appealing to prurient interest" according to community standards.[240]

Black and Douglas JJ consistently rallied against government attempts to ban communication said to be obscene. To some extent, they were able to convince the court to at least narrow its definition of what was obscene. In dissent in *Roth*, Black and Douglas JJ said that it was not legitimate for the government to ban speech or publications that were thought to be non-compliant with that society's existing moral code.[241] It was not tenable for judges to have to determine whether material was offensive to ordinary members of society.[242]

Subsequently it was said that there were three elements to the definition of obscenity—that the dominant theme of the material appeals to prurient interest in sex, the material was patently offensive because it offended contemporary community standards relating to description of sexual matters, and it was utterly without redeeming social value.[243]

Similar argument was evident in *Ginzburg v United States*, where a bare majority of 5:4 confirmed a conviction for distributing obscene material.[244] The defendant was sentenced to a term of five years' imprisonment for distributing material that was said to be obscene. The majority confirmed the material "appealed to the prurient interest," would be offensive and confronting to many, and had little or no redeeming social value.

This was again over a strong dissent of four, Black Douglas Harlan and Stewart. Black and Douglas JJ repeated their absolutist or near absolutist position on freedom of speech. Most of the dissent was based on the highly subjective and uncertain classification of material as obscene and judgments about its social value, and a reiteration of what they saw as the abiding purpose of the *First Amendment*.[245]

The Court clearly struggled with the meaning of the concept of a communication being "utterly without redeeming social value." In *Memoirs* three justices suggested that the circumstances of production, sale and publicity could assist in determining whether the book should enjoy constitutional protection or not. If it suggested the book was targeted as the "prurient interest" to the exclusion of other values, it might not be constitutionally protected.[246] While concurring in their judgment, Douglas J rejected the suggestion that the constitutionality of speech should be dependent on how it was marketed,[247] as did Harlan J in dissent.[248] The dissents also denied that the issue of whether material was utterly without redeeming social value was in fact a third requirement at all; rather they said that *Roth* required a two-stage test only.[249] Some of the difficulties with the "utterly without redeeming social value" were perhaps evident on the facts. The book the subject of the case involved a 1750 story of a prostitute. While some viewed it as simply an example of a collection of soft pornographic stories, some experts who testified in the case claimed it did have social value, describing conditions in Europe in the mid-18th century, and containing a moral story given the development of some of the characters in the book. The efficacy and utility of highly trained lawyers reading and sitting in judgment on the contents of books in order to determine whether or not they were entitled to *First Amendment* protection is perhaps clearer now than it was to some members of the Court in that case.

The Court's clear ambivalence about obscene material continued to be evident.[250] However, the ability of the state to regulate obscenity was narrowed in *Miller v California*,[251] where the Court found the regulatory power was limited to regulating works which described or depicted sexual conduct, which appealed to the prurient interest in sex, which portrayed sexual conduct in a patently offensive way, and which as a whole did not have serious literary, artistic, political or scientific value.[252] This last requirement apparently replaced the "utterly without redeeming social value" requirement from *Memoirs*.

Again, passionate dissent from this view was evident in the judgment of Douglas J, with whom Brennan J joined. Douglas J observed there was nothing in the *Constitution* which specifically mandated differential treatment being given to "obscene" publications or speech, as opposed to other kinds. What shocks some might be of sustenance to others. The fact that some may be angered by speech might reflect personally on the one getting angry, as opposed to the speech itself.[253] The notion of obscenity could not be defined, and it was "monstrous" to jail individuals on such basis.[254] Douglas J continued:

> The idea that the *First Amendment* permits punishment for ideas that are 'offensive' to the particular judge or jury sitting in judgment is astounding. No greater leveler of speech or literature has ever been designed. To give the power to the censor, as we do today, is to make a sharp and radical break with the traditions of a free society. The *First Amendment* was not fashioned as a vehicle for dispensing tranquilizers to the people. Its prime function was to keep debate open to 'offensive' as well as to 'staid' people. The tendency throughout history has been to subdue the individual and to exalt the power of government. The use of the standard 'offensive' gives authority to government that cuts the very vitals out of the *First Amendment*.[255]

The Supreme Court struck out a Florida ordinance prohibiting drive-in theaters from showing movies that included nudity.[256] The majority found the state could not generally censor movies in order to shield the public from speech or communication that the government believed might be offensive. Exceptions that applied when the speaker intruded on the privacy of the home,[257] where the speaker had a captive audience,[258] or where youth were implicated[259] were not applicable to the current situation. It was for the viewer or listener to escape the communication that they found to be offensive, not for the government censor to prevent it being shown. This was a content-based restriction which could not be justified on privacy grounds.

The Supreme Court by bare majority validated a law which regulated the placement of so-called adult establishments such that there would be a minimum distance between each such venue.[260] The majority confirmed that so-called viewpoint discrimination, through which a government might censor particular speech or information based on its viewpoint, was unlikely to survive *First Amendment* challenge. Nor would the government's disagreement with the content permit it to regulate the time, place, or manner of presenting the information. It was not sufficient to curb speech that it would likely rouse anger, dispute, or dissatisfaction.[261] Here the application of the regulation did not depend on the viewpoint expressed.[262] It was a content-based regulation, in that the regulation applied to "adult" films. However, the majority found that content-based regulation could be justified consistently with the *First Amendment*, and was so here. It found that while the *First Amendment* protected all speech, speech that was political in nature enjoyed stronger protection from regulation than the kind of speech implicated here.[263]

Concurring in the result, Powell J used a four-part test: (a) whether the provision was within the constitutional power of the enacting body; (b) whether the provision furthers an important or substantial governmental interest; (c) whether the governmental interest was unrelated to the suppression of free expression; and (d) whether the restriction on freedom of speech was no greater than necessary to further that interest.[264]

For the dissentients, the provision contained time, place and manner regulations based on content, which was offensive to *First Amendment* values, unless in the context of minors or a captive audience, neither of which applied here.[265] The dissentients disagreed with determining the scope of *First Amendment* protections based on justices' perceptions of the "worth" or "value" of what was said or communicated. The dissentients found that the price of the *First Amendment* freedom was that unpleasant speech would enter the "marketplace" of ideas. However, that was the price to be paid, as the founding fathers were aware. They did this knowing that the alternative, of government censorship and control of what could be accessed, was a much worse evil.

Similarly, the refusal of the owner of a theatre space to permit a production to be presented at its premises, on the basis of what the owner thought would involve nudity and obscenity on stage, was held to be contrary to the *First Amendment*.[266] The majority saw it as a kind of prior restraint on communication. It was very difficult, though not impossible, to justify such restraints. The Court noted that it had typically frowned upon prior restraints that were apparently unbounded by clear and precise standards. This was what had occurred here. It was not enough to defend the refusal to say that the production could be held elsewhere.

The exponential growth of the Internet inevitably led to large quantities of pornography being circulated among the general population, and demands for government to respond, particularly to inhibit minors having access to such material. The Clinton administration's *Communications Decency Act* of 1996 attempted to criminalize the knowing distribution of "obscene or indecent" material or that which was "patently offensive." A majority of the Court struck down the provisions as contrary to the *First Amendment*. It was a content-based restriction that was not sufficiently narrowly tailored, suffering from overbreadth and vagueness.[267] The tide had turned against government attempts to censor speech on the basis of obscenity or offense.

Legislation prohibiting the use of offensive or vulgar language is unlikely to be consistent with the *First Amendment*.[268] The Court has emphasized that a real risk of forbidding particular words would be to effectively suppress ideas. Speakers sometimes chose emotive and/or offensive words to reflect the strength of their convictions.[269] The concept of "offensive" was inherently subjective and unworkable as a basis for liability, in any event. For similar reasons, a law forbidding the distribution of written material comprised of "criminal news, police reports or accounts of criminal deeds, or pictures, or stories of deeds of bloodshed, lust or crime" was struck out. Its vague nature was an unacceptable interference with *First Amendment* freedoms. The Court indicated that the legislation was unconstitutional although it could see "nothing of any possible value to society" of such magazines; however they were entitled to as much *First Amendment* protection as the "best of literature."[270] The state may have a stronger argument for censorship when the audience for the apparently obscene speech includes minors at school.[271]

Lastly, a school board attempts to remove books from a school library apparently on the basis of arguably obscene and vulgar language used in the books foundered on a *First Amendment* challenge. There the majority spoke in favor of a "right to receive ideas" as a pre-requisite to an individual being able to exercise their own free speech rights.[272]

Defamation

At one time, it was believed that defamation matter was outside the scope of *First Amendment* protection.[273] Subsequently, in the classic decision of *New York Times Co v Sullivan*, the Court found that the law of defamation must accommodate, and have a restricted interpretation, to communication pertaining to "public figures," to fully preserve and protect the right of an individual to express and hear views. Specifically, a plaintiff in such a case would need to show that, apart from the communication being defamatory, that it was made with actual malice; in other words, that the person making the statement knew it was not true, or was reckless as to its truth or otherwise, in order to succeed against the maker of the statement for defamation.[274] In the context of a plaintiff who was a non-public official who claimed to be defamed, at least proof of negligence would be required, as well as proof of actual damage, before they could recover damages from the defendant.[275]

The Court has accepted that erroneous statements, including about individuals, are protected by the *First Amendment*, to permit freedom of expression to have the kind of "breathing space" needed to function properly. The state cannot prohibit such speech unless there is shown to be no "reasonable basis" for the making of such a statement.[276] However, the line is drawn at deliberate and/or reckless falsehood. Such an approach has also been applied to cases of so-called product disparagement.[277]

The decision in the *New York Times* left many questions unanswered, including whether the precedent applied only to discussion about public officials. Did it apply only to discussion of public affairs? Was it relevant that the defendant, as it was in the facts in the *New York Times*, was a media outlet? Answers were given in subsequent cases, though they would not always be consistent with one another.

In *Curtis Publishing Co v Butts*[278] the Supreme Court found that the principles in the *New York Times* should be applied in defamation cases involving so-called public figures, as well as public officials. The plaintiff in the case was a football coach. He had been accused of corruption in fixing game results. The Court extended the *New York Times* approach to "public figures." It defined public figures as "non-public persons who are nevertheless intimately involved in the resolution of important public questions or, by reason of their fame, shape events in areas of concern to society at large."[279]

The court extended the ambit of the *New York Times* further in *Rosenbloom v Metromedia Inc.*[280] It held that the *New York Times* approach should be applied to discussion about a private figure, provided that the discussion related to matters of public interest. In so doing, the joint reasons rejected the distinction made by the minority between public figures and private figures.[281] The dissentients relied on this distinction in defining the scope of application of the *New York Times* malice standard. The dissenting judges justified more protection being accorded the reputation of private person defamation plaintiffs compared with public figure defamation plaintiffs. They said the latter were better able to access media outlets to defend themselves, and relied on the fact that they had volunteered to become public figures. The joint reasons in *Rosenbloom* rejected these arguments as being based on "unproved and highly improbable generalizations."[282]

Harlan J, part of the joint reasons in the *New York Times*, filed a dissent in *Rosenbloom*. As indicated, as a dissentient he argued that the rationale for the malice test in that case was based on two factors—that public figures were more likely to be able to access public channels to rebut falsehoods uttered against them, and that by volunteering to be a public figure, they knowingly placed themselves in the public spotlight and accepted the associated scrutiny of their activities and lives. These rationales did not apply to private figures. For this reason, he disagreed with the majority's extension of the *New York Times* to private individuals discussing matters of public interest. He concluded that the states were free in these circumstances to determine the relevant standard of care required, as long as they did not impose liability without fault.[283]

Marshall J, joined by Stewart J, also dissented on the basis that the *New York Times* approach did not sufficiently protect the reputation of private figures. He concluded that states should be free to develop their own common law of defamation applicable to private figures, subject to a prohibition on the imposition of strict liability. This was because "the effect of imposing liability without fault is to place the printed or spoken word with the use of explosives or the keeping of dangerous animals."[284] This was quite a radical position at the time, because American states had done precisely that, adopting principles of strict liability in the defamation context, right up until 1964 when the *New York Times* was decided.

The court considered these matters further in *Gertz v Robert Welsh, Inc.*[285] The plaintiff was an attorney representing a family who sought compensation after their child was killed by a police officer. A magazine owned by the respondent carried a story that suggested the plaintiff was part of a plan to introduce communism in the United States. It argued the plaintiff was a socialist and/or communist, and that he had criminal convictions. This was not true. The magazine editors had not made reasonable investigations to determine if their allegations were true or not. Gertz sued the newspaper for defamation. The newspaper proprietor defended the claim by arguing that Gertz was a public figure, so the stricter *New York Times* standard should be applied. It argued Gertz could not meet that standard.

The court re-aligned the law. Powell J delivered the majority judgment, with which Stewart Marshall Blackmun and Rehnquist JJ joined. The joint reasons noted that false statements had no constitutional value. However, it was necessary that the *First Amendment* protect them, because it needed "breathing space" in order to function. If the law imposed strict liability upon a publisher or broadcaster for publishing false material, it would unduly "chill" their freedom of speech.[286] The joint reasons affirmed the decisions in the *New York Times* and *Butts*, but said the principles of the former were limited to cases involving either public officials and public figures.[287] In other words, it disagreed with, and overruled, the extension of the principles in *Rosenbloom* to discussion of private figures, if the matters were issues of public concern. The joint reasons affirmed the reasoning of Marshall J (dissenting) in *Rosenbloom* that the fact that a public figure generally had greater access to communication channels, and that they had voluntarily agreed to enter the public spotlight, meant they should have less of a right to seek redress for defamation than would a private figure.[288] The joint reasons observed it was difficult for judges to determine, as *Rosenbloom* contemplated, whether or not particular topics were of "public concern."

The joint reasons held that as long as states did not impose liability without fault, they had discretion to define as they wished the appropriate law to be applied in respect of defamation regarding a private individual.[289] However, they added that states could not legislate for recovery of punitive or presumed damages where they departed from the *New York Times* standard. Compensation in such circumstances was limited to "actual injury." The court was concerned that if the availability of punitive damages were not capped or limited, it could have the kind of chilling effect on free speech which the courts wished to avoid.[290] The court's finding that plaintiffs could only recover for actual injury was a departure from past practice.

The dissents in *Gertz* were of two different kinds. Douglas and Brennan JJ essentially sought to uphold the law as expounded in *Rosenbloom*. They regarded this case as involving a private citizen in relation to a matter of public concern. They applied the *New York Times* standard. Because the requirement of malice could not be proven, the plaintiff was not entitled to compensation. Brennan J repeated his disagreement with the idea that private plaintiffs deserved greater reputational protection than public figure plaintiffs because they had less access to means of correction and/or that they had voluntarily chosen a public profile.[291] He dissented from the opinion of the majority that permitted states to adopt a negligence rather than actual malice standard as an acceptable basis for a defamation claim by private figures. He concluded that their position did not sufficiently protect freedom of speech. It would not be clear to defendants how much they would need to do by way of background checking before they published material, in order to meet the requirement of "reasonable care."[292]

The other dissent was primarily the judgment of White J, with whom Rehnquist J substantially agreed. White J saw the *New York Times* precedent in narrow terms as "intended to forbid actions for seditious libel."[293] Because he viewed it this narrow light, he disagreed that it should be extended to private citizens suing for defamation. In other words, he partly agreed with the majority's position in *Gertz* in overruling *Rosenbloom*. However, he parted company with the majority in disagreeing that, where states have not applied the *New York Times* standard to defamation actions by private plaintiffs, the claim was limited to "actual injury."[294] He said this was a substantial departure from well-established defamation principles where this was typically not necessary. He also disagreed with how the majority limited recovery of punitive damages.

The Court clarified that in order to meet the standard of actual malice, also expressed as a kind of reckless disregard as to whether particular material published is true or false, or knowledge it was false, it is not enough that the plaintiff the defendant was negligent in publishing. It held that "malice" here does not have its regular meaning as involving evil intent. Rather, it meant knowledge of the falsity of the material, or reckless disregard as to whether or not it was true.[295] It confirmed no special rules should be applied merely because the defendant is involved in the media, as opposed to a non-media defendant.[296]

The exponential growth of online communication has undercut the Supreme Court's reliance on arguments that different rules should apply to public figures because of the assumed ease with which they could access channels of communication to rebut defamatory material. While the argument might have been valid in the past, these days everyone can access communication channels through technology such as twitter and Facebook.[297]

Other Instances Involving Media and the First Amendment

The Court's decision in *New York Times Co v Sullivan* was a major victory for the press, allowing it much greater latitude in its discussion of "public figures." The media also had a major victory in the so-called Pentagon Papers case, *New York Times Co v United States*,[298] where a majority of the court refused attempts by the government to prevent publication of sensitive material about the Vietnam war by the *New York Times* and *Washington Post*. Here members of the Court strongly re-asserted the fundamental role of the media in keeping elected officials accountable for their decision making. Secrecy in government was anti-democratic. The American public were having a robust debate at the time about the Vietnam war, and the material was highly relevant and important to that debate. The government's arguments that suppression of the material was necessary to prevent a "grave and irreparable danger" to American interests, and compromise its relations with other countries, were not accepted.

The Court has also protected the media from laws drafted or applied in a discriminatory manner. It invalidated a state tax provision ostensibly based on a newspaper's circulation.[299] It invalidated taxation on the paper and ink used to produce newspapers, with an exemption for smaller outlets.[300] It invalidated a state sales tax applicable to some magazines but not others.[301] It is very wary of the possibility that states might resort to such measures to indirectly punish or discourage unfavorable coverage of the news, in an effort to censor disfavored speech and encourage preferred voices.

On the other hand, elsewhere in the *First Amendment* case law the Court has been surprisingly less willing to accord substantial *First Amendment* rights to the media. This is surprising given the actual mention of the freedom of the press in the words of the *First Amendment*, and the general acceptance of the pivotal role the media can play in fostering the kind of open communication contemplated and even demanded by a democratic system of government. Whichever view one takes of the purpose of free speech, whether it be the search for truth, marketplace of ideas, self-government, distrust of government, etc., the media has a fundamental role to play in facilitating free speech. This occurs through the speech in which the media is itself engaged, and the speech which will likely result from awareness of the material the media is providing. We want and need debates on a large range of issues, and debates work best when they are informed. The media has an unquestioned fundamental role in providing such information. The media also has a fundamental role in facilitating the exchange of views among other participants. Traditionally this might have been through the letters section of the newspaper, which persists today. Obviously social media has to a large extent complemented the more traditional means of exchange. Radio and television programs also have a fundamental role in terms of both dissemination of information, and exchange of views among participants.

In this light, the Court's decision in *Branzburg v Hayes*,[302] is somewhat difficult to accept. The case involved the issue of the confidentiality of journalists' sources. A grand jury had issued subpoenas to three journalists. Two had written stories on the extent of drug taking within a community, which included interviews with users, suppliers and manufacturers of illicit drugs. Another had attended a gang meeting, and was asked to provide evidence of what was said at the meeting. All three journalists declined to provide the information, arguing that the *First Amendment* protected the confidentiality of their sources, and that they should not be required by legal process to divulge these sources. A majority of 5:4 said that the *First Amendment* did not protect the confidentiality of journalists' sources, and the journalists were required to answer the queries from the grand jury.

The majority stated that the common law had long refused to recognize the right of members of the press to decline to reveal confidential sources to a grand jury. Governments had a legitimate interest in law enforcement to protect the public. The grand jury could play an important role in that regard. It was speculative to say that if journalists were required to divulge the confidentiality of their sources, their ability to do their job would be seriously hampered or that their sources would cease to provide information.[303]

Four justices dissented. Douglas J said that *First Amendment* rights could only be overridden if there were evidence of a compelling need. Here no such need had been demonstrated. He found journalists had an absolute right to refuse to answer questions from a grand jury. He claimed that

> Today's decision will impede the wide-open and robust dissemination of ideas and counter thought which a free press both fosters and protects and which is essential to the success of intelligent self-government. Forcing a reporter before a grand jury will have two retarding effects upon the ear and pen of the press. Fear of exposure will cause dissidents to communicate less openly to trusted reporters. And fear of accountability will cause editors and critics to write with more restrained pens . . . the press has a preferred position in our constitutional scheme, not to enable it to make money, not to set news(people) apart as a favored class, but to bring fulfilment to the public's right to know. The right to know is crucial to the governing powers of the people . . . knowledge is essential to informed decisions.[304]

Douglas J was very concerned with the practical impact of the Court's decision on journalists' access to confidential sources in the future:

> A reporter is no better than (their) source of information. Unless (they have) a privilege to withhold the identity of . . . sources, (they) will be the victim of government intrigue or aggression. If (they) can be summoned to testify in secret before a grand jury, (their) sources will dry up and the attempted exposure, the effort to enlighten the public, will be ended. If what the Court sanctions today becomes settled law, then the reporter's main function in American society will be to pass on to the public the press releases which the various departments of government issue . . . the record in this case is replete with weighty affidavits from responsible news(people), telling how important is the sanctity of their sources of information. When we deny news(people) that protection, we deprive the people of the information needed to run the affairs of the nation in an intelligent way.[305]

Stewart J, with whom Brennan and Marshall JJ agreed, also noted the broad societal interest in the full and free flow of information to the public. The press played a pivotal role in reporting on government operations and activities, exposing corruption and educating the public. As a corollary of the right to publish, journalists had to have a right to gather news. Their ability to do would be seriously crimped if they had to divulge confidential sources. Sources would be fearful of providing information. Journalists would be fearful of publishing stories because of the possible consequences. Stewart J agreed with Douglas J that the protection

> does not exist for the purely private interests of the news(person) or informant, nor even . . . for the *First Amendment* interests of either partner in the news-gathering relationship. Rather it functions to ensure nothing less than democratic decision making through the free flow of information to the public and it serves, thereby, to honor the "profound national commitment to the principle that debate on public issues should be uninhibited, robust and wide open" (citing *New York Times Co v Sullivan*).[306]

The journalists' argument was also unsuccessful in *Houchins v KQED Inc*. There the news organization sought access to a prison facility to take footage and to report on conditions in the jail. A sheriff had refused their request. They unsuccessfully argued that the refusal was an infringement of their *First Amendment* rights. The majority found that the *First Amendment* did not contain a right to access sources of information within government control. It was not a freedom of information provision. The dissenters suggested the *First Amendment* contained at least to some extent a positive right rather than merely a negative right:

> It is not sufficient therefore that the channels of communication be free of governmental restraints. Without some protection for the acquisition of information about the operation of public institutions such as prisons by the public at large, the process of self-governance contemplated by the Framers would be stripped of its substance. For that reason information gathering is entitled to some measure of constitutional protection . . . this protection is not for the private benefit of those who might qualify as representatives of the press but to ensure that the citizens are fully informed regarding matters of public interest and importance.[307]

The dissenters noted that special protection should be accorded to information about conditions in prisons. They were (generally) public institutions financed with public money. They were a fundamental part of the criminal justice system. There was an interest in ensuring that prisoners so detained were not being subject to "cruel and unusual punishment" contrary to the *Eighth Amendment*. Many of those detained had not yet had their cases heard. They were entitled to the presumption of innocence, and should be treated accordingly while on remand. Subsequently, most states legislated to provide journalists with protection.

Some cases have considered issues of equality as they relate to access to media. This issue also relates to the theories and rationale of free speech itself. Some who believe in less robust protection of free speech argue that the marketplace of ideas rationale for free speech is flawed because access to media and the ability to speak, or more importantly the ability to be heard by a significant audience, is limited. Thus it is not a functioning, efficient market, but rather a market dominated by a few powerful players. Of course, there is debate as to whether such arguments are as valid today. One of the positive impacts of social media has been the way in which it has allowed more people to have their views amplified to a broad cross-section of the community. People have access to a very broad range of views, and the kind of market power that newspaper proprietors, and owners of television networks/stations and radio networks/stations had in this regard has been significantly diluted.

Sometimes the court has accepted arguments about equality. It validated federal measures by which holders of broadcast licenses were required to comply with a "fairness" doctrine, under which broadcasters were required to discuss public issues in a fair and balanced way.[308] One of the matters in the case involved a person who had been subjected to a public attack on their honesty and character. The broadcasters refused to air the response of the person attacked. They argued it was their *First Amendment* right to carry or not to carry any communication. The Court found the conditions of the broadcasting license requiring fairness and balance in reporting were valid, and not inconsistent with the *First Amendment*. On the other hand, the court did not accept an equality argument in *Miami Herald Pub Co v Tornillo*,[309] where a newspaper editorial carried strong criticism of a candidate for office. The newspaper refused to publish the response of the attack. The court found the proprietor's refusal to do so did not infringe the *First Amendment* rights of the candidate.[310]

In other respects the court has been more sympathetic to journalists' free speech rights. So, for instance, it is very unlikely to prohibit reporting of a current case, including facts, unless there were strong evidence that such reporting would impede the right of an accused to a fair trial.[311] It will be seen as a prior restraint, and as indicated above, such measures must satisfy a heavy burden of justification. The court will generally find that the court itself can take measures to ensure that the right of an accused to a fair trial will not be compromised by any pre-trial publicity. It will only be where there are no reasonable alternatives open to avoid an unfair trial other than to gag the press that this option will be seriously considered. The court acknowledges the limits of such gags, when individuals typically have access to a range of sources of information.[312]

Laws of general application, whether common law rules[313] or statutory rules,[314] will be applicable to the media. The media has unsuccessfully sought to deny the application of these rules to it on the basis it infringes their *First Amendment* rights.

Government as Speaker

At times, the United States Supreme Court has recognized the right of the government to convey a message, even though recognition of that right might inhibit the right of others to speak. So, for example, in *Rust v Sullivan* it upheld the constitutional right of the legislature to condition funding under a federally-sponsored project on the basis that it would be used only to support preventive family planning activities, and not abortion. Under the project no abortion related counselling could be provided, and no reference to organizations that provided abortions could be made. It did not prevent the organization in receipt of funding from offering abortion services, but these services needed to be clearly separated from the activities funded by the federal government. A majority of the Court rejected a *First Amendment* challenge to this law. The Court found that government was entitled to encourage activity it believed to be in the public interest, and to use funding to do so. It was not required to also fund alternative viewpoints. The fact it only funded one view did not make it unconstitutional viewpoint discrimination.[315] Similarly, it was constitutionally acceptable to condition receipt of federal money to universities on the basis that they would permit military recruiters on their campuses.[316]

The Court draws a line between conditioning funding within a particular government funded program to particular messages, and seeking to control what the grantee organization says or does in relation to activities outside the funded program. The Court will typically accept the validity of the former, but not the latter.[317]

On the other hand, the conditioning of money to public defender type positions on the basis they would limit their arguments in court was held to be an unconstitutional infringement of that attorney's freedom of speech.[318] However, an attempt to discipline an attorney for speaking out about possible irregularities in relation to obtaining a search warrant within his organization was upheld, asserting the right of an employer to discipline staff, even if it was because of something they said,[319] a statement that was arguably in the public interest.

Further, a government body that terminates the employment of a teacher because of the way in which the teacher has exercised their *First Amendment* rights may find itself in *First Amendment* difficulties.[320]

The issue of whether speech is government speech or private speech is often outcome determinative in terms of the *First Amendment* issue, since the *First Amendment* does not generally apply at all to government speech.[321] Further, sometimes the question of whether speech is in fact government speech or private speech is contested. An example of this is the decision in *Walker v Texas Division, Sons of Confederate Veterans Inc.*[322] There the issue was the right of a group of individuals to have personalized number plates issued by the state with the confederate battle flag and the words "sons of confederate veterans" on the number plate. The relevant government authority refused to issue the plates with these inclusions, on the basis that some would find the numberplates offensive and containing a message of hate towards groups. The group claimed that the refusal to issue the numberplates violated their free speech rights. By a majority of 5:4, the Court rejected their claim, on the basis that the speech involved was government speech, such that the *First Amendment* did not apply.

Money and the Political Process

In an earlier case the Court passed judgment on a comprehensive electoral financing law which contained both restrictions on the extent to which an individual could donate money to favored candidates or a favored political party in any particular year, and legislation limiting the extent to which an individual or organization could spend on "campaign expenditure." The Court found that the restrictions on the ability of an individual to donate in a given year were not an infringement of *First Amendment* freedoms, but that restrictions on the amount which could be spend on campaigning each year were.[323] The Court acknowledged that the *First Amendment* had its most urgent application in relation to campaigns for political office. Restrictions on the amount that could be spent on political advertising effectively limited the number of issues discussed, how deeply they were discussed, and how many people got to hear the discussion. On the other hand, a restriction on the amount that an individual could donate effected only a marginal restriction on their right to participate in public debate. The fact a person wished to donate was broadly speech but it did not explain the reason for the support. Thus the impact of a restriction on that form of speech upon freedom of speech generally was marginal.

At one point the Court seemed to accept limitations on the ability of corporations to participate in the political process by way of expenditure to support particular candidates for election. This was on the basis of the presumed large aggregate wealth of corporations, potentially creating a distortion in relation to campaigning, that such influence may not be an accurate reflection of the strength of the view expressed by the corporation in the broader community, and concerns over actual or perceived corruption.[324] However that decision was overruled in *Citizens United v FEC*,[325] where the Court overturned bans on a corporate body incurring independent expenditure for election communication purposed, based on *First Amendment* arguments. The Court there re-affirmed that laws which burdened free speech were subject to strict scrutiny, requiring a compelling justification for the regulation, and evidence that the legislation is narrowly tailored towards achieving that objective. Arguments that independent expenditure should be banned because of their tendency to corruption were rejected. There was a lack of evidence of a link between expenditure and a quid pro quo.

Sometimes the court has distinguished between so-called express advocacy of a particular candidate, or its functional equivalent, and so-called issue advocacy, where the advocacy relates to a particular political issue. It is sometimes argued that the *First Amendment* does and should provide greater protection for issue advocacy, while limits on express advocacy or its functional equivalent should be accorded greater flexibility. For instance, while the Court has sometimes upheld bans on speech that amount to express advocacy, if the government can show a compelling interest and the legislation is narrowly tailored to it, it has not (yet) upheld bans on speech that amount to issue advocacy.[326]

Commercial Speech

At one time, the Court denied that commercial speech warranted *First Amendment* protection.[327] The Court has in more recent years recognized the value of commercial speech in providing information to consumers, and assisting them in making decisions. There is a public interest in decisions about products being informed and intelligent ones. This would increase the likelihood that society's scarce resources would be allocated efficiently.[328] The Court has been prepared to accord commercial speech some protection under the *First Amendment*, though at a lesser level than other types of speech. The government's ability to regulate misleading and unlawful activity in the commercial sphere is well established, though such regulation might technically disrupt speech. Further, measures designed to prevent aggressive sales tactics, or requiring increased disclosure of information, are likely to be supported. Beyond that, it applies an intermediate level of scrutiny; the Court considers whether the government interest served by the regulation would be substantial. The regulation in issue must be tailored in a reasonable manner to meeting that interest.[329] It must directly advance the state interest, and must not go beyond what is necessary to secure the governmental interest.[330] This is something less than strict scrutiny. Complete bans on truthful, non-misleading commercial speech will be very difficult to justify consistent with the *First Amendment*.[331] Thus, a ban on solicitation for customers is constitutionally unsound on *First Amendment* grounds.[332]

There is some overlap between the categories of commercial speech and what some call "obscenity," discussed above. We saw above the difficulties that the court has had in determining what is obscene, and its definition has tended to narrow over the years. The speech sought to be suppressed on this basis was commercial in nature. An example is *Schad v Mt Ephraim*.[333] There the county unsuccessfully sought to prevent the owners of an adult book store from adding to their services a nude live show within their premises. The majority declared the zoning decision to be contrary to the *First Amendment*. It noted that

> by excluding live entertainment throughout the Borough, the Mount Ephraim ordinance prohibits a wide range of expression that has long been held to be within the protections of the *First . . . Amendment*. Entertainment . . . is protected; motion pictures, programs broadcast by radio and television, and live entertainment, such as musical and dramatic works, fall within the *First Amendment* guarantee.[334]

This broad view that the *First Amendment* protected virtually all types of communication, including what some might consider to be obscene and/or pornographic, was not shared by all. In dissent, Burger CJ with whom Rehnquist J agreed, noted that

> The Borough of Mount Ephraim has not attempted to suppress the point of view of anyone or to stifle any category of ideas. To say that there is a *First Amendment* right to impose every form of expression on every community, including the kind of 'expression' involved here, is sheer nonsense. To enshrine such a notion in the *Constitution* ignores fundamental values that the *Constitution* ought to protect. To invoke the *First Amendment* to protect the activity involved in this case trivializes and demeans that great *Amendment*.[335]

Untruths and Fake News

The *First Amendment* clearly contemplates very broad protection of free speech. There is understandable animus towards any attempt by government to censor particular ideas. On occasion, government might attempt to do so by arguing that the speech or idea proposed to be banned should be prohibited because it is not "true." Thus, there is understandable real ambivalence about any regulation of speech on the basis it is not true. It is well summarized in the pithy epithet of Powell J for the majority in *Gertz v Welsh* that "there is no such thing as a false idea."[336] As was demonstrated above in the context of public figures, it is not sufficient for the public figure to recover on the basis of defamation to show that what was said about them was not true.

On one view, the extremism of this position was demonstrated in the case of *United States v Alvarez*.[337] There a member of a government board claimed that he had been awarded the Congressional Medal of Honor, the highest possible military honor for military personnel. His claim was false. The federal *Stolen Valor Act* made it a criminal offense to falsely claim receipt of military medals; the penalty was increased in the case of falsely claiming to have received the Congressional Medal of Honor. Alvarez admitted to breaching the Act, but argued that the Act was inconsistent with the *First Amendment*. His argument was successful in the Supreme Court.[338]

Kennedy J for the majority noted that while there were exceptional categories of case in which content-based speech restrictions had been declared consistent with the *First Amendment*, false statements was not such a category. In doing so, he admitted that other laws did criminalize the telling of untruths, for instance, perjury laws, laws criminalizing the impersonation of a public officer, and laws criminalizing the giving of a false statement to a government official. Laws also made it an offense to make false statements in order to derive commercial gain. The existence of these exceptions did not mean there was a general exception to *First Amendment* principles for false information.[339] The majority was concerned with the potentially broad sweep of this law, and if it struck out this law, the potentially broad sweep of future regulation. Kennedy J for the majority opined that "our constitutional tradition stands against the idea that we need Oceania's Ministry of Truth," a reference to George Orwell's 1984.[340] The Court found that although the government could point to a compelling interest in preserving the integrity of the honor system, it could not link this legislation sufficiently to that objective.[341] The government could not point to evidence that the making of false claims such as Alvarez's claim here diluted the cache accorded to such medals.[342] It could not show that counterspeech would be ineffective in responding to Alvarez's claims.[343] They referred to the marketplace of ideas as the best test of "truth."[344] There were alternative paths to achieving the government's legitimate ends apart from criminalizing falsehood, such as the maintenance of a government database listing actual recipients of military awards.[345]

These precedents are particularly important, acknowledging that online communication has facilitated an exponential expansion in "fake news," material that is demonstrably clearly false. Of course, it is not a public good when individuals are making decisions based on material that is not true. These problems are particularly serious around election time, when powerful and damaging lies about politicians can seriously distort the political decision-making process. Unfortunately, there is no simple solution to this.

Places of Learning

Detailed consideration of the very significant free speech issues associated with universities is reserved for a subsequent book: Anthony Gray, *Freedom of Speech: Contentious Issues* (Lexington Press, Maryland, 2019). I have discussed above the extent to which universities can be seen as public fora. In relation to schools, famously the court upheld the right of students to wear armbands as a protest against war in *Tinker v Des Moines Independent Community School District*.[346] On the other hand, it has generally recognized the right of schools to censor speech in a school setting to a greater extent that it would permit in a university environment, or in the broader community. For instance, the state is not required to tolerate speech that is "inconsistent with its basic educational mission." It need not tolerate speech that it reasonably views as inappropriate in a school setting.[347]

The Court has also distinguished between cases where a school has been asked to tolerate speech, and where a school is asked to affirmatively promote particular student speech. It has concluded that the school's rights to censor views is stronger in the latter case. It has recognized a legitimate interest in the school to ensure that the students are receiving the messages that a particular educational environment is designed to teach, that recipients do not see or hear inappropriate material, or that some might mistakenly attribute the expression to the school. On this contentious basis, a closely divided Court upheld the actions of a school principal in deleting several stories from a student-run school newspaper for which students obtained school credit, and which was managed and overseen by school staff. The principal had vetoed proposed stories dealing with teenage pregnancy and divorce. A bare majority found this action did not contravene the authors' *First Amendment* rights.[348]

Other Categories of Speech

Discussion of other important categories of speech, including so-called hate speech and speech by public employees, is reserved for *Freedom of Speech: Contentious Issues*. Generally, given decisions in cases such as *RAV v St Paul*, it is doubtful that a statute purporting to criminalize so-called hate speech would be constitutionally valid in the United States given the *First Amendment*. The Court has been more forgiving of statutes which seek to curb the right of a public sector employee to speak publicly about matters pertaining to their work, often taking the view that government has a legitimate interest in limiting discussion by their employees of what might be highly contentious issues being considered by government. The fear may be that some might believe that the public sector worker is speaking on behalf of their employer, which is often not the case, that the worker might release information that is sensitive and damaging to government interests to have it made publicly. An employee is on stronger ground when speaking about matters of "public concern" rather than purely internal work-related matters,[349] but the line between the two can sometimes be unclear. In itself, this uncertainty can create a chilling effect on a public sector employee's speech. has found that the rights to free speech of military officers are more limited than for civilians. It has permitted the jailing of military officers because they have criticized operational aspects of the war effort and urged would-be enlisters not to do so.[350]

Reflections

A consideration of the history of the *First Amendment* leads to ambivalence. The precise intent behind inclusion of the provision in relation to free speech is somewhat obscure. While some limit it to an intention to prevent prior restraint of speech, others read it more broadly. Regardless, in its initial application, it did not prevent early attempts to suppress criticism of government.

It is often said that in times of war, the law is silent (*inter arma silent leges*). The opposite has been true in the case of the *First Amendment*. It was federal legislation passed during World War I that forced the Supreme Court to articulate its position on free speech, including whether such rights were absolute in nature, and if limited, what those limits were, and how the court should determine the validity of legislation that restricted free speech in the (supposed) name of the greater good. Initially utilitarian arguments won out, with those criticizing the war effort jailed, and constitutional challenges to the relevant legislation rejected. These arguments again obtained prominence during the World War II era. However, by the late 1960s in the *Brandenburg* decision the Court settled that mere advocacy of dissent, or even general statements around force of violence, could not be the subject of restriction, consistent with the *First Amendment*. At minimum, the speech would have to be directed towards inciting or directing imminent lawless action, and be likely to do so. In that fifty year period, the Court had moved substantially from a position greatly deferential to the legislature and its judgment that speech was harmful to the greater good, in favor of an individual's right to speak.

The Court has struggled to some extent to deal with questions involving speech that might be considered to be low value. It would identify such categories in *Chaplinsky*, including obscene, profane, libelous, and insulting or fighting words. It found that these categories were no essential part of the exposition of ideas and were of "slight social value," so that they should not be protected speech. However, subsequent cases would work to undercut and undermine these supposed categories of non-protected speech. The Court struggled long and hard to attempt to define what was "obscene." Even the now-settled position it arrived at in *Miller*, including a requirement that the material lacks serious literary, artistic, political, or scientific value, is awkward. It is to place judges in an invidious position, for which they have no special expertise, to ask them to determine whether a particular publication has or does not have such value.

Then it gutted the "libelous speech" exception in *New York Times Co v Sullivan*, by providing much more protection for speech that might be defamatory, requiring in the case of public figures and public officials that the publication of the defamatory material was actuated by malice. It is difficult to maintain that profane language is not protected by the *First Amendment* given the decision in *Cohen v California*. The question of fighting words could be adequately dealt with in the exception dealing with speech that is directed to inciting violence and likely to achieve that result. The Supreme Court has itself held in *Stevens* that most of what is said in society lacks value, yet it is protected. Given these sentiments, it seems wise for the Supreme Court to overrule the statements in *Chaplinksy* suggesting categories of speech that are not entitled to any *First Amendment* protection.

Related to questions of whether judges can or should pass judgment on the value of speech is the question whether the *First Amendment* protects statements that are untrue. This is extremely topical at present. The Internet has provided many more opportunities for "fake news" to spread. While some of this is petty, some of it relates to extremely important topics of real public interest, including matters touching on politics, political candidates and political parties. The Supreme Court eventually reached a position in *Alvarez* that the *First Amendment* protected even false statements. This position is supported. It is suggested that the best solution to "fake news" is counter-speech that is true. Past arguments that this does not work because some have more access to media to have their views aired to broader audiences are weaker now, given the growth of the Internet, and social media. There are irreconcilable difficulties in any suggestion of a regulation against "fake news," including who would be the arbiter of what is fake and what is not. Many of these matters are in the margins between fact and opinion. People hold diametrically opposed opinions on many matters. It is extremely difficult, and virtually impossible, to regulate this, in a way that does not create greater problems that it solves. Of course, the specter of a government regulatory in this space raises the abhorrent specter of a totalitarian regime running a "Ministry of Truth," where only certain positions can be articulated on contentious matters. This is not simply the stuff of George Orwell books. We know of government regimes in other parts of the world where this is reality. This is so foreign to American culture that it is considered extremely unlikely that the American people would accept regulation of so-called fake news. And given the court's finding in *Alvarez*, unlikely that the Supreme Court would accept it either.

I will also reserve comments on the categories-based approach that the United States takes to freedom of speech cases, in comparison with the proportionality approach taken elsewhere, for Chapter 6 of this book. I will also reserve comments on the specific questions of the position of the United States on matters of so-called hate speech, questions regarding universities and free speech, and the challenges presented by technology, for the subsequent book *Freedom of Speech in Practice: Controversial Applications of Law and Theory.*

NOTES

1. *Bridges v California* (1941) 314 US 252, 264–265 (Black J, dissenting) ("one of the objects of the Revolution was to get rid of the English common law on liberty of speech and of the press") (quoting Henry Schofield, "Freedom of Press in the United States" (1914) *Publications of the American Sociological Society* 9 (1914): 76.
2. Stewart, "Lennon and the Taxes on Knowledge," *Scottish Historical Review* 15 (1918): 322.
3. 297 US 233 (1936).
4. 246 (Justice Sutherland for the Court).
5. Henry Schofield, "Freedom of the Press in the United States," *Publications of the American Sociological Society* 9 (1914): 76, referred to by the United States Supreme Court in *Bridges v California* 314 US 252, 264 (1941); James Madison "although I know whenever the great rights, the trial by jury, freedom of the press, or liberty of conscience, come in question in

that body (parliament) the invasion of them is resisted by able advocates, yet their Magna Charta does not contain any one provision for the security of those rights, respecting which the people of America are most alarmed. The freedom of the press and the rights of conscience, those choicest privileges of the people, are unguarded in the British Constitution" 1 *Annals of Congress 1789–1790*, 434. Elsewhere, he wrote that "the state of the press . . . under the common law, cannot . . . be the standard of its freedom in the United States": VI *Writings of James Madison 1790–1802*: 387.

6. Article III, s3.

7. William Mayton, "Seditious Libel and the Lost Guarantee of a Freedom of Expression," *Columbia Law Review* 84 (1984): 115; James Madison in *The Federalist Papers*, 43, 310: "as new fangled and artificial treasons have been the great engines by which violent factions, the natural offspring of free government, have usually on wreaked, their alternate malignity on each other, the convention have, with great judgment, opposed a barrier to this peculiar danger, by inserting a constitutional definition of the crime."

8. *Erskine's Speeches*, High's Ed, Vol 1, 525.

9. Stewart Jay, "The Creation of the *First Amendment* Right to Free Expression: From the Eighteenth Century to the Mid-Twentieth Century," *William Mitchell Law Review* 34 (2008): 788.

10. 248; *Bridges v California* 314 US 252, 264–265 (1941): "no purpose in ratifying the *Bill of Rights* was clearer than that of securing for the people of the United States much greater freedom of expression, religion, expression, assembly and petition than the people of Great Britain had ever enjoyed . . . ratified as it was while the memory of many oppressive English restrictions on the enumerated liberties was still fresh, the First Amendment cannot reasonably be taken as approving prevalent English practices. On the contrary, the only conclusion supported by history is that the unqualified prohibitions laid down by the framers were intended to give to liberty of the press, as to the other liberties, the broadest scope that could be countenanced in an orderly society": (Black J, for Reed Douglas Murphy and Jackson; Stone CJ Roberts Frankfurter and Byrnes JJ dissenting).

11. William Mayton, "Seditious Libel and the Lost Guarantee of a Freedom of Expression," *Columbia Law Review* 84 (1984): 120. Bird says that the American colonies which adopted free speech were not primarily concerned with prior restraints, because they had effectively disappeared from British law well prior to 1776: "Liberties of Press and Speech: 'Evidence Does Not Exist to Contradict the. . . . Blackstonian Sense' in Late 18th Century England," *Oxford Journal of Legal Studies* 36(1) (2016): 13; cf Leonard Levy, *Emergence of a Free Press* (Oxford University Press, New York, 1985), 191 who claims that the American colonists used free speech in the Blackstonian sense of a lack of prior restraint, and did not intend it to be a protection against prosecution for seditious libel.

12. "Report Accompanying the Virginia Resolution," Elliot, *The Debates in the Several State Conventions on the Adoption of the Federal Constitution* 4 (1866): 570.

13. Ibid.

14. Zechariah Chafee, "Freedom of Speech in War Time," *Harvard Law Review* 32 (1919): 945 and 947: "two different views of the relation of rulers and people were in conflict. According to one view, the rulers were the superiors of the people, and therefore must not be subjected to any censure that would tend to diminish their authority. The people could not make adverse criticism in newspapers or pamphlets, but only through their lawful representatives in the legislature . . . according to the other view, the rulers are agents and servants of the people . . . the law of sedition was a product of the view that the government was master, and that the American Revolution transformed into a working reality the second view that the government was servant, and therefore subject to blame from its master, the people."

15. Eric Barendt, "Importing United States Free Speech Jurisprudence," in Tom Campbell and Wojciech Sadurski, *Freedom of Communication* (Aldershot, England, 1994), 65: "Americans have always been distrustful of government, an attitude rooted in the origins of the country, the gaining of its independence from a remote and ineffective British regime, and later the pioneering spirit of the nineteenth century. Equally, socialist and egalitarian political theory has exercised relatively little influence on American thinking about fundamental rights"; Grant

Huscroft, "The Constitutional and Cultural Underpinnings of Freedom of Expression: Lessons From the United States and Canada," *University of Queensland Law Journal* 25 (2006): 191.

16. "The Framers seem to have had no coherent theory of free speech and appear not to have been overly concerned with the subject . . . the *First Amendment*, like the rest of the *Bill of Rights*, appears to have been a hastily drafted document upon which little thought was expended": Robert H Bork, "Neutral Principles and Some *First Amendment* Problems," *Indiana Law Journal* 47 (1971): 22.

17. *Patterson v Colorado* 205 US 454, 462 (1907) (Holmes J, for Fuller White Peckham McKenna Day and Moody JJ); *Near v Minnesota* 283 US 697, 713 (1931) (Hughes CJ, for Holmes Brandeis Stone and Roberts JJ).

18. "It (is) difficult to attribute any precise original meaning to the *First Amendment"*: Steven Heyman, "Righting the Balance: An Inquiry Into the Foundations and Limits of Freedom of Expression," *Boston University Law Review* 78 (1998): 1296.

19. William Mayton, "Seditious Libel and the Lost Guarantee of a Freedom of Expression," *Columbia Law Review* 84 (1984): 117; James Madison, "Report Accompanying the Virginia Resolution," in Elliot, *The Debates in the Several State Conventions on the Adoption of the Federal Constitution* 4 (1866): 573.

20. Leonard Levy, *Legacy of Suppression: Freedom of Speech and Press in Early American History* (Harvard University Press, Cambridge, 1960), 186 concluded that the main object of the founding fathers in enacting the *First Amendment* speech provisions was to avoid the doctrine of prior restraint; Norman Rosenberg, *Protecting the Best Men: An Interpretive History of the Law of Libel* (University of North Carolina Press, Chapel Hill, 1986), 100: "to political leaders of Jefferson's generation constitutional guarantees did not require toleration of everything published in the press about the conduct of the best men. Rather, political leaders from both major factions endorsed a quite different proposition: government, if not at the national then at the state level, had a positive responsibility to monitor—and, when necessary, to step in and moderate—political communication"; David Yassky, "Eras of the *First Amendment*," *Columbia Law Review* 91 (1991): 1707: "the Founders did not believe that liberty depended upon the inclusion in public debate of all possible points of view."

21. 1710: "the Founders' intention for the *First Amendment* . . . was not to eradicate censorship. It was to limit central government intrusion into the states' prerogatives. Proponents of the *Bill of Rights* saw it as a guarantee of liberty not because it listed uninfringeable rights but because it set out areas that were left entirely to the states' discretion."

22. Lillian BeVier, "The First Amendment and Political Speech: An Inquiry Into Substance and Limits of Principle," *Stanford Law Review* 30 (1978): 307.

23. Norman Rosenberg, *Protecting the Best Men: An Interpretive History of the Law of Libel* (University of North Carolina Press, Chapel Hill, 1986), 108–120; Leonard Levy, *Legacy of Suppression: Freedom of Speech and Press in Early American History* (Harvard University Press, Cambridge, 1960), 204–212.

24. *Gitlow v New York* 268 US 652 (1925); *De Jonge v Oregon* 299 US 353 (1937).

25. "that if any person shall write, print, utter or publish, or shall cause or procure to be written, printed, uttered or published . . . any false, scandalous and malicious writing or writings against the government of the United States . . . or the President, with intent to defame . . . or to bring them into disrepute . . . then such person . . . shall be punished by a fine not exceeding $2000 and by imprisonment not exceeding two years."

26. David Bogen, "The Origins of Freedom of Speech and Press," *Maryland Law Review* 42 (1983): 462.

27. *New York Times v Sullivan* 376 US 254, 276 (1964) (Brennan J, for Warren CJ Clark Harlan Stewart and White JJ; Black Douglas and Goldberg JJ concurring).

28. David Bogen, "The Origins of Freedom of Speech and Press," *Maryland Law Review* 42 (1983): 461.

29. Robert Bork, "Neutral Principles and Some *First Amendment* Problems," *Indiana Law Journal* 47 (1971): 22.

30. *Debs v United States* 249 US 211 (1919). The Court declared the speech was an attempt "to cause and incite insubordination, disloyalty, mutiny, and refusal of duty in the military and naval forces of the United States" (212).

31. *Cox v Louisiana* 379 US 536, 554 (1965).
32. 379 US 536 (1965).
33. 554.
34. John Stuart Mill, Utilitarianism, *On Liberty, Considerations on Representative Government* (Geraint Williams ed., Everyman, 1972), 82: "the disposition of mankind, whether as rulers or fellow-citizens, to impose their own opinions and inclinations as a rule of conduct on others, is so energetically supported by some of the best and some of the worse feelings incident to human nature, that it is hardly ever kept under restraint by anything other than want of power"; Thomas Emerson, "Towards a General Theory of the *First Amendment*," *Yale Law Journal* 72 (1963): 888: "those who currently dominate a society naturally cling to their economic, political and social position of advantage. Vested interests in the status quo, or in the continuing ignorance of other people, tend to take precedence over the broader interests of society as a whole. Forces of this nature vigorously resist the expression of new ideas or the underprivileged who would change existing conditions"; *Abrams v United States* 250 US 616, 630 (1919) (Holmes J, dissenting).
35. Thomas Emerson, "Towards a General Theory of the *First Amendment*," *Yale Law Journal* 72 (1963): 906: "the court's obligation to bow to the will of the legislature and the executive is at a minimum where a serious claim to infringement of freedom of expression on the part of those institutions is presented."
36. For example, in *Thornhill v Alabama* 310 US 88 (1940) Murphy J for the court referred both to truth (95) and the marketplace of ideas (105) with evident approval. In contrast, the case of *Stromberg v California* 283 US 359 (1931) evidences the democratic self-government idea: "the maintenance of the opportunity for free political discussion to the end that government may be responsive to the will of the people and that changes may be obtained by lawful means, an opportunity essential to the security of the Republic, is a fundamental principle of our constitutional system" (369, Hughes CJ, for Holmes Van Devanter Brandeis Sutherland Stone and Roberts JJ).
37. *American Communications Association v Douds* 339 US 382, 399–400 (1950) (Vinson CJ, for Reed and Burton JJ); see also *Chaplinsky v New Hampshire* 315 US 568, 572 (1942) where Murphy J for the Court referred to cases where the *First Amendment* did not protect speech because "any benefit that may be derived from (it) is clearly outweighed by the social interest in order and morality."
38. William Mayton, "Seditious Libel and the Lost Guarantee of a Freedom of Expression," *Columbia Law Review* 84 (1984): 141; for judicial criticism of balancing in the *First Amendment* context see *Konigsberg v State Bar of California* 366 US 36, 74–75 (1961) (Black J, with whom Warren CJ and Douglas J agreed).
39. O Lee Reed, "A Free Speech Metavalue for the Next Millennium: Autonomy of Consciousness in *First Amendment* Theory and Practice," *American Business Law Journal* 35 (1997): 25: "free speech is anterior to other values and subsumes them."
40. For example, *United States v Stevens* 559 US 460, 470 (2010) (Roberts CJ, for Stevens Scalia Kennedy Thomas Ginsburg Breyer and Sotomayor JJ): "the *First Amendment* guarantee of free speech does not extend only to categories of speech that survive an ad hoc balancing of relative social costs and benefits."
41. *Chaplinsky v New Hampshire* 315 US 568 (1942).
42. William Mayton, "Seditious Libel and the Lost Guarantee of a Freedom of Expression," *Columbia Law Review* 84 (1984): 140–141.
43. "Imperative is the need to preserve inviolate the constitutional rights of free speech, free press, and free assembly in order to maintain the opportunity for free political discussion, to the end that government may be responsive to the will of the people and that changes, if desired, may be obtained by peaceful means. Therein lies the security of the Republic, the very foundation of constitutional government": *De Jonge v Oregon* 299 US 353, 365 (1937) (Hughes CJ).
44. *Garrison v Louisiana* 379 US 64, 74–75 (1964).
45. *First National Bank v Bellotti* 435 US 765 (1978).
46. 319 US 624, 642 (1943) (Jackson J, for Stone, Roberts, Reed and Rutledge JJ; Black Douglas and Murphy JJ concurring; Frankfurter J dissenting).
47. 639–640 (Jackson J).

48. *Palko v Connecticut* 302 US 319, 327 (1937) (the "indispensable condition of nearly every other form of freedom") (Cardozo J).
49. 639–640 (Jackson J).
50. Stanley Ingber, "The Marketplace of Ideas: A Legitimizing Myth," (1984) *Duke Law Journal* (1984): 1; Paul Brietzke, "How and Why the Marketplace of Ideas Fails," *Valparaiso University Law Review* 31 (1997): 951; Catherine MacKinnon, *Only Words* (Harper Collins, London, 1993); Darren Bush, "The 'Marketplace of Ideas'": Is Judge Posner Chasing Don Quixote's Windmills?" *Arizona State Law Journal* 32 (2000): 1107.
51. Kathleen Sullivan, "Two Concepts of Freedom of Speech," *Harvard Law Review* 124 (2010): 143.
52. Mari Matsuda, "Public Response to Racist Speech: Considering the Victim's Story," *Michigan Law Review* 87 (1989): 2320; Richard Delgado, "Words That Wound: A Tort Action for Racial Insults, Epithets and Name-Calling," *Harvard Civil Rights—Civil Liberties Law Review* 17 (1982): 133.
53. Mari Matsuda, "Public Response to Racist Speech: Considering the Victim's Story," *Michigan Law Review* 87 (1989): 2358.
54. 2378–2379: "to allow an organisation known for violence, persecution, race hatred and commitment to racial supremacy to exist openly, and to provide police protection and access to public streets and college campuses for such a group, means that the state is promoting racist speech."
55. Fred McChesney, "A Positive Regulatory Theory of the *First Amendment*," *Connecticut Law Review* 20 (1988): 355; this debate is discussed in Nicholas Wolfson, "Free Speech Theory and Hateful Words," *University of Cincinnati Law Review* 60 (1991): 37–41.
56. Roscoe Pound, "The Scope and Purpose of Sociological Jurisprudence," *Harvard Law Review* 25 (1911): 143.
57. Roscoe Pound, "Interests of Personality," *Harvard Law Review* 28 (1915): 345; Steven Helle, "Whither the Public's Right (Not) to Know—Milton, Malls, and Multicultural Speech," *University of Illinois Law Review* (1991): 1086.
58. 391 US 367 (1968).
59. 377 (Warren CJ, for Black Brennan Stewart White and Fortas JJ; Harlan J concurring; Douglas J dissenting); referred to with approval in *Turner Broadcasting Systems v FCC* 512 US 622, 662 (1994) (Kennedy J, with whom Rehnquist CJ Blackmun Stevens and Souter JJ agreed).
60. *Edenfield v Fane* 507 US 761 (1993). There the Court rejected the government's argument that a ban on professionals soliciting for work was needed to preserve honest practice and the independence of the relevant profession: "the Board has not demonstrated that . . . the ban . . . on solicitation advances its asserted interests in any direct or material way. It presents no studies that suggest personal solicitation of prospective business clients . . . creates the dangers of fraud, overreaching or compromised independence that the Board claims to fear" (771) (Kennedy, for Rehnquist CJ White Blackmun Stevens Scalia Souter and Thomas JJ).
61. *Chaplinsky v New Hampshire* 315 US 568, 571–572 (1942) (noting some utterances were not essential to the expression of ideas and of "slight social value as a step to truth" that they might not enjoy *First Amendment* protection); *Abrams v United States* 250 US 616, 630 (1919): "the ultimate good desired is better reached by free trade in ideas—that the best test of truth is the power of the thought to get itself accepted in the competition of the market, and that truth is the only ground upon which their wishes safely can be carried out. That at any rate is the theory of our *Constitution*" (Holmes J, dissenting); *Thornhill v Alabama* 310 US 88, 95 (1940) (Murphy J, for the Court); *Bose Corp v Consumers Union* 466 US 485, 503 (1984). Obviously the "truth" argument has historical parallels in the writings of Milton and Mill, discussed in Chapter 1.
62. "The constitutional right of free expression . . . is designed and intended to remove governmental restraints from the arena of public discussion, putting the decision as to what views shall be voiced largely into the hands of each of us, in the hope that use of such freedom will ultimately produce a more capable citizenry and more perfect polity and in the belief that no other approach would comport with the premise of individual dignity and choice upon which our political system rests": *Cohen v California* 403 US 15, 24 (1971) (Harlan J, for

Douglas Brennan Stewart and Marshall JJ); "intrinsic to individual liberty and dignity" (*Dun and Bradstreet v Greenmoss Builders* 472 US 749, 787 (1985) (Brennan J, for Marshall Blackmun and Stevens JJ).

63. *Garrison v Louisiana* 379 US 64, 75–76 (1964): "speech concerning public affairs is more than self-expression; it is the essence of self-government"; *Richmond Newspapers v Virginia* 448 US 555, 575 (1980) (Burger CJ White and Stevens JJ), stating that the rights in the *First Amendment* "share a common purpose of assuring freedom of communication on matters relating to the functioning of government"; *New York Times Co v Sullivan* 376 US 254 (1964).

64. "Towards a Metatheory of Free Speech," *Southwestern University Law Review* 10 (1978): 237. His criteria include (a) the theory must describe the premises upon which a free speech should draw; (b) it must take a position on the structure of free speech theory; (c) it must identify acceptable methods; and (d) it must set boundaries of content and substance. He suggests that a free speech theory cannot assume any particular form of economic life, effectively rejecting the "marketplace of ideas" theory; he rejects the self-government justification as hopelessly mired in means and ends confusion and as stretching credibility when it seeks to include certain kinds of speech within free speech protections, according to its tenets, and to apparently arbitrarily exclude others.

65. Lee Bollinger, "Free Speech and Intellectual Values," *Yale Law Journal* 92 (1983): 451 who discusses the "reality of intolerance toward speech, which arises not simply, or even primarily, from unauthorized official censorship but from democracy at work, from a majority demanding or wanting their government to prohibit certain forms of expression from public discourse."

66. Isaiah Berlin, "Two Concepts of Liberty" in *Four Essays on Liberty* (Oxford University Press, London, 1969) 122–131.

67. *New York Times Co v Sullivan* 376 US 254, 270 (1964) (Brennan J, for Warren CJ Clark Harlan Stewart and White JJ; Black, Douglas and Goldberg JJ concurred); *Cantwell v Connecticut* 310 US 296, 310 (1940).

68. *Hustler Magazine v Falwell* 485 US 46, 51 (1988) (Rehnquist CJ for the Court).

69. *Rankin v McPherson* 483 US 378, 387 (1987).

70. *Terminiello v Chicago* 337 US 1, 4 (1949) (Douglas J, for Reed Douglas Murphy Rutledge and Burton JJ; Vinson CJ Frankfurter and Jackson JJ dissenting).

71. *Kingsley International Pictures Corp v Regents of the University of the State of New York* 360 US 684 (1959).

72. Compare, for example, the Court's tolerance for controversial and inflammatory speech in *Terminiello v Chicago* 337 US 1 (1949) (speech warning Americans of a conspiracy against Christian America by Russians and communists, the New Deal, Jew and Eleanor Roosevelt, and denouncing protesters as probably "foreigners" and definitely "scum," with its apparent intolerance for similar natured speech in *Feiner v New York* 340 US 315 (1951) (denouncing various public figures with crude epithets, calling the American Legion the "Nazi Gestapo" and calling for African-Americans to rise up against inequality) only a couple of years later, on the basis of the state's legitimate interest in preserving peace on the streets.

73. *Chaplinsky v New Hampshire* 315 US 568 (1942).

74. *Beauharnais v Illinois* 343 US 250 (1952).

75. *Roth v United States* 354 US 476 (1957).

76. *New York v Ferber* 458 US 747 (1982); subsequently this exception was held not to include cases where real children were not in face used, or cases where those involved may be minors engaged in lawful sexual activity, being of or above the minimum age of consent for lawful sexual intercourse: *Ashcroft v Free Speech Coalition* 535 US 234 (2002).

77. *United States v Stevens* 559 US 460 (2010).

78. *Brown v Entertainment Merchants Association* 564 US 786 (2011).

79. 315 US 568 (1942).

80. 559 US 460 (2010).

81. 572. A different set of so-called exceptions was listed in *United States v Stevens* 559 US 460, 468–469 (2010) (obscenity, defamation, fraud, incitement, and speech integral to criminal conduct) (Roberts CJ, for Stevens Scalia Kennedy Thomas Ginsburg Breyer and Sotomayor

JJ). It also includes "true threats," but there is real uncertainty as to the precise contours of such an exception: *Elonis v United States* 135 S.Ct 2001 (2015).

82. Clay Calvert, "Beyond Headlines and Holdings: Exploring Some Less Obvious Ramifications of the Supreme Court's 2017 Free Speech Rulings," *William and Mary Bill of Rights Journal* 26 (2018): 916: "proportionality is embraced by courts in other nations, but not by the United States Supreme Court," although acknowledging Breyer J's apparent interest in the concept.

83. The difficulties involved in defining this satisfactorily have been acknowledged: *San Diego v Roe* 543 US 77, 83 (2004). In *Connick v Myers* the Court defined public concern to be matters 'relating to any matter of political, social or other concern to the community': 461 US 138, 146 (1983).

84. *Snyder v Phelps* 562 US 443 (2011).

85. *Thornhill v Alabama* 310 US 88, 102 (1940) (Murphy J, for the Court); *Time, Inc v Hill* 385 US 374, 388 (1966): "the guarantees for speech and press are not the preserve of political expression or comment upon public affairs, essential as those are to healthy government. One need only pick up any newspaper or magazine to comprehend the vast range of published matter which exposes persons to public view, both private citizens and public officials": (Brennan J for Warren CJ Clark Stewart White and Fortas JJ; Black Douglas and Harlan JJ concurring).

86. *Dun and Bradstreet v Greenmoss Builders* 472 US 749 (1985) (Powell J, for Rehnquist and O'Connor JJ, Burger CJ and White concurring, found it was not a question of public concern; Brennan J, for Marshall Blackmun and Stevens JJ, said it was).

87. *Abood v Detroit Board of Education* 431 US 209, 231 (1977); *Connick v Myers* 461 US 138, 147 (1983): "we in no sense suggest that speech on private matters falls into one of the narrow and well-defined classes of expression which carries so little social value, such as obscenity, that the state can prohibit and punish such expression by all persons in its jurisdiction" (White J, for Burger CJ Powell Rehnquist and O'Connor JJ).

88. *FCC v Pacifica Foundation et al* 438 US 726, 746 (1978) (Stevens J, with whom Burger CJ and Rehnquist J agreed).

89. *Chaplinsky v New Hampshire* 315 US 568, 572 (1942) (Murphy J, for the Court).

90. *FCC v Pacifica Foundation et al* 438 US 726, 761 (1978): "I do not subscribe to the theory that the Justices of this court are free generally to decide on the basis of its content which speech protected by the *First Amendment* is most valuable and hence deserving of the most protection, and which is less valuable and hence deserving of less protection" (Powell J, with whom Blackmun J agreed); 773: "the idea that the content of a message and its potential impact on any who might receive it can be divorced from the words that are the vehicle for its expression is transparently fallacious. . . . even if an alternative phrasing may communicate a speaker's abstract ideas as effectively as those whose words he is forbidden to use, it is doubtful that the sterilized message will convey the emotion that is an essential part of so many communications" (Brennan and Stewart JJ).

91. *FCC v Pacifica Foundation et al* 438 US 726, 756 (Powell J, with whom Blackmun J concurred) (1978).

92. 479.

93. *New York Times Co v Sullivan* 376 US 254, 271 (1964) (Brennan J); *NAACP v Button* 371 US 415, 433.

94. 379 US 64, 65 (1964); a similar view is evident in *Hustler Magazine v Falwell* 485 US 46, 52 (1988): "false statements of fact are particularly valueless; they interfere with the truth-seeking function of the marketplace of ideas, and they cause damage to an individual's reputation that cannot easily be repaired by counterspeech."

95. *United States v Alvarez* 567 US 709 (2012).

96. *Pickering v Board of Education* 391 US 563 (1968); *City of San Diego v Roe* 543 US 77 (2004); *Rankin v McPherson* 483 US 378 (1987).

97. *Garcetti v Ceballos* 547 US 410 (2006).

98. *Parker v Levy* 417 US 733 (1974).

99. "If there is a bedrock principle underlying the *First Amendment*, it is that the government may not prohibit the expression of an idea simply because society finds the idea itself

offensive or disagreeable": *Texas v Johnson* 491 US 397, 414 (1989); *Police Department of Chicago v Mosley* 408 US 92, 96 (1972); *Perry Education Association v Perry Local Educators' Association et al* 460 US 37, 62 (1983): "viewpoint discrimination is censorship in its purest form and government regulation that discriminates among viewpoints threatens the continued vitality of free speech" (Brennan J, for Marshall Powell and Stevens JJ); *Tinker v Des Moines Independent Community School District* 393 US 503 (1969) (school ban on the wearing of black armbands to protest the Vietnam war held to be inconsistent with *First Amendment* rights, when students in the past had been able to wear buttons in support of national campaigns and to wear the Iron Cross, a symbol of Nazism): "clearly the prohibition of expression of one particular opinion, at least without evidence that it is necessary to avoid material and substantial interference with schoolwork or discipline, is not constitutionally permissible" (510, Fortas J, for Warren CJ Douglas Harlan Brennan and Marshall JJ; Stewart and White JJ concurring; Black J dissenting).

100. *Carey v Brown* 447 US 455 (1980) (general ban on picketing in residential areas, except with respect to labor disputes, struck out as offensive to the *First Amendment* given it discriminated against speech on the basis of content); *Police Department of Chicago v Mosley* 408 US 92, 95–96 (1972): "above all else, the *First Amendment* means that government has no power to restrict expression because of its message, its ideas, its subject matter, or its content . . . any restriction on expressive activity because of its content would completely undercut the profound national commitment to the principle that debate on public issues should be uninhibited, robust and wide-open" (Marshall J, for Burger CJ Douglas Brennan Stewart White and Powell JJ).

101. *Schenck v United States* 249 US 47, 52 (1919).

102. Geoffrey Stone, "Restrictions of Speech Because of its Content: The Peculiar Case of Subject-Matter Restrictions," *University of Chicago Law Review* 46 (1978): 82; *Young v American Mini-Theatres Inc* 427 US 50 (1976).

103. *Widmar v Vincent* 454 US 263 (1981); *Reno v ACLU* 521 US 844, 874 (1997) noting this requires that no alternative is available that is less restrictive of freedom of expression.

104. *Brown v Entertainment Merchants Association* 564 US 786 (2011), where the Court was not convinced of the state's argument that it needed to prohibit the sale of violent video games to minors on the basis that exposure to such material would lead to an increase in anti-social behavior which the state had the right to seek to pre-empt.

105. A recent example is *Williams-Yulee v Florida Bar* 135 S. Ct. 1656 (2015) (legislation prohibiting a candidate for judicial office from directly canvassing for campaign donations held valid on the basis the state had a compelling interest in preserving the actuality and perception of judicial independence, and the provision was narrowly tailored towards that interest).

106. *Renton v Playtime Theatres Inc* 475 US 41 (1986); *Boos v Barry* 485 US 312 (1988).

107. *Boos v Barry* 485 US 312, 334 (1988) (Brennan J, for Marshall J).

108. Clay Calvert and Matthew D. Bunker, "Fissures, Fractures and Doctrinal Drifts: Paying the Price in *First Amendment* Jurisprudence for a Half Decade of Avoidance, Minimalism and Partisanship," *William and Mary Bill of Rights Journal* 24 (2016): 979.

109. *Hill v Colorado* 530 US 703, 726 (2000) (Marshall J, for Rehnquist CJ O'Connor Souter Ginsburg and Breyer JJ).

110. *Ward v Rock Against Racism* 491 US 781, 799 (1989).

111. *Lehman v Shaker Heights* 418 US 298 (1974); *Ward v Rock Against Racism* 491 US 781 (1989); *Members of City Council v Taxpayers for Vincent* 466 US 789 (1984).

112. *Perry Education Association v Perry Local Educators' Association* 460 US 37, 45 (1983) (White J, for Burger CJ Blackmun Rehnquist and O'Connor JJ); *United States v Grace* 461 US 171, 177 (1983).

113. "Wherever the title of streets and parks may rest, they have immemorially been held in trust for the use of the public and, time out of mind, have been used for purposes of assembly, communicating thoughts between citizens, and discussing public questions. Such use of the streets and public places has, from ancient times, been a part of the privileges, immunities, rights and liberties of citizens. The privilege of a citizen of the United States to use the streets and parks for communication of views on national questions may be regulated in the interest of all; it is not absolute, but relative, and must be exercised in subordination to the general comfort

and convenience, and in consonance with peace and good order; but it must not, in the guise of regulation, be abridged or denied": *Hague v Committee for Industrial Organisation* 307 US 496, 515–516 (1939).

114. *Cornelius v NAACP Legal Defense and Education Fund Inc* 473 US 788, 800 (1985).

115. *Packingham v North Carolina* 137 S. Ct. 1730, 1735 (2017) (Kennedy J, for Ginsburg Breyer Sotomayor and Kagan JJ).

116. *Widmar v Vincent* 454 US 263 (1981).

117. An interactive space permitting others to respond to tweets sent from real President Trump twitter account is a designated public forum: *Knight First Amendment Institute at Columbia University v Trump* 302 F. Supp. 3d 541 (2018).

118. *Christian Legal Society Chapter of the University of California v Martinez* 561 US 661, 679 (2010) (Ginsburg J, for Stevens Kennedy Breyer and Sotomayor JJ). In that case a majority of the Court found that the decision of Hastings College of Law to recognize particular student groups on the condition that they accepted "all comers" and complied with state non-discrimination law relating to religion and sexual orientation was valid. The College had denied recognition to a particular group because it had signed a statement of faith indicating it believed sexual intercourse should not occur outside of marriage, that marriage was between one man and one woman, and that anyone engaged in "unrepentant homosexual conduct" could not be a member. A bare majority of the Supreme Court validated the measure against a *First Amendment* challenge, on the basis that the restrictions were non-viewpoint based and reasonable.

119. *Rosenberger v University of Virginia* 454 US 263 (1981).

120. *Perry Education Association v Perry Local Educators' Association et al* 460 US 37 (1983); others argue that free speech that takes place within certain institutional settings, including universities and schools and media organisations, is entitled to special free speech protection: Joseph Blocher, "Institutions in the Marketplace of Ideas," *Duke Law Journal* 57 (2008): 821; Frederick Schauer, "Is There a Right to Academic Freedom?" *University of Colorado Law Review* 77 (2006): 912; Julian Eule and Jonathan Varat, "Transporting First Amendment Norms to the Private Sector: With Every Wish There Comes a Curse," *UCLA Law Review* 45 (1998): 1574–1575.

121. *Board of Education v Mergens* 496 US 226 (1990).

122. *Hazelwood School District v Kuhlmeier* 484 US 260 (1988).

123. *Ward v Rock Against Racism* 491 US 781, 791 (1989).

124. *Rosenberger v Rector and Visitors of the University of Virginia* 515 US 819 (1995).

125. *Widmar v Vincent* 454 US 263, 274 (1981).

126. "The essentiality of freedom in the community of American universities is almost self-evident. No one should underestimate the vital role in a democracy that is played by those who guide and train our youth. To impose any strait jacket upon the intellectual leaders in our colleges and universities would imperil the future of our Nation. No field of education is so thoroughly comprehended by man that new discoveries cannot yet be made. Particularly is that true in the social sciences, where few, if any, principles are accepted as absolutes. Scholarship cannot flourish in an atmosphere or suspicion and distrust. Teachers and students must always remain free to inquire, to study and to evaluate, to gain new maturity and understanding: otherwise our civilization will stagnate and die": *Sweezy v New Hampshire* 354 US 234 (1957).

127. *Widmar v Vincent* 454 US 263, 276 (1981).

128. *Minnesota Voters Alliance v Mansky* 138 S. Ct 1876, 1885 (2018) (Roberts CJ, for Kennedy Thomas Ginsburg Alito Kagan and Gorsuch JJ). In *Minnesota* a majority of the Court found that a ban on the wearing of a political badge, political button or other political insignia within a polling place did not meet the test of reasonableness.

129. *Edwards v South Carolina* 372 US 229 (1963).

130. *Adderley v Florida* 385 US 39 (1966).

131. In *Kingsley v Brown* 354 US 436 (1957) legislation that permitted a public official to confiscate material that is in the possession, or is about to come into the possession, of a person who or organisation that intends to distribute it to the public, if in the opinion of the public official the material was "obscene, lewd, lascivious, filthy, indecent or disgusting." A majority of the Court dismissed a constitutional challenge to the measure.

132. *Niemotko v Maryland* 340 US 268 (1951); *Joseph Burstyn v Wilson* 343 US 495 (1952); *Shuttlesworth v City of Birmingham* 394 US 147 (1969); cf *Cox v New Hampshire* 312 US 569 (1941) where such a scheme was validated. There is a "heavy presumption" that a system of prior restraint is unconstitutional: *Organisation for a Better Austin v Keefe* 402 US 415, 419 (1971).

133. 283 US 697 (1931).

134. 716.

135. *Bantam Books Inc v Sullivan* 372 US 58, 70 (1963).

136. *New York Times Co v United States* 403 US 713 (1971).

137. Thus in *Kingsley v Regents of the University of New York* 360 US 684 (1959) the court overturned a decision to ban the showing of a movie which apparently depicted adultery as acceptable (Lady Chatterley's Lover). The legislation had stated that no film could be shown in New York unless a licence had previously been obtained. A licence would be refused for material judged to be obscene or indecent. The Court said it was unacceptable to ban a communication based on the messages it contained.

138. *Hill v Colorado* 530 US 703, 716 (2000) (Stevens J, for Rehnquist CJ O'Connor Souter Ginsburg and Breyer JJ).

139. *Rowan v United States Post Office Department* 397 US 728 (1970).

140. *Janus v AFSCME* 138 S. Ct 2448 (2018).

141. *Smith v Goguen* 415 US 566 (1974).

142. *Stromberg v California* 283 US 359 (1931).

143. *Coates v Cincinnati* 402 US 611 (1971).

144. *Lanzetta v New Jersey* 306 US 451 (1939); somewhat surprisingly, a closely divided court in *Parker v Levy* 417 US 733 (1974) upheld military provisions providing for jail terms for military personnel found guilty by court-martial of conduct "unbecoming of an officer and a gentleman" and conduct "of a nature likely to bring discredit upon the armed forces," rejecting a *First Amendment* challenge. The appellant had been convicted of these offenses for imploring other African-Americans not to join the war effort because in his view they would suffer racial discrimination. By a majority of 5:3 the court rejected an argument that the provisions were void for vagueness.

145. *Reno v ACLU* 521 US 844 (1997).

146. *Connally v General Construction Co* 269 US 385, 391 (1926).

147. *Smith v Goguen* 415 US 566, 573 (1974) (Powell J, for Douglas Brennan Stewart and Marshall JJ).

148. *United States v Robel* 389 US 258 (1967); *Keyishian v Board of Regents* 385 US 589 (1967).

149. *Thornhill v Alabama* 310 US 88 (1940); *Virginia v Black* 538 US 343 (2003).

150. *Shuttlesworth v Birmingham* 394 US 147 (1969); *Cox v Louisiana* 379 US 536 (1965).

151. *McCullen v Coakley* 134 S. Ct 2518 (2014) (invalidating a statute creating a buffer zone around an abortion clinic. The statute prohibited a person from "knowingly standing on a public way or sidewalk within 35 feet of an abortion clinic." The majority concluded the legislation burdened substantially more speech than was necessary to achieve its objective; cf *Hill v Colorado* 530 US 703 (2000). Similarly legislation prohibiting a convicted sex offender from accessing a social networking site frequented by minors was invalid due to overbreadth: *Packingham v North Carolina* 137 S. Ct. 1730 (2017).

152. *Hill v Colorado* 530 US 703, 732 (2000).

153. *Healy v James* 408 US 169, 192 (1972).

154. *Giboney v Empire Storage and Ice Co* 336 US 490 (1949).

155. *Texas v Johnson* 491 US 397 (1989); *Tinker v Des Moines Independent Community School District* 393 US 503 (1969).

156. *FCC v Pacifica Foundation et al* 438 US 726, 745 (1978) (Stevens J, with whom Burger CJ and Rehnquist J agreed).

157. *Expressions Hair Design v Schneiderman* 137 S.Ct 1144, 1152 (2017) (Breyer J).

158. *Cox v Louisiana* 379 US 536, 555 (1965) (Goldberg J); *Tinker v Des Moines School District* 393 US 503, 505–506 (1969) (Fortas J).

159. *Thomas v Collins* 323 US 516, 537 (1945): "we do not mean to say that, in many circumstances, a difference between urging a course of action and merely giving and acquiring information . . . but the protection they (founding fathers) sought was not solely for persons in intellectual pursuits. It extends to more than abstract discussion, unrelated to action. The *First Amendment* is a charter for government, not for an institution of learning. 'Free trade in ideas' means free trade in the opportunity to persuade to action, not merely to describe facts" (Rutledge J, Douglas Black Murphy and Jackson JJ concurring).

160. *Madsen v Women's Health Center* 512 US 753 (1994) (Rehnquist CJ, for Blackmun O'Connor Souter and Ginsburg JJ, Stevens J concurring; Scalia J, with whom Kennedy and Thomas JJ agreed, dissenting on point); *Schenck v Pro-Choices Network of Western New York* 519 US 357 (1997).

161. Thomas Emerson, "Towards a General Theory of the *First Amendment,*" *Yale Law Journal* 72 (1963): 891–893.

162. Zechariah Chafee, "Freedom of Speech in War Time," *Harvard Law Review* 32 (1919): 965.

163. Stewart Jay, "The Creation of the *First Amendment* Right to Free Expression: From the Eighteenth Century to the Mid-Twentieth Century," *William Mitchell Law Review* 34 (2008): 830.

164. *Schenck v United States* 249 US 47 (1919); similarly *Pierce v United States* 252 US 239 (1920) and *Gilbert v Minnesota* 254 US 325 (1920) and *Schaefer v United States* 251 US 466 (1920).

165. 52. The test has been strongly criticized: see, for example, Paul Freund, *On Understanding the Supreme Court* (Greenwood Press, Connecticut, 1950), 27–28; Benjamin DuVal, "Free Communication of Ideas and the Quest for Truth: Towards a Teleological Approach to *First Amendment* Adjudication," *George Washington Law Review* 41 (1972): 166–170; Stanley Ingber, "The Marketplace of Ideas: A Legitimizing Myth," *Duke Law Journal* (1984): 18: "speech is constitutionally protected under the clear and present danger test as long as it is either ineffective or insignificant. In either instance the test creates an establishment bias."

166. 250 US 616 (1919); there Holmes J developed his "marketplace of ideas" theory of free speech that would subsequently prove to be very influential, that the best test of truth was the ability of an idea to gain traction in the marketplace of ideas: 630.

167. Some credit the approach of Hand J in *Masses Publishing Co v Patten* 244 Fed. 535 (S.D.N.Y 1917) and his chance meeting with Holmes on a train with the Supreme Court's restricted view of the ability of the state to regulate speech: Gerald Gunther, "Learned Hand and the Origins of Modern *First Amendment* Doctrine: Some Fragments of History," *Stanford Law Review* 27 (1975): 719.

168. Thomas Emerson, "Towards a General Theory of the *First Amendment*," *Yale Law Journal* 72 (1963): 877, 910–911 says that the test is too focussed on the effectiveness of speech, and bans speech that is likely to be effective, leaving only innocuous speech available to the public, criticizes the test for vagueness, and suggests it is unworkable in requiring the Court to consider a whole range of non-legal factors which it is ill-equipped to complete in order to apply the test.

169. *Abrams v United States* 250 US 616, 628 (1919).

170. 268 US 652 (1925).

171. 667 (Justice Sanford, for the Court).

172. 667 (Justice Sanford, for the Court).

173. Henry Schofield, *Proceedings of the American Sociological Society* 9 (1914): 86 spoke of the "great danger . . . that men will be fined and imprisoned, under the guise of being punished for their bad motives or bad intent and ends, simply because the powers that be do not agree with their opinions, and spokesmen of minorities may be terrorized and silenced when they are most needed by the community and most useful to it, and when they stand most in need of the protection of the law against a hostile, arrogant majority"; Thomas Emerson, "Towards a General Theory of the *First Amendment*," *Yale Law Journal* 72 (1963): 910.

174. *Whitney v California* 274 US 357 (1927).

175. 375–378.

176. 299 US 353 (1937).

177. 364–365 (Hughes CJ, for Van Devanter, McReynolds, Brandeis, Sutherland Butler Roberts and Cardozo JJ).

178. See to like effect *Herndon v Lowry* 301 US 242 (1937) (offense of attempting to incite insurrection, punishable by the death penalty, petitioner sentenced to a minimum eighteen year jail period for attending meetings of the Communist Party and possessing written material espousing its doctrines, overturned by the Supreme Court on *First Amendment* grounds).

179. *Dennis v United States* 341 US 494 (1951); in dissent Black and Douglas JJ observed there was no evidence of positive acts of espionage against the United States, seemingly in contrast with Article III's confinement of the treason offense to overt acts.

180. 501 (Vinson CJ, for Reed Burton and Minton JJ; Frankfurter and Jackson JJ concurring; Black and Douglas JJ dissenting).

181. *Yates v United States* 354 US 298 (1957).

182. *Garner v Board of Public Works* 341 US 716 (1951); *Adler v Board of Education* 342 US 485 (1952).

183. *Wieman v Updegraff* 344 US 183 (1952).

184. 360 US 109 (1959).

185. Harlan J, for Frankfurter Clark Brennan Whittaker and Stewart JJ; Warren CJ Black and Douglas JJ dissenting. Legislation requiring union officials to utter an oath of allegiance to the United States government, and state that they are not members of the Communist Party, was validated against a First Amendment challenge in *American Communications Association v Douds* 339 US 382 (1950). Similarly, legislation requiring that public employees declare whether they have been members of a party which advocated or taught the overthrow by force or violence the government of the United States or California was validated by majority in *Garner v Board of Public Works* 341 US 716 (1951). A researcher at a hospital who refused to utter an oath undertaking to uphold and defend the United States Constitution and oppose the overthrow of the government by force, or illegal or unconstitutional means was dismissed. Her argument that such action interfered with her First Amendment freedoms was rejected in *Cole v Richardson* 405 US 676 (1972). Compare *Watkins v United States* 354 US 178 (1957), where the petitioner's conviction for refusing to answer questions posed by Congress' Committee on UnAmerican Activities was overturned on due process grounds.

186. 367 US 203 (1961).

187. *In Re Summers* 325 US 561 (1945) (legislation under which admitting authorities denied admission of a would-be lawyer on the basis that he refused to agree to be loyal to the state's *Constitution* and to fight for his country if asked, on the basis he was a conscientious objector, held to be consistent with *First Amendment* requirements).

188. *Speiser v Randall* 357 US 513 (1958).

189. "I believe that the *First Amendment* grants an absolute right to believe in any governmental system and (to) argue for desired changes in the existing order. This freedom is too dangerous for bad, tyrannical governments to permit" (quoting *Carlson v Landon*).

190. 531.

191. *Brandenburg v Ohio* 395 US 444 (1969).

192. 447–448 (Warren CJ Harlan Brennan Stewart White and Marshall JJ, Black and Douglas JJ concurring).

193. 454.

194. 454.

195. 278 US 63 (1928).

196. *NAACP v Alabama* 357 US 449 (1958).

197. 347 US 483 (1954).

198. 417 US 733 (1974).

199. Rehnquist J, for Burger CJ White Blackmun and Powell JJ.

200. 776; see Pauline Collins, *Civil-Military Relations: Where to From Here?* (Brill Nijhoff, Netherlands, 2018).

201. 310 US 296, 308 (1940) (Roberts J, for the Court). The Court concluded Cantwell's speech was not likely to provoke an immediate violent response in the circumstances.

202. 310 (Roberts J, for the Court).

203. *Chaplinksy v New Hampshire* 315 US 568 (1942).

204. 572.
205. *Beauharnais v Illinois* 343 US 250 (1952).
206. "No legislature is charged with the duty or vested with the power to decide what public issues Americans can discuss. In a free country that is the individual's choice, not the state's. State experimentation in curbing freedom of expression is startling and frightening doctrine in a country dedicated to self-government by its people. I reject the holding that either state or nation can punish people for having their say in matters of public concern" (270).
207. 274.
208. 275.
209. Douglas J expressed dismay with the creeping trend in *First Amendment* cases to permit the legislature to 'reasonably regulate' free speech: "this to me is an ominous and alarming trend. The free trade in ideas which the Framers of the *Constitution* visualized disappears. In its place there is substituted a new orthodoxy—an orthodoxy that changes with the whims of the age of the day, an orthodoxy which the majority by solemn judgment proclaims to be essential to the safety, welfare, security, morality, or health of society. Free speech in the constitutional sense disappears": 285.
210. 383 US 131 (1966).
211. *Hess v Indiana* 414 US 105, 108 (1973) (Rehnquist J, with whom Burger CJ and Blackmun J agreed, dissenting).
212. *Gregory v Chicago* 394 US 111 (1969) ("improper noise, riot, disturbance, persons who 'collect in bodies' . . . to the annoyance or disturbance of other persons").
213. *Gooding, Warden v Wilson* 405 US 518 (1972); *Ashton v Kentucky* 384 US 195 (1966).
214. *Doe v University of Michigan* 721 F. Supp. 852 (E.D, Mich, 1989). On the other hand, the Supreme Court has validated hate crime sentencing enhancement regimes against *First Amendment* challenge: *Wisconsin v Mitchell* 508 US 476 (1993).
215. *Grayned v City of Rockford* 408 US 104, 108–109 (1972): "it is a basic principle of due process that an enactment is void for vagueness if its prohibitions are not clearly defined. Vague laws offend several important values. First, because we assume that man is free to steer between lawful and unlawful conduct, we insist that laws give the person of ordinary intelligence a reasonable opportunity to know what is prohibited, so that he may act accordingly. Vague laws may trap the innocent by not providing fair warning. Second, if arbitrary and discriminatory enforcement is to be prevented, laws must provide explicit standards for those who apply them. A vague law impermissibly delegates basic policy matters to policemen, judges, and juries for resolution on an ad hoc and subjective basis, with the attendant dangers of arbitrary and discriminatory application. Third, but related, where a vague statute 'abuts upon sensitive areas of basic first amendment freedoms,' it operates to inhibit the exercise of (those) freedoms. Uncertain meanings inevitably lead citizens to 'steer far wider of the unlawful zone' . . . than if the boundaries of the forbidden areas were clearly marked."
216. 283 US 697 (1931).
217. *Edwards v South Carolina* 372 US 229 (1963).
218. *Kunz v New York* 340 US 290 (1951). This includes a requirement that a person using a loudspeaker obtain a permit: *Saia v New York* 334 US 558 (1948).
219. *Thornhill v Alabama* 310 US 88 (1940); see similarly *Madsen v Women's Health Center* 512 US 753 (1994), but a prohibition on protesting outside a doctor's home was upheld: *Frisby v Schultz* 487 US 474 (1988).
220. 102 (Justice Murphy for the Court); "matters of public concern" (104).
221. 95 (Justice Murphy for the Court).
222. *Snyder v Phelps* 562 US 443 (2011).
223. *Street v New York* 394 US 576 (1969); *Texas v Johnson* 491 US 397 (1989); *United States v Eichman* 496 US 310 (1990).
224. 505 US 377 (1992).
225. 69 Ill. 2d 604 (1978), affirmed *National Socialist Party v Skokie* 432 US 43 (1977).
226. See also *Virginia v Black* 538 US 343 (2003), where the Court invalidated a law which criminalized the burning of a cross with the intent to intimidate another. The legislation provided that the burning of the cross would be prima facie evidence of an intention to intimidate. The Court found the prima facie evidence provision rendered the law unconstitutional, making

it potentially applicable to behavior where the requisite intention was lacking, thus impinging on constitutionally protected speech.

227. 505 US 377, 382–383 (1992) (Scalia J, for Rehnquist CJ Kennedy Souter and Thomas JJ; White Blackmun O'Connor and Stevens JJ concurring in the judgment).

228. 390.

229. 393.

230. 389.

231. 395.

232. 391.

233. 615.

234. *Roth v United States* 354 US 476 (1957).

235. 485 (Brennan J, for Frankfurter, Burton, Clark, and Whittaker JJ; Warren CJ concurring and Harlan J concurring in part; Black and Douglas JJ dissenting).

236. *Kingsley v Brown* 354 US 436 (1957).

237. *Kingsley v Regents of the University of New York* 360 US 684 (1959). Subsequently it would accept a system of prior licensing of films prior to their being shown, but only where the onus was on the regulator to bring proceedings to have the film banned, where the burden of proof was on the regulator to show the material was unlawful under any applicable statute (for instance, on the basis it was obscene), and only where the time frame during which the regulator would consider whether or not the film should be licensed was strictly confined: *Freedman v Maryland* 380 US 51 (1965).

238. As noted in *Paris Adult Theatre I v Slaton* 413 US 49, 103 (1973): "I am forced to conclude that the concept of obscenity cannot be defined with sufficient specificity and clarity to provide fair notice to persons who create and distribute sexually oriented materials, to prevent substantial erosion of protected speech as a byproduct of the attempt to suppress unprotected speech, and to avoid very costly institutional harms" (Douglas J, dissenting); *Milller v California* 413 US 15, 22 (1973): "apart from (*Roth*), no majority of the Court has at any given time been able to agree on a standard to determine what constitutes obscene, pornographic material" (Burger CJ, for White Blackmun Powell and Rehnquist JJ); 37: "the court has worked hard to define obscenity and concededly has failed" (Douglas J, dissenting).

239. *Smith v California* 361 US 147 (1959).

240. 487.

241. 513.

242. 508; see also their dissent in in *Ginsberg v New York* 390 US 629 (1968).

243. *A Book Named 'John Cleland's Memoirs of a Woman of Pleasure' v Attorney-General of Massachusetts* 383 US 413 (1966). The state could not criminalise the mere private possession of pornography: *Stanley v Georgia* 394 US 557 (1969).

244. 383 US 463 (1966).

245. "Under our charter all regulation or control of expression is barred. Government does not sit to reveal where the 'truth' is. People are left to pick and choose between competing offerings. There is no compulsion to take and read what is repulsive any more than there is to spend one's time poring over government bulletins, political tracts, or theological treatises. The theory is that people are mature enough to pick and choose, to recognise trash when they see it, to be attracted to the literature that satisfies their deepest need, and hopefully to move from plateau to plateau and finally reach the world of enduring ideas. I think this is the ideal of the Free Society written into our *Constitution*. We have no business acting as censors or endowing any group with censorship powers. It is shocking to me to send to prison anyone for publishing anything, especially tracts to distant from any incitement to action as the ones before us" (Douglas J dissenting, 492); "censorship reflects a society's lack of confidence in itself. It is a hallmark of an authoritarian regime. Long ago those who wrote our *First Amendment* charted a different course. They believed a society can be truly strong only when it is truly free. In the realm of expression they put their faith, for better or for worse, in the enlightened choice of the people, free from the interference of a policeman's intrusive thumb or a judge's heavy hand. So it is that the *Constitution* protects coarse expression, as well as refined, and vulgarity no less than elegance. A book worthless to me may convey something of value to my neighbour. In the

free society to which our *Constitution* has committed us, it is for each to choose for himself" (Stewart J dissenting, 498).

246. *A Book Named "John Cleland's Memoirs of a Woman of Pleasure" v Attorney-General of Massachusetts* 383 US 413, 420 (1966) (Warren CJ Brennan and Fortas JJ).

247. 427.

248. 459.

249. 441 (Clark J), 459 (Harlan J), and 461 (White J).

250. *Paris Adult Theatre I v Slaton* 413 US 49 (1973), explaining the state's interest in regulating obscenity as based on "quality of life . . . the tone of commerce . . . and possibly, the public safety itself" (58), entitling the state to make a "morally neutral judgment" that material might "injure the community as a whole" by "polluting the public environment" (68–69), again over the strong dissent of Black and Douglas JJ.

251. 413 US 15 (1973).

252. 24 (Burger CJ, for White Blackmun Powell and Rehnquist JJ).

253. 40–41.

254. 44.

255. 44–45.

256. *Erznoznik v Jacksonville* 422 US 205 (1975).

257. *Carey v Brown* 447 US 455, 471 (1980).

258. *Consolidated Edison Co v Public Service Commission of New York* 447 US 530, 542 (1980); *Frisby v Schultz* 487 US 474 (1988).

259. *Ginsberg v New York* 390 US 629 (1968); *New York v Ferber* 458 US 747 (1982).

260. *Young v American Mini Theatres* 427 US 50 (1976).

261. 63–64 (Stevens J, for Burger CJ White and Rehnquist JJ; Powell J concurring in the judgment).

262. 70.

263. 70–71.

264. 79–80 (citing the test as applied in *United States v O'Brien* 391 US 367, 377 (1968)).

265. 85–86 (Stewart J, with whom Brennan Marshall and Blackmun JJ agreed).

266. *Southeastern Promotions Ltd v Conrad* 420 US 546 (1975).

267. *Reno v ACLU* 521 US 844 (1997). Similarly a ban on child pornography that included cases where actual children were not used, as well as minors engaged in sexual conduct, was struck out on *First Amendment* grounds on the basis of overbreadth: *Ashcroft v Free Speech Coalition* 535 US 234 (2002).

268. *Lewis v City of New Orleans* 415 US 130 (1974); the unconstitutional ordinance had made it a crime for a person to "wantonly curse or revile or to use obscene or opprobrious language."

269. *Cohen v California* 403 US 15 (1971).

270. *Winters v New York* 333 US 507, 509–510 (1948) (Reed J, for Vinson CJ Black Douglas Murphy and Rutledge JJ; Frankfurter Jackson and Burton JJ dissenting).

271. *Bethel School District v Fraser* 478 US 675 (1986).

272. *Board of Education v Pico* 457 US 853, 867 (1982) (Brennan J, for Marshall and Stevens JJ; Blackmun and White JJ concurring in the judgment).

273. *Beauharnais v Illinois* 343 US 250, 266 (1952).

274. *New York Times Co v Sullivan* 376 US 254, 279–280 (1971); *Gertz v Robert Welch* 418 US 323 (1974).

275. *Gertz v Robert Welch* 418 US 323 (1974).

276. *Garrison v Louisiana* 379 US 64 (1964).

277. *Bose Corp v Consumers Union* 466 US 485 (1984).

278. 388 US 130 (1967).

279. 164 (Warren CJ, concurring in the result).

280. 403 US 29 (1971).

281. The joint reasons rejected the argument that the distinction between public and private figures was justified because of the likely ability of the former to access channels of communication to rebut statements made about them as "unproved and highly improbable" (46) (Brennan J, for Burger CJ and Blackmun JJ, Black and White JJ concurring in the judgment). They

also rejected the argument that a public figure should be subject to different rules because they had voluntarily placed themselves in the public eye as being inconsistent with *First Amendment* values (47) (Brennan J, for Burger CJ and Blackmun JJ, Black and White JJ concurring in the judgment).

282. 363.

283. 64.

284. 86–87, quoting William Prosser's, *The Law of Torts* (1964).

285. 418 US 323 (1974).

286. 340.

287. 342.

288. 344–345.

289. 347.

290. 349–350; subsequently the Court clarified that this principle only applied to public figures. States were free to legislate so as to permit the award of punitive damages to private plaintiffs in defamation cases in the absence of proven malice: *Dun & Bradstreet v Greenmoss Builders* 472 US 749 (1985).

291. 363–364.

292. 366.

293. 386.

294. 392–393.

295. *Masson v New Yorker Magazine Inc* 501 US 496, 510–511 (1991) (Kennedy J, for all members of the Court); see for discussion Denis Boivin, "Accommodating Freedom of Expression and Reputation in the Common Law of Defamation," *Queen's Law Journal* 22 (1997): 246–248.

296. *Dun and Bradstreet Inc v Greenmoss Builders Inc* 472 US 749 (1985).

297. Aaron Perzanowski, "Relative Access to Corrective Speech: A New Test for Requiring Actual Malice," *California Law Review* 94 (2006): 836. Perzanoswki suggests the focus should not be on whether the plaintiff has access to fora within which they can rebut the allegedly defamatory material (because they undoubtedly will), but rather on the extent of disparity of access to such fora between the plaintiff and the defendant (861–862).

298. 403 US 713 (1971).

299. *Grosjean v American Press Co* 297 US 233 (1936).

300. *Minneapolis Star and Tribunes Co v Minnesota Commissioner of Revenue* 460 US 575 (1983).

301. *Arkansas Writers' Project Inc v Ragland* 481 US 221 (1987).

302. 408 US 665 (1972).

303. Burger CJ, White Blackmun Powell, and Rehnquist JJ.

304. 720–721.

305. 722–723.

306. 737–738. Stewart J did not find that the journalists' protection from answering questions of a grand jury was absolute, as had Douglas J. Rather he said that journalists could only be required to answer such questions consistently with the *First Amendment* where there was probable cause to think the journalist had information relating to a specific likely breach of the law, that the information could not reasonably be obtained in any other way, and that there was a compelling and overriding interest in the relevant information (743). These requirements were not met on the facts. On the other hand, where a media outlet breaches a promise that it made to preserve the confidentiality of a source, and the source sues it for breach of promise, it cannot use the First Amendment as a defense: *Cohen v Cowles Media Co* 501 US 663 (1991).

307. 32 (Stevens J, with whom Brennan and Powell JJ agreed).

308. *Red Lion Broadcasting Co v FCC* 395 US 367 (1969).

309. 418 US 241 (1974).

310. Similarly, a condition attached to a license to a cable television operator requiring them to carry free to air channels was not a breach of their *First Amendment* rights. It was not content-based and was justified by substantial public interests in ensuring a diversity of media outlets, competition among them, and preserving local programming: *Turner Broadcasting Systems v FCC* 512 US 622 (1994).

311. *Nebraska Press Association v Stuart* 423 US 1327 (1975); cf its earlier view that "the propriety and necessity of preventing interference with the course of justice by premature statement, argument or intimidation hardly can be denied": *Patterson v Colorado* 205 US 454, 462 (1907) (Holmes J, for the Court). A rare case where the Court was convinced that the actions of the media had precluded the right of a defendant to a fair trial was *Sheppard v Maxwell* 384 US 333 (1966), but the facts were extreme, including extensive media coverage prior to trial suggesting the accused was guilty, media suggestions of a possible motive for the accused to commit the crime, overwhelming media presence in and around the courtroom during the trial, the evidence of witnesses being given to the media before they had given it in court, and jurors having extensive contact with the outside world while considering their verdict.

312. *Nebraska Press Association v Stuart* 427 US 539 (1976).

313. *Cohen v Cowless Media Co* 501 US 663 (1991).

314. *Lorain Journal Co v United States* 342 US 143 (1951); *Associated Press v United States* 326 US 1 (1945).

315. *Rust v Sullivan* 500 US 173 (1991).

316. *Rumsfeld v Forum for Academic and Institutional Rights* 547 US 47 (2006).

317. *Agency for International Development v Alliance for Open Society International Inc* 570 US 205 (2013). In that case the Court found that conditioning federal funding on the recipient adopting a particular government policy was unconstitutional, because its impact went beyond the specific activities funded, and applied to all of the recipient's activities.

318. *Legal Services Corp v Velazquez* 531 US 533 (2001).

319. *Garcetti v Ceballos* 547 US 410 (2006); Steven Guy, "Why Should the *First Amendment* Protect Government Speech When the Government Has Nothing to Say?" *Iowa Law Review* 95 (2010): 1259.

320. *Mt Healthy Board of Education v Doyle* 429 US 274 (1977); *Pickering v Board of Education* 391 US 563 (1968).

321. The Court found in *Matal v Tams* 137 S. Ct 1744 (2017) that a trademark was commercial, rather than government, speech.

322. 135 S. Ct. 2239 (2015).

323. *Buckley v Valeo* 424 US 1 (1976).

324. *Austin v Michigan State Chamber of Commerce* 494 US 652 (1990).

325. 558 US 310 (2010).

326. *FEC v Wisconsin Right to Life Inc* 551 US 449, 476 (2007) (Roberts CJ, with whom Alito J concurred; Scalia Kennedy and Thomas JJ concurring in the judgment).

327. *Valentine v Chrestensen* 316 US 52 (1942).

328. *Virginia State Board of Pharmacy v Virginia Citizens Consumer Council* 425 US 748 (1976)

329. *Edenfield v Fane* 507 US 761, 767 (1993) (Kennedy J, for Rehnquist CJ White Blackmun Stevens Souter and Thomas JJ).

330. *Central Hudson Gas & Electric Corp v Public Service Commission* 447 US 557, 566 (1980); *Matal v Tam* 137 S.Ct 1744, 1764 (2017) (Alito J, for Roberts CJ Thomas and Breyer JJ); see Thomas Jackson and John Jeffries, "Commercial Speech: Economic Due Process and the *First Amendment*," *Virginia Law Review* 65 (1979): 1; Jonathan Weinberg, "Constitutional Protection of Commercial Speech," *Columbia Law Review* 82 (1982): 20.

331. *44 Liquormart v Rhode Island* 517 US 484 (1996) (there a ban on price information about liquor was held to be constitutionally invalid. It was a restriction on truthful, non-misleading commercial speech which could not be justified. The state's claim that its legislation was intended to induce temperance was not supported by any evidence that withholding of the price of liquor would in fact achieve this objective.

332. *Edenfield v Fane* 507 US 761 (1993).

333. 452 US 61 (1981).

334. 65 (White J, for Brennan Stewart Marshall Blackmun and Powell JJ). On the other hand, a state law prohibiting nude dancing was upheld against *First Amendment* challenge in *Barnes v Glen Theatre* 501 US 560 (1991).

335. 88.

336. 418 US 323, 339 (1974) (Powell J, for White Marshall Blackmun and Rehnquist JJ).
337. 567 US 709 (2012).
338. Kennedy J, for Roberts CJ Ginsburg Sotomayor JJ, Breyer and Kagan JJ concurring in the judgment; Alito J (with whom Scalia and Thomas JJ joined) dissenting.
339. 720–722.
340. 723.
341. 725.
342. 725.
343. 726.
344. 728.
345. 729.
346. 393 US 503 (1969).
347. *Bethel School District No. 403 v Fraser* 478 US 675 (1986).
348. *Hazelwood School District v Kuhlmeier* 484 US 260 (1988).
349. *Pickering v Board of Education* 391 US 563 (1968).
350. *Parker v Levy* 417 US 733 (1974).

Chapter Three

Australian Case Law

This chapter is structured as follows. Firstly, I will provide relevant background to the Australian *Constitution* as it pertains to freedom of speech. Secondly, I will describe the development of free speech case law prior to landmark decisions in 1992. Then I will explain the landmark "political communication" cases of that year, and how the law in this area developed subsequently. Finally, I will offer some critique on the existing Australian jurisprudence.

INTRODUCTION TO THE AUSTRALIAN CONSTITUTION AND RIGHTS PROTECTION

A discussion of Australian case law in this area should begin with an acknowledgment that the drafters of the Australian *Constitution* sought to combine the best of two great models of constitutional governance in the Australian *Constitution.* The founding fathers were of course well aware of the United Kingdom Westminster system, featuring a largely unwritten constitution, and heavy emphasis on parliamentary supremacy. The common law of the United Kingdom would recognize freedom of speech as a common law right, but as has been noted in Chapter 1, British legal history is replete with examples of cases where the right of an individual to speak had been abrogated, and persons punished for what they said.[1] The founding fathers were also well aware of the United States *Constitution*, including its written nature, judicial review, federal system of government, and enshrined bill of rights.

In the area of human rights protection, the founding fathers who crafted the Australian *Constitution* leaned towards the British approach of common law protection of human rights. A few human rights were expressly scattered throughout the *Constitution*, including freedom of religion and freedom from discrimination on the basis of residence, and free movement around Australia. By and large, these were borrowed from the United States *Constitution*. An equal protection clause was debated but not eventually included in the Australian *Constitution*. A common law approach to human rights protection generally starts with an individual's liberty, but this is subject to override by legislation. In other words, it effectively leaves human rights protection in the hands of the legislature, in that human rights are only recognized as part of a country's legal system to the extent they are not abrogated or removed by parliament.[2]

However, the experience of the founding fathers had not taught them the need for a written, entrenched bill of rights. They generally had not experienced a foreign government grossly abusing human rights, as had those in the American colonies. It has been noted that the Australian *Constitution* reflects an evolution, away from a disparate set of colonies and towards a new central government, primarily as a result of concerns about defense and free trade among the colonies. Its writing and creation was not motivated by a strong desire to protect for fundamental human rights that the previous regime had suppressed. In that light, a lack of concern to enshrine fundamental human rights is not altogether surprising.

The writers of the Australian *Constitution* were evidently much more exercised by economic issues, and these concerns provided the impetus for the movement to federation, along with defense concerns. The other concern very evident in the document is the power that the new central government would have. This explains why, of the few protections it contains for human rights, almost all of them are targeted at the federal government.[3] The founding fathers were either not concerned with the potential for the state governments to breach these rights, or were overborne with their fears about the power of the new central government they were creating, and hence did not focus on the ability of states to legislate in precisely the same ways they were determined the new federal government would not.

It is also noteworthy that the tone of philosophical debate about governance had evolved substantially during the 19th century. In the second half of the 18th century, social contract theory of Locke and Rousseau was prevalent. Concern for human rights fit well within that theory; it could accommodate notions that the right of individuals to freedom of speech had not been ceded to the elected legislature. The people had not agreed to relinquish their right to speak, and to hear a range of views. On one view, such a consensual view of government actually contemplated broad protection for freedom of speech. The people had to speak, and to have the opportunity to hear a range of views, in order to properly determine how their representative government should be comprised.

On the other hand, by the mid-19th century the philosophy of Albert Vere Dicey had become very prevalent.[4] Dicey was a legal positivist who espoused a parliamentary supremacy model, pursuant to which everything that an elected parliament did was legally valid, and could not be legally questioned or overturned by a court. The remedy for any alleged wrongdoing by a legislature was to remove the offending individuals at the subsequent election. This was the means by which government was accountable to the people. As indicated in Chapter 1, this bore resemblances to the classic Hobbesian view of society, pursuant to which a strong sovereign was needed in order to bring individuals within a society to heal. In such a regime, freedom of speech was not essential in order for that model of government to function. The freedom of speech that an individual enjoyed could be removed by an authoritarian legislature. This cohered with another strain of thought that gained prominence in the 19th century, that of utilitarianism, the idea of the greatest good for the greatest number. Again, this would not strongly support notions of an individual's freedom of speech. A utilitarian would be prepared to sacrifice the individual right of a person to speak, if it led to a safer society overall.

It is the legal positivist and utilitarian view that is more prevalent in the text and structure of the Australian *Constitution.* Firstly, the document is very sparse, imposing very few legal restrictions on the ability of legislatures to pass laws. In itself, this is instructive, positioning the document as primarily an enabler of governments to function, as opposed to a restricter of government power with an eye to liberty protection. In Chapter I of the *Constitution*, which establishes the new federal parliament, an intention to give that body very strong power over electoral matters is very clear. Section 7 states that the people of one state shall vote as a bloc on the senators to represent them, until parliament otherwise provides. It states the starting number of senators, until parliament otherwise provides. Parliament has the right to choose the qualification of electors for the parliament. Parliament has power to choose the method by which senators and members of the House of Representatives are chosen. Section 24 permits parliament to make provision for the division of Australia into a number of electorates. Parliament can provide for the qualifications of a member of parliament.

Thus, as has been noted by High Court justices, the Australian *Constitution* accords great freedom to elected bodies in terms of determining how members of parliament are chosen, who gets to vote, and how the nation is divided into electorates.[5] The founding fathers intended that the kind of representative government contemplated by the *Constitution* would be an evolving one.[6] This fact presents some challenges in seeking to ascribe some minimum baseline content to it, although the High Court has done so to some extent. For instance, it found, somewhat surprisingly in the context of a relatively conservative court with a modest record of protecting fundamental human rights, an implied right to vote. It did this in the course of striking down legislation prohibiting prisoners from voting at a federal election, on the basis it was contrary to the requirements of the *Constitution*.[7] Similarly, the Court found that legislation providing for a closing of the electoral rolls a couple of days after an election was announced was constitutionally invalid, because it effectively denied the franchise to a large number of people, and could not be justified.[8]

The Australian *Constitution* does not contain an express right to vote,[9] does not preclude the withholding of the franchise to members of society,[10] and does not guarantee something like one-vote, one-value voting.[11] At the time of federation, women did not generally have the right to vote in Australia. Indigenous Australians were also disenfranchised.[12] Legislative changes would subsequently correct these deficiencies.

These facts enliven a debate about the proper role of parliament as compared with the courts in terms of determining issues relative to voting. On one hand is the argument that parliament should be left broad discretion here, partly on the basis that this was the system envisaged by the founding fathers. Advocates of this position would point to the fact that it has been the legislatures that have been primarily responsible for broadening the franchise, to women, to indigenous Australians, and to younger Australians, by lowering the voting age from 21 to 18. Such advocates would deny that the *Constitution* enshrines any particular form of representative government or representative democracy, permitting it to evolve over time as society changes. Under this model, the courts have a minimal role to play in preserving the constitutional franchise.[13]

Others would say that since the exercise of political power is dependent upon access to the franchise, this is an area in which courts must be at their most vigilant. Even if we accept a Diceyan type philosophy that parliament is the democratic body in terms of lawmaking and is entitled to settle most contentious issues for its society, this theory presupposes free and fair elections, and a broad franchise. These conditions may not be present when parliaments are making laws which inhibit the franchise, laws that may frustrate the democratic will. Thus the argument from Ely and the courts, on occasion,[14] that due deference to the democratic nature of the legislature and the laws it passes is at its minimum in relation to laws that impact on the access of an individual to the franchise.[15] There is also evidence of this occurring. So it was by High Court decision, that in *Roach*, that Australian law "came to accept" a constitutionally enshrined right to vote. This was not conferred by legislation; on the contrary, it was in response to a parliamentary attempt to remove the right to vote from all prisoners that triggered the litigation in *Roach* culminating in the constitutional finding.

This can be coupled with the argument that the case for judicial scrutiny in this context is at its highest because politicians have a natural inclination to silence dissenting voices. They are motivated, as most are, by self-interest, and it is not in their interest to have critical communication about them said or published. In such cases, we cannot rely on parliaments to do the right thing, even if typically we can. In other words, this is a kind of "failure" of the system that can only be remedied by court supervision to ensure minimum requirements are met.[16]

The Australian *Constitution* does not expressly guarantee the kind of freedom of speech that one might argue is necessarily inherent in a democratic nation which our founding fathers clearly intended Australia to be. The founders viewed freedom of speech as a common law right.[17] Like all common law rights, it would be subject to being overridden by valid statute.[18] There was also a suggestion in the Australian case law that Australia had inherited existing British law regarding sedition. Some readers will be aware of the *Australian Courts Act 1828* (Imp), under which all laws then existing in the United Kingdom and "applicable" to the then Australian colonies were imported into and adopted as "Australian" law. Some have argued that the United Kingdom law of sedition as it existed in 1828 may have been imported into the law of the colonies that would later unite to form Australia.[19]

The reverence that the founding fathers had for the United Kingdom model of parliamentary supremacy overwhelmed their intention to create and enshrine Australian governance in a democratic form, with all that that necessarily entailed. However, this traditional conception of the Australian *Constitution* and its protection of freedom of speech was controversially abrogated in two leading cases in 1992, at the height of the Mason Court. Non-Australian readers may not be familiar with the Mason Court. Sir Anthony Mason became Chief Justice of the High Court of Australia in 1987. The next eight years heralded a series of controversial decisions, in constitutional law and other areas. The Court was not afraid to jettison existing legal doctrine that it believed had surpassed its use-by date. It employed controversial legal reasoning in particular cases, embodying a "living tree" method of constitutional interpretation, as opposed to an emphasis on originalist and/or literalist interpretation.

This debate continues apace in constitutional law. Those who complain about the High Court's use of implications in relation to the *Constitution*, usually to protect human rights, do so on the basis that the founding fathers did not intend such rights to be enshrined in the *Constitution*.[20] They argue that the founding fathers considered, and rejected, a bill of rights in the *Constitution*.[21] For some, this fact, together with other evidence of their intention, for instance, to leave large aspects of electoral law and governance in the hands of parliament rather than making them justiciable, greatly crimps the role of the court in defending and protecting fundamental human rights, including those associated with governance such as freedom of speech. Those of this conservative view will criticize judges who imply rights and freedoms in the *Constitution* as going beyond the judicial remit and engaging in judicial activism (a label generally intended by those who use it in a pejorative sense). Those of this persuasion will sometimes deny the efficacy of the implied freedom of political communication altogether,[22] or seek to limit it to a significant extent, arguing that it was never intended by the founding fathers, and/or that it cuts across British constitutional traditions of deference to parliament, including notions that common law rights only exist in the negative, to the extent that parliament does not abrogate them.[23]

They will argue that the only legitimate implications that can be made are based on the intentions of the founding fathers.[24] This can lead them to quite extraordinary conclusions, for instance, that any "right to vote" implicit in the Australian *Constitution* could only refer to those who had such a right at the time of federation. On this reasoning, men, and more particularly men who owned property, would have an implied constitutional right to vote. Women would not have an implied right to vote, and nor would propertyless men, if the intention of the founding fathers truly did control the content and scope of implications.[25] This example surely shows the fallacy of the argument that implications drawn from the *Constitution* must be based on the founding fathers' intention. It is in reality just an extension of an originalist argument towards constitutional interpretation more generally, an argument that the High Court has generally rejected,[26] and an argument which becomes progressively less tenable as the years go on.

Implicit (pardon the pun) in this reasoning is that the High Court should when interpreting the *Constitution* give effect to the view of the founding fathers.[27] Further, it assumes there is one agreed collective view of what the founding fathers intended, which is much disputed, and it assumes that the founding fathers themselves intended that their intentions would be controlling of subsequent interpretation, which is also much disputed.[28]

There is also the fact that founding fathers themselves, including John Quick and Robert Garran, specified some implications that should be drawn from the Australian *Constitution.*[29] Early justices of the High Court, some of whom were also founding fathers, suggested particular implications that should be drawn from the document.[30] Perhaps Australia's most revered jurist Sir Owen Dixon drew implications from the *Constitution.*[31] The drawing of an implication from Australia's federal structure was made in 1947, and has been applied since then.[32] The High Court has implied a separation of powers from the structure of the *Constitution* which can and has operated to invalidate state legislation.[33] The High Court has implied that a nationhood power inheres in the federal government by virtue of its status as the nation's government, quite apart from the text of the *Constitution.*[34] The fact that founding fathers, High Court justices, including some justices who were founding fathers, and later courts in a range of settings have drawn implications from the *Constitution* creates serious difficulties for those who would deny the efficacy of doing so.

Now frustratingly, the High Court seems to have an ambivalent attitude towards the importance of the founding fathers' intentions. In some cases they give great deference to the views of the founding fathers[35]; in others, they dismiss them as a "mirage" that is not of particular importance.[36] The High Court in *Theophanous v Herald and Weekly Times* dismissed suggestions that the "dead hands" of the founding fathers could or should rise from the grave to control constitutional interpretation.[37]

Further, many scholars do not favor giving controlling influence to the views of the founding fathers, including their decision not to include an express bill of rights. This is the "living tree" view of constitutional law, that the document was deliberately sparse. For some, this is evidence that the founding fathers intended it to be a living, breathing document capable of evolving as the fundamental legal document of a nation, as the nation itself evolves.[38] It was not designed to be a code. It is a special document. Arguably, traditional rules of statutory interpretation, such as would favor resort to the object of legislation (as, for instance, evidenced by parliamentary debate), might be inapt in the context of constitutional law. This is on the basis that an argument about the intention of the founding fathers is analogous in some ways to an argument about the intention of parliamentarians who passed a law. However, it may be a mistake to treat ordinary rules of statutory construction as being applicable to a document as fundamental as the *Constitution*. For some, this is particularly important given the very strict hurdles in place in s128 to formally amend the Australian *Constitution*.

Another argument made against focusing too heavily on the intention of the founding fathers, and specifically their intention not to enact an express bill of rights, is to point out the unacceptable and ugly basis upon which they made that decision. Constitutional law scholar George Williams points out that the founding fathers knew well that the new system would protect their own personal rights. They also "sought to establish the means by which the rights of other sections of the community could be abrogated. In this respect the framers were driven by a desire to maintain race-based distinctions, which today would undoubtedly be regarded as racism."[39] Specifically, there is evidence the founding fathers wished to continue to permit discriminatory treatment on the basis of race in relation to working conditions and entitlements, and this was at least one of the reasons for eschewing broad-based rights protection.

Of most relevance for current purposes, in 1992 the High Court of Australia discerned an implied freedom of political communication, and was much criticized for doing so.[40] The implied freedom is now enshrined in Australian constitutional law, operating as a defacto, if more muted, freedom of speech provision than its American counterpart.[41] Given the momentous change to the existing law made by the Australian High Court in 1992 in this area of law, it is appropriate to discuss how Australian law protected that freedom in the era prior to 1992, what was decided in the landmark 1992 cases, and how the freedom has been employed since that time.

PROTECTION OF FREEDOM OF SPEECH IN AUSTRALIA PRIOR TO 1992

During this period, while freedom of speech was recognized as a common law right, it would generally be subject to being overridden by valid legislation. In relation to state legislatures, they had (and still have) extremely broad, plenary power to pass laws for the "peace, welfare and good government" of the state. These are not words of limitation, but rather a plenary conferral of power.[42] This gave them very broad power to restrict freedom of speech. In the case of the federal government, it would need to show a head of power in the *Constitution* that permitted it to pass certain laws. This imposed the greatest practical constraint on the ability of the Commonwealth to pass laws invasive of common law rights, including the freedom of speech. Further, even if a head of power were available, the High Court would sometimes take into account the extent to which a law impacted on established fundamental human rights in determining whether or not a head of power existed to support the Commonwealth's legislation.[43] This approach to constitutional interpretation continues today.[44] Through this indirect channel, the Court could (and can) in a limited way protect fundamental human rights like freedom of speech.

The other main way in which the High Court could protect fundamental human rights was through principles of statutory interpretation. Specifically, the Court adopted a principle of presumption that a given statutory provision did not interfere with established human rights, unless parliament's will to do so was irresistibly clear. The best exposition of this position is found in the judgment of O'Connor J in *Potter v Minahan*. O'Connor stated that in cases where statutes affected civil rights, the principle of construction stated by Maxwell on Statutes was apposite. This principle was that:

> There are certain objects which the legislature is presumed not to intend; and a construction which would lead to any of them is therefore to be avoided . . . one of these presumptions is that the legislature does not intend to make any alteration in the law beyond what is explicitly declares . . . it is in the last degree improbable that the legislature would overthrow fundamental principles, infringe rights, or depart from the general system of law, without expressing its intention with irresistible clearness.[45]

Relatedly, where a provision was ambiguous, the Court would lean to an interpretation which favored the protection of the right where reasonably possible, or minimal infringement of it. A factual example of this occurred in

Melbourne Corporation v Barry,[46] where a majority of the High Court interpreted the statutory power of a local government body to regulate street marches so as not to support a regulation which prohibited them, unless relevant consent had been obtained. In the view of the majority, the power to regulate did not include the power to prohibit, or prohibit in the absence of consent.

The Court is also sometimes troubled by the provision of broad discretion to members of the executive, without defined criteria by which that discretion is to be exercised. In *Melbourne Corporation v Barry*,[47] members of the High Court noted this in determining that the regulation prohibiting street marches was invalid.[48] This fact is utilized by the Court to conclude that the legislature did not intend to confer such broad regulation making power upon the local government body.[49] These are obvious parallels with this decision in the American doctrine of void for vagueness, and more general principles of the rule of law. However, the Court is typically shy about actually making decisions to invalidate legislation based on the rule of law, as opposed to acknowledging its importance.

In *Australian Communist Party v Commonwealth*,[50] the High Court considered the validity of legislation which provided for the dissolution of the Communist Party. The Governor-General was authorized to make a declaration that a group sympathetic to communism should be declared unlawful, on the basis it was prejudicial to the war effort. The effect of such a declaration would be to provide for the dissolution of the body, and the distribution of its assets. The Governor-General was also empowered to declare that an individual associated with such an organization should be banned from working in particular industries. There were no stated criteria for the exercise of the Governor-General's declaratory power. A majority of the High Court, Latham CJ dissenting, declared the legislation to be constitutionally invalid.[51] This was on the basis that it was not supported by the defense power. One of the reasons the law was invalid was the lack of express criteria governing the exercise of the decision maker's discretion.[52]

From earliest times the High Court appeared to broadly interpret the Commonwealth's defense power, particularly in war times. Obviously, that power could be used to effectively silence speech or other activity considered to be subversive. An example during World War I was the decision in *Lloyd v Wallach*,[53] where the High Court upheld against constitutional challenge a provision permitting the Minister for Defense to detain an individual for the duration of the war if they believed the person was "disaffected or disloyal." The Minister ordered the detention of Wallach on this basis. The judgments do not disclose the basis upon which the Minister established the view that Wallach was disaffected and/or disloyal. It is likely that such evidence was not disclosed to the Court. Thus, the case may have involved something that

Wallach said, that indicated to persons in authority that he was disaffected and/or disloyal. However, it cannot be said with certainty that he did so.

In any event, members of the Court made it clear that the question of whether Wallach was in fact "disaffected or disloyal" was immaterial to the court's consideration. The court pointedly declined to review the exercise of the Minister's discretion; essentially it found that his decision was unreviewable by the court. The legislation was a valid exercise of the Commonwealth's defense power.

At the start of the Cold War, two communist sympathizers were charged with the offense of sedition under s24 of the *Crimes Act 1914* (Cth), as it then was. Section 24D made it an offense for a person to write, print, utter, or publish any seditious words. Section 24B(2) defined seditious words as those used with the intention of exciting disaffection with the government or constitution of Australia, against the government of the United Kingdom, or against the monarch. A good faith defense was provided in relation to the pointing out of perceived defects in the system, advocacy of law reform, or pointing out matters with which members of the public were unhappy.

The first case involved Gilbert Burns.[54] He attended a public meeting as a representative of the Australian Communist Party (ACP). He was asked what the attitude of the ACP would be to any possible future war between Russia and Western powers. He replied the ACP would oppose the war, but indicated that members would fight for Russia in such a war. He was charged with the offense of sedition under s24 of the *Crimes Act 1914* (Cth).

All members of the High Court found that the section was constitutionally valid. This was primarily on the basis of the executive power contained in s61 of the *Constitution*, together with the Commonwealth's incidental power in s51(39). Latham CJ concluded

> The Commonwealth Parliament . . . has power to make laws to protect them and itself, not only against physical attack and interference, but also against utterance of words intended to excite disaffection against the Government . . . and to prevent or impede the operation of governmental agencies which prepare for defense and conduct warlike operations . . . the encouragement of internal disloyalty is a grave obstacle to effective defense against an external enemy . . . protection against fifth column activities and subversive propaganda may reasonably be regarded as desirable or even necessary for the purpose of preserving the constitutional powers and operations of governmental agencies and the existence of the government itself. The prevention and punishment of international excitement of disaffection against the sovereign and the government is a form of protective law for this purpose which is to be found as an element in most, if not all, organized societies. I agree that the Commonwealth Parliament has no power to pass a law to suppress or punish political criticism, but excitement to disaffection against a Government goes beyond political criticism.[55]

Dixon J agreed with the Commonwealth having broad constitutional power to deal with sedition, saying it would include suppressing actual incitement to antagonism towards constitutional government. It was not necessary to show the antagonism had led, or would be likely to lead, to overt acts of resistance or resort to violence.[56]

Sharkey, the General Secretary of the ACP, was also charged with sedition. In an interview, Sharkey said that if Soviet forces entered Australia "in pursuit of aggressors," Australian workers would welcome them, as the Soviets had been welcomed in Europe against the Nazis. He indicated that the communists generally opposed war, and wanted to bring the working class to power. However, if "fascists in Australia" used force to prevent workers from obtaining that power, he indicated communists would advise the workers to meet force with force. A constitutional challenge to the validity of the sedition provisions was again dismissed.[57]

Latham CJ confirmed the Commonwealth had the legislative power constitutionally to punish "any utterance or publication which arouses resistance to the law or excited insurrection against Commonwealth Government or is reasonably likely to cause discontent with and opposition to the enforcement of Federal law or the operations of the Federal government." He said it was inherent in the very existence of the Commonwealth government that it had the constitutional power to deal with such speech.[58] He also referred to the fact that the United Kingdom common law offense of seditious libel did not require evidence that the accused actually incited or counseled actual opposition to the government in the performance of its functions, and claimed United States law at the time also permitted serious incursions into freedom of speech on the basis of preventing speech which brings a government into disrepute or scorn, at least during wartime.[59]

As discussed above, the High Court held to be constitutionally invalid the Commonwealth Parliament's legislative attempt to ban the Communist Party and like organizations, and to prevent communists working in particular occupations in Australia.[60] This was primarily because the legislation was not supported by the defense head of power. The Government had not demonstrated why such legislation was necessary for Australia's defense, in a period where the country was not at war. In addition, the lack of express criteria for the decision maker to make their decision, rendering their decision effectively not reviewable judicially, told against its constitutionality. In the course of declaring the legislation to be invalid, members of the Court made some observations of more general application to regulation of speech. Dixon J was clearly alert to the lessons of history in terms of government censorship:

> In point of constitutional theory the power to legislate for the protection of an existing form of government ought not to be based on a conception, if other-

> wise adequate, adequate only to assist those holding power to resist or suppress obstruction or opposition or attempts to displace them or the form of government they defend.[61]

On the other hand, he confirmed the constitutional power of the federal government to punish treason and suppress insurrection or rebellion, and to put down any attempts to obstruct or interfere with the discharge of proper government functions.[62] In so confirming, he expressly referred to a textbook on American constitutional law.[63] He seemed to possibly confine the federal government's power in this sphere to cases involving the suppression of violence or disorder or some ascertained and existing condition of disturbance, or alternatively legislation which proscribed specified conduct with objective standards.[64] The legislation here did not do either of those things, but rather proceeded against particular bodies by name or characterization. It was relevant that the sanctions against them were not provisional or tentative, but ones which directly and finally affected their status, rights, and liabilities.[65]

One issue with which the Court had to grapple was the apparent acceptance by the High Court in *Lloyd v Wallach*[66] of unbridled executive discretion in the context of a defense purpose. Recall that all members of the Court in *Lloyd* validated legislation which permitted the Minister of Defense to order the incarceration of a person they had declared to be disaffected or disloyal. The Court refused to even consider questioning the validity of the Minister's belief. The legislation specified no criteria for the making of the Minister's declaration. This was declared constitutionally valid. Was this materially different from the legislation being challenged in the *Australian Communist Party* case, pursuant to which another member of the executive, this time the Governor-General, also had unbridled discretion to make a decision that was effectively unreviewable? Some thought the *Lloyd* decision suggested the validity of the legislation in the *Communist Party* case.

However, for the majority, a fundamental point of differentiation was the different times. The decision in *Lloyd* was rendered in the early part of World War I. The *Australian Communist Party* case was being considered after World War II had ended. For some judges, this explained the different outcomes.[67] McTiernan J said that during "periods of grave emergency" a person's civil liberties came under the control of the Commonwealth.[68] Williams J agreed that powers such as that in Lloyd and here, depriving individuals of fundamental human rights, could only be constitutionally valid as being supported by the defense power during times of grave crisis involving large-scale hostilities.[69] Fullagar J tended to agree that such measures might be valid during times of "clear and great national danger," but not otherwise.[70]

In two High Court decisions prior to the 1992 revolution, the court found defendants guilty of a contempt of court for comments they had made that were perceived to be critical of judges. In one case, a newspaper lamented how the High Court had "punched holes" in the government's legislation, and that the law "which was relied on to keep Australia white had been put in suspended animation" due to decisions of the High Court. The editor and proprietor were found guilty of a contempt.[71] The Court found that power existed over comments that amounted to a contempt of court. These were comments which tended to deflect the court from its proper role, to detract from the authority and influence of judicial determination, calculated to impair the confidence of the public in the judiciary, or to "excite misgivings as to the integrity, propriety and impartiality" of the judges.[72]

In *Gallagher v Durack*,[73] the High Court confirmed the conviction of a trade union official for contempt. He had originally been convicted of an offense of contempt by a single judge, but the decision was overturned by an appeal court. The official was asked about the appeal, and claimed that it was influenced by demonstrations of trade union officials. He was then charged with, and convicted of, contempt for that comment. Upholding the conviction, the High Court noted that:

> The law attempts to reconcile two principles, each of which is of cardinal importance, but which, in some circumstances, appear to come in conflict. One principle is that speech should be free, so that everyone has the right to comment in good faith on matters of public importance, including the administration of justice, even if the comment is outspoken, mistaken or wrongheaded. The other principle is that it is necessary for the purpose of maintaining public confidence in the administration of law that there shall be some certain and immediate method of repressing imputations upon courts of justice which, if continued, are likely to impair their authority (quoting Dixon J in *Dunbabin*).[74]

The Court expressed concern that the authority of the court not be undermined by baseless attacks on the judiciary.

Prior to 1992, the only other development in relation to freedom of speech in High Court decisions was the suggestion of one member of the Court, Murphy J, that freedom of speech, among other rights, was fundamental to a democratic society, and necessary for the system of representative government to work as intended.[75]

It is also worth mentioning that Australia has had somewhat of an ambivalent attitude towards issues of "sovereignty." The question of whether Australia accepts the doctrine of parliamentary sovereignty remains surprisingly contentious. It would seem very difficult to accept parliamentary sovereignty, and the notion that all laws passed by parliament are valid for that reason, in the context of a written constitution and the acceptance of judicial review.[76] Of the three criteria that the architect of parliamentary sovereignty gave for such a parliament, no Australian parliament could fulfil at least two of the three conditions, and there is a good argument that no Australian parliament meets any of them.[77] However, many commentators continue to refer to Australia as accepting notions of parliamentary sovereignty.[78] With respect, this is a serious error.

It has only been in recent years that the High Court has made explicit that Australia's system of governance does not reflect a parliamentary sovereignty model.[79] It is not surprising that this has occurred during the pivotal 1990s on the High Court. Some of the judges in the pivotal 1992 decisions, to be discussed presently, referred to notions of popular sovereignty,[80] in contradistinction to suggestions of parliamentary sovereignty. Notions of sovereignty are very closely linked with freedom of speech. As Weinstein put it:

> The commitment to popular sovereignty alone arguably creates a narrow but very powerful right of free speech. If the people are the ultimate source of political authority, they must be able to speak to each other about all matters within the scope of this authority, that is, on all matters of public concern. If, to the contrary, the government were able to prohibit speech on the ground that it will persuade the populace to formulate erroneous public policy, then the government, not the people, would be the ultimate sovereign. As James Madison argued over two centuries ago, a logical consequence of a commitment to popular sovereignty is that 'the censorial power is in the people over the government and not in the government over the people.[81]

A parliamentary sovereignty model would only accept the right to free speech to the extent parliament did not take it away. In contrast, a popular sovereignty model could much more significantly protect freedom of speech, at a constitutional level, from parliamentary interference. In that system, parliamentary attempts to take away free speech rights could be declared constitutionally invalid.

THE FUNDAMENTAL CHANGES TO THE LAW IN 1992

In 1991, the federal government sought to respond to concerns around the increased influence of money in electioneering with its amendments to the *Broadcasting Act 1942* (Cth). These amendments effectively banned electronic political advertising during election periods. They also required broadcasters to allocate particular periods of "free time." The amount of free time to which a party would be entitled would be dependent on the extent of their vote at the previous election, with 90 percent going to parties already represented in parliament. A number of television broadcasters challenged the legislation in the High Court, arguing it was constitutionally invalid. A majority of the Court found the legislation to be constitutionally invalid.[82] In doing so, the Court recognized an implied freedom of political communication contained in the Australian *Constitution*. This was a landmark decision; no previous decision had discerned such a freedom, though as indicated above Murphy J in dissent in previous decisions had claimed that freedom of speech was fundamental in a democracy. He did not show how such a freedom was implicit in the *Constitution*, for example, in relation to its text or structure. It was pivotal to a broader acceptance of the principle in *Australian Capital Television* that a majority tied the implication to the text and structure of the *Constitution*.

Mason CJ explained that implications had in the past been drawn from the text and structure of the *Constitution*. An example was the so-called *Melbourne Corporation* principle, prohibiting one level of government from legislating in a manner which discriminated against the other level of government.[83] While implications could more easily be drawn from the text of the *Constitution*, implications could also be drawn from the structure of the *Constitution*, at least those which were "logically or practically necessary" for that structure to survive.[84]

Mason CJ explained that it was the founding fathers' unshaken belief in responsible government, that the executive was answerable to the legislature, which explained their lack of enthusiasm for an express bill of rights.[85] He noted the comments of perhaps Australia's most revered justice, Sir Owen Dixon, that the history of the founding fathers had not taught or shown them the need for express rights protection. He noted the founding fathers believed the best protection of rights was the common law system, in accordance with parliamentary supremacy, and regular free and fair elections at which politicians would be accountable to the people for their decision making.

Mason CJ said that a different argument was being made here. It was that the Australian *Constitution* was premised on a system of representative government. Provisions of the *Constitution*, including s24 which provided for the House of Representatives to be comprised of representatives voted directly by the people and the equivalent for the Senate in s7, contemplated a representative system of government. Mason CJ said that in constitutional terms, representative government meant that the people were sovereign, and their power was exercised through their representatives in parliament. Their representatives were accountable to the people they served, and had to take account of their views.[86] Mason CJ said that it was indispensable to that system of government that there be freedom of communication. Through this means, an individual could communicate their views on a range of matters relevant to political action or decision. They could criticize government action, seek change and influence elected representatives. This freedom was necessary in order that representatives could do their jobs. Communication here was a two-way street; it also gave representatives a chance to explain and account for their decisions and actions in government, permitting the public to make an informed opinion on relevant matters. If freedom of communication did not exist, representative government could not work.[87] However, the freedom was not confined to communication between the voting public and representatives; it had to include communication among the voting public. An individual's judgment on many issues turned on public discussion of all views of individuals, groups and organizations. Mason CJ cited the position in other countries which had recognized the essentiality to a functioning democracy of free communication, including the United States *New York Times v Sullivan*[88] and the judgment of Rehnquist J in *Smith v Daily Mail Publishing Co.*[89] Mason CJ said that because the federal parliament could discuss the fullest range of matters, the freedom extended to "all matters of political affairs and political discuss." It was irrelevant whether the topic was one assigned to the federal government in terms of legislative responsibility, or which was one not assigned, and thus within exclusive state control.[90]

Mason CJ confirmed that freedom of political communication was not absolute in nature. He suggested a distinction between regulation of communication on the basis of ideas or information, and those laws of general application concerning a particular mode of communication. Laws of the former kind were more difficult to justify—only a compelling justification would warrant the burden of communication, and the restriction could not be more than was reasonably necessary to achieve that public interest objective. In conducting the relevant balancing exercise, the need to protect freedom of communication would be paramount.[91] In contrast, laws which related to communication generally without regard to the particular ideas conveyed would be more easily justified. It would be considered whether such regulation was reasonably necessary to achieve a stated public interest, and whether the burden was disproportionate to attainment of the legitimate objective.[92] This has obvious close parallels with American *First Amendment* case law, which considers content-based discrimination and viewpoint-based discrimination to be highly relevant in determining the validity of legislation which impinges on free speech.

Mason CJ categorized the laws here as belonging to the second category—they related to communication about issues generally. He acknowledged the claimed government interest in safeguarding the integrity of the political process, and that the need to raise substantial moneys in order to effectively compete raised the specter of corruption. Thus, some restriction on political advertising might be valid, although it did restrict the freedom of political communication to some extent. However, generally the benefits obtained by freedom of communication outweighed possible detriment. He noted that all too often attempts to restrict the freedom due to some imagined necessity have stifled public discussion and criticism of government. The court should not simply accept at face value government assertions of the need to curb freedom of expression.[93] Here the impact on freedom of communication was very significant, with claimed benefits marginal and speculative. By giving free time based on past political performance, it discriminated against new voices.

Other judges in the case would confirm the essentiality of public discussion of political issues in terms of democracy,[94] and that the Australian *Constitution* contemplated a representative parliamentary democracy,[95] would confirm the applicability of the freedom to what might be considered state political issues,[96] as opposed to federal political issues, and would confirm that the freedom was not absolute in nature.[97] The freedom extended to communication among voters.[98] Similarly to Mason CJ, judges accepted a tiered system of enquiry. Laws which restricted or prohibiting freedom of political communication due to the nature of the communication would be much more difficult to justify. It would need to be shown that they were reasonably necessary for the preservation of an ordered and democratic society or to protect legitimate claims of individuals to leave peacefully and with dignity in society.[99] Like Mason CJ, Deane and Toohey JJ were skeptical that the challenged laws were conducive to counteracting corruption activity. The other argument, that the laws created a level, or more level, playing field, could support some restrictions, but not to the extent of the regulation here. Likewise, McHugh J distinguished between laws which restricted freedom of political communication due to their content, and laws which incidentally affected that freedom by regulating time, place or manner of communication (citing the United States decision in *Buckley v Valeo*).[100] Laws of the former category could only be validated on a showing of compelling justification; laws of the latter type may well be valid if they were tailored to a legitimate objective and the measures were not disproportionate to that end.

While a majority of the Court was content to frame the freedom in terms of political communication, at least two justices countenanced the suggestion that the freedom could apply to speech more generally. Gaudron J said that the freedom could "perhaps" be framed as freedom of speech generally, rather than being confined to the political sphere.[101] This was part of her conception of a free society governed in accordance with principles of parliamentary democracy, rather than a more constrained function-based freedom. Gaudron J did not tie her conception of the freedom to the text and structure of the *Constitution* as did the other justices. Mason CJ said it was not necessary to consider whether there was a significant difference between the implied freedom of political communication and "an unlimited freedom of communication."[102]

In the companion case, the High Court considered the constitutional validity of provisions of industrial relations legislation making it an offense to by writing or speech use words calculated to bring a member of the Industrial Relations Commission into disrepute.[103] A majority of the Court struck out the legislation as invalid. Some of the reasoning related to whether the law was supported by a head of power, which is not of immediate relevance here. However, some judges based their decision partly on the basis of the implied freedom of political communication.

For example, Brennan J found the law was invalid because it precluded fair and reasonable public discussion about public figures. Free speech in this context was essential to expose defects in, and preserve the integrity of, a public institution. The institution could affect the lives of many Australians. While the government could point to preserving public confidence in the Commission and the authority of its members as a legitimate interest to which the legislation was directed, it went beyond what was necessary to achieve that objective, and interfered substantially with an individual's freedom to discuss the Commission.[104] Deane and Toohey JJ confirmed the implied freedom was based on a notion of the sovereignty of the people, that the politicians represented the people, and derived their power from the consent of the people. The people could not perform their essential function within our system of government if they were "islands" unable to communicate with others.[105]

Deane and Toohey JJ referred with evident approval to remarks in a Canadian case which had referred to a right of free expression of opinion and criticism regarding public policy and public administration, and the right to discuss such matters, whether they be social, economic, or political, on the basis they were essential to the working of a parliamentary democracy.[106] Much of the debate involved contested notions, so the fact that particular assertions or opinions are rejected by government and/or proven to be mistaken did not of itself justify laws suppressing their communication.[107]

There was some disagreement evident in the court about the test to determine whether or not a law was consistent with the implied freedom. At some points a test of "reasonably appropriate and adapted to a legitimate purpose" was suggested[108]; at others, a test of whether the law was "reasonably proportional" to a legitimate purpose was used.[109]

SUBSEQUENT DEVELOPMENTS

The interaction between the implied freedom and common law doctrine was explored in *Theophanous v Herald and Weekly Times Limited and Anor*.[110] There a majority of the Court found that the common law of defamation had to cede to the implied freedom.[111] The case involved a letter published in a newspaper which was critical of the plaintiff's views of defamation, accusing him of being in favor of things most Australians were against, was biased in favor of Greeks, and was an idiot. The court adapted the ordinary law of defamation, providing further defense in the context of discussion of political figures where the defendant could show they were not aware the material was false, did not publish recklessly, and publication was reasonable.

The joint reasons emphasized that the freedom related to communication that was political in nature, rejecting the more general terms in which the freedom was discussed by Gaudron J in an earlier case. It confirmed the freedom applied to all those who participated in "political discussion." This allowed electors to make better decisions and choices, thus enhancing the efficacy of representative government. The joint reasons stated that the concept of "political discussion" was not limited to matters relating to the Commonwealth government. There was too much of an inter-relation between federal and state matters and discussion about topics that slid across the different tiers of government to insist upon a differentiation.[112] The reasons defined political discussion for current purposes as relating to the conduct, policies or fitness for office of government, political parties, public bodies, public officers, and candidates for public office. It included discussion of the political views and public conduct of those engaged in activities the subject of political debate, including trade union leaders, indigenous leaders, political, and economic commentators. They referred with evident approval to the statement of Barendt that political speech referred to "all speech relevant to the development of public opinion on the whole range of matters which an intelligent citizen should think about."[113] They now referred to Meiklejohn's conception of freedom of speech as that relating solely to speech which bears relation, directly or indirectly, to issues upon which voters have to deal.[114] The joint reasons did not note that Meiklejohn eventually accepted a much broader conception of free speech than the merely political in a more traditional sense, agreeing that works of art and literature warranted constitutional *First Amendment* protection.

Evident in the judgments in *Theophanous* is a tentative embrace of the freedom as more of a freestanding freedom based on a philosophy of representative democracy, and what it might entail. This was evidently a broader construction than had been placed on the freedom just a couple of years prior.

The joint reasons left open the question whether the freedom was a source of positive rights, or was a freedom that was negative in nature.[115] Brennan J denied that it was a personal right.[116] The joint reasons confirmed that the implied freedom was protected against intrusion by either statute law or the common law. It confirmed it provided protection from both civil law and criminal law.[117]

The Court addressed itself to arguments that the founding fathers had deliberately chosen not to include an express bill of rights in the *Constitution*, and thus had not intended to constitutionally protect rights such as freedom of speech. The joint reasons acknowledged that the founding fathers had placed their faith in the political process as the best means by which rights would be protected. However, for a majority of the Court, the intention of the founding fathers here was irrelevant; specifically, it did not preclude acceptance of the implied freedom of political communication. The majority pointed out that some founding fathers who ended up on the High Court had themselves drawn implications from its text and structure,[118] as had original constitutional textbook writers who were also founding fathers.[119] Further, the founding fathers did not have the right to control how constitutional interpretation might evolve over the years.[120] Deane J's judgment was broadly congruent with that of the joint reasons, though he would not apply the absence of recklessness or reasonableness requirements in order that the defendant be able to defend themselves on the basis of the implied freedom in a political defamation case.[121]

In dissent in the result, McHugh J espoused what he saw as some important limits on the implied freedom of political communication. He said that representative government was not a freestanding implied constitutional principle, but was restricted to that required by the text of the *Constitution*, specifically ss1, 7, 24, 30, and 41. He also rejected the interchangeable use of the phrases "representative government" and "representative democracy," stating that the latter had a broader meaning than the former, and contemplated notions of equality. Some said that free and regular elections, political equality, political freedoms and majority rule were implicit in representative democracy. Its meaning was contested and had changed over time. For these reasons, he preferred the concept of "representative government" to explain the implication to be drawn.[122]

The views of McHugh in *Theophanous* would gain influence among other members of the Court. In *McGinty v Western Australia,*[123] the High Court rejected a suggestion that an electorate system involving significant disparities in the numbers of voters in electorates involved a breach of the implied freedom. In so doing members of the Court determined that the implication to be drawn from the *Constitution* of a system of representative government was not a freestanding principle involving a general political theory, but could only be derived from the text and structure of the *Constitution.*[124] Obviously, this narrowed the scope of the freedom. For these judges, this defeated an argument in favor of a constitutionally guaranteed system of one-vote, one-value, since in their view, such could not be implied from the text and structure of the Australian *Constitution.* Two of the six judges dissented, holding that the text and structure of the *Constitution*, providing for a democratic system of government and that the legislature be chosen directly by the people, found that this implied something like equality in relation to electorate numbers.[125]

The Court further considered the interplay between the implied freedom and the law of defamation in *Lange v Australian Broadcasting Corporation.*[126] There a unanimous court accepted the proposition of a majority in *Theophanous* that the common law of defamation had to yield to the requirements of the *Constitution.*[127] The Court now confirmed unanimously that the freedom was a negative one, in the sense of a protection against laws which impacted it, rather than a positive right that might give rise to compensation in damages for breach.[128] The Court confirmed the implied freedom was not absolute. In determining whether or not it was breached two questions should be asked:

a. Does the law effectively burden freedom of communication about government or political matters either in its terms, operation, or effect? and
b. If the law effectively burdens that freedom, is the law reasonably appropriate and adapted to serve a legitimate end to the fulfilment of which is compatible with the maintenance of the constitutionally prescribed system of representative and responsible government?

If the answer to the first question was yes and the answer to the second was no, the challenged provision was constitutionally invalid. Note the unanimous court's apparent embrace of the concept of "reasonably appropriate and adapted." However, the Court appeared to take a more confined view of the freedom than had been evident in *Theophanous*. By this time, Brennan had succeeded Mason as Chief Justice. A more literalist, text, and structure basis of the freedom is clearly evident in *Lange*, as opposed to a more free-flowing freedom based on notions of representative democracy as was evident in *Theophanous*. The text and structure basis served to limit the scope and extent of the freedom. It has persisted in subsequent decisions.

The Court noted a material difference between the law of the United States and the law of Australia in that, in the latter case, there was one unified common law for the nation.[129] A material difference between the law of Australia and that of the United Kingdom was the rejection in Australia of notions of parliamentary supremacy:

> The (Australian) *Constitution* displaced, or rendered inapplicable, the English common law doctrine of the general competence and unqualified supremacy of the legislature.[130]

Subsequently the Court would clarify that the freedom could extend to non-verbal communication, such as protest.[131] Some judges highlighted in that case that the infringement of the freedom was no greater than necessary to achieve the government's legitimate objective.[132] This indicates the challenged measure is likely to survive a constitutional challenge on the basis of interference with the implied freedom. McHugh J confirmed that the freedom protected "false, unreasoned and emotional communications," as well as those which were well reasoned, truth and/or detached. Citing American decisions like *Cohen*, McHugh J confirmed that invective speech was entitled to protection, just as calm and reasoned analysis was.

The Court considered its major "breach of the peace" case in the context of the implied freedom in *Coleman v Power*.[133] There the legislation made it unlawful for a person in a public place to use any threatening, abusive, or insulting words to another. The maximum penalty for breach was a fine of $100 or six months' jail. Coleman was arrested after handing out written pamphlets naming police officers who he alleged were corrupt. A majority of the Court set aside the conviction on the basis of the implied freedom.

A majority of the Court slightly modified the two-step test adopted by the High Court in *Lange* for determining whether laws were invalid on the basis they infringed the implied freedom. In relation to the second of the steps, the words "in a manner" should replace the words "the fulfilment of."[134] The Court found that the freedom extended to matters involving the executive, including discussion of the fitness for office of members of the executive arm of government.[135] Police officers were within the executive arm.

Gummow and Hayne JJ referred to the classic American decisions of *Chaplinsky v New York* and *Cantwell v Connecticut*, where the Supreme Court had carved out the "fighting words" exception to *First Amendment* freedoms, permitting the state to punish the expression of such words on the basis they were likely to lead to a breach of the peace. Gummow and Hayne JJ acknowledged that the American *First Amendment* was materially different from the Australian implied freedom, but suggested that just as in the United States where the ability of the state to regulate speech was held to be narrowly limited to preventing a breach of the peace, by an analogy the Australian implied freedom should be read so as to prevent broadly worded provisions such as the one in issue here, criminalizing the use of insulting or offensive words. Gummow and Hayne JJ concluded the broad words of the offense should be read down so as to be limited to speech likely to provoke a breach of the peace. Here Coleman's speech was unlikely to so lead, so those justices overturned his conviction. Kirby J expressed agreement with the reading down of the provision by Gummow and Hayne JJ in order to make the provision constitutionally valid.[136] McHugh J found the provision to be constitutionally invalid because it was too broad in the type of behavior it criminalized, substantially interfering with the implied freedom.

Several members of the Court reflected on the nature of the speech here, in so far as that was relevant to the implied freedom. McHugh J said the fact that the comments were an insult did not deny the communication constitutional protection, on the basis that insults were just as much part of political communication as irony, humor, or criticism.[137] Kirby J said that from earliest times, Australian politics had included "insult and emotion, calumny and invective, in its armory of persuasion."[138] The freedom was not confined to the "whispered civilities of intellectual discourse."[139] This was in contrast to the view of Heydon J in dissent. He concluded that insult was not part of political debate. It did not generally assist electors to make informed choices. Due to its nil value, it was outside the protection of the implied freedom, according to Heydon J.[140] Callinan J took a similar position.[141]

The Court has subsequently maintained its distinction between laws which have a direct and substantial effect on political communication, and laws which focus on other topics, and whose impact on political communication is indirect and/or incidental. Laws of the first type will be much more difficult to justify than laws of the latter type.[142] Again, the United States approach of wariness towards content-based and viewpoint-based discrimination is evident.

The Court has reiterated that the discussion of what some might consider to be state political issues has become so intertwined with what some might consider to be federal political issues that the distinction had become virtually meaningless in current discourse.[143]

The Court considered the application of the implied freedom to laws providing for the registration of political parties.[144] Under the rules a political party could be registered either if it had an existing member of parliament or had at least 500 members. A party which was registered had the right to have its name included against the name of a candidate on the ballot paper; a party that was not registered was not entitled to place its name against the name of a candidate on the ballot paper. A majority of the Court found the implied freedom of political communication did not even apply to the ballot paper. There was no burden on the implied freedom at all, according to the majority, because a person had no common law right to have their party name appear on the ballot paper. The right to have a party name appear on the ballot paper was purely a creature of the statutory framework, and parliament was free to condition placement of a party name on the ballot paper as it wished.[145] Two justices found that a ballot paper was a political communication, and a law conditioning what could be placed on it did burden it. However, those justices validated the measures on the basis they were justified in terms of a compelling objective and proportionality.[146]

In *Hogan v Hinch*, a very broad conception of the concept of "political communication" was evident in the judgment of French CJ. French CJ said it was "difficult to identify subjects not capable or potentially capable of discussion as matters which are or should be or could be of concern to the national government."[147] He said that the meaning of "government and political matters" for the purposes of the implied freedom "arguably include social and economic features of Australian society."[148]

The joint reasons in *Hogan v Hinch* highlighted a distinction made by some of the judges in the 1992 implied freedom cases between the likely constitutionality of laws which directly targeted freedom of political communication, as opposed to those with a different focus, but with an incidental effect on the freedom. The joint reasons in *Hogan* maintained this distinction between laws which directly burdened the freedom, and those which did so incidentally.[149] It did not expressly refer to the requirement of Mason CJ in *ACTV* that the former laws would have to be shown to have "compelling justification" in order to be valid; the joint reasons was simply content to note that laws of that kind were more difficult to validate against a constitutional challenge on the basis of the implied freedom, compared with laws with a merely incidental impact on the freedom.

The equivalent to some extent of the United States decision in *Snyder v Phelps* is the Australian decision in *Monis v The Queen*. There Monis was charged with a breach of the *Criminal Code*, s471.12 of which stated that a person committed an offense if they used a postal service in a way that a reasonable person would regard as being menacing, harassing, or offensive. Monis had sent letters to the families of dead soldiers in which he criticized Australia's involvement in Afghanistan. He argued that the dead soldiers had killed innocent civilians, comparing them to pigs and dirty animals. He referred to the bodies of the dead soldiers as being "contaminated" and compared the dead soldiers to Hitler. The High Court split 3:3 on the question of whether the provision was invalid as being contrary to the implied freedom of political communication.

French CJ, in finding the provision invalid, stated that political discussion would often include "unreasonable, strident, hurtful and highly offensive" communication.[150] It might include words likely to induce significant anger, outrage, resentment, hatred, or disgust. He found the provision did burden freedom of communication about political matters, and that the legislation was not compatible with the system of representative government. It was not a legitimate end of legislation to seek to shut down communication on the basis it was, or was likely to be considered by some or many, offensive.[151] Hayne J agreed that the protection of others from offense was not a legitimate end, and was not compatible with representative government.[152] He disagreed with the suggestion that the fact that the burden on freedom of communication was relatively slight or little, and the fact that there were other ways in which the accused could communicate their views other than through the post, indicated the law was valid.[153] He alluded to the dangers involved in distinguishing between "orthodox" and "unorthodox" views for the purposes of the implied freedom. The whole point of the implied freedom was to ensure that unpopular views could be and were expressed.[154]

Crennan Kiefel and Bell JJ validated the provision. In so doing, they clearly adopted a German-style proportionality analysis, considering whether the law was proportionate to the attainment of a legitimate objective.[155] This was a significant development in the implied freedom jurisprudence. If there were other, less drastic means available to attain the legitimate objective, the law might not have the required proportionality.[156] The joint reasons said that the law's purpose was to protect individuals from the intrusion of highly offensive material into a person's home or workplace.[157] The joint reasons said that "considerable ingenuity" would be required to argue that the accused's use of the postal service was in the course of a reasonable discussion of political matters.[158] Protecting citizens from offensive communication was a legitimate objective of legislation, and was not incompatible with the system of representative government.[159] The joint reasons relied upon the distinction between laws which directly impacted on freedom of political communication, and laws which did so indirectly and incidentally. The latter were more easily justified. This law was of the latter variety.

While the other jurisdictions studied will generally prohibit systems of prior restraint on speech, the High Court validated a statutory provision which prevented a person on a thoroughfare from distributing printed matter to passers-by and prevented a person preaching, canvassing, touting for business, or conducting a survey on such thoroughfare without permission of Council.[160]

The application of the implied freedom to matters of political funding was considered in a couple of cases. Firstly, the court decided the case of *Unions NSW and Others v State of New South Wales*.[161] The legislation there provided that only a person on the electoral roll could donate to a political party, and capped the level of electoral communications expenditure. For the purposes of calculating the level of expenditure, the legislation provided for "aggregation," whereby expenditure of a political party would be aggregated with expenditure by a third party that was affiliated to that political party. All members of the High Court declared the legislation to be constitutionally invalid.

Again the Court dismissed an argument that the implied freedom of political communication did not apply here because the provisions were included in state legislation and dealt with politics at a state level. The joint reasons reiterated that a broad view should be taken of the implied freedom, because of the impossibility of separating political discussion at the federal and state levels. The joint reasons noted it was

> difficult to identify subjects not capable of discussion as matters which do or could potentially concern a federal governmental or political matter. Social, economic and political matters in Australia are increasingly integrated.[162]

The Court found that the limitation of the right to donate to individuals on the electoral roll burdened the freedom of political communication. It restricted the funds available to political parties to campaign, which involved communicating. Thus, it burdened the political party's freedom to communicate. It also burdened freedom of communication of a donor by limiting the amount of the donation they could make.[163] In relation to the second *Lange* limb, considering whether the legislation was directed to a legitimate purpose compatible with the system of representative government, this was an impossible inquiry. The section did not disclose what its purpose was. It was not clear why the ability to donate was restricted to those on the electoral roll.[164] Given the lack of evident purpose, the section was constitutionally invalid.

A similar conclusion was reached with respect to the "aggregating provisions" regarding expenditure caps, seeking to aggregate the expenditure of third party affiliates with that of political parties for the purposes of determining whether the expenditure gap had been breached. The Court noted the legislation did not explain why it was appropriate to consider separate organizations as effectively one and the same for the purposes of the cap. It was not clear that the aggregating provisions related to any purpose, and particularly the anti-corruption purpose evident elsewhere in the Act.[165]

The Court reached a different view when other provisions of the electoral law were challenged in *McCloy v New South Wales*.[166] At issue there was the validity of (a) limits on the extent to which an individual could make a political donation in any given year; (b) bans on political donations by developers; and (c) bans on the making of indirect campaign contributions, for instance, the use of office accommodation, vehicles, computers, or other equipment at no cost or below market rates. All members of the Court validated provisions (a) and (c),[167] and all but one members of the Court validated provision (b) against a challenge on the basis of the implied freedom of political communication.[168] The Court accepted that the provisions were reasonably appropriate and adapted to achieving a purpose of preventing the actuality and appearance of corruption and undue influence, and adequately tailored to that end.

In so deciding, a majority of the Court settled upon a three stage inquiry to determine whether a law was consistent with the implied freedom, building, and expanding upon the former *Lange* two-stage test. The first stage was to consider, as had the court in *Lange*, whether the challenged provision burdens the freedom in its terms, operation of effect. If yes, the second stage considered whether the purpose of the law and the means adopted to achieve that purpose were legitimate. In other words, whether the laws were compatible with our system of representative government in that they did not adversely impinge upon such system. This was known as "compatibility testing."

The third stage considered whether the challenged law was reasonably appropriate and adapted to advance that legitimate object. This stage was also known as "proportionality testing." It would consider the extent to which the challenged law burdened the freedom. The majority took the opportunity to lay out in more detail the kinds of considerations that would be relevant in making this determination. They were threefold: whether the law was suitable, necessary, and adequate in its balance.

The majority explained that a law was "suitable" if it bore a rational connection to the purpose of the provision. It was "necessary" if there was no obvious and compelling alternative, reasonably practicable way of achieving the same purpose which had a less restrictive impact on the freedom. It was "adequate in its balance" if it was reasonable considering the importance of the purpose served by the restriction, and the extent to which it impacted on the freedom. This three-stage approach, including a more specific focus on proportionality, is reminiscent of the *First Amendment* case law during its so-called "ad hoc balancing" era.[169] Subsequently the American case law would evolve further into a category rule-based system, with some balancing involved and some generic principles applied universally.

Three judges continued to apply the two-stage *Lange* test, and expressed disagreement with the use of proportionality analysis in the way accepted by the majority of the court.[170] There was evident disagreement among the judges as to whether a political donation was a form of communication.[171] Nettle J would have invalidated the provision banning donations by property developers because it was discriminatory and distortionary.

Recently the High Court considered the validity of the *Workplaces (Protection from Protesters) Act 2014* (Tas).[172] Section 6 stated that a protester must not enter or do an act on business premises if that hinders or obstructs the conduct of a business activity on those premises, where the protester knows or could reasonably be expected to know their entry or act would likely hinder or obstruct the carrying out of a business activity on those premises. The Act defined "business premises" in such a way as to apply to lands upon which Forestry Tasmania might conduct logging operations. Section 11 of the Act permitted a police officer to direct a person on business premises to leave those premises immediately, if the officer reasonably believed the person has committed, is committing, or would commit an offense against the Act. Such a notice could include a requirement that the person not commit an offense against the Act for the following three months. The direction could be issued either to a person or a group of persons. If a direction were given to a group of persons, it would be taken to have been given to each of them. Section 8 made it an offense for a person to fail to comply with a direction by police to remove themselves from business premises. It also made it an offense to return to premises upon which a direction had been given within four days. A protester was defined as a person engaging in a protest activity that takes place on business premises. Protesters who had been arrested under the legislation challenged its constitutional validity. By a majority of 5 to 2, the High Court invalidated the challenged provisions.[173]

A majority of the Court, comprising the joint judgment of Kiefel CJ Bell and Keane JJ, and the separate judgment of Nettle J, applied the three stage proportionality approach identified in *McCloy*. In relation to the stages, firstly the law burdened the freedom of communication about political matters.[174]

It was aimed directly at protesters who wished to challenge an existing government practice. Secondly, in relation to compatibility, the majority found that the legislation was directed to a legitimate purpose, that of public safety and preservation of government equipment, and disruption to lawful government activity. The joint reasons concluded that the law satisfied the compatibility test[175] although the burden it placed on political communication was significant, given the size of land affected and the fact that the notice not to revisit an area could be applied to large groups of people and could endure for three months.

In terms of proportionality testing, the majority considered whether the law was suitable, necessary, and adequate in its balance. The majority found the law was largely suitable for its intended purpose. Thus, s6 and s11 met this requirement.[176] However, s8 did not. It provided for the detention of anyone given a notice, though they were not there in order to protest and posed no risk of causing damage or disruption.[177]

The majority considered s6 and s11 in terms of "necessity." The joint reasons noted that this test involved a consideration of the existence of alternative measures that could have been taken to achieve the legitimate objective that were less invasive of the freedom. Here the joint reasons noted the legislation operated more widely than its purpose required. It operated across a broad area, and there was uncertainty as to the precise scope of the ambit of the legislation in terms of geography. The Tasmanian Government had not shown that previous laws were ineffective in dealing with protesters. The Act contained special offenses and heavy penalties. The joint reasons concluded the legislation was not reasonably necessary to achieve its legitimate purpose, meaning it was invalid.[178] It was thus not necessary for them to consider whether the legislation was adequate in its balance.

Nettle J noted the restrictions on protest were substantial. Someone could be ordered to be removed from the relevant area based solely on a police officer's reasonable belief. There need not be evidence that the person had caused damage or disruption in the past, or would likely do son in future. The burdens on the implied freedom were substantial.[179] In contrast to the joint reasons, Nettle J found the legislation was reasonably necessary. He accorded parliament substantial deference in making this assessment.[180] There were not compelling and obvious measures of significantly less restrictive effect to meet the government's legislative objectives.[181]

For Nettle J, the constitutional difficulty was that the law was not adequate in its balance. It permitted a police officer to exclude a person from a designated area for four days simply based on the officer's reasonable belief. The belief may well be mistaken. The Act provided for a direction to be provided to what could be a broad range of people that would effectively preclude them from returning to the area within three months, although only one member of the group was thought to have engaged in, or be likely to engage in, damaging or disruptive behavior.[182] The fact discretion was broad-ranging made it more likely the legislation would be found to have offended the implied freedom.[183]

The final member of the majority, Gageler J, also invalidated the legislation. However, he did not accept the three-stage proportionality testing, favoring the more traditional two-stage *Lange* test, as modified in *Coleman.* Applying this test, the laws substantially burdened communication about political matters. He accepted the traditional distinction between laws which directly burdened communication about political matters, and laws about another subject matter which incidentally burdened such communication.[184] Traditionally, the former were more difficult to justify, and according to Mason CJ in the *ACTV* case, would require a compelling justification. Gageler J said the laws operative here were of the former variety, directing targeting the expression of particular views (content and/or viewpoint discrimination). He concluded there was no compelling justification for them. The specific provisions did not fit well with their purpose. They applied to a very broad area, applied to individuals who were not shown to have actually caused damage or disruption, and permitted police to effectively remove individuals from areas for a lengthy period.[185] The penalties were severe. Thus the burden imposed on political communication was well beyond what was necessary in order to achieve the legitimate objective, and the legislation was invalid. Gageler J also rejected the suggestion that the implied freedom of political communication was confined to activities for which individuals had a legally enforceable right to engage.[186]

In dissent, Gordon J concluded the legislative measures were reasonable "time, place and manner" restrictions on just one aspect of the right to protest.[187] She found the challenged provisions were not significantly more onerous than pre-existing regulations which were not the subject of challenge.[188] She discussed the proportionality testing approach in unfavorable terms.[189] Edelman J in dissent did not discuss the question of proportionality. He said there was no relevant freedom, so there could be no question of whether the law burdened it. A person did not necessarily have the legal right to be on Crown land; parliament could legitimately condition or limit the right of an individual to be on Crown land.[190] A person could not base a claim of breach of the implied freedom on conduct that was unlawful.[191]

Most recently in *Clubb v Edwards; Preston v Avery*,[192] all members of the High Court rejected a constitutional challenge to state legislation which prohibited communicative activity within 150 meters of an abortion clinic. The court found that to some extent what those charged did not meet the definition of "political activity." Even if it did, the laws were directed towards a legitimate objective of public safety for those wishing to access such clinics, to prevent harm to vulnerable individuals. They were not excessive in scope given that legitimate objective. There were sufficient alternative channels of protest available to those who objected to the laws. Again, difference of opinion on the efficacy of a proportionality approach is evident. A majority, Kiefel CJ, Bell Keane Nettle, and Edelman JJ accepted and applied a proportionality approach; Gageler and Gordon JJ declined to apply such an approach. However, the decision to reject the challenge was unanimous.

The cases have considered to some extent whether the implied freedom of political communication includes freedom of association, given that often individuals will associate in order to communicate. In *Kruger v Commonwealth*,[193] two justices accepted,[194] and four rejected,[195] the suggestion that the implied freedom of political communication included an implied freedom of association. There was some support for an implied freedom of association in *Mulholland v Electoral Commissioner*.[196] There Gummow and Hayne JJ said that there was no freestanding right of association, but suggested it might to some degree be a "corollary" of the implied freedom of communication.[197] This view was repeated by four members of the Court in *Wainohu v New South Wales*.[198]

The matter was considered again in *Tajjour v New South Wales*,[199] where the Court validated consorting legislation, providing for an offense of habitually consorting with convicted offenders, after having being issued with a notice by police to refrain from such association. Six members of the Court, Gageler J dissenting, validated the legislation. While the Court agreed that the challenged section did, or could, burden the implied freedom of political communication, the measures were reasonably appropriate and adapted to the achievement of a legitimate end, namely deterring further criminal conduct.[200]

Currently there are significant restrictions on freedom of speech in Australian legislation. The most high profile example is s18C of the *Racial Discrimination Act 1975* (Cth), making it unlawful to do an act in public because of a person's race, color or national and ethnic origin which is likely to insult, offend, intimidate, or humiliate, subject to a good faith defense in s18D. There are state equivalents.[201] Other examples include the offense of treachery in the Crimes Act 1914 (Cth),[202] and limitations on speech which could impact on Australia's border security.[203] In 2018 new legislation requiring foreign principals to register with the government if they wish to conduct political activity in Australia was introduced.[204] Communication activity by such an entity would also need to be registered, in a limited throwback to the system of prior restraints that applied in England until 1694. Individual states retain legislation dealing with sedition,[205] pornography-type activity,[206] breach of the peace[207] and, in one case, blasphemy.[208]

Critique of the Current Australian Position

Freedom is Confined to the "Political"

One critique of the current Australian implied freedom of political communication is the emphasis that it places on the nature of the communication being "political" in nature. The reason why the High Court sought to impose this limit on the freedom is understood. It sourced the freedom in the system of representative government for which the *Constitution* provided, and viewed the freedom as being necessary to preserve the essential attributes of that system. In order that a democratic system of government could function, individuals had to have freedom to discuss political matters among themselves, and to express and receive political information and views.

The problem is that the distinction may not be able to practically handle the weight being placed on it. The view perhaps assumes that a nice distinction can be made between what are "political" communications and what are "non-political" communications. What if a given communication combines both political communication and non-political communication? Does the constitutional freedom only extend to part of some messages, some speeches, and some conversations? The line-drawing can become very difficult.[209] At one time "political" communication was held to involve the "whole range of issues which an intelligent citizen should think about."[210] As Kirk observes:

> any public communication is potentially a political matter, at least when it involves the communication of ideas. As every area of human activity is potentially subject to government intervention, communication on any subject could be covered.[211]

French CJ in *Hogan v Hinch* adopted a very similar idea, stating that political matters could include social and economic features of Australian society, being matters "potentially within the purview of government."[212]

If this breadth is considered a problem, possible solutions to this definitional problem exist. Kirk suggests one. He says that the freedom should be limited to communication which is "primarily" aimed at or relating to government activity. So, for example, he concludes that artistic expression, at least most of such expression, would not be covered by the implied freedom,[213] because the artist generally did not create it with the intention of making political commentary, at least usually. With respect, it may often be very difficult to discern the intention of someone who communicates in a particular way. Their intention in communicating as they did should not be fulcrum upon which their constitutional freedom in doing so should depend.

Similarly Dan Meagher notes the potential indeterminacy of the concept of "political communication."[214] His solution is to define the concept of "political communication" to be where "the subject matter of the communication is such that it may reasonably be relevant to the federal voting choices of its likely audience." That can include an audience of one.[215]

Adrienne Stone suggests four categories of communication that should be regarded as political: (a) explicitly political communication—concerning speech about individuals within government, and policy, and communication about how citizens are governed; (b) potential subjects of government action; (c) communication that does or may influence attitudes about public issues; and (d) communication that develops qualities desirable in a voter.[216]

Category (d) is the most contentious. It apparently reflects a much broader conception of the freedom of communication than the kind of functionalist, consequentialist argument that the High Court has typically accepted in narrowly crafting the scope of the implied freedom of political communication. Having said that, broad iterations of the scope of political communication do appear occasionally. So, for instance, in *Theophanous v Herald and Weekly Times Ltd*,[217] Mason CJ Toohey and Gaudron JJ quoted with evident approval from the work of Barendt to the effect that political speech "refers to all speech relevant to the development of public opinion on the whole range of issues which an intelligent citizen should think about."[218]

In that case, Mason CJ Toohey and Gaudron JJ specifically equated their view with that of Meiklejohn. This is particularly important to current discussion. Meiklejohn favored the functionalist, consequentialist view of freedom of speech as being confined to political communication. However, in his later writings he took a broader view. He said that education, science, philosophy, art and literature were protected by the *First Amendment*. He accepted that the *First Amendment* required an informed citizen, and that citizens needed to have access to a very broad range of materials to permit the kind of self-development that would shape them and permit them to carry out their role as voters.[219] Arguably, one of the problems with the High Court's jurisprudence in this area is that, although some of the leading progenitors of the freedom espouse the views of Meiklejohn, an author who did at one time emphasize the functionalist view of freedom of speech, Australian case law has not evolved in the way that Meiklejohn's thinking on the issues did, moving from a narrow consequentialist conception to a very broad conception of what freedom of speech required in order to fulfil its place in the constitutional scheme.

Stone is not supportive of a narrow view of what is political communication, concluding that "much apparently non-political communication is relevant to th(e) rationale for the freedom."[220]

It is interesting to briefly consider here overlap between the Australian and American positions. While the *First Amendment* has been interpreted more broadly than the Australian equivalent, in some contexts it has been limited by notions of "public concern," particularly in the realm of speech by public servants,[221] and in the area of defamation.[222] There is equivalence between notions of "political speech" and what is of "public concern."[223] Just as there is significant criticism of notions of "political" communication on the basis of its indeterminacy, there is substantial criticism of the use of the concept "public concern" in the context of some categories of *First Amendment* speech.[224]

Freedom of Association is Not Protected

As stated above, some judges have suggested that freedom of association and assembly could be seen as being part of the implied freedom of political communication. Gaudron J in *Kruger* did seem to suggest that an implied freedom of association might be separate from the implied freedom of political communication,[225] but other justices did not share her view, and any (hypothetical) freedom of association (for no cases have yet been decided on the basis of it) appears to be limited and linked to freedom of communication, in the minds of the High Court justices.

It is easy to see how they are linked. Some people need to associate in order to communicate effectively. The mere fact that a large number of people associate for a common purpose could itself be a communication about the depth of community feeling about an issue. However, when the High Court of Australia has been confronted with questions about the validity of laws directly targeting association, for example, anti-association laws literally criminalizing acts of association per se, and consorting laws which do the same, the High Court has, in the former case, decided the case on other grounds,[226] or in the latter case, validated the provisions despite constitutional challenge.[227] In the rare case where justices have spoken favorably about a possible right to associate, apart from the original case law in 1992, it has been a hypothetical, brief statement that any right to associate could only exist as a corollary to a freedom of political communication.[228] Such a "corollary" argument is never justified or explained, but simply asserted.

Other scholars support notions of a guaranteed constitutional freedom of association in the Australian context. Kirk says that a right to form or join any association with potentially political aims should be recognized.[229] Constitutional scholar George Williams agrees,[230] as do Tham[231] and Gray.[232]

As indicated, there is a lack of explanation from the judges as to why they arrived at the position that a freedom to associate could only be a corollary to a freedom to communicate ("the corollary limitation"). It is not clear whether the purpose of claiming it could only exist in that light is to limit the scope of freedom to associate. Is it to prevent an argument that a freedom of association has been infringed by a law that does not say anything about communication? For instance, the anti-association laws, literally criminalizing acts of association, in *Totani* and *Wainohu*. Is the argument that these laws cannot be challenged on the basis of an implied freedom to associate, because they do not implicate (at least directly) freedom to communicate? It is not entirely clear what the reason is for the corollary limitation. Clearly, the democratic structure of our system of government has been the source of more than one implied limitation, it being utilized to determine that Australians had an implied right to vote. So clearly democracy can and does implicitly mean more than freedom to communicate. Thus, it is not entirely clear why the judges have baldly asserted the corollary limitation. It is suspected that this has been done with the unstated purpose of limiting the extent to which an individual can mount a constitutional argument that their freedom of association has been infringed by a law. While of course the justices have not openly admitted that this is the case, it is perhaps no coincidence that while applying the corollary limitation, the courts have not actually struck out legislation which arguably infringes the implied freedom to associate on that basis. And that cases which directly raise association issues, literally laws that criminalize mere acts of association, are decided on other grounds. Arguments about association tend to be discouraged during oral argument, and if they are considered by the judges, given very limited treatment.

Does it make any practical difference that an implied freedom to associate is seen merely as a corollary to a freedom to communicate, as opposed to a freedom in its own right. Presumably the judges think so, otherwise they would not have crafted it in such a fashion. The argument here is that it does make a substantive difference. It effectively buries freedom of association under the freedom of political communication. This makes it easier to ignore arguments about association, in cases where a law is challenged that makes no ostensible reference to communication, such as laws criminalizing association. Since the legislation does not deal directly with communication, political or otherwise, it is difficult to succeed on any argument about an implied freedom of political communication. In turn, this has apparently hobbled any argument about freedom of association in such cases. It is considered that if freedom of association were considered as a standalone freedom, it would be given more substance and attention by the courts. Thus, laws which directly targeted association, and not speech, would be seriously considered in terms of the standalone freedom. In contrast, at present the association argument is considered marginal, because the challenged law does not target communication, and the judges see association as being a subset of the communication freedom.

Another practical benefit of providing for a freestanding association freedom is recognized by Kirk. He concludes that an individual should have a "right to form any association with even potentially political aims."[233] In so stating, he perhaps unconsciously provides another reason for separating the freedom of association with freedom of communication. His argument recognizes that laws exist which might inhibit freedom of association but which might not inhibit freedom of communication. Thus, it does make a practical difference to recognize the right to associate as a standalone freedom, as opposed to a derivative corollary right.

Unclear Philosophical Basis of the Implied Freedom

While the High Court sought to position the Australian implied freedom of political communication in the text and structure of the Australian *Constitution*, it has not particularly engaged with the more general freedom of speech scholarship. Specifically, of the various rationales for freedom of speech generally, including search for truth, marketplace of ideas, self-actualization, autonomy, and functional democracy, it has not generally chosen any one of these philosophical underpinnings of the freedom.[234] At times, it seems to have embraced different philosophical underpinnings. For instance, a comparison of the decision in *Theophanous* in 1994 and that of *Lange* in 1997 seems to suggest a shift from a broader conception of the rationale for the freedom, "development of public opinion on the whole range of issues which an intelligent citizen should think about,"[235] to a narrower conception, based on what is "necessary" for representative and responsible government.[236] At times, it is criticized for quickly adopting United States doctrine that reflects the kind of deep-seated suspicion and distrust of government that is embedded in United States culture but finds little equivalent in Australia, due to the very different circumstances in which the countries' constitutions were forged.[237] Sometimes the High Court itself eschews reference to the American *First Amendment* case law; at other times, it openly embraces it.[238]

One would have thought that the Meiklejohn line, that freedom of speech is a purely functions doctrine required by democracy and thus limited to the political context, would have best suited the High Court of Australia's interpretation, and its constant emphasis that the freedom is confined to the political context, and does not have broader application. However, the High Court has not relied on the work of Meiklejohn in framing its jurisprudence in this regard, apart from in the joint reasons in *Theophanous*.[239] And further complications arise because although Meiklejohn did espouse a narrow functionalist and consequentialist argument about free speech initially, later in his career he accepted a much broader conception, arguing that free speech had to include a broad variety of sources from which an individual could draw intellectual sustenance, including arts and literature. He did relate that development back to the role that the voter played in the system of government, rather than a broader conception of individual self-development. Thus, individual self-actualization was not an inherent good, in the view of Meiklejohn, which should be supported by the *First Amendment*, but self-actualization of a voter, in order to permit them to play their proper role within a system of democratic government.[240]

Stone argues that the autonomy justification for freedom of speech can also support the Australian implied freedom, concluding that "arguments for autonomy and arguments for democratic government are rather closely linked, and it is possible to draw similar links between autonomy and the apparently narrower justification behind the Australian doctrine."[241]

Another complication is that even if it is agreed that the Australian *Constitution* contemplates a system of representative democracy, there is no agreement as to what that necessarily requires. For instance, Glen Patmore has identified at least three models of representative democracy, including a protective theory, a participatory theory, and an elite theory.[242] The first two would require a strong freedom of speech in order to function effectively; the third is more focused on the breadth of the franchise. Michael Chesterman refers to a participatory conception of democracy and an institutional, or top-down, version. The former is broader, similar to goals of individual self-fulfilment. It supports the ability of individuals to express their views on any topic within the purview of government as they see fit, in a way, and in a place, and at a time, they see fit. There would be a virtually unregulated public forum to allow this to take place. An institutional approach would be narrower, merely requiring that the government provide access to a reasonable level of public debate so that voters could exercise an informed choice while voting.[243]

It has also been pointed out that the founding fathers left many of the rules relating to the democratic process up to future parliaments to determine.[244] This makes it very difficult, even if it is accepted that the Australian *Constitution* contemplates a system of representative democracy, to move from that overarching principle to specific requirements.

"Text and Structure"

While at some point there was a suggestion that the implication regarding freedom of political communication could be more of a freestanding right, by the time of *Lange v Australian Broadcasting Corporation* in 1997, a more conservative view was evident. According to this view, any implications to be drawn had to be closely related with the text and structure of the *Constitution*.[245] This view was likely taken in order to narrow the extent of the implied freedom[246]; it has certainly had this effect. It fits with the High Court's general antipathy towards any notion that a particular political theory underpins or explains the Australian *Constitution*, or should be used in its interpretation.[247] Stone claims members of the High Court intended to preclude development of a theoretical or philosophical basis of the implied freedom.[248]

Related to questions regarding "text and structure" are arguments about the very nature of implied freedoms. Some espouse a narrow view regarding the making of implications. For instance, Windeyer J stated that "I would prefer not to say 'making implications' because our avowed task is simply the revealing or uncovering of implications that are already there."[249] Similarly, Brennan CJ in *McGinty v Western Australia* stated that "implications are not devised by the judiciary; they exist in the text and structure of the *Constitution* and are revealed or uncovered by judicial exegesis."[250] On the other hand, some might suggest that this kind of reasoning is reminiscent of the "declaratory theory" of law more generally, that the law exists, but sometimes it takes some time for judges to discover what was always the legal position about a particular matter.[251] That theory has, in my view, rightly been discredited, and a more realistic view taken about the true nature of the judicial function.[252] Judges make law.[253]

If the High Court's use of "text and structure" as a means of narrowing the scope of the implied freedom was designed to provide certainty, demonstrably it has failed to do so. Cases like *Roach* and *Rowe* demonstrate this, where a majority of the High Court discerned in the words "directly chosen by the people" in ss7 and 24 (the same sections from which the implied freedom of political communication is derived) an implied right to vote and an implied right to join the electoral roll at a time quite close to when the election was being held. It is arguably somewhat difficult to discern from the words "directly chosen by the people" that individuals should have a right to vote and a right to join electoral rolls at a certain time. Certainly, nothing in the text requires that it be so interpreted. Thus, the ability of the concepts of "text and structure" to provide the kind of certainty that doubters about implied freedoms and rights pine for is seriously in question.[254] Now, presumably they would have the same difficulty with arguments for a more freestanding right like representative democracy, but the point is that these definitional and scope issues are hardly assuaged by an insistence that any implied freedoms must be drawn from the text and structure of the *Constitution*.[255]

There is likely to be a link between arguments that implications should be limited to text and structure and an argument in favor of interpreting the *Constitution* in accordance with the view of the founding fathers. Goldsworthy is most open about this, arguing that any constitutional implications to be drawn must reflect the founding fathers' intention, presumably to the extent that such is reflected in the text and structure.

However, Stokes suggests links between an argument about internationalism and a contractual view of the *Constitution*. Typically, in the law of contract, the parties' intentions, or presumptions about the parties' intentions, govern interpretation. Stokes suggests that originalists may see the *Constitution* in contractual terms, and this may be one reason for their favoring an originalist interpretation. There is evidence of this. Goldsworthy has suggested the use of the concept "so obvious that it goes without saying," taken from the realm of contract law, to seek to articulate strict limits on the extent to which courts might legitimately draw implications from the *Constitution*.[256]

Stokes has cogently argued that it is mistaken to see the *Constitution* in a contractual sense.[257] Contracts are private agreements between parties about their rights and obligations to each other. He argues it is inappropriate to extend this concept to a constitution. For instance, a contract between parties generally does not bind parties who were not privy to it. Given this, why would the *Constitution* be binding on Australian governments and individuals living in Australia today? None of us were parties to the original agreement; nor could the Australian Government have been party to it, because it did not exist at the time. Some see the *Constitution* as an agreement among the states; others as an agreement between individuals living in the colonies at the time. Others seem to see it as an agreement among the founding fathers.

Stokes argues that it is incorrect, and leads to undesirable outcomes, to see the *Constitution* in contractual terms. It would mean that current members of society would not be bound by the *Constitution*, since they were not parties to it and they have not "accepted" or "ratified" it. Silence does not constitute acceptance in the law of contract. It would preclude changes in the meaning of the document over time. And it would give controlling influence in interpreting the *Constitution* to the intention of the founding fathers, because they wrote the contract and/or because they were parties to the contract.

Stokes says it is better to see the *Constitution* as a commitment to government in accordance with particular values, including federalism, the rule of law and representative government. These values can provide guidance in cases where laws are challenged as being unconstitutional. Stokes says that, by seeing the *Constitution* in this way, interpretation of the *Constitution* can change over time. It will be a gradual process over time, a process very familiar to the common law, by which the implications of those values are worked out. We would not necessarily be limited by how the founding fathers viewed or interpreted those values. Such reasoning is said to better explain why the *Constitution* binds us today. It binds us not because it is a contract and we are said to be bound by a contract to which we were not a party, undermining basic privacy principles, but because we have made a "social commitment to co-operate" along the lines of what is contained in the *Constitution*. It is not an individual commitment as implied by the contract theory, but a social commitment to the principles enshrined in the *Constitution*. Arguably, this was the essence of the original implied freedom case law in 1992, basing the implied freedom of political communication on values of representative democracy and representative government, before the black-letter, positivistic approach began to undermine that approach, eventually leading to the "text and structure" limit of the implied freedom heralded just five years later in *Lange*.

Similarly, Kirk is not convinced that the desired clarity can be obtained by an overt reliance on the text and structure of the *Constitution*. He argues that in order to make sense of representative government it is necessary to look beyond the terms of the *Constitution*, regardless of what the judges who hold to this view claim:

> The necessary line-drawing is guided by the text of the *Constitution*, the content of the external doctrine and the usual factors determining the recognition of implications . . . the relevant question when it comes to such matters as recognizing or delimiting a guarantee of free political communication is not 'what do the terms and structure of the *Constitution* prohibit, authorize or require?' as the Court suggests, for this cannot provide the necessary answers. The question is more along these lines: 'what conditions and requirements are constitutionally entrenched as part of the system of representative democracy or government in the form, and to the extent, that it is adopted in the *Constitution*?'[258]

A Negative Freedom Not a Positive Right

The High Court announced that the implied freedom was negative in nature, in that it was a defense against a law which impacted the freedom, rather than a source of positive rights. In other words, it was a shield rather than a sword. The High Court merely announced this, without justification or explanation.

Subsequently, scholars have attempted to justify and explain the decision to cast the freedom in a negative way. Certainly, on one view it fits the United Kingdom common law liberal tradition, that a person has a right to do something, unless parliament takes it away with legislation.[259] On the other hand, the Australian *Constitution* does not completely embrace the traditional British common law position in relation to protection of rights, because it contains express protection of a limited number of human rights in a way that has no constitutional equivalent in the United Kingdom. In other cases in which rights have been implied, there is no mention of their being "negative" in nature.[260] In relation to the express rights, while in a sense they are negative, in that a person will complain about a breach of s80, s116, or s117 in order to have the legislation struck out as invalid, in other ways specific express sections can be a positive source of rights. For instance, s92 confers a positive right on an individual to move among and between states. Section 51(31) effectively confers a positive right on an individual to obtain fair compensation, in cases where their property is compulsorily acquired by the Commonwealth.

Thus, at the very least there is no inevitability about human rights at the constitutional level in Australia inevitably being seen as "negative" in nature, in the sense that the High Court has used it in order to constrain the implied freedom of political communication.

Adrienne Stone has attacked the High Court's use of "text and structure" to constrain the implied freedom. She opines that it was probably adopted by the High Court in the hope of constraining the implied freedom; however its utility in doing so is very limited, because the text of the *Constitution* is very sparse, inevitably leading to different judges taking different approaches. She says this is borne out by the divergent views that have been taken to an interpretation of the freedom.[261] She concludes "the text and structure method itself provides no principled limits on the category of political communication and little guidance for the resolution of particular cases."[262]

The Concept of "Necessary"

In seeking to explain the scope of possible constitutional implications drawn from the structure of the *Constitution*, Mason CJ in *ACTV* embraced the concept of "necessity":

> Where the implication is structural rather than textual it is no doubt correct to say that the term sought to be implied must be logically or practically necessary for the preservation of the integrity of that structure.[263]

This iteration of the scope of the freedom has inevitably generated significant controversy and academic literature, on the basis of what is "necessary" to preserve a system of representative government. Of course, legally conservative jurists use it to attack the implied freedom of political communication, pointing out the Australian democracy worked reasonably well prior to recognition of the implied freedom in 1992, so that it cannot be said that it is "necessary" to preserve the system of representative government that such an implied freedom exists.

A leading example is Jeffrey Goldsworthy, a long-term opponent of the High Court's implied freedom jurisprudence. He dismisses the notion that the implied freedom is necessary for the existence of representative democracy as involving "sheer effrontery."[264] He says that while the implied freedom might have improved Australian democracy, in no sense did its existence or survival depend on such recognition.

There is certainly some difficulty in articulating the precise basis upon which implications can or should be made from the *Constitution*. It is probably best assessed on a case by case basis. Perhaps it should be recognized that the contours of what is considered "necessary" can and should change over time. The High Court determines what is "necessary." It suggests some minimum content, though precisely what that content is admittedly hard to articulate. It might, for example, be that which enables the democratic system which the *Constitution* contemplates to operate functionally, in the sense that the people are able to make informed judgments between and among political options, and have access to the kind of information needed to do that, such that the people's views on particular matters can be known by their elected representatives in parliament when it comes to voting.

It should also be noted that the High Court has accepted the use of concepts of "necessity" in the current law relating to the implied freedom. While Mason CJ used the concept of "necessity" to justify the making of constitutional implications generally, in the specific context of the implied freedom of political communication, the now-accepted three stage test to determine the validity of a law challenged on the basis of the implied freedom embraces the concept of what is "necessary." The interference with the implied freedom must be necessary to achieve the legitimate objective of the law, and no reasonable alternatives that are less invasive of the implied freedom must be available.[265] A majority of the High Court evidently believes that the concept of "necessity" is workable in the context of implied freedoms. It does involve value judgments, about which minds might reasonably differ. So does much of constitutional law. Certainty is elusive. We must accept that this is the nature of constitutional law, and indeed our common law.

NOTES

1. Section 9 of the *Bill of Rights 1689* (Eng) does protect freedom of speech, but only in relation to parliament. This would be received law into Australia (*R v Smith; ex parte Cooper* (1992) 1 QdR 423), but is not entrenched and would be subject to override by inconsistent legislation.

2. Geoffrey Kennett, "Individual Rights, The High Court and the *Constitution*," *Melbourne University Law Review* 19 (1994): 582; Michael Chesterman, *Freedom of Speech in Australian Law: A Delicate Plant* (Aldershot, Ashgate, 2000), 7.

3. For example, the right to trial by jury applies only to Commonwealth offenses (s80), freedom of religion relates only to Commonwealth laws (s116), and the right to fair compensation when property is compulsorily acquired applies only when it is the federal government, rather than state governments, doing the acquiring (s51(31)).

4. *An Introduction to the Study of the Law of the Constitution* (Macmillan, London, 1959).

5. *Rowe v Electoral Commissioner* (2010) 243 CLR 1, 22 (French CJ), 69 (Hayne J), 106 (Crennan J), 129 (Kiefel J).

6. *Mulholland v Australian Electoral Commission* (2004) 220 CLR 181, 237: "the recurrent phrase in the Constitution 'until the Parliament otherwise provides' accommodates the notion that representative government is not a static institution and allows for its development by changes . . . some of these changes would not have been foreseen at the time of federation or, if foreseen by some, would not have been generally accepted for constitutional entrenchment" (Gummow and Hayne JJ); "no written constitution can provide for the detail essential to the conduct of a modern election that carries into effect all of the requirements of a representative democracy such as the Constitution establishes . . . representative government is also an evolving concept . . . the *Constitution* does not impose rigid limitations on the power of the Federal Parliament, in enacted electoral law, to respond to changing attitudes concerning the conduct of elections" (Kirby J, 255).

7. *Roach v Electoral Commissioners* (2007) 233 CLR 162, where Gleeson CJ concluded that ss7 and 24 of the *Constitution* had "come to be a constitutional protection of the right to vote." For the other members of the majority, Gummow Kirby and Crennan JJ, the question

was whether denial of the franchise was for a substantial reason. It would be so if the measure was reasonably appropriate and adapted to serve an end compatible with the constitutional system of representative government. They likened it to considerations of arbitrariness and proportionality (199). These justices apparently used the *Lange* test, traditionally applied to test whether laws were compatible with the implied freedom of communication found in the system of representative government reflected in ss7 and 24 of the *Constitution* and its mandate that parliament be chosen directly by the people, to the question of whether a law was compatible generally with ss7 and 24. Roach was not run on the basis that voting was a political communication, so denial of the franchise was a burden on freedom of communication. Rather, it was an alleged case of direct breach of the requirements of ss7 and 24, upon which the implied freedom was based.

8. *Rowe v Electoral Commissioner* (2010) 243 CLR 1 per French Gummow Crennan and Bell JJ; Hayne Heydon and Kiefel JJ dissenting.

9. Section 41 does, but it has been rendered effectively useless by the High Court's determination in *R v Pearson; Ex Parte Sipka* (1983) 152 CLR 254 that s41 refers only to citizens who were on the electoral roll as at the date of federation. Subsequently the High Court would discern an implied right to vote: *Roach v Electoral Commissioner* (2007) 233 CLR 162.

10. "If a State wishes to have a system of one party government, to abolish one or both of its legislative chambers or to deny significant sections of its population the right to vote, nothing in the *Constitution* implies that it cannot do it": *Theophanous v Herald and Weekly Times Ltd* (1994) 182 CLR 104, 201 (McHugh J, dissenting), although see now *Roach v Electoral Commission* (2007) 233 CLR 162, 174: "because the franchise is critical to representative government and lies at the centre of our concept of participation in the life of the community and of citizenship, disenfranchisement of any group of adult citizens on a basis that does not constitute a substantial reason for exclusion from such participation would not be consistent with choice by the people" (Gleeson CJ).

11. *McGinty v Western Australia* (1996) 186 CLR 140.

12. In classic understatement Kiefel J in *Rowe v Electoral Commissioner* (2010) 243 CLR 1, 130: "at the time of federation, democracy was not a perfectly formed concept."

13. An example of this reasoning appears in *Rowe v Electoral Commissioner* (2010) 243 CLR 1, 71–72 (Hayne J).

14. *United States v Carolene Products* 304 US 144, 152 (1938): "it is unnecessary to consider now whether legislation which restricts those political processes which can ordinarily be expected to bring about repeal of undesirable legislation, is to be subjected to more exacting judicial scrutiny . . . than are most other types of legislation" (Stone J, for the Court).

15. John Hart Ely, *Democracy and Distrust: A Theory of Judicial Review* (Harvard University Press, Cambridge, 1980).

16. Wojciech Sadurski, "Offending With Impunity: Racial Vilification and Freedom of Speech," *Sydney Law Review* 14 (1992): 178–179; Jeremy Kirk, "Constitutional Implications II: Doctrines of Equality and Democracy," *Melbourne University Law Review* 25 (2001): 54–55.

17. *Burns v Ransley* (1949) 79 CLR 101, 115 Dixon J referred to the "principles of the common law . . . governing the freedom of criticism and of expression."

18. *Australian Capital Television Pty Ltd v Commonwealth* (!992) 177 CLR 106, 182: "the Australian *Constitution* . . . does little to confer upon individuals by way of positive rights those basic freedoms which exist in a free and democratic society. They exist, not because they are provided for, but in the absence of any curtailment of them" (Dawson J, dissenting).

19. *The King v Sharkey* (1949) 79 CLR 121, 163 (Webb J), to like effect 148 (Latham CJ), referring to the United Kingdom common law of sedition.

20. Jeffrey Goldsworthy, "Implications in Language, Law and the *Constitution*," in Geoff Lindell ed, *Future Directions in Australian Constitutional Law* (Federation Press, Sydney, 1994).

21. One example appears in a speech by Cockburn at the Convention Debates. Wondering whether a colonial government had ever sought to deprive an individual of life, liberty, or property without due process, he thought an attempt to enshrine such rights expressly would be mocked by others, that they would comment something like "pretty things these states of

Australia; they have to be prevented by a provision in the *Constitution* from doing the grossest injustice": *Convention Debates* (1898) Melbourne, Vol. 1, p. 688; although see Jeremy Kirk, "Constitutional Implications II: Doctrines of Equality and Democracy," *Melbourne University Law Review* 25 (2001): 27: "it appears the framers never actually discussed whether to adopt a bill of rights."

22. *Monis v The Queen* (2013) 249 CLR 92, 183–184 (Heydon J), dismissing the implied freedom as unnecessary for representative government and a "noble and idealistic enterprise which has failed, is failing and will go on failing"; Tom Campbell and Stephen Crilly, "The Implied Freedom of Political Communication, Twenty Years On," *University of Queensland Law Journal* 30 (2011): 59; Nicholas Aroney, "Towards the Best Explanation of the Constitution: Text, Structure, History and Principle in *Roach v Electoral Commissioner*," *University of Queensland Law Journal* 30 (2011): 145; Grant Huscroft, "Romance, Realism and the Legitimacy of Implied Rights," *University of Queensland Law Journal* 30 (2011): 35; George Winterton, "Extra-Constitutional Notions in Australian Constitutional Law," *Federal Law Review* 16 (1986): 223.

23. Dan Meagher, "What is 'Political Communication'? The Rationale and Scope of the Implied Freedom of Political Communication," (2004) 28 *Melbourne University Law Review* 28 (2004): 454–456.

24. Jeffrey Goldsworthy, "Implications in Language, Law and the *Constitution*," in Geoff Lindell ed., *Future Directions in Australian Constitutional Law* (Federation Press, Sydney, 1994).

25. See for discussion Patrick Emerton, "Political Freedoms and Entitlements in the Australian *Constitution*—An Example of Referential Intentions Yielding Unintended Legal Consequences," *Federal Law Review* 38 (2010): 199–200.

26. *New South Wales v Commonwealth* (2005) 229 CLR 1, 97 (Gleeson CJ Gummow Hayne Heydon and Crennan JJ).

27. Greg Craven, "Original Intent and the Australian *Constitution*—Coming Soon to a Court Near You?' *Public Law Review* 1 (1990): 178 claims it is: "the duty of the courts to give effect to the intentions of the Founders, as those intentions were ultimately backed by the last authentic expression of the will of the Australian people on the subject of their constitutional dispositions"; Jeffrey Goldsworthy, "Originalism in Constitutional Interpretation," *Federal Law Review* 25 (1997): 1.

28. Stephen Donaghue, "The Clamour of Silent Constitutional Principles," *Federal Law Review* 24 (1996): 151–154. Donaghue says that one of the practical consequences of the High Court finding that sovereignty resided in the Australian people was that the intention of the founding fathers became irrelevant to constitutional interpretation: "There is no need to focus upon what the framers thought the *Constitution* meant, for their intentions are not relevant to the reasons the *Constitution* binds present generations" (146).

29. *Annotated Constitution of the Australian Commonwealth* (Angus and Robertson, Sydney, 1901), 958.

30. *R v Smithers; Ex Parte Benson* (1912) 16 CLR 99, 108–109 (Griffith CJ) and 109 (Barton J).

31. *West v Commissioner of Taxation* (NSW) (1937) 56 CLR 657, 681; see also Evatt J (687)

32. *Melbourne Corporation v Commonwealth* (1947) 74 CLR 31.

33. *Kable v Director of Public Prosecutions* (NSW) (1996) 189 CLR 51; Anthony Gray *Criminal Due Process and Chapter III of the Australian Constitution* (2016).

34. *Davis v Commonwealth* (1988) 166 CLR 79.

35. *Cole v Whitfield* (1988) 165 CLR 360, 385–391.

36. *New South Wales v Commonwealth* (*WorkChoices Case*) (2006) 229 CLR 1, 97: "to pursue the identification of what is said to be the framers' intention, much more often than not, is to pursue a mirage. It is a mirage because the inquiry assumes that it is both possible and useful to attempt to work out a single collective view about what now is a disputed question of power, but then was not in the minds of those who contributed to the debates . . . the answer to the question is not to be found in attempting to attribute some collective subjective intention to

all or any of those who participated in the Convention Debates" (Gleeson CJ Gummow Hayne Heydon and Crennan JJ).

37. (1994) 182 CLR 104, 128 (Mason CJ Toohey and Gaudron JJ): "what the framers of the *Constitution* thought, but did not provide in the *Constitution*, 100 years ago is hardly a sure guide in the very different circumstances which prevail today"; "to construe the Constitution on the basis that the "dead hands" of those who framed it reached from their graves to negate or constrict the natural implications of its express provisions or fundamental doctrines would deprive what was intended to be a living instrument of its vitality and its adaptability to serve succeeding generations" (Deane J, 171).

38. This was noted by Dixon J in *Australian National Airways Pty Ltd v Commonwealth* (1945) 71 CLR 29: "it is a *Constitution* we are interpreting, an instrument of government meant to endure and conferring powers expressed in general propositions wide enough to be capable of flexible application to changing circumstances"; Marshall CJ in *McCullough v Maryland* 17 US 316, 407 (1819): "we must never forget that it is a *Constitution* we are expounding."

39. George Williams, *Human Rights Under the Australian Constitution* (Oxford University Press, Melbourne, 1999) 25; *Convention Debates* (1898) Melbourne 665–666, 669 and 686–687; John Williams, "Race, Citizenship and the Formation of the Australian *Constitution*: Andrew Inglis Clark and the 'Fourteenth Amendment,'" *Australian Journal of Politics and History* 42 (1996): 110.

40. Nicholas Aroney, "A Seductive Plausibility: Freedom of Speech in the Constitution," *University of Queensland Law Journal* 18 (1995): 249; Andrew Fraser, "False Hopes, Implied Rights and Popular Sovereignty in the Australian *Constitution*," *Sydney Law Review* 16 (1994): 213; H P Lee, "The Australian High Court and Implied Fundamental Guarantees," *Public Law* [1993]: 606.

41. Anthony Gray, "Freedom of Association in the Australian Constitution and the Crime of Consorting," *University of Tasmania Law Review* 32(2)(2013): 149.

42. *Union Steamship Co of Australia v King* (1988) 166 CLR 1.

43. *Australian Communist Party v Commonwealth* (1951) 83 CLR 1; *Davis v Commonwealth* (1988) 166 CLR 79, 100 (Mason CJ Deane and Gaudron JJ); Geoffrey Kennett, "Individual Rights, The High Court and the *Constitution*," *Melbourne University Law Review* 19 (1994): 597.

44. *Nationwide News Pty Ltd v Wills* (1992) 177 CLR 1.

45. *Potter v Minahan* (1908) 7 CLR 277, 304; see also *Melbourne Corporation v Barry* (1922) 31 CLR 174, 206 (Higgins J) ("if a statute is capable of being interpreted without supposing that it interferes with the common law right, it should be so interpreted").

46. (1922) 31 CLR 174 (Isaacs and Higgins JJ; Knox CJ dissenting).

47. (1922) 31 CLR 174.

48. "No one desiring to take part in a procession has any opportunity by way of right of knowing what matters the Council will consider fatal" (Isaacs J, 198).

49. "Common justice . . . dictates that except where the legislature has clearly empowered a council to make its own unfettered and unregulated will . . . the test of legality, a council having the power . . . should state its requirements . . . as explicitly as circumstances reasonably permit. Otherwise, how are individuals to attempt to conform to law without a total surrender of their right innocently and unaggressively to use the King's highway in company on occasions that frequently represent great and important national, political, social, religious or industrial movements or opinions? It would require very explicit words in an Act of Parliament to induce me to believe the Legislature, in the name of regulation, contemplated such unregulated authority" (Isaacs J, 197).

50. (1951) 83 CLR 1.

51. Dixon McTiernan, Williams Webb Fullagar, and Kitto JJ; Latham CJ dissenting).

52. 185–187 (Dixon J), 258 (Fullagar J), 282–283 (Kitto J).

53. (1915) 20 CLR 299.

54. *Burns v Ransley* (1949) 79 CLR 101.

55. 110; similarly Rich J (111): "these sections do not purport to prevent or punish mere criticism of a political nature but are intended to defend the existing regime against its overthrow or suppression."

56. 116. All four members of the Court (Latham CJ, Rich Dixon, and McTiernan JJ) confirmed the Commonwealth had constitutional power to legislate with respect to sedition.
57. *The King v Sharkey* (1949) 79 CLR 121.
58. 148; similarly 158 (Dixon J) and 163 (where Webb J said that in order to protect a government against violent overthrow, it might be necessary to prevent the incitement of feelings that might lead to that).
59. 148.
60. *Australian Communist Party v Commonwealth* (1951) 83 CLR 1.
61. 187–188.
62. 188.
63. 188.
64. 192.
65. 192.
66. (1915) 20 CLR 299.
67. 194–195 (Dixon J), 282 (Kitto J).
68. 206.
69. 227.
70. 268.
71. *R v Dunbabin; Ex Parte Williams* (1935) 53 CLR 434.
72. 442 (Rich J, with whom Dixon Evatt and McTiernan JJ agreed).
73. (1983) 152 CLR 238.
74. 243 (Gibbs CJ Mason Wilson and Brennan JJ. Murphy J dissented, concluding the majority's approach was an oppressive limitation on free speech (248).
75. *Miller v TCN Channel Nine Pty Ltd* (1986) 161 CLR 556, 581–582 (dissenting in the result).
76. *Australian Communist Party v Commonwealth* (1951) 83 CLR 1, 262 where Fullagar J described the judicial review principle of *Marbury v Madison* (1803) 5 US (1 Cranch) 137 as "axiomatic."
77. The three criteria Dicey gave were: (a) there was no law that parliament could not change; (b) there was no real distinction between laws that were fundamental and those that were not; and (c) no person or body could void legislation for constitutional reasons: Albert Vere Dicey, *An Introduction to the Study of the Law of the Constitution* (Macmillan, London, 1959), 37–39. See Anthony Gray, *Criminal Due Process and Chapter III of the Australian Constitution* (Federation Press, Sydney, 2016), 6–7: "it is clear, from the words of the progenitor of the theory of parliamentary sovereignty, that the concept never described the Commonwealth Parliament or those of the State parliaments in Australia."
78. Jeremy Kirk, "Constitutional Implications (II): Doctrines of Equality and Democracy," *Melbourne University Law Review* 25 (2001): 54: "Australia inherited the doctrine of parliamentary supremacy from Britain"; Julie Taylor, "Human Rights Protection in Australia: Interpretative Provisions and Parliamentary Supremacy," *Federal Law Review* 32 (2004): 57; *Kartinyeri v Commonwealth* (1998) 195 CLR 337, 355 (Brennan CJ and McHugh J).
79. "The (Australian) *Constitution* displaced, or rendered inapplicable, the English common law doctrine of the unqualified supremacy of the legislature": *Lange v Australian Broadcasting Corporation* (1997) 189 CLR 520, 564 (all members of the Court).
80. *Australian Capital Television Pty Ltd v Commonwealth* (1992) 177 CLR 106, 138 (Mason CJ); *Theophanous v Herald and Weekly Times Ltd* (1994) 182 CLR 104, 171 (Deane J).
81. James Weinstein, "Extreme Speech, Public Order and Democracy: Lessons from The Masses," in Ivan Hare and James Weinstein, *Extreme Speech and Democracy* (Oxford University Press, New York, 2009), 26.
82. *Australian Capital Television Pty Ltd v Commonwealth* (1992) 177 CLR 106.
83. (1947) 74 CLR 31.
84. 135. Jeffrey Goldsworthy criticizes this position, arguing that judicially enforceable freedom of political communication is demonstrably not "necessary" in order that representative government or representative democracy function. This is clear because it was not recognized by the Australian High Court until 1992, yet no-one would argue that Australia did not have a system of representative government until then: "Constitutional Implications and Free-

dom of Speech: A Reply to Stephen Donaghue," *Monash University Law Review* 23 (1997): 372; Jeffrey Goldsworthy, "Constitutional Implications Revisited," *University of Queensland Law Journal* 30 (2011): 28: "the sheer effrontery of the claim that a constitutional right to freedom of political speech is necessary for the existence of representative democracy should be emphasised." He says all that can be said is that our system of representative government and/or representative democracy has been improved by the Court's recognition of the implied freedom, not that its very existence or survival depended on it.

85. 135–136.

86. 138.

87. 139.

88. (1964) 376 US 254.

89. (1979) 443 US 97.

90. Subsequently the freedom was applied to discussion of state political matters, and a majority of the court found that state constitutions also contained an implicit freedom of political communication: *Stephens v West Australian Newspapers Ltd* (1994) 182 CLR 211.

91. 143.

92. 143–144.

93. 145.

94. 159 (Brennan J), 169 (Deane and Toohey JJ), 231 (McHugh J)

95. 168 (Deane and Gaudron JJ); 210 (Gaudron J), 228 (McHugh J).

96. 169 (Deane and Toohey JJ), 216 (Gaudron J).

97. 169 (Deane and Toohey JJ).

98. 174 (Deane and Toohey JJ).

99. 169 (Deane and Toohey JJ).

100. 424 US 1 (1976).

101. 212 (Gaudron J).

102. 141 (Mason CJ).

103. *Nationwide News Pty Ltd v Wills* (1992) 177 CLR 1.

104. 52–53.

105. 72.

106. 74–75.

107. 75.

108. *Nationwide News Pty Ltd v Wills* (1992) 177 CLR 1, 95 (Gaudron J).

109. *Australian Capital Television Pty Ltd v Commonwealth* (1992) 177 CLR 106, 143–144 (Mason CJ) and 157 (Brennan J). Similarly Deane and Toohey JJ referred to laws that did not go beyond what was reasonably necessary to achieve the legitimate objective.

110. (1994) 182 CLR 104.

111. "the law of defamation . . . must conform to the implication of freedom" (136, Mason CJ Toohey and Gaudron JJ); Deane J (178); Brennan Dawson and McHugh JJ dissenting.

112. 122 (Mason CJ Toohey and Gaudron JJ).

113. 124 (Mason CJ Toohey and Gaudron JJ), citing Barendt, *Freedom of Speech* (1985) 132.

114. Alexander Meiklejohn, *Political Freedom: The Constitutional Powers of the People* (Oxford University Press, New York, 1960), 42.

115. 125–126.

116. 148.

117. 130; to like effect Deane J (166).

118. *R v Smithers; Ex Parte Benson* (1912) 16 CLR 99, 108–109 (Griffith CJ) and 109 (Barton J).

119. John Quick and Robert Garran, *Annotated Constitution of the Australian Commonwealth* (Angus and Robertson, Sydney, 1901), 958.

120. 128 (Mason CJ Toohey and Gaudron): "what the framers of the *Constitution* thought, but did not provide in the Constitution, 100 years ago, is hardly a sure guide in the very different circumstances which prevail today"; "to construe the Constitution on the basis that the dead hands of those who framed it reached from their graves to negate or constrict the natural implications of its express provisions or fundamental doctrines would deprive what was in-

tended to be a living instrument of its vitality and its adaptability to serve succeeding generations" (171, Deane J).

121. 188.

122. Anthony Gray, "The Protection of Voting Equality in Australia," *Federal Law Review* 44(3)(2016): 557.

123. (1996) 186 CLR 140.

124. 170–171 (Brennan CJ), 185 (Dawson J), 232 (McHugh J).

125. "A general principle of equal electorates is a minimal requirement for a representative democracy. In that event the principle is part of the Australian Constitution, even if not expressed in any provision. It derives from s24 but more fundamentally from the very structure of the system of government enshrined in the *Constitution*" (203, Toohey J); "persons elected under a system involving significant disparity in voting value could not, in my view, now be described as chosen by the people (in s24)" (222, Gaudron J).

126. (1997) 189 CLR 520.

127. 556 (Brennan CJ Dawson Toohey Gaudron McHugh Gummow and Kirby JJ).

128. 560.

129. 563–564.

130. 564 (Brennan CJ Dawson Toohey Gaudron McHugh Gummow and Kirby JJ).

131. *Levy v Victoria* (1997) 189 CLR 579.

132. 614–615 (Toohey and Gummow JJ).

133. (2004) 220 CLR 1.

134. 50 (McHugh J), 78 (Gummow and Hayne JJ) and 82 (Kirby J).

135. 45 (McHugh J) made this express, the others implicitly agreed.

136. 87.

137. 45.

138. 91.

139. 91.

140. 126.

141. 113–114: "insulting or abusive words will no doubt generate heat, but it is equally unlikely that they will . . . throw light on (anything, let alone) government or political matters."

142. *Hogan v Hinch* (2011) 243 CLR 506, 555 (Gummow Hayne Heydon Crennan Kiefel and Bell JJ).

143. Unions NSW (2013) 252 CLR 530.

144. *Mulholland v Australian Electoral Commission* (2004) 220 CLR 181.

145. McHugh J (223), Gummow and Hayne (247–248), Callinan J (298) and Heydon J (303).

146. Gleeson CJ (200) and Kirby J (279).

147. (2011) 243 CLR 506, 543.

148. 544.

149. (2011) 243 CLR 506, 555–556 (Gummow Hayne Heydon Crennan Kiefel and Bell JJ).

150. 131.

151. 133–134; Heydon J agreed with the judgment of French CJ (178).

152. 139.

153. 146.

154. 146.

155. 214.

156. 214.

157. 214–215.

158. 215.

159. 215.

160. *Attorney-General (SA) v Corporation of the City of Adelaide* (2013) 249 CLR 1.

161. (2013) 252 CLR 530.

162. 549; to like effect Keane J (583).

163. 544–545 (French CJ Hayne Crennan Kiefel and Bell JJ).

164. 557–558; to like effect Keane J (580).

165. 560–561.

166. (2015) 257 CLR 178. A similar decision was reached in *Spence v Queensland* [2019] HCA 15.

167. French CJ Kiefel Bell Gageler Keane Nettle and Gordon JJ.

168. French CJ Kiefel Bell Gageler Keane and Gordon JJ; Nettle J dissenting.

169. Adrienne Stone, "The Limits of Constitutional Text and Structure: Standards of Review and the Freedom of Political Communication," *Melbourne University Law Review* 23 (1999): 692. Stone suggests use of the proportionality doctrine will, in time, lead to adoption of a rules-based approach (704). Sometimes there is evidence of the use of categories in the Australian case law, for instance, the distinction between content-based restrictions and content-neutral restrictions (*Hogan v Hinch* (2011) 243 CLR 506), use of the "fighting words"' category of speech by some members of the court in *Coleman v Power* (2004) 220 CLR 1, and the occasional reference to the place at which the communication occurs as being relevant to constitutionality (*Levy v Victoria* (1997) 189 CLR 579, 642 (Kirby J)).

170. Gageler J 235–236; Gordon J 282. Nettle J expressly left the matter open, but did not apply a proportionality analysis to resolved the matters at hand.

171. Compare Gageler J: "the plaintiffs eschew any argument that the payment of money . . . could itself be political communication. They are right to do so. Whether or not in might in another context be capable of being characterised as a form of expression, mere payment of money can hardly be regarded as form of communication. The mere fact of making a political donation communicates nothing" (241) (Gordon J to like effect at 289) with Nettle J: "in the practical reality of the political system, the ability of a corporation to make a political donation is likely to be considered as important a method as any of expressing ideas about politics and government. As the Supreme Court of the United States recognised in *Buckley v Valeo*, the fact of a political contribution, as opposed to its amount, serves as a general expression of support for a candidate and his or her views" (263).

172. [2017] HCA 43.

173. Kiefel CJ Bell Gageler Keane and Nettle JJ; Gordon and Edelman JJ dissenting.

174. [95].

175. [123].

176. [134].

177. [136].

178. [146].

179. [264].

180. [286].

181. [289].

182. [292].

183. [293].

184. [200].

185. [225]–[230].

186. [188].

187. [420].

188. [411].

189. [427]–[436].

190. [561].

191. [567].

192. [2019] HCA 11.

193. (1997) 190 CLR 1.

194. Gaudron J (115–116); Toohey J (91).

195. Brennan CJ (45); Dawson J (70); McHugh J (142); and Gummow J (157). While McHugh rejected an argument that there was an implication in the Constitution of a right to movement and association "for political, cultural and familial purposes," he did accept a freedom to associate with other persons for the purposes of the system of government, though the precise scope of this is not entirely clear.

196. (2004) 220 CLR 181, 225 (McHugh J) and 277 (Kirby J).

197. 234, with whom Heydon J agreed (306).

198. (2011) 243 CLR 181, 230 (Gummow Hayne Crennan and Bell JJ).

199. (2014) 254 CLR 508.

200. This view has been substantially criticized: Jeremy Kirk, "Constitutional Implications from Representative Democracy," (1995) 23 *Federal Law Review* 23 (1995): 53–56.

201. See *Criminal Code Act 1913* (WA) s 77—conduct intended to incite racial animosity, and ss78–80, *Racial and Religious Tolerance Act* 2001 (Vic) s7+8; *Summary Offences Act* 1988 (NSW) s4A; *Summary Offences Act* 1966 (Vic) s17; *Summary Offences Act* 2005 (Qld) s56(3).

202. Section 24AA makes it an offense to do an act or thing with intent to overthrow the Australian *Constitution* by revolution or sabotage, or to overthrow the government by force or violence (max life jail term).

203. Section 42 of the *Border Force Act 2015* (Cth) makes it an offense for an immigration or border force worker to disclose information likely to prejudice Australia's defense and security, prejudice the investigation of a possible breach, likely to affect protection of public health or the health and wellbeing of individuals, or likely to cause "competitive detriment" to a person (max 2 year jail term).

204. *Foreign Influence Transparency Scheme Act 2017* (Cth).

205. *Criminal Code 1899* (Qld) s 52; *Criminal Code Act 1913* (WA) s 52; *Criminal Code Act 1924* (Tas) s 67 (see also offenses of treason (s59), inciting treasonous conduct (s62), and libelling a foreign power (s68); *Crimes Act 1900* (NSW) s 12 ("compassing" or "imagining" disposition of the sovereign); *Criminal Law Consolidation Act 1935* (SA) s 7 ("compassing" or "imagining" disposition of the sovereign).

206. *Criminal Code 1899* (Qld) s 228; *Classification of Computer Games and Images Act* 1995 (Qld) s 24; *Classification of Publications Act 1991* (Qld) s 13; *Criminal Code Act 1913* (WA) s 220, *Classification (Publications, Films and Computer Games) Enforcement Act 1996* (WA); *Criminal Code Act 1924* (Tas) child exploitation material (s130C) and obscene publications (s138); Crimes Act 1958 (Vic) s51G (child exploitation material); *Crimes Act 1900* (NSW) s91H (child abuse material) and s91P and Q (pornography).

207. *Summary Offences Act 2005* (Qld) s 6.

208. Section 119 *Criminal Code Act 1924* (Tas).

209. George Williams, "Sounding the Core of Representative Democracy: Implied Freedoms and Electoral Reform," *Melbourne University Law Review* 20 (1996): 860: "a question still before the High Court is whether the ambit of political discussion can be pared back to less than a general freedom of speech without resorting to arbitrary distinctions."

210. *Theophanous v Herald and Weekly Times Ltd* (1994) 182 CLR 104, 124 (Mason CJ Toohey and Gaudron JJ) (quoting Eric Barendt, *Freedom of Speech* (1985) 152). In *Cunliffe v Commonwealth* (1994) 182 CLR 272 a majority of the High Court found that legal practitioners consulting with clients with respect to immigration legal advice were involved in political communication (1994) 182 CLR 272, 298–299 (Mason CJ), 336 (Deane J), 379–380 (Toohey J), and 387 (Gaudron J).

211. Jeremy Kirk, "Constitutional Implications from Representative Democracy," *Federal Law Review* 23 (1995): 53; Tom Campbell and Stephen Crilly, "The Implied Freedom of Political Communication, Twenty Years On," *University of Queensland Law Journal* 30 (2011): 60: "twenty years on, there is little progress in identifying what counts as 'political communication' . . . the High Court has consistently dodged this question, perhaps because there is no way to answer it from the Constitution alone, so that addressing it directly would bring their political function squarely into the open."

212. (2011) 243 CLR 506, 544.

213. "It is arguable that . . . artistic free speech . . . may enhance the democratic process to some small extent. But such matters are not sufficiently central to the operation of the democratic process to justify the judicial review of laws in such areas"': Jeremy Kirk, "Constitutional Implications from Representative Democracy," *Federal Law Review* 23 (1995): 76.

214. Dan Meagher, "What is Political Communication—The Rationale and Scope of the Implied Freedom of Political Communication," *Melbourne University Law Review* 28 (2004): 465: "if the argument is taken to its logical conclusion, every communicative act could be political . . . the implied freedom becomes a comprehensive and autonomous guarantee or free

communication . . . this conception cannot be supported by either the textual origins and limited purpose of the implied freedom."

215. 467–468.

216. Adrienne Stone, "Rights, Personal Rights and Freedoms: The Nature of the Freedom of Political Communication," *Melbourne University Law Review* 25 (2001): 383–390.

217. (1994) 182 CLR 104.

218. 124.

219. Alexander Meiklejohn, "The *First Amendment* is an Absolute," [1961] *Supreme Court Review* [1961]: 255, arguing that the *First Amendment* had to be interpreted so as to protect the process by which the voter "acquire(d) the intelligence, integrity, sensitivity and generous devotion to the general welfare that, in theory, casting a ballot is assumed to express"; and that "people do need novels and dramas and paintings and poems, because they will be called upon to vote" (263).

220. Adrienne Stone, "Rights, Personal Rights and Freedoms: The Nature of the Freedom of Political Communication," *Melbourne University Law Review* 25 (2001): 390.

221. *Connick v Myers* 461 US 138 (1983).

222. *New York Times Co v Sullivan* 376 US 254 (1964).

223. Cynthia Estlund, "Speech on Matters of Public Concern: The Perils of an Emerging *First Amendment* Category," *George Washington Law Review* 59 (1990): 35–36: "the (Supreme) Court use(s) the term 'political' almost interchangeably with the 'public issue' or 'public concern' formulation."

224. Toni Massaro, "Significant Silences: Freedom of Speech in the Public Sector Workplace," *Southern California Law Review* 61 (1987): 4; Michael Wells, "Section 1983, the *First Amendment*, and Public Employee Speech: Shaping the Right to Fit the Remedy (and Vice Versa)," *Georgia Law Review* 35 (2001): 952: "*Pickering* offers little guidance as to what subject matter falls within the public concern category"; Cynthia Lee, "Freedom of Speech in the Public Workplace: A Comment on the Public Concern Requirement," *California Law Review* 76 (1988): 1110; D Gordon Smith, "Beyond "Public Concern": New Free Speech Standards for Public Employees," *University of Chicago Law Review* 57 (1990): 258: "no-one knows what 'public concern' is."

225. (1997) 190 CLR 1, 126–127.

226. *South Australia v Totani* (2010) 242 CLR 1; *Wainohu v New South Wales* (2011) 243 CLR 181.

227. *Tajjour v New South Wales* (2014) 254 CLR 508.

228. *Wainohu v New South Wales* (2011) 243 CLR 181, 230 (Gummow Hayne Crennan and Bell JJ).

229. Jeremy Kirk, "Constitutional Implications From Representative Democracy," *Federal Law Review* 23 (1995): 56.

230. "It is difficult to see how some version of a freedom to associate could not be implied given the approach of the majority in *McGinty* and the existence of a freedom of political discussion. The ability to associate for political purposes is obviously a cornerstone of representative government in Australia. How could people 'directly choose' their representatives if denied the ability to form political associations and to collectively seek political power? The ability to choose must entail the ability to be chosen and to seek power. A freedom to associate for political purposes is likely to be a basic element of the system of representative government established by the *Constitution*": "Sounding the Core of Representative Democracy: Implied Freedoms and Electoral Reform," *Melbourne University Law Review* 20 (1996): 861.

231. Joo-Cheong Tham, "Possible Constitutional Objections to the Powers to Ban Terrorist Organisations," *University of New South Wales Law Journal* 27 (2004): 495: "the question whether a freedom of political association should be implied from the *Constitution* has yet to be settled by the High Court. Such an implication can be plausibly argued on the basis it arises independently from the constitutionally prescribed system of representative democracy."

232. Anthony Gray, "Freedom of Association in the Australian Constitution and the Crime of Consorting," *University of Tasmania Law Review* 32(2)(2013): 149.

233. Jeremy Kirk, "Constitutional Implications from Representative Democracy," *Federal Law Review* 23 (1995): 56.

234. "The High Court has not expressly relied on any political or philosophical theory of freedom of speech": Michael Chesterman, *Freedom of Speech in Australia: A Delicate Plant* (Aldershot, Ashgate, 2000), 19; Deborah Cass, "Through the Looking Glass: The High Court of Australia and the Right to Political Speech," in Tom Campbell and Wojciech Sadurski, *Freedom of Communication* (Aldershot, England, 1994), 188: "no attempt is made (by the High Court) to elucidate the type of democracy envisaged under this particular constitutional protection."

235. *Theophanous v Herald and Weekly Times Ltd* (1994) 182 CLR 104, 124 (Mason CJ Toohey and Gaudron JJ).

236. *Lange v Australian Broadcasting Corporation* (1997) 189 CLR 520, 561 stating that the implied freedom of political communication "is limited to what is necessary for the effective operation of that system of representative and responsible government provided for by the *Constitution*" (Brennan CJ Dawson Toohey Gaudron McHugh Gummow and Kirby JJ).

237. Adrienne Stone, "Freedom of Political Communication, the *Constitution* and the Common Law," *Federal Law Review* 26 (1998): 235.

238. Anthony Gray, "The *First Amendment* to the United States *Constitution* and the Implied Freedom of Political Communication in the Australian *Constitution*," *Common Law World Review* 49 (2019) (forthcoming).

239. William Buss, "Constitutional Words About Words: Protected Speech and Fighting Words Under the Australian and American Constitutions," *Transnational Law and Contemporary Problems* 15 (2006): 493: "the High Court adopted the reasoning of Alexander Meiklejohn, the influential American political philosopher (but) . . . the High Court did not cite Meiklejohn in its first two ground-breaking cases (regarding the implied freedom of political communication)." Meagher points out there is some connection between the High Court's implied freedom of political communication case law and the theory of Meiklejohn. However, the fit is not a precise one. Meiklejohn's theory would not see the freedom as a negative freedom; it would see it as a positive right. Meagher says the purpose of the implied freedom in Australia is much more limited than the First Amendment's purpose, thus Meiklejohn's theory is inapt to describe the Australian position: Dan Meagher, "What is Political Communication—The Rationale and Scope of the Implied Freedom of Political Communication," *Melbourne University Law Review* 28 (2004): 450.

240. For an alternative argument that it is the end of personal autonomy that justifies the Australian freedom of political communication see Adrienne Stone, "Rights, Personal Rights and Freedoms: The Nature of the Freedom of Political Communication," *Melbourne University Law Review* 25 (2001): 374.

241. Adrienne Stone, "Rights, Personal Rights and Freedoms: The Nature of the Freedom of Political Communication," *Melbourne University Law Review* 25 (2001): 391.

242. "Making Sense of Representative Democracy and the Implied Freedom of Political Communication in the High Court of Australia," *Griffith Law Review* 7 (1998): 97. Chesterman says the freedom of political communication cases have veered from a participatory version of democracy to a more institutional approach, but without clear articulation that this was occurring, or why: *Freedom of Speech in Australia: A Delicate Plant* (Aldershot, Ashgate, 2000), 31.

243. 29.

244. *Mulholland v Australian Electoral Commission* (2004) 220 CLR 181, 189–190 (Gleeson CJ), 206 (McHugh J), 237 (Gummow and Hayne JJ) and 254 (Kirby J).

245. *Lange v Australian Broadcasting Corporation* (1997) 189 CLR 520, 567 (Brennan CJ Dawson Toohey Gaudron McHugh Gummow and Kirby JJ).

246. Adrienne Stone believes so: "Post's argument (in favour of an autonomy rationale for freedom of speech) is exactly the kind of argument that the High Court intended to exclude by its adoption of the text and structure interpretive method,": "Rights, Personal Rights and Freedoms: The Nature of the Freedom of Political Communication," *Melbourne University Law Review* 25 (2001): 395.

247. *McGinty v Western Australia* (1996) 186 CLR 140, 232 (McHugh J).

248. Adrienne Stone, "The Limits of Constitutional Text and Structure: Standards of Review and the Freedom of Political Communication," *Melbourne University Law Review* 23 (1999): 696.

249. *Victoria v Commonwealth* (1970) 122 CLR 353, 402. There are critics. Referring to Windeyer J's view, Neil Douglas, "Freedom of Expression Under the Australian *Constitution*," *University of New South Wales Law Journal* 16 (1993): 344 referred to it as "nonsense."

250. (1996) 186 CLR 140, 168; see also *Kruger v Commonwealth* (1997) 190 CLR 520, 567 (Gummow J).

251. For example, Tom Campbell, "Democracy, Human Rights and Positive Law," (1994) 16 *Sydney Law Review* 16 (1994): 197: "many judges have ceased even to pretend that they are not making law."

252. Lord Reid, "The Judge as a Lawmaker," *Journal of the Society of Public Teachers of Law* 12 (1972): 25–26: "those with a taste for fairy tales seem to have thought that in some Aladdin's cave there is hidden the common law in all its splendour and that on a judge's appointment there descends on him (sic) knowledge of the magic words 'open sesame.' Bad decisions are given when the judges muddle their password and the wrong doors open. But we do not believe in fairy tales any more."

253. Michael McHugh, "The Law-Making Function of the Judicial Process—Part I," *Australian Law Journal* 62 (1988): 17: "judging is not always value-free . . . only in comparatively recent times have the judges . . . acknowledged their law-making function and the influence of values outside the legal system." My reading of the work of Tom Campbell suggests he disagrees with the notion that judges make (or should make) law, evidenced by his comment that "many judges have ceased even to pretend that they are not making law": "Democracy, Human Rights and Positive Law," (1994) 16 *Sydney Law Review* 16 (1994): 197 and discussing the judges' "prime role of administering rules chosen for them in an impartial and non-political manner" (210).

254. James Allan, "The Three Rs of Recent Australian Judicial Activism: Roach, Rowe and (No) 'Riginalism,'" *Melbourne University Law Review* 36(2) (2012): 743.

255. Nicholas Aroney, "Towards the Best Explanation of the *Constitution*: Text, Structure, History and Principle in *Roach v Electoral Commissioner*," *University of Queensland Law Journal* 30 (2011): 156: "the bare text and structure of the *Constitution* provides little guidance about the substantive issues to which the application of the implied freedom of political communication unavoidably gives rise . . . the Court's continued application of an implied freedom of political communication remain(s) illegitimate because it is not properly grounded in the text and structure of the *Constitution*, and problematic because 'text and structure' does not provide sufficient conceptual resources when it comes to applying the implied constitutional guarantee to contested cases."

256. Jeffrey Goldsworthy, "Constitutional Implications Revisited," *University of Queensland Law Journal* 30 (2011): 20: "instead of asking whether the alleged implication is practically necessary for the instrument to operate effectively, we should ask whether or not it is so obvious as not to be reasonably deniable."

257. Michael Stokes, "Constitutional Commitments Not Original Intentions: Interpretation in the Freedom of Speech Cases," *Sydney Law Review* 16 (1994): 250.

258. Jeremy Kirk, "Constitutional Implications II: Doctrines of Equality and Democracy," *Melbourne University Law Review* 25 (2001): 52.

259. Adrienne Stone, "Rights, Personal Rights and Freedoms: The Nature of the Implied Freedom of Political Communication," *Melbourne University Law Review* 25 (2001): 401–402.

260. For example, in *R v Smithers; Ex Parte Benson* (1912) 16 CLR 99, Griffith CJ referred to various implied rights, including the right to come to the seat of government, the right to access government-controlled seaports and the right to access courts of justice (108), with whom Barton J agreed (109). Neither Griffith CJ nor Barton J referred to these rights as being negative in nature, as opposed to positive. In *Theophanous v Herald and Weekly Times Ltd* (1994) 182 CLR 104 Deane J (170) refers to many implicit rights in the *Constitution* identified by founding fathers Quick and Garran. Again, there is no mention of these rights being negative in nature. They are referred to as "rights" rather than "freedoms." In subsequent discourse on the implied "freedom" of political communication, the High Court has conspicuously referred to it as a freedom rather than a right in order to emphasise its supposedly negative nature. On that basis, one wonders what they make of earlier iterations of rights implicit in the *Constitution* espoused by founding fathers, some of whom became members of the High Court.

261. Adrienne Stone, "The Limits of Constitutional Text and Structure Revisited," *University of New South Wales Law Journal* 28 (2005): 845.
262. 849.
263. (1992) 177 CLR 106, 135; to like effect *McGinty v Western Australia* (1996) 186 CLR 140, 231 (McHugh J).
264. "Constitutional Implications Revisited," *University of Queensland Law Journal* 30 (2011): 28.
265. In turn, some have argued that it is illegitimate for the High Court to determine the constitutional validity of a law on the basis that alternatives less invasive of constitutional freedoms are available: *Levy v Victoria* (1997) 189 CLR 579, 598 (Brennan CJ); Dan Meagher, "The Brennan Conception of the Implied Freedom: Theory, Proportionality and Deference," *University of Queensland Law Journal* 30 (2011): 128.

Chapter Four

Canadian Case Law

The passage of the *Canadian Charter of Rights and Freedoms* in 1982, including the enshrining of freedom of expression and freedom of the press in s2(b) of the *Charter*, fundamentally altered the extent to which Canadian law approached freedom of speech. The *Canadian Bill of Rights 1960* does not refer to freedom of speech. As such, it is appropriate to discuss Canadian law relating to freedom of speech prior to 1982, and since 1982. Further, the Australian High Court relied on the Canadian case law prior to 1982 when it discerned in the Australian *Constitution* an implied freedom of political communication in its 1992 decision, as discussed in Chapter 3.[1] Further, it should be acknowledged that many of the cases to be discussed below were decided on a range of grounds. For the purposes of current discussion, those grounds relating to constitutional protection of freedom of speech will be the primary focus of the discussion.

FREE SPEECH CASES DECIDED PRIOR TO THE *CHARTER*

The first important Canadian case in which freedom of speech rights were discussed was *In the Matter of Three Bills Passed by the Legislative Assembly of Alberta*.[2] The relevant challenge for current purposes was to Bill No. 9. The relevant scheme had established an Alberta Social Credit Board. Clause 3 empowered the Chair of that Board to order a newspaper proprietor to publish any "correction or amplification" of any statement relating to government policy published by that newspaper within the previous 31 days. Clause 4 empowered the Chair to request from a newspaper proprietor details of all sources used for particular stories published within the past 60 days, and their names, addresses and occupations. The same obligation could apply to any writer of an editorial, article, or news item. Clause 6 stated that if a newspaper breached any requirement of the legislation, the Governor could order that the newspaper not be published until further order.

The Supreme Court of Canada declared the law to be constitutionally invalid. Much of the reasoning relates to whether the province had a head of power to support the legislation, and this part of the reasoning does not concern us here. Of more interest are the comments made by several justices as to the extent to which Canadian constitutional documents protected freedom of speech.

Duff CJ (with whom Davis J joined) noted that the preamble to the *British North America Act 1867* (Imp) reflected an intention that the Canadian constitutional arrangements were to reflect a similar style of government to that of the United Kingdom. A parliament was to be established, and it was to be a body representative of the people. Duff CJ noted that parliaments "derived their efficacy" from the free public discussion of public affairs, policy, and administration.[3] Reform proposals should receive the "freest and fullest" analysis.[4] Duff CJ said that the practice of free discussion was the "breath of life" for parliamentary institutions.[5] He found that "powers requisite for the protection of the constitution itself arise by necessary implication" from the 1867 Act.[6] At one point Duff CJ appeared to view the freedom as virtually absolute, but then conceded provinces had some power to regulate speech, but not such as would substantially interfere with workings of the parliamentary institutions of Canada, as contemplated by its foundation legal documents.

Cannon J expressed similar views:

> Under the British system, which is ours, no political party can erect a prohibitory barrier to prevent the electors from getting information concerning the policy of the government. Freedom of discussion is essential to enlighten public opinion in a democratic state; it cannot be curtailed without affecting the right of the people to be informed through sources independent of the government concerning matters of public interest . . . at the time of Confederation the United Kingdom was a democracy. Democracy cannot be maintained without its foundation: free public opinion and free discussion throughout the nation of all matters affecting the state . . . the province cannot interfere with (a person's) status as a Canadian citizen and (their) fundamental right to express freely (their) untrammeled opinion about government policies and discuss matters of public concern.[7]

The next case which considered freedom of speech in Canada was *Boucher v The King*.[8] The case concerned the validity of legislation proscribing seditious libel. The section defined sedition as involving the publication or circulation of written material which advocates the use, without legal authority, of force as a means of accomplishing government change in Canada. The section expressly stated that it was not intended to limit the meaning of sedition. A defense was provided for someone who in good faith intended merely to point out matters which were producing or had the tendency to produce feelings of hatred and ill-will between individuals. Difficulties arose because, historically, sedition had sometimes been defined as involving mere intent to bring the sovereign or government into hatred or contempt, or to invite disaffection with them. Alternatively, historically it was sometimes defined to be merely promoting feelings of ill-will and hostility between different individuals. In both of these iterations of the offense, there was no requirement of an intention to incite violence in order to secure government change. The issue was whether the Canadian version of the sedition law should be interpreted narrowly on its terms, to be confined to cases where it could be shown the publisher or circulator of the material intended it to lead to government change through violence, or whether the broader view of sedition was also part of Canadian law.

The factual context was an adherent of the Jehovah's Witness religion who distributed pamphlets. The pamphlets contained statements which firstly called for calm and reason. It then discussed victimization and persecution of Jehovah's Witness followers. It called for a closer reading of God's word.

A majority of the Court interpreted the sedition offense in Canada as being limited to circumstances in which the person charged intended to bring about government change through force.[9] Rand J tied the changing conception of the meaning of sedition with changes in the way government was viewed. At a time when government was seen as comprising superior beings exercising a divine mandate, and a Hobbesian view of human nature taken, a broad conception of sedition, and a strong legal prohibition against criticism of government action was explicable. With the growth of ideas of representative government and the people as sovereign, criticism of government action became more acceptable.[10]

Rand J pointed out that Stephen had historically defined sedition as involving any of the following: (a) bringing into hatred or contempt, or exciting disaffection against, the monarch or government or constitution of the United Kingdom, either House of Parliament, or the administration of justice; (b) to excite the monarch's subjects, other than through lawful means, to alter any law; (c) to incite any person to commit a crime in disturbance of the peace; (d) to raise discontent or disaffection among citizens; or (e) to promote feelings of ill-will or hostility between different classes of subjects.[11]

Rand J pointed out that no modern authority had included within the concept of sedition the mere fact of a person creating discontent or disaffection among citizens, without the further element of inciting illegal conduct. He was not surprised by this because

> Freedom in thought and speech and disagreement in ideas and beliefs, on every conceivable subject, are of the essence of our life. The clash of critical

> discussion on political, social and religious subjects has too deeply become the stuff of daily experience to suggest that mere ill-will as a product of controversy can strike down the latter with illegality . . . our compact of free society accepts and absorbs . . . differences and they are exercised at large within the framework of freedom and order on broader and deeper uniformities as bases of social stability. Similarly in discontent, affection and hostility: as subjective incidents of controversy, they and the ideas which arouse them are part of our living which ultimately serve us in stimulation, in the clarification of thought and . . . in the search for the constitution and truth of things generally.[12]

These statements appear to reflect a broader view of freedom of speech, not confined to the political process, but more towards the self-actualization perspective of freedom of speech as an intrinsic good.

Locke said it was now "very much too late in the day" to say that it was a crime for a person to publish something calculated to alienate the affections of people by bringing the government into disrepute or ridicule.[13] In contrast, four dissenting justices found that a broader definition of sedition should apply, not necessarily requiring proof of an intention in the defendant to cause the overthrow of government by unlawful means.[14]

The Canadian Supreme Court overturned a Canadian version of prior restraint laws in *Saumur v City of Quebec*.[15] The challenged provision there had conditioned lawful distribution of a book or pamphlet on the permission of the Chief of Police. Petitioners, who were Jehovah's Witnesses, were denied permission to circulate material. Thus the case raised consideration of both freedom of speech and freedom of religion, together with other issues of constitutional powers. Statements by the justices regarding freedom of speech are of most importance here. Rand J stated that the Canadian *Constitution* contemplated freedom of speech regarding political issues. A system of prior restraint was fundamentally at odds with this system of government. He lauded freedom of speech in terms of "steadily advancing enlightenment for which the widest range of controversy is the sine qua non."[16] He referred to the book of Jeremiah in the Bible to the effect that dissemination of ideas was the 'breath of life' for society's political institutions.[17] Locke J agreed with the judgment of Duff CJ in the Alberta case to the effect that the right to public discussion was implicit in the *British North America Act*.[18]

At the start of the Cold War, the Supreme Court of Canada next dealt with a law making it illegal for the owner of premises to use it or allow any person to make use of it to propagate communism.[19] The Act also made it unlawful to publish or distribute any newspaper, pamphlet, or document propagating communism. A majority of the Court found the legislation to be invalid. Some of the reasoning was based on the constitutional issue that the province lacked the power to pass the law. Of more interest here again is the reasoning of some judges that the law was invalid because of its impact on freedom of speech.

Rand J, with whom Kellett J agreed, stated that the founding fathers of Canada intended to build a system of representative parliamentary government similar to that of the United Kingdom:

> This means ultimately government by the free public opinion of an open society . . . public opinion, in order to meet such a responsibility, demands the condition of a virtually unobstructed access to and diffusion of ideas. Parliamentary government postulates a capacity in (persons), acting freely and under self-restraints, to govern themselves; and that advance is best served in the degree achieved of individual liberation from subjective as well as objective shackles . . . this constitutional fact is the political expression of the primary condition of social life, thought and its communication by language. Liberty in this is little less vital to man's mind and spirit than breathing is to his physical existence.[20]

A very different view of the extent to which Canadians enjoy a right to freedom of speech was evident in *Attorney-General (Canada) and Dupond v Montreal*.[21] There a majority of the Court upheld a Montreal ordinance prohibiting the holding of an assembly, parade, or gathering for 30 days on land owned by the city. The government justified its restrictions on the basis there had been numerous demonstrations in recent times, with increasing levels of associated aggression and violence. In rejecting a constitutional challenge to the legislation, a majority of the Court concluded that the right to free speech, assembly, and association was not enshrined in the Canadian *Constitution*.[22] The majority also held that demonstrations were not a form of speech, but rather a display of force.[23] They added that the right to hold meetings on a highway or in a park was unknown to English law.[24] As such, it did not form part of Canadian law.

Even after the passage of the *Canadian Charter of Rights and Freedoms*, the Canadian Supreme Court would continue to emphasize the fundamental nature of freedom of speech in Canada, and the fact it was required by any system of representative democracy.[25]

CANADIAN *CHARTER* DECISIONS ON FREE SPEECH

Obviously, in 1982 the Canadian constitutional landscape changed significantly with the passage of the *Constitution Act 1982* and the *Canadian Charter of Rights and Freedoms*, section 2(b) of which protects freedom of thought, belief, opinion, and expression, section 2(c) of which protects freedom of assembly, and section 2(d) freedom of association. These rights are not absolute, with s1 stating that the rights enshrined in the *Charter* are subject to reasonable limits prescribed by law that can be demonstrably justified in a free and democratic society. This requires a test of proportionality, involving questions as to whether the measure can be justified on the basis of a legitimate objective, and whether the measure which impacts the right is carefully tailored to meeting the relevant objective, rather than being arbitrary, unfair, or based on irrelevant considerations, whether the provision minimally impairs the fundamental right, and whether there is proportionality between the effects of the measures and the state's legitimate objective.[26] It was always going to be interesting to observe the extent to which Canadian judges approached the role of interpreting these provisions, individually and in concert. As others have noted, Canadian jurisprudence started in a much different place than the American *First Amendment* jurisprudence.[27] The Canadian tradition of parliamentary supremacy and deference to the legislature had no equivalent in the case of the American *Bill of Rights*.[28] It must also be emphasized that the position of the common law in the United States differs from the position in Canada, and indeed Australia. In the United States the common law is primarily state law. In Canada and Australia there is one national common law, and the highest court has a substantial role to play in developing and refining it, and in this context, in determining the interplay between common law principles and freedom of speech rights. Furthermore, the Canadian *Charter* applies only to government action, not private disputes.[29]

Early in its *Charter* jurisprudence, the Canadian Supreme Court set the course of Canadian precedent on a different path to American *First Amendment* case law. For example, as indicated in Chapter 2, the United States Supreme Court settled on a category-based system, under which some types of speech would be entitled to greater constitutional protection than other speech. Specifically, commercial speech was considered to be of lesser value than speech that was more political in nature; as such, greater regulation of commercial speech would be consistent with the *First Amendment*.[30]

The Canadian Supreme Court set its face against such an approach in one of its first free speech cases following the passage of the *Charter*.[31] It acknowledged that most of the pre-*Charter* Canadian case law had concerned free speech in the political context. However, even if this were a feature of the pre-*Charter* law, as opposed to merely the factual context in which statements had been made, it would not be a feature of free speech jurisprudence in Canada following the passage of the *Charter*. This was because "political expression is only one form of the great range of expression that is deserving of constitutional protection because it serves individual and societal values in a free and democratic society."[32] The Canadian Court rejected a differential approach to free speech according to whether the speech was commercial in nature or non-commercial, including political. In so doing, the Canadian Court linked its broader conception of free speech in Canada to the various rationales presented for freedom of speech. It indicated it did not agree with the Meiklejohn functionalist justification for free speech related to the democratic process, but favored a broader view:

> Over and above its intrinsic value as expression, commercial expression which . . . protects listeners as well as speakers plays a significant role in enabling individuals to make informed economic choices, and important aspect of individual self-fulfillment and personal autonomy. The Court accordingly rejects the view that commercial expression serves no individual or societal value in a free and democratic society and for this reason is undeserving of any constitutional protection.[33]

A very strong attitude of protection of free speech is also evident in the decision in *Irwin Toy Ltd v Quebec.*[34] The legislation at issue there sought to restrict the extent to which business could advertise to children under the age of 13.

The majority summarized the nature and principles underlying protection of free speech in Canada as including (a) that seeking and attaining truth was self-evidently good; (b) that participation in social and political decision making should be encouraged; and (c) that diversity in individual self-fulfilment should be cultivated in a tolerant environment for both those who wish to speak and those who wish to listen.[35] As with the American jurisprudence, the Canadian court would frown upon content-based restrictions, whether direct or indirect, and regulation which sought to influence how the content affected behavior.[36] Generally all speech was protected by s2 regardless of content, with the exception of expression that incited violence, which was not accorded any constitutional protection.[37] The majority said that in considering the extent to which regulation impacted the human right, both its purpose and its effect had to be considered.[38] If a law had the purpose of infringing freedom of expression, a s2 breach would be established. If a law did not have that purpose but had that effect, a s2 breach would be established if the speech at issue was connected with at least one of the three established objectives of freedom of expression, namely search for truth, participation in political and social life, and self-actualization.

The majority indicated it would accord the legislature a margin of appreciation in determining that a particular legislative response was the way in which the human right was minimally impaired. It would be sufficient if the legislature had a reasonable basis for regulating in the way that it did in terms of minimal impairment of free expression.[39] Subsequent cases have confirmed that the Court will not strike down a law on the basis it does not minimally impair free expression rights simply on the basis it can think of another way to manage the identified the problem that is considered less invasive of the right. It is sufficient if the court is satisfied the legislature has tailored its legislation to its objective in a reasonable manner.[40]

While the bare majority was satisfied that the regulation was saved pursuant to s1 of the *Charter,* an even stronger defense of free speech is evident in the judgment of the dissentients, who would not have saved the measure under s1. McIntyre J in dissent noted that

> Freedom of expression is too important to be lightly cast aside or limited. It is ironic that most attempts to limit freedom of expression and hence freedom of knowledge and information are justified on the basis that the limitation is for the benefit of those whose rights will be limited. It was this proposition that motivated the early church in restricting access to information, even to prohibiting the promulgation and reading of the scriptures in a language understood by the people. The argument that freedom of expression was dangerous was used to oppose and restrict public education in earlier times. The education of women was greatly retarded on the basis that wider knowledge would only make them dissatisfied with their role in society . . . our concern should be to recognize that in this century we have seen whole societies utterly corrupted by the suppression of free expression . . . (freedom of expression is) not absolute (but) . . . whether political, religious, artistic or commercial, should not be suppressed except in cases where urgent and compelling reasons exist and then only to the extent and for the time necessary for the protection of the community.[41]

Subsequent case law on freedom of speech in the commercial sphere suggested that commercial speech may warrant less s2 protection than other kinds of speech.[42] This would be through the use of the s1 exception to freedom of speech rights. The Court might more readily accept that a law impacting commercial speech was tailored to a legitimate objective and passed proportionality analysis than a law impacting other kinds of speech. However, this did not mean that an American-style category approach should be adopted, in which different rules were applied to assess free speech claims depending on the nature of the speech.[43] Total bans on a form of expression, as opposed to partial bans, will be more difficult to justify under s1.[44]

Strict restrictions on the extent to which an organization such as a media outlet could report on current family law proceedings, as well as other civil proceedings, were successfully challenged on the basis of s2(b) of the *Charter*.[45] The regulations prohibited disclosure of details relating to family law proceedings, except the names, addresses and occupations of the parties and witnesses, and brief descriptions of the allegations and issues raised in the case. A majority of the Court found the regulations breached s2(b) of the *Charter*, and could not be saved under s1 as justified restrictions on expression. The majority again emphasized the importance of free speech in a democracy.[46] This included the right to publicly express views about public institutions. It included that courts had to function openly.[47]

The measures could not be saved under s1. Even if the government could show a legitimate objective for its legislation, and that the legislation was rationally connected to that objective, the legislation was not minimally invasive of the fundamental right, and was not proportional having regard to the objective sought and the interference with freedom of speech. It operated a very substantial restriction on freedom of speech. While privacy concerns were legitimate, they could be secured with legislation much less sweeping in impact, for instance, conferring discretion on a judge in an individual case to order suppression of material in limited cases, rather than a general prohibition. The fourth member of the majority, Wilson J, generally agreed with the majority's decision. She favored a contextual approach to freedom of speech, rather than an approach in the abstract. By this, she suggested that the extent to which the law protected freedom of speech should be context specific; in some cases, the law would defend freedom of speech more stoutly than others.[48] This approach has been adopted in subsequent cases. While virtually all speech and communication will be protected by s2 of the Canadian *Charter*, some speech will be protected to a greater extent than others. Specifically, speech close to what is considered to be the core of freedom of speech and the rationales for its existence will be accorded greater protection; speech considered to be at the margins and not valuable in terms of the purposes that freedom of speech is said to serve will be accorded lesser protection.[49]

The Canadian Supreme Court was called upon to consider the constitutionality of that nation's hate speech laws in *R v Keegstra*.[50] The accused was charged with an offense of communicating statements in public that willfully promoted hatred against an identified group. The maximum penalty for the offense was two years' imprisonment. Defenses were available based on truth, that the expression was a good faith opinion on a religious subject, or were matters of public interest, and the expression was for the public benefit, if the accused reasonably believed they were true, or if the accused had in good faith pointed out matters tending to produce hatred towards an identifiable group in Canada, with the purpose of removing such hatred. Mr. Keegstra, a teacher, was charged after communicating anti-Semitic statements in class, calling Jews treacherous, subversive, money loving, power hungry, and child killers. He claimed the Jews had invented the Holocaust in order to garner sympathy. He expected students to adopt and reflect his views in assessment; if they did not do so, their marks suffered. A bare majority of the Supreme Court validated the relevant statutory provision against a free speech challenge.[51]

The majority was satisfied that s2 had been breached. A breach of s2 could be found regardless of the content of the expression, as long as it did not incite violence. The majority found that the legislature had a legitimate objective in passing its legislation, given the demonstrated harm and hurt that hate speech could cause to those at whom it was directed, and society more generally. This had been reflected in international covenants to which Canada was a party. The legislation was rationally connected with that legitimate end. The majority found, of the objectives of free speech accepted in *Irwin Toy*, none were furthered by permitting hate speech.[52] Hate speech did nothing to pursue goals of truth; speech that was almost certainly false did not move a society towards truth, thus the argument for its protection was weaker.[53] Its dissemination would not "lead to a better world."[54] Such speech did not further self-actualization; on the contrary, it could impede the self-actualization of members of the marginalized group.[55] The majority also denied the contribution of the relevant speech to political and social discussion, as part of a democracy. They concluded that democracy was premised on the equal participation of those in society to political and social debates, and the view that each person was equally deserving of respect and dignity. Hate speech had the potential to impede democracy in that form, according to the majority.[56]

The majority was satisfied the law met the minimal impairment requirement. It was narrowly tailored to speech that was willful. This imported an appropriate mens rea requirement that served to significantly narrow the breadth the provision might otherwise have. So too the requirement that the person communicate with the intention of inciting "hatred," and that the communication be in public. This, together with the defenses available, meant the provision satisfied the minimum impairment requirement. That requirement did not mean that on every occasion where parliament was faced with a range of options to meet its legislative requirements, it must always choose the mode of intervention that was least intrusive on *Charter* rights or freedoms.[57] The provision passed proportionality testing given the very strong value that Canadian society applied to inclusiveness and non-racism, and the marginal extent to which the speech affected by the provision contributed to any recognized free speech purpose.[58] For similar reasons, a general human rights provision banning the use of a telephone to communicate messages likely to expose a person to hatred or contempt on prohibited grounds was upheld against a freedom of expression challenge.[59]

In dissent, the majority emphasized that speech was entitled to protection under s2 regardless of its content, provided it did not incite violence. The speech here was not in that category. They rejected an argument that speech "without redeeming value" was not entitled to s2 protection.[60] They agreed that the government had a legitimate objective with its legislation of seeking to reduce racism and prejudice. The minority was not convinced that the legislation was sufficiently connected with its purpose. There was not strong evidence that suppressing racist comments actually reduced levels of racism in society.[61] Pre-Hitler Germany had the kinds of laws currently at issue. Demonstrably, they were ineffective in suppressing race and religion-based hatred of the worst kind.

The dissenters were not satisfied the legislation met the "minimum impairment" requirement. It used the concept of "hatred," which was broad and subjective in nature. They were not satisfied that the concept of "willful" sufficiently narrowed the provision, in the absence of a requirement to prove actual harm or incitement to hatred be shown.[62] The very fact of the subjectivity of the requirements of the offense, together with the possibly very serious consequences of breach (jail terms), was likely to produce the kind of "chilling effect" on free speech that American courts had come to recognize in *First Amendment* cases. In other words, the fact that the legislation was vague or ambiguous would often lead citizens to shy away from debate on contentious topics, for fear of crossing the (hard to discern) line. This in itself was insidious, but was relevant to the determination of the constitutionality of the provision. Other remedies were available for offensive speech, not involving jail terms. Thus, the challenged legislation did not minimally invade the human right.[63] The dissentients also found the legislation failed the third requirement of proportionality analysis. It severely impacted a fundamental human right, for very marginal and speculative gain.[64]

A slightly different result occurred in the context of hate speech laws in *Saskatchewan Human Rights Commission v Whatcott*.[65] There the relevant part of the legislation prohibited the distribution of written material that "exposed or tends to expose to hatred, ridicules, belittles, or otherwise affronts the dignity of any person or class of persons on the basis of a prohibited ground." A prohibited ground included sexuality. Whatcott distributed several flyers in his neighborhood. One was entitled "Keep Homosexuality out of Saskatoon's Public Schools" and the other entitled "Sodomites in our Public Schools." Whatcott's flyers included allegations that homosexuals "want to share their filth and propaganda with Saskatchewan's children," referred to "ex-Sodomites and other types of sex addicts who have been able to break free of their sexual bondage and develop wholesome and healthy relationships," gay people who wanted to "remain in their lifestyle and proselytize vulnerable young people," claimed that children "will pay the price in disease, death and abuse," said the Bible was clear that homosexuality was an "abomination," and that God had destroyed Sodom and Gomorrah due to homosexual perversion. Whatcott defended his right to circulate the flyers on free speech and other grounds. He challenged the relevant statutory provision of which he was accused of breaching.

The Court found that the measure breached s2. It clearly impacted on the ability of a person to express themselves. Consideration of the location and manner of the speech did not change this. Handing out flyers was clearly a common form of communication, which advanced the objectives of free speech. Location was irrelevant. The legislation had the purpose of partly infringing the right of a person to free speech. Clearly, s2 was breached.

In terms of s1 analysis, the Court accepted that the statutory provision was intended to reduce levels of hate speech and the associated harm that such speech could well cause to targeted groups. In so finding, the Court emphasized that it was necessary to focus on the likely effect of the hate speech, rather than the content of what was said.[66] This required an objective test, based on the likely impact of the speech on the targeted group, rather than individual effects. The important consideration was whether the speech was reasonably likely to lead to hatred of the targeted group. In other words, an objective test of "hatred" should be applied.[67] Further, the Court acknowledged the limits of hate speech law, conceding that its prohibition would not remove hatred from the range of human emotions.[68] That said, the Court agreed that the legislature had legitimate objectives in passing these laws.

However, the Court was not satisfied that the entire law satisfied the requirement of a rational connection between the measures used and the overall objective of the legislation. Focusing on the likely impact of the targeted group, rather than the individual, the Court determined that the part of the legislation which prohibited behavior that "ridicules, belittles, or otherwise affronts the dignity of any person" did not meet this requirement. Comments meeting this description could be repugnant, hurtful and/or offensive. However, speech at that level was not sufficiently connected with avoidance of hatred and the associated harm to the targeted group.[69] As a result, the Court determined that that part of the legislation should be struck out, while the provision targeting "hate speech" did meet the requirement of sufficient connection.

The Court rejected an argument that the remaining provision prohibiting communication that would likely foment hatred against the targeted group was not "minimally invasive." There were arguments that the legislation was overbroad, that it should be narrowed to circumstances where it was shown the defendant intended to incite hatred, had threatened, advocated or justified violence, or had caused actual harm to the targeted group. Such groups suggested the "marketplace of ideas" would resolve differences and tensions among groups.

In response, the Court said it was for parliament to choose among competing policy options in terms of how it framed its legislation. It was sufficient that the means chosen by the legislature was one of the reasonable choices it could make. The Court was not satisfied it was sufficient to rely on the marketplace of ideas to resolve such controversies in society. They expressed concern with the insidious nature of hate speech, in that it tended to silence and marginalize the target group, such that the marketplace of ideas would not work to resolve the difficulty. Again, that part of the provision which prohibited "ridicule, belittling or otherwise affronts the dignity of" the group did not meet the minimal impairment requirement.[70] In terms of proportionality between the objective of the legislation and its impact on free speech, the Court said that hate speech was low value speech. It was only barely related to the purposes of free speech, or was sometimes at odds with principles of free speech, in that it often silenced the targeted group, inhibiting rather than encouraging freedom of discussion.[71] Thus, part of the provision survived the constitutional challenge, and part of it was struck out.

As the Canadian jurisprudence developed, that country's Supreme Court was asked to consider adopting various American *First Amendment* concepts, including so-called reasonable time and place restrictions, the concept of a "public forum," and concepts of "vagueness" and "overbreadth." A good example of this is *The Queen in Right of Canada v Committee for the Commonwealth of Canada and Others*.[72] At issue there were regulations applying to an airport, government controlled property, preventing a person from conducting any business or undertaking, commercial or otherwise at an airport, and from soliciting there. Individuals handing out non-commercial pamphlets of a religious nature at the airport were alleged to have breached the regulation. They challenged the regulation on the basis it restricted their freedom of speech. There were statutory interpretation issues involved in the resolution of the case, but the focus here will be on the freedom of speech discussion.

All members of the Court found that the law infringed the applicants' right to freedom of expression in s2(b), and could not be saved under s1. However, a range of approaches was taken to various issues.

The first issue where division was evident was on the use of the so-called public forum doctrine in *First Amendment* analysis. Succinctly put, this suggests that courts should more readily uphold *First Amendment* challenges to laws which impact on speech in areas where traditionally citizens have gathered to discuss issues, such as sidewalks/footpaths, parks, streets, and public meeting places. Lamer CJ reinterpreted this doctrine to refer to places where public access for the purposes of communication was consistent with the state's use of the place. He agreed that individuals had an interest in the greatest possible dissemination of their ideas, and (at least in the early 1990s) this was mostly possible in public places. This gave individuals a legitimate interest in their use to discuss ideas. On the other hand, the government had an interest in the proper use of its property for the benefit of all, not just those who wished to gather. Lamer CJ reconciled these interests by stating that an individual had a right to gather in a public place to discuss ideas that would be recognized by s2 of the *Charter*, provided this use was compatible with the principal function of that place.[73]

L'Heureux-Dube J also indicated that special rules should apply to the right of individuals to conduct speech on government-owned property. She indicated that such a right was imperative; if individuals could not exercise communication rights on government property, their practical ability to exercise their right to freedom of speech would be substantially curtailed (at least, in 1991).[74] On the other hand, the *Charter* did not confer upon an individual the right to enter upon any property, public or private, to express their views. L'Heureux-Dube J adopted a list of factors that would be applied in order to determine whether a place would qualify as a "public arena" for the purposes of s2.[75] Speech within such an arena would qualify for special s2 protection, in her view.[76]

McLachlin J seemed to chart a middle position, rejecting the view that s2 automatically protected speech on government property, and the view that public speech on government property was only protected if it was not incompatible with the government's use of the property. She discussed the distinction between content-based restrictions on speech, and content-neutral restrictions on speech. In her view, a restriction of the first kind automatically breached s2 of the *Charter*, and the analysis should proceed to s1.[77] In respect of content-neutral regulation, the question was whether the particular speech involved (having regard to its time, place, and manner) furthered at least one of the purposes identified for free speech in *Irwin Toy*, namely search for truth, participation in political and social decision making, or self-actualization.[78] By this means, the fact that the particular place in which the individual sought to express themselves was one where speech typically occurred would be relevant. This explained why, for example, a person could not demand the freedom to speak in private places such as the Prime Minister's office or judges' private chambers, but may legitimately demand it in a public park or thoroughfare. Subsequent cases involving free speech on public property have also emphasized whether the place historically served as a place where free expression would occur, and whether other aspects of the place suggest that communication there would further, or impede, the values underlying free expression.[79]

L'Heureux-Dube J said that the American "void for vagueness" doctrine applied to consideration of free speech rights in Canada, through the s1 limit which permitted interference with fundamental rights within "limits prescribed by law." She indicated that a vague law would not amount to a limit prescribed by law.[80] She also connected "void for vagueness" doctrine with the rule of law.[81] She found the law challenged her was "void for vagueness" due to the uncertain scope of the prohibition.[82] Vagueness was particularly insidious in relation to laws impacting human rights, because the very uncertainty of their scope would itself lead to individuals choosing not to exercise the freedoms conferred upon them by the *Charter*.[83]

L'Heureux-Dube J also adopted the American "overbreadth" doctrine as applicable in the Canadian context. Issues relevant to overbreadth in the American context were particularly relevant to the kind of proportionality analysis undertaken by the Canadian courts pursuant to s1, including whether the law was minimally invasive of fundamental rights. She found the regulation was overbroad, applicable to a very large range of potential activities at airports.[84] Regulation of this full range of activities went well beyond any legitimate interest the government might have in regulating airports, for instance, safety considerations.[85]

One aspect of the American case law that the Canadian Supreme Court has rejected concerns the law of defamation/libel and freedom of expression.[86] As discussed in Chapter 2, *First Amendment* case law creates a significant exception to American defamation law with respect to "public figures."[87] In relation to such individuals, they could only successfully show they had been legally defamed if they could prove either that the defendant made the relevant statement knowing that it was false, or had been reckless in not knowing whether or not the statement was false. The Canadian Supreme Court refused to adopt that approach with respect to defamation and the Canadian *Charter*, or the common law right to freedom of speech.[88] Nor did the Canadian court accept that those who were classed as "public figures" should be treated differently in terms of the law of defamation than those who were not public figures.[89]

The Court also confirmed in that case that where the express terms of the *Charter* did not apply to a situation, for example, because the particular dispute did not involve state action, although this meant that *Charter* rights were not in play, the *Charter* was not completely irrelevant. Specifically, the litigants might argue that the common law was inconsistent with *Charter* values, and might therefore need to be re-shaped.[90] Here the Court noted that defamation did not contribute to healthy participation in community affairs. It was harmful to the interests of a free and democratic society.[91]

The limits of free speech in Canada were tested when the Supreme Court considered the constitutionality of legislation criminalizing the spreading of "fake news."[92] The relevant provision made it an offense to publish a false statement or news, knowing it was false, in such circumstances as to cause or likely cause an injury or mischief to the public interest. Zundel had been charged after spreading a publication which apparently questioned whether 6 million Jews had in fact been killed in the Holocaust, and claiming it was a myth created and maintained by a worldwide Jewish conspiracy. A constitutional challenge to the validity of the measure was upheld 4:3.[93]

Invalidating the legislation, the majority rejected the argument that a deliberate lie met no value underlying freedom of speech, so that it did not warrant protection. In many cases, there might be an issue about whether a statement was true of false, particularly in the realm of opinion. Even if the statement were clearly false, exaggeration or lies could serve useful purposes relative to broad free speech goals.[94] The fact the section under which Zundel had been prosecuted had been so rarely used in the near century during which it had been on the statute books suggested it was not necessary for a free and democratic society, in terms of the s1 exception to the s2 protection of free speech.[95] The provision was overbroad in terms of any legitimate objective of securing social harmony or general peace in society.[96] It was not minimally invasive of the right in order to secure the legitimate objective.[97]

While the dissenters recognized that extreme speech also warranted free speech protection, they concluded that preserving the kind of speech at issue here met none of the objectives of free speech. It was not part of a search for truth, did not assist in political deliberation,[98] and did nothing for self-actualization.[99] The speech had potentially very severe emotional impact on Jewish people. It could substantially harm individuals.[100]

The interplay between the right of an accused to a fair trial, the common law doctrine of contempt of court, and the right to free speech was at issue in *Dagenais v CBC*.[101] While criminal proceedings were pending against various religious individuals for alleged abuse of children within their care, a Canadian broadcaster sought to broadcast a television program involving abuse of children within a religious institution. While the program was said to be fictional, it also claimed to be inspired by recent events in Canada. Those charged with offenses sought to stop the airing of the program, on the basis that it would or may infringe their right to a fair trial. The broadcaster argued that they had a right to broadcast the material as a freedom of speech issue. A majority of the Supreme Court overturned the ban on airing of the program.[102]

The majority noted that the common law of Canada had to yield to interpretation of the Canadian *Charter*, in the event of conflict. As a result, it modified the law with respect to pre-trial publication of material, so that publication would only be banned where it was necessary to prevent a real and substantial risk to a fair trial, because other less invasive means were not reasonably available,[103] and where the salutary effects of the publication ban outweighed the negative effects on freedom of expression.[104] In so doing, members of the Court said that this comparison of the salutary effects of the infringement of free speech with its negative impacts should be used in general proportionality analysis under s1, and was not confined to publication bans.[105] In a later case, it dismissed a *Charter* challenge to a law imposing a mandatory publication ban on evidence produced at a bail hearing. The ban was justified because material contained in a bail hearing often went to character, material which may or may be used at a subsequent trial. The publication of this could prejudice the ability of the accused to obtain a fair trial. Further, such a ban permitted an accused to concentrate on their liberty interests, rather than their privacy interests, at what could be a very stressful time for them, and during which they may or may not be legally represented. The ban was only temporary in that case.[106]

The Court has considered freedom of expression and its application to court proceedings on a few other occasions. It considered a power in criminal legislation for a judge to order members of the public from a court room if it was considered necessary in the interests of public morals, maintenance of order, or proper administration of justice.[107] Pursuant to this power, a judge ordered the removal of members of the media when announcing a sentence for a sex offender. A broadcaster challenged the legislation on constitutional grounds. The Supreme Court emphasized how fundamental the notion of open courts was in the Canadian legal tradition. It was a hallmark of a democratic society and the "very soul of justice."[108] As part of this, it was also necessary that members of the press be ordinarily able to attend court proceedings. Often, it was only through the means of the press (at least in 1996) that the public would be made aware of legal proceedings. In terms of the freedom of expression, the court noted that discussion of court proceedings was part of the core values, given it concerned a key institution within the democratic structure.[109] While the provision did breach s2(b) freedom of expression rights, the court upheld it as a reasonable limit under s1, on the basis that sometimes openness could conflict with the due administration of justice.[110] Privacy was an important interest protected by such orders.[111] The discretion had been carefully limited and the legislation showed due deference to the important free expression rights in play. While the provision was valid, its exercise in this particular case was problematic. The Supreme Court did not agree that the proper administration of justice would be imperiled here if the press were present in court. It was during a sentencing hearing, rather than the actual trial, so concerns about media interference with the administration of justice were less real. Already, suppression orders were in place in relation to the identities of the victims.[112]

The Supreme Court upheld a criminal law provision prohibiting the possession of child pornography. The accused had argued that the provision breached s2 of the Canadian *Charter*, and was not justified by s1. A majority of the Court found that the measure interfered with the accused's right to expression.[113] While truth and engagement in the political process were not implicated, the Court found that individual self-fulfilment was.[114] It found that without the right to possess expressive material, an individual's right to freedom of thought, belief, opinion, and expression would be compromised. In determining whether or not s2 had been breached, it was not necessary to consider the content of the material, as offensive as the material currently at issue obviously was, provided the material did not incite violence. Thus, it was protected by s2. However, the Court found that the criminal provisions were justified in terms of s1 analysis. The government's legitimate objective with the legislation was to reduce the harm around the use of children in pornography. The Court was satisfied that the legislation was rationally connected with prevention of harm to children. While there was a lack of strong evidence that those in possession of child pornography went on to commit child sexual abuse, their attitudes towards potential victims may change. The fact they possess such material might normalize the content, in their mind. It might reduce their inhibitions towards committing abuse. Further, criminalizing possession of such material might reduce the market for it, and in turn its supply. The government did not have to prove this with certain scientific evidence; it was sufficient there was a "reasonable apprehension of harm."[115]

On the minimum impairment question, the majority clarified that the government did not have to show in all cases that it had chosen the option least invasive of rights. It was sufficient for it to show that it impeded the right no more than was reasonably necessary to secure their legitimate objective/s. Here the majority had some concerns with overbreadth, specifically that the criminal provision could catch materials created and held by the accused alone, for personal use, and visual recordings created by or featuring the accused, that depicted lawful sexual activity and was held by them exclusively for private use. The majority solved this overbreadth problem by interpreting the offense such that these types of activities fell outside the offense provision.[116] The dissentients differed from the majority in refusing to graft two exceptions onto the provision in order to overcome overbreadth; they would have validated the provision in its entirety. In so doing, the dissentients emphasized that *Charter* jurisprudence suggested that the fact that a restriction on one *Charter* right served to enhance other express *Charter* rights was relevant; here the restriction would enhance rights to equality and security. Further, the Court had been sensitive to the fact that the challenged legislation protected vulnerable groups in conducting its proportionality testing. Few, if any, groups in society were more vulnerable than children.

The Court's position on morality-based provisions and their compatibility with freedom of expression provisions has altered to some extent. For instance, in *Butler v The Queen*,[117] the Court considered an obscenity offense in the federal criminal code. The provision made it an offense to publish, distribute or possess any obscene written matter. It defined obscene matter as a publication which had a dominant characteristic of undue exploitation of sex, or sex together with crime, horror, cruelty, and/or violence. The owner of a video store who stocked pornographic videos was charged with a breach of the provision. He sought to defend himself on the basis of s2(b) of the *Charter*. All members of the Court found that the provision infringed s2(b), but was justified under s1.

The Court noted that artistic expression was at the heart of freedom of expression. Expression here was of some value, albeit low-level in nature. It did not concern the heart of freedom of expression. It was directed, at least marginally, towards "base" aspects of human fulfilment.[118] It disfavored justifying legislation which impacted freedom of expression on the basis of a moral view of a certain section of society.[119] On the other hand, the state had a legitimate interest in intervening regarding expression that was "harmful."[120] Harm involved predisposing someone to act in an anti-social manner, for example, mistreatment of others. Anti-social behavior was behavior contrary to the proper functioning of society. In so deciding, the Court applied a community standards test, whether members of the community would tolerate others viewing the material at issue, given possible harm associated with it.[121] The Court categorized pornography as involving (a) explicit sex with violence; (b) explicit sex without violence but which subjects people to treatment that is degrading or dehumanizing; and (c) explicit sex without violence that is neither degrading nor dehumanizing. The legislation in question dealt with categories (a) and (b).

The Court was satisfied that the state had a legitimate objective in tackling some of the harm associated with pornography, including changing attitudes towards women. It conceded that the evidence connecting pornography with violent crimes, sexual abuse of others, or failure of societies was not particularly strong. However, it was reasonable for parliament to assume some connection between them, such that parliament's laws were reasonably tailored to a legitimate objective. The Court also found the laws passed the minimal impairment requirement, given that it primarily focused on categories (a) and (b) above. It was proportional to the objective sought.

The Court re-considered the use of the community standards test in *R v Labaye*.[122] The factual scenario was the prosecution of individuals who were running a "swinger's club" in Montreal. They were charged with the offense of keeping a bawdy-house at which indecent acts were committed. The Court overturned the convictions of the accused. In so doing, it explained how the law had moved away from a morality-based approach to criminality to one focused on harm. The community standard of tolerance was designed to emphasize harm, and sought to apply an objective test. However, the Court expressed concern that, as applied, the test had become an effective proxy for judges' own moral views.

As a result, the Court reconceptualized the notion of "harm" as the basis for criminal conviction. The Court said that two issues were relevant: (a) nature of the harm—the government had to show that the proscribed activity was harmful or created a significant risk of harm to others grounded in societal norms and reflected in the Constitution and other fundamental laws. This harm could be an affront to the autonomy and liberty of those confronted with the conduct, harm to society by pre-disposing others to antisocial conduct, or harm to participants; and (b) degree of harm—this must be incompatible with the proper functioning of society. Both would need to be shown in order that the activity could be deemed "indecent" in terms of the criminal law.[123]

The Court seemed to set the requirements of evidence at a higher level than had previously been thought to be the case:

> Incompatibility with the proper functioning of society is more than a test of tolerance. The question is not what individuals or the community thinks about the conduct, but whether permitting it engages a harm that threatens the basic functioning of our society . . . if the harm is based on predisposing others to anti-social behavior, a real risk that the conduct will have this effect must be proved. Vague generalizations that the sexual conduct at issue will lead to attitudinal changes and hence anti-social behavior will not suffice. The causal link between images of sexuality and anti-social behavior cannot be assumed . . . in most cases expert evidence will be required to establish that the

> nature and degree of the harm makes it incompatible with the proper functioning of society.[124]

On the facts, the majority found none of the harms discussed had been established. Only voluntary members of the club were exposed to the relevant conduct. Members were aware of the kind of activity conducted prior to seeing it. No-one was being pressured or coerced to have sex, and no-one was being subject to humiliation or degradation.[125] Further, the degree of harm (if any) was not incompatible with Canadian society or values.[126]

Some free speech cases have involved the context of elections. Obviously political discussion is a key part of democracy, and protection of aspects of the electoral process as part of an effective democracy a core goal of freedom of expression. Governments must be very careful with legislation in this area given the strength of the free speech objectives in play.

A majority of the Court found legislation which prohibited the publication of electoral polling in the days leading up to a general election breached freedom of expression in s2(b) of the *Charter* in a manner which could not be justified under s1.[127]

In terms of the s1 analysis, the government suggested the limits were necessary in order that Canadians have a certain quiet period in which to reflect on their vote prior to polling day, and that the publication of polls could disturb the kind of quiet reflection needed. A second purpose was that opinion polling results had been shown to affect the actual voting patterns of some voters, and given concerns that the polling results might be inaccurate, it was thought that this problem was a legitimate object of regulation. The majority accepted the second but not the first of these arguments was a pressing and legitimate objective, in terms of the first part of s1 analysis.[128]

However, the legislation foundered at the second and third stages of proportionality analysis, in the view of the majority. It did not minimally impair freedom of expression.[129] In doing so, the majority articulated various factors which might impact the extent to which parliament should be given a margin of appreciation with its regulation. These factors included whether the group affected by the regulation was vulnerable, that group's subjective apprehension of harm, whether a particular harm from the speech was quantifiable, and the extent to which a remedy would be effective.[130] Here the group affected, Canadian voters, were not vulnerable. The majority noted that in some cases it had accepted less than scientific evidence said to justify the regulation of speech. The Court sought to limit the categories of case in which this had occurred, to occasions where such evidence as there was not refuted by notions of logic or common sense, or in cases where the affected group was vulnerable, or where the interests of the person speaking were in conflict with the interests of those who might hear the expression.[131] Here, a suggestion that voters would be influenced by a late, inaccurate opinion poll was not logical.[132] There was no conflict between those who took opinion polls, those who published the results and those who read and interpreted the results, excepting the odd occasion where a pollster had a political bias or agenda.[133] The legislation was both overbroad, in prohibiting polls near election day although they could be shown to be highly accurate, and underbroad, permitting polls outside this time which could be wildly inaccurate, and at the same time not requiring pollsters to explain their methodology, such that an individual could themselves ask questions about their authenticity.[134]

A majority of the Court upheld under s1 restrictions on the ability of third parties to spend money on election advertising.[135] The challenged law prohibited a third party from spending more than $3,000 with respect to any one district, and a total of $150,000 nationally. The government argued the limits were necessary to create an equal playing field, to avoid corruption of the electoral process, and to preserve public confidence in such process. All judges agreed that the section infringed freedom of expression under s2, but a majority validated it under s1. It was designed to meet a legitimate objective of equality and fairness, and to avoid elections being unduly influenced by the wealthy. The majority conceded the evidence that the legislation corrected a current problem of lack of equality and fairness in Canadian elections was somewhat scant, but they countered that such harm was difficult to measure tangibly.[136] The measures were sufficiently connected with their legitimate objective. While the right to participate in elections was at the heart of s2, and should be accorded significant protection, it was not absolute. The restraints were minimally invasive, because third parties had many other options open to them to get their message across.[137]

In terms of the final proportionality question, comparing the benefits with the disadvantages, the court concluded the measures were proportional and justified.[138] McLachlin CJ and Major J, with whom Binnie J agreed, noted the effect on freedom of speech was significant. Effectively, it meant only political parties could effectively communicate during election periods. This was a significant restriction on freedom of speech in an area where its constitutional importance was at its highest.[139] The dissenters thought that the legislation was aimed at legitimate objectives, but was not convinced that the measures chosen were sufficiently connected with meeting that objective. The government had not demonstrated a positive link between limits on spending and electoral fairness.[140] There was no demonstrated problem that required addressing.[141] The legislation could actually increase inequality, by allowing the voice of those whose beliefs were actually mirrored in what political parties might communicate to be heard, but silencing those who had other views. In terms of proportionality, the impact on speech was significant, and the benefits of the legislation tendentious, according to the dissent.[142]

The Court has drawn a distinction between a positive right and a negative right.[143] This is important given it is found that the *Charter* is primarily concerned with protecting negative rights, in the sense of protecting existing rights from interference, as opposed to creating new rights. A positive rights claim is one that requires government legislation for its existence. At least in the vast majority of cases, a positive rights claim is not one which will be protected by the *Charter*. The Court has determined that in assessing a positive rights claim, it must consider whether the activity for which the applicant seeks protection is a form of expression. If so, it must then ask three questions:

a. Whether the claim is grounded in a fundamental freedom of expression, as opposed to mere access to a particular statutory scheme;
b. Whether the claimant can show that exclusion from a statutory scheme substantially interferes with freedom of expression; and
c. Whether the government is responsible for the claimant's inability to exercise their fundamental freedom.[144]

A claimant must show each of the three requirements, in order to show a breach of s2 of the *Charter*. In that case, the Court rejected a challenge to Alberta legislation which precluded teachers from nominating to be a member of a school board in the province. The Court said that the claim involved mere access to a statutory scheme, the school boards set up by provincial legislation, as opposed to a fundamental right. The legislation did not limit the extent to which the claimants could communicate about educational issues.

The Court considered the application of freedom of expression rights to advertising on public transport in *Greater Vancouver Transportation Authority v Canadian Federation of Students*.[145] The transit authority had adopted a policy of not accepting any political advertising. The Court found that the policy effected a breach of s2 which could not be justified under s1 of the *Charter*.

In terms of the s2 analysis, the Court found that the policy restrained expressive content. Secondly, the court considered the *method* and *location* of the expression. The expression was not objectionable in terms of its method, since it did not advocate or incite violence. In terms of its location, there was a history of advertising on public transport. Nothing in the location suggested that to permit expression there would undermine free expression values. And the transit authority's policies did have the purpose or effect of infringing free expression—they had this purpose. As a result, a s2 breach was made out.

The transit authority did not succeed in having its measures validated through a s1 analysis. The Court heard argument that the relevant policy was not a "law" within s1. It found that, in order to determine whether a policy was a "law" for the purposes of s1, it must be considered whether the government entity was authorized to enact the relevant policies, and whether the policies were general rules of binding application. If they were, they met the requirements of s1 in terms of "law." It would then be necessary to see whether they were "prescribed." This required consideration of whether the policies were sufficiently precise and accessible to others.[146] The Court found that the policy was a measure prescribed by law in terms of s1—it was a rule of general application pursuant to delegated statutory authority which the authority had to make rules for its management and organization. It was not a rule designed for internal management only, and it was a rule that was both accessible and precise.[147]

In terms of s1 analysis, the policy was accepted as being designed to provide a safe and welcoming public transit system. However, the measures were not rationally connected with that objective.[148] It was unlikely that political messaging on a bus would compromise public safety. Nor were the measures minimally invasive or proportionate.[149]

Reflections on the Canadian Freedom of Expression Jurisprudence

Section 2(b) and its Relation With Section 1

When the Canadian *Charter* was introduced, one of its laudable features was the way in which it expressly provided for the limitation of the fundamental human rights. This is on the basis that most accept the position that human rights, while of paramount importance, are not absolute in nature, and must on some occasions yield in relation to other values. Some had suggested that the American experience was pivotal to the way in which the Canadians framed their constitutional rights protection. The rights enshrined in the United States *Bill of Rights*, including the *First Amendment*, are typically cast in absolute or near-absolute terms. They do not expressly permit of exceptions. Not surprisingly, this has led some justices in the United States to an absolutist position, including on free speech. Since a majority of the justices have not accepted this position, this has required the United States Supreme Court, over a long period, to develop a sophisticated range of jurisprudential doctrine which essentially seeks to map out the principles by which the reasonableness of governmental interference with freedom of speech might be measured and assessed. Inevitably, there have been many twists and turns during this time, with evident great deference to the interests of the state during some periods, a period of so-called ad hoc balancing for a period, followed by a category-based system under which different kinds of speech are accorded different ranges of protection, and are exposed to different ranges of scrutiny. In addition, it has been evident that the *First Amendment* was and is part of a culture and system of government involving deep distrust of government, a product of dissatisfaction with English authoritarian rule, and a focus on individual rights typical of the philosophical era in which it was crafted.

The challenge for the drafters of the Canadian *Charter* was to learn from the American experience, to secure the benefits derived by a constitutional expression of fundamental principles of government like democracy, in which freedom of expression is essential, but to imbue the *Charter* with the characteristics of Canadian governance and culture. Clearly, the Canadians retained significant features of Westminster type governance, including a significant fusion between the roles of executive and legislature, responsible government, and parliamentary sovereignty and supremacy. They retained significant collegiality with the United Kingdom and its system of governance. It is not surprising that the Canadians did not opt for a full-throated *Bill of Rights* in the mold of the United States, but a hybrid document which sought to expressly articulate and enshrine fundamental rights (a significant departure from the traditional common law means of protecting rights), but to balance it with the right of parliament to override fundamental rights in particular cases. Thus, the inclusion of s1 of the Canadian *Charter* provided the authority, and also the limits, of parliamentary interference with human rights in a manner that is conspicuously absent in the American version. I would laud this as a feature of the Canadian approach to human rights.[150] Others have criticized the lack of clarity as to how s1 and s2 are to be practically reconciled in particular cases.[151] Some have expressed fears that the effective quarantining of the two risks sidelining freedom of expression as a fundamental value, rendering it more liable to be overridden during a s1 analysis in favor of other values, such as equality or multiculturalism.[152]

The other particularly noteworthy feature of the s1 analysis is the structured way in which the Court considers the legislation. Prima facie legislation which interferes with fundamental human rights is in breach of the *Charter*, a subject to which I return below. Most of the analysis occurs at the second stage, where the Court considers whether the restriction on the right can be justified by the government. Here, a relatively structured analysis takes place. The government is forced to articulate the pressing objectives which animated its legislation. If it can do that, then it must further articulate how the legislation is tailored towards meeting this objective. Upon reading a good proportion of the Canadian case law, it has been surprising, not to say perplexing, the number of occasions when the government has not been able to articulate a pressing and substantial objective for its legislation, or that the legislation is carefully tailored towards meeting its objective. That said, the idea that governments should have to justify interferences with fundamental freedoms, to precisely articulating what its legislation is designed to achieve, and how the specific provisions will do that, is a good one. It is thought to lead to better legislation and better policy outcomes. The idea that legislation should be held invalid if it does not meet these hurdles is justified on the basis of public policy. It is no-one's interests to have poorly thought out, or poorly drafted, legislation, particularly legislation which interferes with human rights.

Further, the idea that once a law has been shown to interfere with fundamental human rights, the onus is placed on the government to justify this interference is a good one. It reflects the starting point of liberty. Interferences with fundamental liberties ought to be justified and justifiable.

Minimally Invasive

Another laudable feature of the Canadian approach is its concern with whether the legislation is minimally invasive of human rights. I will consider the specific mechanics of how this test is applied below, but the notion that drafters of legislation which impacts human rights must be mindful to consider how they can minimally impair the fundamental freedom in the course of legislating to achieve their legitimate objectives is a good one. Again, this is a rights-defensive approach. It forces human rights to be front and center of government thinking about its proposed legislation. And in the last stage of proportionality, the court explicitly undergoes a balancing exercise, considering the benefits of the legislation in the light of its negative impacts on rights. Again, this is considered to be a very valuable exercise, consciously recognizing the difficult trade-offs involved in many of these policy areas, seeking to take account of the democratic franchise which entitles the government's policy decisions to some deference, but also recognizing the need to uphold fundamental Canadian values.

That having been said, some confusion regarding the role of the s2 analysis, and its link with s1 analysis, is evident. It seems that in the s2 analysis the Court is mainly concerned with the question whether the particular action in dispute conveys expression. If it does, this will usually be enough to indicate a s2 breach, and then the conversation turns to whether there is a s1 justification. One of the advantages of this approach is the court's repeated concern that content-based restrictions not be imposed. It has repeatedly emphasized that the s2 analysis does not involve any consideration of the content of the speech, and whether the speech is of a nature or quality that "deserves" constitutional protection. These would be questions better left for the proportionality analysis in s1.

However, arguably the Court has progressively diluted this potentially very clear demarcation between s2 issues and s1 issues. It has done this by, for example, considering whether the relevant law has either the purpose or the effect of regulating expression. The particular concern arises with provisions which in effect (though presumably not in purpose) operate as a restriction on expression. The Supreme Court has found that laws which only burden free expression in effect only involve s2 breach where the speech concerned furthers at least one of the stated purposes of free speech protection, namely search for truth, political and social decision making, and self-actualization. It has not been clearly explained, let alone justified, why laws which affect free expression must meet this further requirement at the s2 stage, but laws with that purpose do not. Others have also been critical of this distinction.[153]

There has also been criticism of the Court's statement that violence is not protected by the s2 freedom of expression. While instinctively one can understand a revulsion for violence, and any notion that violence should ever be recognized by the law as a right, some have argued that conceptually it would be better to recognize that at least in some cases violent acts do count as expression in s2, before a s1 analysis that would in all probability find regulation of such violence to be eminently defensible.[154] Thus the overall outcome would not change, but some say this different approach would reflect a purer distinction between matters relevant to s2, and matters relevant to s1, and avoid contamination.

Another area of criticism is that in conducting the balancing that s1 requires, the Court seems very prepared to accept the government's assertions that it is necessary to proscribe the particular speech on the basis of its "harm." It has rejected arguments that strong and/or scientific evidence is needed for the government to show the harm of the expression it seeks to proscribe. It has accepted justifications based on a "reasonable apprehension" of harm,[155] well short of proof of actual harm or likely harm. It has not generally insisted on a certain level of harm, though this should be taken into account in the balancing required at the last stage of proportionality analysis. It has accepted arguments based around "common sense" or "logic,"[156] or what is "reasonable to assume,"[157] and apparently required less evidence where the group possibly affected by the speech is "vulnerable."[158] This approach has been criticized on the basis it does not sufficiently protect the fundamental right of freedom of expression.[159] Often research into the impact of particular expression is inconclusive.[160] Cameron would require proof of demonstrable harm.[161]

Contextual Approach to Speech

Another area of criticism has been with the shift in the Court's approach from a more literal interpretation of the *Charter* provisions to the "contextual" approach favored by Wilson J in *Irwin Toy* and subsequently adopted by the Court.[162] As was discussed above, a contextual approach in effect accords greater protection for some speech as opposed to other speech. Specifically, for example, speech that is political in nature will be valued more highly, and thus entitled to greater legal protection and respect, than commercial speech. Cameron has stated that by adopting the contextual approach, under which some speech is valued more than other speech in terms of s1 analysis, the Court undermined its view in *Irwin Toy* that freedom of expression was content-neutral.[163] So either it is content-neutral or it is not, but Cameron says that there is an inherent contradiction between, for the purposes of s2 analysis, stating that content is irrelevant, but then for the purposes of s1 analysis, adopting a contextual approach where content is relevant. Moon also expresses concern with distinctions based on the perceived "value" of speech.[164] Thus, while content-based restrictions are very unlikely to survive "compelling reasons" scrutiny in the United States, they have been upheld regularly in Canada.[165]

It is argued that the Court has allowed its opinion of the inherent value of particular speech to skew its view of whether to uphold it in s1 analysis, reducing s1 to a subjective analysis which fails to uphold the fundamental nature of freedom of expression.[166] In order to fix this, Cameron suggests that where a particular restriction on freedom of expression is content-based, it must be presumed to be not justifiable under s1. The state would have to show that, although its legislation does infringe s2(b), it is justified on the basis of a legitimate, non-censorial objective that is not based on the content being offensive or valueless.[167]

Moon criticizes the Canadian Supreme Court's approach to s1 analysis on the basis that it is too ready to abandon protection of freedom of expression as soon as someone who has been affected by the speech is able to show they have suffered "harm" as a result. Rather than weigh up the harm caused to that person or others with the values of free speech, and what he calls the emergence and development of "human agency" provided by free speech, the Court immediately sides with the one seeking to censor the speech, in Moon's view. He says that protection of freedom of expression needs to be broader:

> Freedom of expression has little substance if our trust in the 'autonomous' judgment of the individual is the exception—a condition that must be established. It has no substance if it is 'protected' only when we agree with the message or consider the message to be harmless. A commitment to freedom of expression means defining a reasonably clear space for freedom of expression that does not depend (simply) on our agreement with the message communicated or our judgment that no harm will be caused if the message is accepted. There is no avoiding the difficult task of identifying contextual factors that justify removing an act of expression from the scope of constitutional protection, of isolating situations in which individual 'rationality' is distorted or 'autonomous judgment' is constrained, even if this is a relative judgment that is difficult to make in an adjudicative framework.[168]

In conclusion, Canada represents a good example of a country that has moved from a tradition of parliamentary supremacy towards a situation where rights are given express recognition and protection at constitutional level. This has permitted the court to engage in an overt form of structural proportionality in assessing laws that impinge on freedom of speech, which is supported. The way in which its jurisprudence connects protection of free speech with the objectives of free speech is laudable. Its use of the concept of minimally invasive is a rights-protective doctrine. On the other hand, the Court has sometimes mixed issues more relevant to s1 in its s2 discussion, sometimes seems ready to accept the argument of legislatures that relevant speech causes "harm" with little reflection, and is prone to making judgment on whether particular speech is "valuable" that some find problematic in the free speech space.

NOTES

1. *Australian Capital Television Pty Ltd v Commonwealth* (1992) 177 CLR 106; *Nationwide News v Wills* (1992) 177 CLR 1.
2. [1938] SCR 100.
3. 133.
4. 133.
5. 133.
6. 133–134.
7. 146.
8. [1951] SCR 265.
9. Kerwin Rand Kellock Estey and Lock JJ; Rinfret CJ Taschereau Cartwright and Fauteux JJ dissenting.
10. 285–286.
11. 287.
12. 288; see to like effect Locke J (330). Similar comments appear in the judgment of Dickson J (for Spence and Estey JJ) in *Cherneskey v Armadale Publishers Ltd* [1979] 1 S.C.R. 1067, 1096: "a free and general discussion of public matters is fundamental to a democratic society. The right of persons to make public their thoughts on the conduct of public officials, in terms usually critical and often caustic, goes back to earliest times in Greece and Rome. The Roman historian, Tacitus, spoke of the happiness of the times when one could think as her wished and could speak as he thought . . . citizens, as decision makers, cannot be expected to exercise wise and informed judgment unless they are exposed to the widest variety of ideas, from diverse and antagonistic sources. Full disclosure exposes, and protects against, false doctrine."
13. 331.
14. For example, Cartwright J (for Fauteux J): "at common law an intention to bring into hatred or contempt or to create disaffection against the administration of justice is a seditious intention" (342).
15. [1953] 2 SCR 299.
16. 330.
17. 332.
18. 375. Locke J also referred to a reference by Galt CJ in *In Re Cribbin and the City of Toronto* (1891) 21 O.R. 325 to the constitutional right of all persons to hold meetings and make speeches in public places (376).
19. *Switzman v Elbling and Attorney-General of Quebec* [1957] S.C.R. 285.
20. 306; to like effect Abbott J (326, 328).

21. [1978] 2 S.C.R. 770.
22. 796 (Beetz J, for Martland Judson Ritchie Pigeon and de Grandpre JJ; Laskin CJ Spence and Dickson JJ dissenting).
23. 797.
24. 797.
25. *Retail, Wholesale and Department Store Union, Local 850, Al Peterson and Donna Alexander v Dolphin Delivery Ltd* [1986] 2 S.C.R. 573, 583–584 (McIntyre J, for Dickson CJ Estey Chouinard and Le Dain JJ).
26. *R v Oakes* [1986] 1 S.C.R. 103, [134].
27. Kent Greenawalt, "Free Speech in the United States and Canada," *Law and Contemporary Problems* 55 (1992): 8.
28. Charles Tingley, "Reputation, Freedom of Expression and the Tort of Defamation in the United States and Canada: A Deceptive Polarity," *Alberta Law Review* 37 (1999): 635.
29. S32 *Charter*. Issues have arisen as to whether *Charter* protections apply to Universities: Sarah Hamill, "Of Malls and Campuses: The Regulation of University Campuses and Section 2(b) of the *Charter*," *Dalhousie Law Journal* 40 (2017): 157.
30. *Central Hudson Gas & Electric Corp v Public Service Commission of New York* 447 US 557 (1980); see Robert Sharpe, "Commercial Expression and the *Charter*," *University of Toronto Law Journal* 37 (1987): 229.
31. *Ford v Quebec* [1988] 2 S.C.R. 712. Here the Court invalidated a Quebec statute requiring any business operating in that province to display business signage only in the French language. A unanimous court found that a direction to a business as to which language to communicate is restricted their freedom of expression under s2(b), and could not be justified under s1. In terms of commercial speech, picketing can amount to a kind of such speech, and could warrant s2 protection: *Retail, Wholesale and Department Store Union, Local 580, Al Peterson and Donna Alexander* [1986] 2 S.C.R. 573. However, the same case found the Charter did not apply to disputes between private parties, as opposed to the government; cf *Pepsi Cola Canada Beverages (West) v Retail, Wholesale and Department Store Union and Others* [2002] 1 S.C.R. 156 where the court interpreted the common law so as to conform with the requirements of the Charter, such that the general position was that picketing per se, both primary and secondary and whether involving a labor or non-labor dispute, was protected by the *Charter*.
32. 764 (Dickson CJ Beetz McIntyre Lamer and Wilson JJ).
33. 767 (Dickson CJ Beetz McIntyre Lamer and Wilson JJ).
34. [1989] 1 S.C.R. 927.
35. 976.
36. 976.
37. 970.
38. 973–976.
39. 994.
40. *City of Montreal v 2952–1366 Quebec Inc* [2005] 3 S.C.R. 141, 178 (McLachlin CJ and Deschamps JJ, for Bastarache Le Bel Abella and Charron JJ).
41. 1008–1009.
42. *Rocket v Attorney General of Quebec* [1990] 2 S.C.R. 232, 247 (McLachlin J, for the Court); RJR-Macdonald Inc v Canada [1995] 3 S.C.R. 199, 347 (McLachlin J, with whom Major Sopinka JJ agreed, and Iacobucci J generally agreed).
43. On the facts, the Court found that strict restrictions on dentist advertising breached s2(b) and could not be saved under s1. While they were targeted at a legitimate objective (preserving professional standards) and were adequately tailored to that objective, they were not minimally invasive of the right, and failed proportionality analysis (250–251).
44. *RJR-Macdonald Inc v Canada* [1995] 3 S.C.R. 199, [343] (McLachlin J, with whom Major and Sopinka JJ agreed, and Iacobucci J generally agreed). In that case, a majority of the Court struck out legislation which generally prohibited tobacco advertising and which required cigarette packets to display health warnings, on the basis that the provisions impacted free speech and the government could not show its legislation was tailored to achievement of its claimed public health objective, nor that freedom of speech rights had been minimally im-

paired, or that it was proportionate in the achievement of its objective, given its impact on the fundamental right (McLachlin Sopinka Iacobucci and Major JJ, Lamer CJ agreeing with the outcome; La Forest J L'Heureux-Dube Gonthier and Cory JJ dissenting). A revised version of the legislation withheld constitutional challenge: *Attorney-General of Canada v JTI-Macdonald Corp and Others* [2007] 2 S.C.R. 610.

45. *Edmonton Journal v Attorney General for Alberta and the Attorney General of Canada* [1989] 2 S.C.R. 1326.

46. "It is difficult to imagine a guaranteed right more important in a democratic society than freedom of expression. Indeed a democracy cannot exist without that freedom to express new ideas and to put forward opinions about the functioning of public institutions. The concept of free and uninhibited speech permeates all truly democratic societies and institutions": 1336 (Cory J, for Dickson CJ and Lamer).

47. 1339.

48. 1355.

49. *R v Lucas* [1998] 1 S.C.R. 439, 459 (Cory J, for Lamer CJ Gonthier Iacobucci and Bastarache JJ) (joint reasons). In this context, defamatory material is considered to be "low value" (466). This assists in determination of whether the law minimally infringes the right (466) (joint reasons) or in the last stage of proportionality reasoning (487) (McLachlin J, with whom L'Heureux-Dube agreed).

50. [1990] 3 S.C.R. 697.

51. Dickson CJ Wilson L'Heureux-Dube and Gonthier JJ; La Forest Sopinka and McLachlin JJ dissenting.

52. 69.

53. 69–70.

54. 70.

55. 70.

56. "Expression can work to undermine our commitment to democracy where employed to propagate ideas anathemic to democratic values. Hate propaganda works in just such a way, arguing as it does for a society in which the democratic process is subverted and individuals are denied respect and dignity simply because of racial or religious characteristics. This brand of expressive activity is thus wholly inimical to the democratic aspirations of the free expression guarantee": 71.

57. 91.

58. 94.

59. *Taylor v Canadian Human Rights Commission and the Attorney-General of Canada* [1990] 3 S.C.R. 892, 919: "it can thus be concluded that messages of hate propaganda undermine the dignity and self-worth of target group members and, more generally, contribute to disharmonious relations among various racial, cultural and religion groups, as a result eroding the tolerance and open-mindedness that must flourish in a multicultural society which is committed to the idea of equality" (Dickson CJ, for Wilson L'Heureux-Dube and Gonthier JJ). The joint reasons in that case rejected an argument that the provision did not minimally impair freedom of expression because it did not require intent in order to prove a breach had been committed (932).

60. 149.

61. 162.

62. 165.

63. For another related example see *Attis v Board of School Trustees District No 5* [1996] 1 S.C.R. 825 where a school board dismissed a teacher who had expressed anti-semitic views to their students. While the Court found that the teacher's comments were harmful, and his comments could legitimately be seen as undermining the kind of equality and respect and dignity for others that was a hallmark of Canadian culture and values, their actions in dismissing him were a breach of his free speech rights, because the actions were not minimally invasive of his free speech rights; alternative action to address their legitimate objectives, but not in such a way as to suppress his free speech rights unnecessarily, were available.

64. 172.

65. [2013] 1 S.C.R. 467.

66. 499 (Rothstein J, for the Court).
67. 501 (Rothstein J, for the Court).
68. 499 (Rothstein J, for the Court).
69. 512 (Rothstein J, for the Court).
70. 516–520 (Rothstein J, for the Court).
71. 521–522 (Rothstein J, for the Court).
72. [1991] 1 S.C.R. 139.
73. 154–156. La Forest J (166) expressed a similar view, as did Cory J (226).
74. 198.
75. These were: (a) the traditional openness of such property for expressive activity; (b) whether the public is ordinarily admitted to the property as of right; (c) the compatibility of the property's purpose with expressive activities; (d) the impact of the availability of such property for expressive activity on the purposes of s2; (e) the symbolic significance of the property for the message being communicated; and (f) the availability of other public arenas in the area for expressive activities (203).
76. 225.
77. 240; Gonthier J concurred with McLachlin J's reasons (226) and La Forest J expressed support for the manner in which McLachlin J approached the issues (166).
78. McLachlin J endorsed three rationales for protection of free speech, including the pursuit of truth, encouragement of social and political decision making, and the encouragement of a tolerant and welcoming environment which promotes diversity in self-development and the maximization of human potential and happiness (241).
79. *City of Montreal v 2952–1366 Quebec Inc and Attorney General of Ontario* [2005] 3 S.C.R. 141, 172 (McLachlin CJ and Deschamps J, for Bastarache Le Bel Abella and Charron JJ).
80. 209.
81. 210.
82. 213.
83. 214. McLachlin J also noted that overbreadth was an indication of constitutional invalidity (248). Gonthier and La Forest JJ supported the approach and reasons of McLachin J.
84. 217.
85. 223. McLachlin J also noted that vagueness was an indication of constitutional invalidity (248). Gonthier and La Forest JJ supported the approach and reasons of McLachlin J. Similar reasoning led to the invalidity of regulations preventing public servants from engaging in work for or against a political party, candidate for political office, or to be a candidate. While the government could point to some legitimate interest, in terms of public servants providing independent advice, and being, and being seen to be, independent of the government of the day, the regulation was over-broad in that its reach extended to a large number of public servants whose work could not reasonably be influenced by any personal political views they had, including clerical, technical or industrial duties. The regulation thus failed the "minimal impairment" requirement and was invalid: *Public Service Commission v Miller and Others* [1991] 2 S.C.R. 69. On the other hand, in a case decided on the law as it was prior to the Charter, the Court dismissed an appeal of a dismissed public servant, whose service was terminated after he repeatedly publicly criticized the government that employed him, including comparing the Prime Minister's government with a totalitarian regime. There the Court concluded that "a public servant must not engage . . . in sustained and highly visible attacks on major government policies. In conducting himself in this way, the appellant . . . displayed a lack of loyalty to the government that was inconsistent with his duties as an employee of the government": *Fraser v PSSRB* [1985] 2 S.C.R. 455, 470 (Dickson CJ, for the Court). Another example of a provision that was void for overbreadth was a provision which outlawed picketing. Union members who sought to hand out pamphlets outside of a business of an employer with whom they were in dispute were accused of a breach of a statute which prevented "picketing." They argued the provision infringed their right to free speech. A unanimous court agreed. It found that the provision was overbroad. While it might be legitimate for parliament to prohibit "picketing" activities, these were thought to involve prevention of egress or access to sites, and threatening behavior against one who might otherwise be tempted to cross the picket line. This was

materially different from what those accused of wrongdoing here were doing, which was handing out pamphlets. The Court found the definition of picketing was overbroad. It suspended the declaration of invalidity for six months to permit parliament to draft the definition of "picketing" in much narrower terms: *United Food and Commercial Workers, Local 1518 v Kmart Canada Ltd and the Labour Relations Board of British Columbia* [1999] 2 S.C.R. 1083.

86. *Hill v Church of Scientology* [1995] 2 S.C.R. 1130.

87. *New York Times Co v Sullivan* 376 US 254 (1964).

88. 1187 (Cory J, for La Forest Gonthier McLachlin Iacobucci and Major JJ).

89. 1161 (Cory J, for La Forest Gonthier McLachlin Iacobucci and Major JJ).

90. 1171 (Cory J, for La Forest Gonthier McLachlin Iacobucci and Major JJ).

91. 1174–1175.

92. *R v Zundel* [1992] 2 S.C.R. 731.

93. La Forest L'Heureux-Dube Sopinka and McLachlin JJ; Gonthier Cory and Iacobucci JJ dissenting.

94. 754 (McLachlin J, for La Forest L'Heureux-Dube and Sopinka JJ).

95. 766.

96. 768.

97. 775.

98. "intentional and harmful falsehoods repudiate democratic values by denying respect and dignity to certain members of society" (828, Gonthier Cory and Iacobucci JJ).

99. "Self-fulfilment and human flourishing can never be achieved by the publication of statements known to be false" (828, Gonthier Cory and Iacobucci JJ).

100. Gonthier Cory and Iacobucci JJ (808–809).

101. [1994] 3 S.C.R. 835.

102. Lamer CJ Sopinka Cory Iacobucci Major and McLachlin JJ; La Forest L'Heureux-Dube and Gonthier JJ dissenting.

103. Subsequently, this was adapted to consider whether such an order was necessary to prevent a serious risk to the proper administration of justice, because reasonably available alternatives would not prevent the risk: *R v Mentuck* [2001] 3 S.C.R. 442, 462 (Iacobucci J, for the Court).

104. Lamer CJ (878) (for Sopinka Cory Iacobucci and Major JJ). These were subsequently adapted so as to specifically consider the right of an accused to a fair trial, and the efficacy of the administration of justice: R v Mentuck [2001] 3 S.C.R. 442, 462 (Iacobucci J, for the Court). In *Mentick* the Supreme Court struck out a ban on media coverage of police investigatory methods. The Court found this was a very important topic of public debate, that the media could play a role in curbing possible abuse of power, and that without media coverage, citizens would probably not be sufficiently aware of the issue to carefully consider it (471–472).

105. Lamer CJ (887); at 889, "there must be a proportionality between the deleterious effects of the measures which are responsible for limiting the rights or freedoms in question and the objective, and there must be a proportionality between the deleterious and the salutary effects of the measures" (for Sopinka Cory Iacobucci and Major JJ); Gonthier J agreed (929).

106. *Toronto Star Newspapers Ltd v Canada* [2010] 1 S.C.R. 721.

107. *Canadian Broadcasting Corporation v Attorney General for New Brunswick and Others* [1996] 3 S.C.R. 480.

108. 495 (La Forest J, for the Court).

109. 514.

110. 506.

111. 504.

112. 521–523. On the other hand, limits on the locations in which media could take photographs or conduct interviews within the court precinct, and a ban on media broadcasting the official audio recording of hearings, was validated in *Canadian Broadcasting Corporation v Attorney General of Canada* [2011] 1 S.C.R. 19 on the basis that the presence of media was impeding egress to courts, and their presence was exacerbating the stress and anxiety of those who had to attend court to give evidence.

113. *R v Sharpe* [2001] S.C.R. 45, McLachlin CJ, for Iacobucci Major Binnie Arbour and Le Bel JJ (72); L'Heureux-Dube Gonthier and Bastarache JJ denied that what the defendant possessed had communicative qualities (128).
114. 71 (McLachlin CJ Iacobucci Major Binnie Arbour and Le Bel JJ); 145 (L'Heureux-Dube Gonthier and Bastarache JJ).
115. 98.
116. 119.
117. [1992] 1 S.C.R. 452.
118. 509 (Sopinka J, for Lamer CJ La Forest Cory McLachlin Stevenson and Iacobucci JJ).
119. The historical view of obscenity drew on notions of morality, considering whether the relevant material would result in "corruption of morals": *R v Hicklin* (1868) LR 3 QB 360.
120. 479; the "harm" approach was also applied in *Little Sisters Book and Art Emporium v Canada* [2000] 2 S.C.R. 1120. Bans on street prostitution were also upheld against s2 challenge: *Reference Re Criminal Code (Manitoba)* [1990] 1 S.C.R. 1123; *The Queen v Skinner* [1990] 1 S.C.R. 1235; *Stagnitta v The Queen* [1990] 1 S.C.R. 1226.
121. 485.
122. [2005] 3 S.C.R. 728.
123. 744 (McLachin CJ, for Major Binnie Deschamp Fish Abella and Charron JJ; Bastarache and LeBel JJ dissenting).
124. [2005] 3 S.C.R. 728, 751–752 (McLachlin CJ, for Major Binnie Deschamps Fish Abella and Charron JJ).
125. 755.
126. "Consensual conduct behind code-locked doors can hardly be supposed to jeopardize a society as vigorous and tolerant as Canadian society": 756.
127. *Thomson Newspapers Coy Ltd v Attorney General of Canada* [1998] 1 S.C.R. 877.
128. 949–954 (Bastarache J, for Cory McLachlin Iacobucci and Major JJ).
129. 955.
130. 942.
131. 957–961.
132. 957.
133. 958.
134. 963.
135. *Attorney-General of Canada v Harper* [2004] 1 S.C.R. 827, Iacobucci Bastarache Arbour Le Bel Deschamps and Fish JJ; McLachlin CJ Major and Binnie JJ dissenting.
136. 875.
137. 890.
138. 892–893.
139. 836. Similarly, a provision regarding referenda pursuant to which those wishing to incur expenditure on electioneering were required to channel their funds through a national committee system, and could not directly incur election expenditure themselves, was declared invalid due to a breach of s2, which could not be saved under s1 because it did not minimally impair election speech: *Libman v Quebec* [1997] 3 S.C.R. 569.
140. 846.
141. 847.
142. 850.
143. *Baier v Alberta* [2007] 2 S.C.R. 673.
144. 691 (Rothstein J, for McLachlin CJ Binnie Deschamps and Charron JJ).
145. [2009] 2 S.C.R. 295.
146. 323 (Deschamps J, for McLachlin CJ Binnie Le Bel Abella Charron and Rothstein JJ).
147. 328–331.
148. 333.
149. 333.
150. Kent Roach refers to it as the "genius" of the Canadian approach: *The Supreme Court on Trial* (Irwin Law, Toronto, 2001) 291; Kent Roach, "American Constitutional Theory for Canadians (And the Rest of the World)," *University of Toronto Law Journal* 52 (2002): 503.

151. Jamie Cameron, "The Original Conception of Section 1 and Its Demise: A Comment on *Irwin Toy Ltd v Attorney-General of Quebec*," *McGill Law Journal* 35 (1990): 262–263: "the *Charter*'s equivocation between individual liberty and collective values stems from a conception of their relationship that is more organic and symbiotic than static and confrontational . . . however by attempting to join that organicism with the positivism of entrenched rights, the *Charter* created an unresolved contradiction. It is sometimes portrayed as shifting Canada into the direction of American constitutional culture, but although the institutions of rights review may formally be in place, its ideological values are not. Unfortunately, instead of making a choice between these conceptions, the text delegates the task of grappling with this contradiction to the Canadian judiciary. The *Charter* has not only forced the judiciary to adopt an institutional role that compromises its self-image as a neutral and apolitical body, it also abdicates much of the responsibility for a Canadian ideology of rights"; Jamie Cameron, "The Past, Present and Future of Expressive Freedom Under the *Charter*," *Osgoode Hall Law Journal* 35 (1997): 7; Denise Meyerson, "The Legitimate Extent of Freedom of Expression," *University of Toronto Law Journal* 52 (2002): 333 refers to the "mismatch" between the Court's approach to s1 and s2.

152. Jamie Cameron, "The Past, Present and Future of Expressive Freedom Under the *Charter*," *Osgoode Hall Law Journal* 35 (1997): 26; Grant Huscroft, "The Constitutional and Cultural Underpinnings of Freedom of Expression: Lessons from the United States and Canada," *University of Queensland Law Journal* 25 (2006): 194: "equality and expression are seen as coming into conflict in Canada in the way that Isaiah Berlin thought inevitable, and typically the reconciliation works in favour of equality"; Peter Hogg, *Constitutional Law of Canada* (Carswell, Ontario, Fifth Edition 2007): "it is arguable that the scope of s2(b) should be narrowed to make way for a ban on expression that has as its purpose the advancement of equality."

153. Jamie Cameron, "The Original Conception of Section 1 and its Demise: A Comment on *Irwin Toy Ltd v Attorney-General of Quebec*," *McGill Law Journal* 35 (1990): 271: "the attempt to isolate an act of communication from its consequences is artificial and formalistic"; Richard Moon, *The Constitutional Protection of Freedom of Expression* (University of Toronto Press, Buffalo, 2000), 51.

154. Jamie Cameron, "The Original Conception of Section 1 and its Demise: A Comment on *Irwin Toy Ltd v Attorney-General of Quebec*," *McGill Law Journal* 35 (1990): 268.

155. *R v Sharpe* [2001] S.C.R. 45, 98 (McLachlin CJ Iacobucci Major Binnie Arbour and Le Bel JJ).

156. *Thomson Newspapers Coy Ltd v Attorney-General of Canada* [1998] 1 S.C.R. 877, 957–961 (Bastarache J, for Cory McLachlin Iacobucci and Major JJ).

157. *R v Butler* [1992] 1 S.C.R. 452, 502 (Sopinka J, for Lamer CJ La Forest Cory McLachlin Stevenson and Iacoubucci JJ).

158. *Thomson Newspapers Coy Ltd v Attorney-General of Canada* [1998] 1 S.C.R. 877, 942 (Bastarache J, for Cory McLachlin Iacobucci and Major JJ).

159. Denis Meyerson, "The Legitimate Extent of Freedom of Expression," (2002) 52 *University of Toronto Law Journal* 52 (2002): 338: "freedom of expression has the status of a constitutional guarantee. This means that the mere fact that there is some evidence suggesting that a particular form of expression carries some risk of danger will not yield sufficient reason to restrict it. Rather, one would need strong, if not conclusive, evidence that the exercise of the freedom increases to a large extent the probability of damage to other important individual or collective interests. Yet the only circumstance in which the Supreme Court appears willing to invalidate restrictions on expression is when it is satisfied that the expression in question is harmless . . . freedom of expression has no substance if it is protected only when we consider the message to be harmless"; Richard Moon, *The Constitutional Protection of Freedom of Expression* (University of Toronto Press, Buffalo, 2000), 54–55.

160. Richard Moon, "Justified Limits on Free Expression: The Collapse of the General Approach to Limits on *Charter* Rights," *Osgoode Hall Law Journal* 40 (2002): 361.

161. Jamie Cameron, "The Past, Present and Future of Expressive Freedom Under the *Charter*," *Osgoode Hall Law Journal* 35 (1997): 64. She rejects a standard based on common sense: "a common sense standard is inherently problematic because the purpose of the *Charter*'s

guarantees is to protect certain rights and freedoms from unfounded perceptions of good and bad, value and harm, or cause and effect. Simply believing that expression is harmful or has a bad influence is not sufficient to justify limits under s1 of the *Charter.*"

162. *Rocket v Royal College of Dental Surgeons of Ontario* [1990] 2 S.C.R. 232, 246–247 (McLachlin J).

163. Jamie Cameron, "The Past, Present and Future of Expressive Freedom Under the *Charter*," *Osgoode Hall Law Journal* 35 (1997): 14; and criticizing *Keegstra* on this basis: "a definition of freedom which deemed the content of expression irrelevant under s2(b) supported the converse proposition under s1 ie that valueless expressive activity is entitled to little or no protection under the *Charter*" (18). Cameron also criticizes the Court for collapsing the distinction between something that is valueless and something that is harmful (19).

164. Richard Moon, "Justified Limits on Free Expression: The Collapse of the General Approach to Limits on *Charter* Rights," *Osgoode Hall Law Journal* 40 (2002): 357: "there is no bright line between expression that contributes to insight and understanding and expression that is deceptive or manipulative."

165. Grant Huscroft, "The Constitutional and Cultural Underpinnings of Freedom of Expression: Lessons from the United States and Canada," *University of Queensland Law Journal* 25 (2006): 186–187.

166. Jamie Cameron, "The Past, Present and Future of Expressive Freedom Under the *Charter*," *Osgoode Hall Law Journal* 35 (1997): 53: "controversial views have virtually no protection under the *Charter* . . . the Court's aversion to unpopular and offensive expression is entrenched in a methodology that treats context as a proxy for content under s1, equates subjective perceptions of value with constitutional principles, and dilutes s1's requirements of harm and proportionality to the vanishing point."

167. Jamie Cameron, "The Past, Present and Future of Expressive Freedom Under the *Charter*," *Osgoode Hall Law Journal* 35 (1997): 60–61.

168. Richard Moon, *The Constitutional Protection of Freedom of Expression* (University of Toronto Press, Buffalo, 2000), 75.

Chapter Five

European Case Law

This chapter is structured as follows. Firstly it provides an introduction to the protection of free speech in "Europe." As presently advised, this is taken to include the United Kingdom. Secondly, the general principles applied to the relevant provision of the *European Convention on Human Rights* are discussed. Thirdly, the approach of the United Kingdom courts to interpretation of the provision is considered. Fourthly, the approach of the Strasbourg court to interpretation of the provision is considered. This bifurcated treatment is justified by the differences in approach (and sometimes, result). Finally a critique of some of the European principles is offered.

INTRODUCTION TO FREE SPEECH IN EUROPE

The lengthy history of freedom of expression in Great Britain was discussed in Chapter 1. It was noted there that systems of prior restraint existed until 1694, and prosecutions were brought both before and after that time for seditious libels, treason, *Scandalum Magnatum*, and blasphemy. Sir William Blackstone denied that freedom of speech existed as a general principle of British law, apart from prohibiting prior restraint, in the late 18th century. A different attitude towards freedom of speech, caused by larger changes in how society viewed the relationship between the government and the governed, and a broad switch from a Hobbesian view to a Lockean view, led to a different approach, and by 1832 prosecutions for seditious libel had largely ceased. Courts began to laud the general importance of freedom of speech by the latter part of the 19th century. From that time freedom of speech was largely protected by the common law, as opposed to a specific statute or bill of rights document. It must also be emphasized that the United Kingdom applies/has applied the doctrine of parliamentary supremacy, under which all statutes passed by parliament are valid. A court under such a system does not possess the power to strike down legislation as being invalid because it removes or abrogates fundamental principles such as freedom of speech. They are not enshrined rights, in the way of the United States *Bill of Rights*, and specifically the *First Amendment*. While the *Bill of Rights 1688* (Eng) does refer to a right to freedom of speech, this is limited to parliament, and the English *Bill of Rights* is not equivalent to the United States *Bill of Rights* in that in the event that legislation is inconsistent with the former, it is not for that reason valid. So to hold would undermine the principle of parliamentary supremacy or sovereignty which is axiomatic in the United Kingdom legal system.

Freedom of speech was effectively a negative right, in that it existed only so far as parliament did not take it away or abrogate it with legislation.[1] This is consistent with a parliamentary supremacy or parliamentary sovereignty model. Under such a model, parliament, and not the people, is sovereign. This system naturally limits the extent to which the law protects freedom of expression, as opposed to a system of popular sovereignty that is evident in the United States, and to some extent Australia and Canada.[2]

Nevertheless, some judges have referred to freedom of expression as a constitutional right in the United Kingdom.[3] There is also a longstanding practice of interpreting statutes in a way that is minimally invasive of rights, and a related presumption that parliament did not intend to alter or remove fundamental legal rights, of which freedom of speech is one, unless their intention to do so is very clear.[4] These are often called the principle of legality. This way of thinking about freedom of speech naturally spread to the countries which were based on United Kingdom common law, including Australia and Canada.

In relation to judicial review of an administrative decision which impacted human rights such as freedom of speech, the United Kingdom Courts settled on the *Wednesbury* unreasonableness approach in 1948.[5] Under this approach, an administrative decision could only be overturned if it was so unreasonable that no decision maker acting reasonably could have made it. Of course, this greatly limited the extent to which an aggrieved person could challenge the decision on this ground.

Matters changed with the implementation by the United Kingdom of the European Convention on Human Rights, which occurred with the passage of the *Human Rights Act 1998* (UK). As we will see presently, that *Convention* expressly protects freedom of expression and related rights, though not without exception. Courts will interpret legislation compatibly with the *Convention* where it is possible to do so, and can declare legislation to be incompatible with the Convention. There is debate as to the precise extent of change to United Kingdom law relating to freedom of expression heralded by the *Human Rights Act 1998* (UK). One view is that freedom of expression in the

United Kingdom has changed "radically" as a result.[6] Another is that the actual change is relatively minimal, on the basis that United Kingdom common law robustly protected freedom of expression prior to the 1998 legislation.[7] On any view, the kind of proportionality analysis undertaken in terms of whether a prima facie breach of convention rights is necessary in a democratic society reflects a significantly broader scope of review of a decision than was applied to review of administrative decisions in the *Wednesbury* case.[8]

It was always going to be a challenge for Europe to establish something of a common position on fundamental human rights, including freedom of expression, given the range of different nations with long histories and established cultures. As indicated in Chapter 1 and above, the United Kingdom had come from a system of prior restraint, as well as prosecutions for seditious libel, treason, *Scandalum Magnatum*, blasphemy, obscenity, etc., but by the mid-19th century had in broad terms settled on recognition of the fundamental nature of freedom of speech, even if it was not expressly enshrined in a legally protected manner. The United Kingdom had also adopted principles of democracy, extending the franchise to a broad range of individuals, adopting relatively fair electoral boundaries, etc.

There is some contrast here with mainland Europe. Free expression is enshrined in Articles 10 and 11 of the *Declaration of the Rights of the Man and of the Citizen of 1789* (France), though this is constrained by an express contemplation of legal regulation of "abuses" of this liberty. Mainland European nations were typically very concerned with attacks on the nobility, so they created laws which protected against "insult."[9] This was extended in some nations to insults of police officers and other public officials. There was expressed concern that public criticism of the government and its officials could undermine public confidence in these institutions.[10] Some European countries continue to criminalize insult towards public officials and public servants, as well as the government, royal family (if any), and the armed forces.

This attitude has persisted to some extent in the legal systems of mainland European nations, which often continue to outlaw "insult" at a more general level. In other words, European systems have transferred the idea of "insult" and "honor" as a source of legal rights and obligations from the aristocratic class to all members of society.[11] Respect is at the heart of such concepts.[12] Further, they often view it as a criminal matter, rather than a civil matter, as the common law tradition would. Truth was not always a defense in relation to such matters. One current example is s185 of the German *Criminal Code*, which criminalizes insult, and makes it punishable by one year in jail or fine. Another is s130, dealing with "inciting the public to hatred," punishable by imprisonment from three months to five years.[13] That jurisdiction also recognizes a crime of "sexual insult" and of "collective insult," which finds its most controversial application in areas such as Holocaust denial and so-called hate speech.

Further, mainland European states did not traditionally embrace the kind of democratic culture of which freedom of expression would form a pivotal part. Heinze points out that in the Weimar Republic, the pre-cursor to Nazi Germany, democratic institutions existed, but they were of recent origin. He notes that the German people "had never been raised in generations-old habits and traditions of open and candid dissent, debate and political participation"[14]; rather autocratic leaders who commanded unquestioning assent were more the norm. This underlying popular culture provided fertile ground for a demagogue who promises a return to imperial greatness and who ruthlessly cut down dissenters. Heinze reminds us that although today we are infused with the commitment to human rights enshrined in the *European Convention on Human Rights*, we should not forget that this culture was largely forged in the shadows of World War II, and did not precede it.[15]

Obviously, notions of freedom of speech would also be anathema to totalitarian regimes. Lenin thought that freedom of the press was dangerous, because it could overthrow the post-1917 government.

The other important principle of mainland Europe is that of proportionality. This concept apparently originated in German administrative law, applied to curtail broad discretion that had been given to police officers, in order to protect the liberties of individuals. The means adopted by the police officer in a particular case had to relate to the object of the law. If a less invasive way to meet the object of the law was available, this should be taken, in preference to a more invasive way. The court was asked to balance the intrusiveness of the law on human rights with its legitimate objective.[16] At this time, the doctrine operated in a society which lacked formal human rights protections. The doctrine seemed to morph into a constitutional law concept in the German legal system after the passage of the *Basic Law* in 1949, a document which does embrace formal human rights protections. A strong focus on human rights in the *Basic Law* was understandable, given then recent events in Europe. In this respect the German system differed significantly from the United Kingdom system, based on a system of parliamentary sovereignty. As indicated above, that system limited review of the exercise of administrative power to a *Wednesbury*-unreasonableness analysis. Similarly, the French and Italian civil law systems adopted standards of review much more limited than the kind of proportionality analysis undertaken in German courts.[17] It was an important decision as to which of the disparate approaches the European Court of Human Rights would take to the question of human rights. It accepted the proportionality approach applied in Germany.

Under that approach, the court considers whether the legislature is constitutionally empowered to enact the law that it has. Assuming it is, the court next considers the suitability of the law, in terms of the connection between the law and the legitimate objective the government claims it is designed to serve. It considers the necessity of the law, in terms of its impact on rights. A law will pass a necessity test if it is minimally invasive of the human right impacted. Finally, the court undertakes balancing, to determine whether the challenged measure is justified in terms of its legitimate objective, having regard to its impact on human rights. This proportionality approach, originating in Germany, was adopted for the *European Convention on Human Rights*.[18] It was then subsequently adopted in other nations that are the focus of this book, including Canadian[19] and Australian[20] constitutional law. It has not generally been adopted in the United States, though for a time that country seemed to adopt an "ad hoc balancing" approach. This contrast will be considered further in the final chapter of this book.

Some have continued to practice prior restraint, at least with regard to some categories of publication.[21] Obviously the content of the *European Convention on Human Rights* represents a compromise of these different legal systems. It certainly provides for a greater recognition of the value of freedom of expression than was apparent in the approach of the national law of most of the nations comprising Europe.

The European flavor of the *Convention* is evident in terms of its focus on equality and egalitarianism.[22] Clearly, this reflects that the Convention was written in the aftermath of World War II, when the world had witnessed racial and religion-motivated violence of the very worst kind. It is not surprising that this sharpened the participants' focus on regulating in such a way as would reduce, so far as regulation could, the chances of this happening again within a member state or states.[23] This philosophy has facilitated subsequent state regulation of hate speech including Holocaust denial, such regulation being generally supported by institutions such as the Council of Europe.[24] Obviously, the background of criminalizing notions of "insult" feeds into this, in the way that hate speech and Holocaust denial can be seen as insulting speech of a kind worthy of legal censure.[25] Recent controversy has involved the publication of cartoons as satire in respect of the Prophet Mohammed.[26] These cartoons were extremely offensive to Muslims. Merely drawing Mohammed in a physical form is considered highly offensive, let alone the content of some of the cartoons at issue.

This provides a marked contrast with the position in other jurisdictions studied, particularly the United States,[27] where the only case in which limits on race-based speech were upheld against *First Amendment* challenge[28] is now widely regarded as bad law.

There is debate over whether such restrictions are "democratic." The *European Convention on Human Rights* reflects a fundamental commitment to democracy. The constitutions of many member states also enshrine democratic principles into their governance.[29] Clearly, most European states believe that restrictions on race-based or racist speech are consistent with democracy. In contrast, the United States, which would see itself as the prime example of democracy, believes that free speech with few limits is fundamental to democracy, and would not for that reason countenance restrictions on racist speech. In fact, that nation believed so strongly about this matter that it specifically derogated from provisions in the discrimination convention which required signatory states to prohibit hate speech.[30] How can this divergence be explained? Two jurisdictions which laud themselves as exemplars which take fundamentally opposed views to a matter such as hate speech? It may be that they conceive of democracy in different terms; some have suggested that the Europeans favor what is termed substantive democracy, while the American model reflects procedural democracy.[31] It may also be that the experience of World War II seared into the consciousness of Europeans how ideology can subvert democracy, with the rise of Hitler, and the relatively easy destruction of institutions that might have otherwise been thought to contain features that would prevent what occurred from occurring.[32] As indicated above, it must also be acknowledged that European states had a long history of regulating "insult" not matched in the United States.

SUMMARY OF PRINCIPLES APPLICABLE TO FREE SPEECH IN THE *EUROPEAN CONVENTION*

Article 10 of the *European Convention on Human Rights* states that individuals have the right to freedom of expression, including the right to hold opinions and to receive and impart information and ideas without interference by government authorities. Article 10(2) states that with the right to freedom of expression comes duties and responsibilities. As such, it is subject to limits prescribed by law and necessary in a democratic society. It gives examples of contexts in which limits may be imposed, including the interests of national security or public safety, prevention of "disorder" or crime, protection of health or morals, protection of reputation, maintenance of confidentiality, and maintenance of the authority and impartiality of the judiciary.

As many decisions of the European Court of Human Rights express themselves in very similar terms, it is possible to state how Article 10 has been interpreted very succinctly. In essence, the Court has consistently observed that freedom of expression is one of the essential foundations of a democratic society, and a basic condition for the progress of society and for an individual's self-fulfilment.[33] Article 10 applies to a broad range of expression, including ideas that shock, offend, or disturb.[34] While freedom of expression is not absolute, exceptions must be construed strictly and justified thoroughly.[35] The mere fact that the expression is in a particular form, for example, emotive or extreme words, does not preclude it having Article 10 protection.[36] Courts are not arbiters of how particular opinions should be expressed.[37] Contributions to debates on matters of public interest are entitled to strong freedom of expression protection.[38] Most especially this protects expression which conveys ideas which "offend, shock or challenge the established order."[39] Although it has emphasized that the form of the expression is protected, it has also taken into account the fact that a media organization chose to run a story on the front page of its largest circulation outlet in applying proportionality analysis.[40] The Court also noted in that case that the circumstances in which the media outlet came to acquire confidential information was also relevant in proportionality analysis.[41] The Court does not accord protection to the expression of violent intentions, or those which deny the foundation of a democratic society. Occasionally it suggests that right may be positive in nature, rather than just a negative protection from interference.[42]

The Court has given specific meaning to various concepts within Article 10(2), including whether a limit is "prescribed by law," whether it has been passed for legitimate reasons, and whether it is "necessary," which has been held to engage a proportionality analysis. In terms of whether a limit is prescribed by law, the Court will consider whether the law (whether it be statute or the common law) is specific enough, so that individuals reasonably could be aware of their obligations under the law, and whether the law and its application to a particular situation is accessible and reasonably knowable by individuals.[43] In other words, a person must be able to reasonably foresee the consequences that a given action will entail.[44] This will depend on the identity of the person expressing the relevant view. So, for instance, where they are a professional or media organization, they might be generally considered to better be able to foresee the application of the law to them and to obtain legal advice.[45]

This requirement has usually, if not always, been satisfied. In one rare case, the court found that the exercise of a magistrate's discretion to bind a person over to be of good behavior and not breach the peace was not "prescribed by law."[46] It would not have been clear to those affected by the order what the behavior was that was being prohibited.[47] The measure was prospective in nature there, applying to possible future acts, rather than past acts.[48] This gave it the essence of a "prior restraint" on freedom of expression, requiring even more justification in proportionality analysis.[49] The government could not meet this proportionality requirement on the facts. In another case, the court found that someone reading the defendant public authority's advertising policy could not reasonably foresee that it might reject advertising on the basis that it referred to a region that was not officially recognized as a separate jurisdiction from the rest of the nation.[50]

The Court will also consider whether the relevant provision was "necessary." Here, the Court considers whether the legislation is targeted to a pressing social need.[51] The Court's role here has been carefully delineated. It is not to take the place of the national authority, and determine whether it would have legislated as the national authority did.[52] It accords the relevant legislature a "margin of appreciation" in terms of its legislative choices. The extent of this margin of appreciation is context-specific,[53] so that the court might accord a legislature a greater margin of appreciation in some contexts than in others. For example, the Court has accorded special significance to speech in the political context, such that it will be very difficult for a legislature to justify curbs on political speech,[54] or criticism of a politician who is acting in a public capacity.[55] On the other hand, a legislature might be more able to curb freedom of speech in a non-political context, for example, defamation, or criticism of court decisions (if these are not seen as political). It has been noted that the concept of what is speech in the political context has been stretched to include matters of general public debate and interest,[56] and including commercial communication. Discussion of matters of general concern is given very strong protection.[57]

Article 10 protects both the substance of the expression and its form. This means that the person communicating enjoys wide latitude in terms of how they express themselves, as well as the content. A person may choose to express themselves in a sarcastic, exaggerated, or provocative way.[58] The fact speech is one-sided in nature and/or virulent does not deny it Article 10 protection.[59] Article 10 protects the expression regardless of the form chosen by the one communicating.[60] This can include non-verbal communication, for example, flags or other symbols which convey meaning.[61] However, many jurisdictions prohibit the showing of Nazi symbols such as the swastika. These bans have been upheld against freedom of expression challenges.[62]

The Court engages in proportionality analysis in terms of the goals of the legislation and the extent to which it interferes with freedom of expression. This is broader than simply enquiring as to whether the legislature exercised its judgment reasonably, carefully and in good faith.[63] The Court considers the legislature's justification for the legislation, whether it is legitimate, and whether the legislation is carefully tailored and proportionate to meeting this objective.[64] The reasons given by the state for the legislation must be "relevant and sufficient."[65] It is not a positive obligation on the state to provide information.[66] The extent of the penalty imposed on the alleged wrongdoer is an important part of proportionality analysis.[67] It is very unlikely that any jail term for mere expression which does not involve violence or a call to violence will survive proportionality analysis.[68] The fairness of the proceeding, including the extent of procedural fairness accorded, is relevant.[69] So is the reach of the expression; the more far-reaching it is, the more the government may be able to justify its regulation.[70] Similarly, the identity of the speaker is important. It might view differently speech by a low-profile person which is unlikely to make much impact than speech by a high-profile, influential person.[71] The extent to which the banned expression which is the focus of the current dispute could be articulated in other channels is also relevant in the court's proportionality analysis.[72]

The Court has played special regard to restrictions which impact freedom of the press, in recognition of the fundamental role that the press play in maintaining a democratic system of government, and holding governments accountable to the electorate.[73] Such measures are approached with the utmost caution. The court is conscious that even the possibility of sanctions, including jail terms, for journalism could have a significant chilling effect on the exercise of journalistic freedom of expression.[74] It will be very rare that imposing a jail term on a journalist for exercising their freedom of expression will be consistent with Article 10.[75] One possible example would be where the expression at issue infringed other convention rights, for example, hate speech or incitement to violence. Similarly, it is very unlikely that a "prior restraint" on a journalist, in the form of banning them from working for one year, will be consistent with convention rights.[76] The extent of protection of journalists will depend to a large extent on the nature of their topic. While significant protection will be accorded a journalist's investigation and reporting of significant political and social issues, much less protection will be given in relation to coverage of a non-politician's private life.[77]

The court has expressed itself more generally also about the danger that punishment of someone because of something they said will create a chilling effect beyond the impact on the particular person involved in the case at hand.[78] This is relevant in proportionality analysis.

The Court also routinely observes that the government enjoys a dominant position within legal systems of a country, and has special power to curb freedom of expression of individuals living within the country. The court notes this in observing that this requires governments to exercise restraint in curbing freedom of expression, particularly with criminal sanctions, and particularly when alternatives are available to meet the objectives said to justify the curbs on speech.[79] However, the Court also typically accepts the right of legislatures to limit speech, even through criminal sanctions, that poses a legitimate threat to public order. Criminal sanctions for defamation are not, for that reason alone, prohibited.[80]

The federal nature of Europe is important in how the Court conducts proportionality analysis. In applying proportionality analysis, the Court faces a delicate balance between enforcing the rights in the Convention but also paying due regard to the sovereignty of member nations, and their approaches to a range of public policy issues. Member states have many historical, cultural, and political differences.[81] It is a delicate balance to respect this, while remaining faithful to the ambitious intent of the *European Convention on Human Rights*.

It seeks to pay heed to the sovereignty of member nations through its "margin of appreciation" in applying the terms of the Convention to their legislation.[82] Further, it is also relevant in applying this margin of appreciation the extent to which there is, or is not, relative consensus in European nations as to a particular issue. So, for instance, the Court is likely to provide a greater margin of appreciation for a measure that is broadly mirrored across European states,[83] and a lesser margin of appreciation for a measure that is unusual and more invasive of a particular convention right than is typically seen across Europe. It also pays regard to the federal nature of Europe in its repeated observations that there is no concept of general morality in Europe.[84] A lack of consensus across Europe about a particular issue will typically in practice mean the margin of appreciation is greater for member states to regulate as they see fit.[85] This is a specific example of the Court's attempt to pay due deference to the sovereignty of nation states, and a greater margin of appreciation in areas of significant policy difference across the continent. Further, the Court will take into account a particular state's political history and development in the proportionality analysis. Measures that might be justified as proportionate in one state given its political history and circumstances are not necessarily proportionate in another.[86]

A greater margin of appreciation is also given in circumstances where there is a clash of competing convention rights. Here the court will consider whether it believes a fair balance has been achieved, in accordance with past guidance given in the case law.[87] It considers national authorities to usually be in the best position to balance the competing interests, including threats to national security and continued risks.[88]

The timing of comments in relation to events to which they are connected is relevant in proportionality analysis. Consider a case where, for example, a conflict is ongoing, where an ex-politician expresses support for a revolutionary group at the precise time that the group is engaged in guerrilla warfare with government forces. The Court found the applicant's comments were likely to exacerbate existing tensions. A jail term of about two months for the person uttering the statements was upheld.[89] In contrast, comments about events of 40 years ago were not likely to stir up violence, so punishment for the maker of such statements could not be justified given Article 10.[90] Timing is relevant in another way, for instance, if speech is made during the course of an election campaign, it will be accorded even greater protection than it might enjoy during other times.[91]

The existence of Article 17 must be noted. It provides that nothing in the Convention implies the right to do anything aimed at the destruction of other rights in the Convention. This has particular application to controversial areas of speech such as Holocaust denial or so-called hate speech. In effect, the Court has said that denial of historical truths and hate speech is, or may be, incompatible with other parts of the Convention, for example, non-discrimination rights under Article 14, or respect for private and family life under Article 8. As such, the Article 10 right to freedom of expression has been held not to extend to speech such as Holocaust denial[92] or hate speech[93] against groups in society. This has been explained on the basis that the Convention contemplates a democratic society which tolerates and respects the dignity of all human beings.[94]

To the extent that the previous two categories do not catch it, nor are statements in favor of Nazi or neo-Nazi policy or practice.[95]

In relation to hate speech, in December 2015 the Council of Europe Commission Against Racism and Intolerance adopted recommendations on combating hate speech. It recommended that member states take appropriate actions against the public use of hate speech intended or reasonably likely to incite acts of violence, intimidation, hostility, or discrimination through the criminal law, provided no other less restrictive measure would be effective.[96] In determining whether such risk is likely to materialize, various factors must be considered. These include (a) the context in which the hate speech concerned is occurring, and whether it is linked to existing serious tensions within the community; (b) the capacity of the person using the hate speech to influence others (e.g., that they are a community or political leader); (c) the nature and strength of the language used (e.g., whether it is provocative, direct, involved use of misinformation, negative stereotyping, stigmatization, or otherwise capable of inciting acts of violence, intimidation, hostility, or discrimination); (d) context of the remarks, including whether they were isolated in nature or recurrent, and whether or not they are balanced by other speech uttered by the relevant person or someone else, for example, in the course of a debate; (e) the medium used, in particular the resulting ability of the speech to bring about an immediate response from an audience (e.g., the contrast between speaking at a live event, and part of a book); and (f) the nature of the audience, particularly bearing on the likelihood that the speech would likely incite violence, intimidation, hostility, or discrimination.[97] Some suggest that sentiment against hate speech, including on racial or religious grounds, has now become part of international customary law, so that even nations which have not acceded to the relevant Conventions would be required to act.[98]

Holocaust denial is not accorded freedom of expression protection, because the Court has determined there is a category of "historical facts" about which denial may be criminalized. Of course, this does not mean that everything about World War II or everything about Nazism is forbidden. For instance, it was permissible to express an opinion regarding matters of the French resistance, and to speculate as to who might have informed the Nazis about details of the resistance. This remained a topic of legitimate public debate that had continued since the war.[99] Hate speech is also prohibited by other international human rights instruments.[100]

Other forms of speech may also be denied protection under Article 10 due to Article 17, including the expression of violent intentions, or denying the foundations of a democratic society,[101] glorification of war crimes, crimes against humanity, genocide, or contempt to victims of totalitarianism.[102] The Court has explained that this latter restriction is necessary because the convention is based on notions that democracy is fundamental and essential in order to secure the liberties specifically expressed in the document, so that someone who denies or seeks to undermine the democratic basis of government falls within the kind of behavior dealt with in Article 17.[103] By this type of reasoning, a ban on active members of the Communist Party running for government office was justified in Latvia, because the Communist Party had attempted to overthrow the newly established democratic regime in that country in the early 1990s after the disintegration of the USSR and its former annexation of Latvia to that nation. The person concerned was a senior member of the Communist Party and had not expressly disavowed that party's policy platform.[104]

We will consider now how these principles have been applied in various specific contexts. I will consider firstly how freedom of expression has been interpreted in the United Kingdom courts, and then how it has been interpreted by the *European Court of Human Rights*.

UNITED KINGDOM COURT DECISIONS

> We may pride ourselves on the fact that freedom of speech has existed in this country (England) perhaps as long as, if not longer than, it has existed in any other country in the world.[105]

As indicated above, the first bone of contention is the extent to which the United Kingdom common law of freedom of expression is in fact congruent with Article 10. Here we have statements by several courts that the principles are effectively the same.[106] On the other hand, we have skepticism by learned commentators that this was/is in fact the case, or whether courts have been guilty of some kind of retrofitting of the common law principle in order to make it congruent with the *Convention* right, without wishing to appear to be doing so.[107] And clearly there have been cases decided differently under the common law of the United Kingdom and the *Convention*.[108]

It is considered important to discuss the United Kingdom court decisions separately from the Strasbourg decisions for at least three reasons. Firstly, their approach is, though similar, in some ways different, as the following discussion will tease out. Secondly, with the so-called Brexit decision of 2016, and subsequent ongoing legal machinations in terms of separating the

United Kingdom from Europe, it is not at this time precisely clear how the United Kingdom courts will take account of Strasbourg decisions going forward. In addition, the current United Kingdom government has a policy to change the existing arrangements in terms of the *Human Rights Act 1998* (UK) and that jurisdiction's accession to the *European Convention on Human Rights*, though at the time of writing, just what this change will involve is not precisely clear.

The highest United Kingdom courts has in modern times emphasized the fundamental place of freedom of expression in a democracy. It has discussed the intrinsic importance of freedom of expression, and instrumental justifications for it in terms of self-fulfilment of individuals, the search for truth, and its contribution to democracy.[109] It has noted that individuals are more likely to accept decisions with which they do not agree if they have had the opportunity for input. It helps protect against abuse of power by public officials, and assists in correcting errors. The context was a case in which prison authorities sought to prevent journalists from talking with prisoners, unless they agreed not to use information garnered. The court heard evidence that in the past through this channel, many wrongful convictions had been overturned.[110] Elsewhere, it has emphasized that attempts to place limits on freedom of speech are likely to founder due to the inherent difficulty in framing them appropriately.[111] The English court has noted that Article 10 enshrines both a right to speak, and a right to hear.[112] As with the United States, British law frowns upon content-based restrictions.[113] The mere fact that speech is offensive is not sufficient, of itself, to justify an abrogation of Article 10 rights,[114] although expression that causes an "affront to human dignity" may be considered differently.[115]

There is apparently broad similarity, and some divergence, in how United Kingdom courts and the European Court on Human Rights apply proportionality analysis.[116] Specifically, in both cases the court will consider whether the legislation is designed to meet a pressing social need. In the European court, proportionality analysis will then involve consideration of whether the legislation is carefully tailored to that need, and will balance this with the infringement of freedom of expression. In contrast, the United Kingdom courts have considered whether the limits on freedom of expression chosen by the legislature are "rational, fair and not arbitrary."[117] This phrase does not appear in the Strasbourg jurisprudence. It has identified a four-stage approach, asking the following: (a) whether the objective of the interference with freedom of expression is sufficiently important to justify limiting a fundamental right; (b) whether the means used to achieve that objective are rationally connected to it; (c) whether the means used to impair the right or freedom are no more than necessary to achieve that objective[118]; and (d) there is a fair balance between the rights of individuals or groups and the interests of the community.[119] This approach to proportionality was substantially derived from the classic judgment of Dickson CJC in the Canadian decision of *R v Oakes*.[120]

The United Kingdom Court generally prefers not to use the phrase "margin of appreciation" which appears throughout the Strasbourg jurisprudence, as will be seen below; instead it prefers concepts such as "appropriate weight" to decisions of the legislature or executive.[121] This decision will be appropriately sensitive to "national traditions and institutional culture."[122] Some have been critical that United Kingdom's highest court has been overly deferential, or accorded too much weight, to parliament's decisions about the balancing of various rights.[123] This may be related to the strong tradition of parliamentary supremacy in that jurisdiction.

The courts' answer to the question of whether different categories of speech warrant different protection by the law has been inconsistent. So, for example, in *Reynolds v Times Newspapers Ltd* there are indications that no special rules should be applied to different categories of speech, all of it being subject to the Article 10 proportionality analysis. That was in the context of a suggestion in that case that political speech should be subject to special consideration in terms of the law of defamation.[124] On the other hand, there is evidence that speech will be categorized in determining the extent to which it should be accorded Convention protection: "it can be appropriate to take into account the general character of the views whose expression the *Convention* is being invoked to protect . . . political and economic views are at the top end of the scale, and pornography and vapid tittle-tattle is towards the bottom."[125]

The House of Lords was quite accommodating to parliament's attempts to strictly limit political advertising. It rejected a challenge to a ban on political advertising on the basis of a suggested infringement of Article 10.[126] The appellant wished to show an anti-animal cruelty advertisement. The European Court of Human Rights had found an equivalent ban to be contrary to Article 10, and not justifiable as being necessary in a democratic society.[127] The United Kingdom court had a different view, upholding a ban on political advertising because:

> It is highly desirable that the playing field of debate should be so far as practicable level. This is achieved where, in public discussion, differing views are expressed, contradicted, answered and debated . . . it is not achieved if political parties can, in proportion to their resources, buy unlimited opportunities to advertise in the most effective media, so that elections become little more than an auction. Nor it is achieved if well-endowed interests which are not political parties are able to use the power of the purse to give enhanced prominence to views which may be true or false . . . the risk is that objects which are essentially political may come to be accepted by the public not because they are shown in public debate to be right but because, by dint of constant repetition, the public has been conditioned to accept them. The rights

> of others which a restriction on the exercise of the right to free expression may properly be designed to protect must . . . include the right to be protected against the potential mischief of partial political advertising.[128]

Somewhat surprisingly, the European Court dismissed a challenge to this decision.[129]

The Court rejected a freedom of expression challenge to a decision of a television broadcaster to refuse to show ads prepared by an anti-abortion political organization.[130] The ads included images of fetuses. The broadcaster refused to run the ads during an election campaign, based on relevant guidelines which required them to take into account whether proposed advertisements would be "offensive to public feeling." It decided they were, and refused to broadcast them. The political organization argued that this decision infringed its Article 10 rights. A majority of the House of Lords found in favor of the broadcaster. The majority emphasized the negative nature of the right,[131] emphasizing there was "no human right to use a television channel."[132] The broadcaster had not prevented the political association from communicating its message through other means, merely through the broadcast medium. The court merely required that access not be denied on discriminatory or arbitrary grounds, and this had not occurred on the facts. Lord Scott wrote a spirited dissent, stating that the United Kingdom was a mature democracy, and this meant political organizations were entitled to communicate their opinions to the public.[133] Elsewhere it has elaborated upon the important role played by media in a democracy, and the need to minimize restrictions on the ability of media to facilitate and contribute to important public debates.[134]

The Court upheld the refusal of a public transit authority to run controversial advertisements on its buses.[135] The authority had an advertising policy which said that advertising would not be accepted if it condoned or provoked anti-social behavior or contained images or messages relating to matters of public controversy and sensitivity. The authority was bound by relevant provisions of the *Equality Act 2010* (UK) which stated that public authorities were required in exercising their functions to have due regard to the need to eliminate discrimination, harassment and victimization, advance equality of opportunity, foster good relations among individuals, tackle prejudice and promote understanding. The public transport authority had previously run advertising on its buses stating "Some people are gay, get over it." An organization wished to respond to those ads with ads of their own stating "Not gay! Ex-Gay, Post-Gay and Proud. Get Over It!" The organization's statement of belief stated that Christ supported those who struggled with "sexual brokenness, including homosexuality." Its Change Statement included the following:

> There is a growing body of research evidence indicating that sexual preference is neither immutable, innate nor chosen. As a consequence of our basic sinfulness we all have desires that we do not choose to have but we do have choices with respect to what we do about them. As a consequence our sexual identity can be reinforced or altered by either gender-affirming or gay-affirming lifestyles or therapies. CORE works with people who voluntarily seek to change from a 'gay' lifestyle to a gender-affirming one. This is sometimes referred to as a 'sexual re-orientation process.'

The case refers to a Guardian newspaper report of the incident. The ads had been requested by both Core Issues Trust and Anglican Mainstream. The Guardian reported that in a statement, Core Issues Trust and Anglican Mainstream claimed the first ad represented an attempt to shut down critical debate about being gay, and those who authored it were dismissive of those who sought to "move out of homosexuality." The judgment quotes the statement from Core Issues Trust and Anglican Mainstream directly to the effect that both organizations believe that those who were "unhappy with their homosexuality should be supported in developing their heterosexual potential where this is the appropriate life choice for them. Current scientific research says there is no gay gene." The public transport authority declined to run the proposed ad by Core Issues Trust. The Trust brought legal action, arguing the authority's refusal to do so breached their freedom of expression rights under Article 10.

The court rejected the argument. The decision related to a pressing social need. Its policy required it to avoid advertising likely to cause widespread and serious offense. The ads would have been in a highly visible place and could not be avoided by those who did not want to hear it. Core Issues Trust could express their views via different channels other than advertising on buses.[136] There had been a large number of complaints about the proposed advertising.[137] It contained a "confrontational assertion, not a reasoned, informed contribution to a debate . . . it is liable to encourage homophobic views."[138] The public authority would be acting in breach of its obligations under the *Equality Act 2010* (UK) if it ran the ads.[139] The court claimed that "the case law of the ECHR shows that reasoned debate is likely to be more deserving of protection under Article 10 than slogans and abusive messages."[140]

The Court has significantly deferred to executive will in other contexts relating to freedom of speech. So it rejected a challenge to a determination of the Secretary of State denying entry to the United Kingdom to Louis Farrakhan.[141] Mr. Farrakhan had wished to visit the country to conduct a speaking tour. He had controversial views. Those which appear in the judgment, which appear to be the basis of the decision, are Mr. Farrakhan's accusations "in extreme language" that wealthy Jews had exploited African-American people. In his talks he also emphasized the need for African-American people to build self-esteem, dignity and self-discipline.[142] The Secretary of State personally decided to exclude Mr. Farrakhan from the United Kingdom, on the basis that his presence would pose a significant threat to community relations, including relations between Jewish and Muslim people, that his presence would be "deeply offensive to large sections of the population," and a potential threat to public order. The Court found that five factors combined led to the conclusion that a wide margin of appreciation ought to be given to the executive here—it involved an immigration decision, it was a decision made personally by the Minister involving detailed consultation and consideration, and that the Minister was better able to assess the likely consequences of Mr. Farrakhan's presence in the United Kingdom than the court. Further, the Minister was democratically accountable for the decision. Finally, Mr. Farrakhan's freedom of expression was only marginally restricted. He could communicate his opinions in the United Kingdom by means other than doing so in person.[143]

Similar deference to the will of the executive is clear in *R v Secretary of State for the Home Department,* where a majority of the Supreme Court upheld a decision refusing entry to the United Kingdom of a dissident Iranian politician living in France. The Home Secretary had decided that the politician's entry to the United Kingdom to speak with a number of United Kingdom politicians could jeopardize the United Kingdom's economic interests and diplomatic relationship with Iran, and create possible violence in Iran, including against British residents living there. A majority of the Court said that in a case such as this, the executive was in the better position to make a reasoned assessment of the extent of this likely risk. It would be very difficult for a court to do so. A court's interference would only be justified in exceptional circumstances, and this was not the case here. This did not mean that the court simply "franked" the decision of the executive. Here, there were many other ways in which British politicians could engage with the Iranian dissident.[144] In dissent, Lord Kerr stated emphatically that it was the duty of the court to assess whether the interference with the Article 10 right was necessary, justified, and proportionate, and that courts should not genuflect to the executive on such matters.[145]

The Court has to some extent adopted the kind of categories approach to speech, in finding that Article 10 has differential application in terms of different categories of speech.[146] For example, it has found that pornography might engage Article 10 issues, but only at a "low level."[147] This presumably has the impact that regulation of it is less likely to infringe freedom of expression. This result could be achieved by various paths, by finding that regulation of pornography is likely to reflect a "pressing social need" and by weighting the value of the free speech involved at a lesser level in the proportionality and balancing stage. Another way of expressing it is to say that in such an area of regulation, states should be given a broader margin of appreciation to make appropriate decisions, than they would in areas involving other kinds of expression.[148] In contrast, political speech is "top of the list" in terms of importance.[149] The Court has also recognized the importance of speech that is not political in nature, in terms of goals of freedom of expression more generally.[150] Commercial speech, though expressed as being of "lesser value," is also protected.[151]

Other points about the United Kingdom approach to interpretation of Article 10 may be noted:

- it has suggested that where there is a wide divergence of legislative approaches to a particular public policy issue, the Court should adopt a wider margin of appreciation to the ability of states to legislate on the matter as they see fit, in contrast with a situation where there was reasonable consensus[152];
- it has been suggested that states be given a wider margin of appreciation in immigration cases, giving due respect to the right of a state to control its borders[153];
- the court has shaped principles of the common law so as to accord with Article 10[154];
- substantial importance has been placed on the freedom of the press to report court proceedings, in terms of transparency and accountability.[155]
- the government has a clear and legitimate interest in restricting expression connected with possible terrorism.[156]

In terms of protest, the English courts have taken into account numerous factors in determining whether it is protected expression within Article 10. Firstly, they have drawn a distinction between a protest which is merely asking a government to reconsider a particular decision, and a protest which is actively preventing the government from implementing a decision taken.[157] The former will be given more protection. The court has distinguished between short-term and long-term protests.[158] The fact that a protest infringes the law will be relevant, as will the extent to which the protest disrupts the lawful activities of others, and the extent to which the precise location of the protest is important in terms of its communicative value.[159] The ability of protesters to conduct their protest in another way will also be important.[160] In another cases the courts have been surprisingly unprepared to protect the right to (peaceful) protest.[161]

The delicate balance of freedom of expression with freedom of religion and equality rights was considered in the recent decision of *R (Ngole) v University of Sheffield.*[162] Ngole was a mature student enrolled in the University's master's program in social work. Completion of this qualification would lead to registration and practice as a qualified social worker. The profession of social work was regulated by a Health and Care Professions

Council. The Council produced a document entitled Standards of Conduct, Performance and Ethics which set out the duties of registered social workers. This included a requirement that a registered person's behavior not damage public confidence in the profession. It also had a social media policy, which advised about how to use such an outlet in a way that would comply with professional obligations. It stated that individuals should think before they posted, and should not use offensive or inappropriate language. It gave specific examples of the use of racist or sexist language, pointing out that the body may need to take action if individuals did this.

The University's handbook for social work students reiterated the expectation that students were expected to act in a professional manner both at University and in their personal life, including social media. It indicated that students had in the past been the subject of disciplinary proceedings because of things they posted. At the time of admission, students, including Mr. Ngole, signed a document indicating they would uphold the above standards, not compromise trust in the profession, not allow views about a person's lifestyle, culture, beliefs, race, ethnicity, color, gender, sexuality, age, social status, or perceived economic status prejudice their interaction with service users, university staff or colleagues. Mr. Ngole acknowledged that his conduct outside of the program of study may compromise his ability to remain in the program of study.

There was a news story about the release from prison in the United States of a registrar who refused to provide same-sex marriages. The news feeds permitted readers to comment. Mr. Ngole made several posts in response. He said that same-sex marriage was a sin. When challenged by another user, he provided Biblical references. These included claims that homosexuality was detestable to God, that homosexuality was a sin, and a claim that the devil had hijacked the Constitution of the United States, a country built on Christianity. He claimed the United States was now worse than a country worshipping idols. He cited the book Leviticus for the claim that homosexuality was an abomination, that homosexual acts were wicked and that God hated the acts, and that God would judge all those who had participated in wicked acts like homosexuality. After complaints, the University launched an internal investigation and invited him to various meetings. At each meeting he reiterated the views he expressed in the posts, and did not resale from them or apologies for them. He did not appreciate the possible impact of such views on others, including homosexuals. The University decided to exclude him from the program. He appealed on the basis that his Article 10 rights had been breached.

The original court found the restrictions pursued a legitimate aim. It was legitimate for a professional body to impose behavioral standards on members or would-be members of that profession. Though Ngole did not identify himself as a social worker in the posts, the posts were freely available and anyone could see them and, if they knew Ngole, connect him with them. The court noted a reasonable observer might wonder how someone with such hardline views could behave appropriately in the area of social work, a profession involving vulnerable individuals, and the need for a high degree of trust between worker and client. The objective of the regulations was important, in terms of public trust in the profession and the interests of users. There was a rational connection between the objective and the regulation.

The measure taken, excluding him from the program, was not overly invasive. The University was justifiably concerned not only with the comments, but Mr. Ngole's failure to apologies for or resale from the comments, and continued lack of insight as to why his posts were being questioned by the University given his enrolment in a social work program. The Court concluded that the University's decision to disenrol him was entitled to significant deference, since they had the expertise in terms of what was required for a social worker to be able to function adequately in their position. Further, the decision was overall a fair one. The University was entitled to take steps to ensure that only students committed to the ethos of the profession continued in this professional degree. It was entitled to be concerned with the perception that these comments would create. There was no inherent inconsistency between social work and religious views; many excellent social workers had strong religious views. However, in this case the University was entitled to take the position that Ngole's views, in conjunction with his lack of insight and remorse, made him an unsuitable candidate for registration as a social worker. This decision was successfully appealed. The Court of Appeal[163] found that the University had a legitimate interest in maintaining confidence in the profession in which graduates would work. However,

> It must equally be the case that the obligation to maintain confidence cannot extend to prohibiting any statement that could be thought controversial or even to have political or moral overtones . . . the expression of such views in offensive language, however, might well damage confidence . . . (arguments about preservation of confidence) cannot extend to preclude legitimate expression of views simply because many might disagree with those views: that would indeed legitimise what in the United States has been described as the "heckler's veto."[164]

One difficulty for the University is that they had taken inconsistent positions in relation to Mr. Ngole. At some points it was suggested that the University did not welcome any negative expression about homosexuality, at other points it was apparently not the content, but the manner and language used by Mr. Ngole. At other points, the concern was apparently with Mr. Ngole's lack of insight into how his comments could affected others, and that his views were "entrenched."

The Court was concerned about the implications for religious freedom and free speech, if the original decision were upheld:

> The implication of the University's submission is that such religious views as these, held by Christians in professional occupations, who hold to the literal truth of the Bible, can never be expressed in circumstances where they might be traced back to the professional concerned. In practice, this would seem to mean expressed other than the professional concerned. And if that proposition holds true for Christians with traditional beliefs about the literal truth of the Bible, it must arise also in respect of many Muslims, Hindus, Buddhists and members of other faiths with similar teachings. In practice, if such were a proper interpretation of professional regulation supported by law, no such believing Christian would be secure in such a profession, unless they resolved never to express their views on this issue other than in private . . . in our view, such a blanket ban on the freedom of expression of those who may be called "traditional believers" cannot be proportionate.[165]

The United Kingdom courts have jealously guarded the public nature of court proceedings, stating that it is a general principle of that jurisdiction's constitutional law that courts are to operate in public, allowing scrutiny of its decisions and processes.[166] This as inherent characteristic of the dispensation of justice in a modern democratic state.[167] Exceptions must be tightly contained. The right of the media to report on court proceedings was an aspect of this.[168] Exceptionally in *A* the Court dismissed an Article 10 challenge to a court order preventing disclosure of the name of a convicted sex offender. The government was in the process of deporting the offender to their country of origin. The offender had been resisting on the basis that disclosure of his identity would lead to a very dangerous situation for him in his country of origin. The court was satisfied that in those circumstances the Article 10 infringement was justified, proportionate, and minimally invasive of the media's right to freedom of expression.[169]

EUROPEAN COURT OF HUMAN RIGHTS DECISIONS

In an early case the Court considered a prosecution under the *Incitement to Disaffection Act 1934* (UK).[170] The Act created an offense for someone to attempt to seduce a member of the armed forces from their duty or allegiance. An offense was punishable by a jail term. The accused was a pacifist who sought to discourage British soldiers from travelling to Northern Ireland. She distributed flyers at an army barracks which contained statements of ex-soldiers who had deserted army ranks due to their objections to army policy. The flyer contained details of countries to which deserters from the army might travel safely, where they could obtain legal advice and social help. The flyer expressly stated that the hope of the authors of the flyer was that soldiers would avoid participating in the conflict in Northern Ireland. The accused refused a police request to stop distributing the flyers, and she was then arrested and charged with a breach of the legislation. She was convicted and sentenced to 18 months' jail, reduced to 7 months' jail on appeal. She argued the legislation breached her Article 10 freedom of expression rights.

The Court accepted that the Article 10 rights of the accused had been breached, but that the government succeeded in showing the limitation on freedom of expression was a proportional response to a legitimate interest. It accepted that expression of the kind at issue could weaken national security, specifically mentioned in Article 10 as a context in which limits might be justified, and the ability of the nation to defend itself from external threats. The flyers were directly targeted at soldiers soon to be posted to Northern Ireland. It went beyond mere comment about the politics of the conflict, and involved a direct incitement to soldiers to desert their positions. The Court found there was no breach of Article 10 rights on the facts.

The European Court has considered on many occasions freedom of expression in the context of media reporting. It has generally been sensitive to the important role played by the media in acting as a conduit for information about important matters of public interest. So, for instance, it lifted an injunction against a newspaper which sought to publish material on an upcoming case against a drug manufacturer involving the thalidomide case. The Court emphasized that the article was written in such a way as to make it unlikely to affect the outcome of the upcoming trial. It was reasonably balanced, did not prejudge or suggest outcomes, and was on a matter of very strong public interest.[171] Similarly it found that a prosecution of a journalist for writing stories about thuggish behavior within the ranks of Icelandic police was protected by Article 10, and a provision of the Criminal Code which made it an offense to insult a public servant or make defamatory comments about them infringed the freedom of expression rights of the accused.[172] The Court concluded that the provisions were not necessary in a democratic society. A conviction in such circumstances could discourage open discussion on legitimate topics of public debate. It was unreasonable to expect the accused to prove their allegations; the articles complained of consisted mainly of reports of what others had told him.

In other ways, the court has been sensitive to the special role of the media in relation to discussion of matters of public concern. The Court has also protected the confidentiality of journalists' sources.[173] The Court has also acknowledged the importance of topicality in media reporting, so that it will require very strong justification for attempts to delay media reporting of ongoing issues.[174]

On the other hand, the Court found that the relevant law did not infringe a journalist's freedom of expression in *Prager and Oberschlick v Austria*.[175]

Here a journalist wrote a 13 page article heavily critical of the Austrian judiciary. He claimed that they started with a presumption of guilt, acquitted accused individuals only as a last resort, bullied and harassed the accused, extended remand detention for longer than was permitted, and who disregarded the verdict of a jury when they disagreed with it. He said they were unaccountable and arrogant. The journalist was charged under the Austrian criminal code with accusing another of having a contemptible character or attitude contrary to honor or morality. This offense could attract a jail term or fine, subject to a defense of truth or fair comment.

The court again emphasized the critical role of media in a democracy, in terms of providing information about matters in the public interest. As part of this, questions about the functioning of the system of justice were important in a democracy. Judges had to be accountable to the people for decisions made, and the media could play an important role in that regard.[176] On the other hand, it was imperative that courts enjoy public confidence in order to do their job properly.[177] It was legitimate for a government to protect the judiciary against destructive attacks that were essentially unfounded, particularly when the ability of judges to respond to allegations was severely circumscribed.[178] Here the journalist had made very broad allegations of wrongdoing among the judiciary, with little factual basis or semblance of credibility. He had not attended any hearing of a judge who he personally denigrated and criticized, and did not afford any judge an opportunity to respond.[179] As a result, there was no breach of Article 10. On the other hand, a five day jail term for a lawyer for contempt was held to breach Article 10. The Court found that it would only be in exceptional circumstances that a jail term, albeit short, for a lawyer because of something they said in court would survive proportionality analysis.[180]

The right to freedom of expression extends to the commercial realm. In one case, a prosecution against a veterinarian for speaking with a journalist about his night clinic, on the basis that it was advertising contrary to the professional standards of that field, was overturned. The Court found that the regulations impacted on an individual's freedom of expression and could not be justified. The journalist's animal had been treated by the vet. He was interviewed about the fact he offered a night service, and had unsuccessfully sought to convince other vets to do the same. If he could be prosecuted for saying such things, the ability of professionals such as him to participate in community debates and discussions would be severely curtailed. This would in turn impact the ability of the press to provide information to the public.[181] On the other hand, an Article 10 challenge to restrictions on the ability of a professional to advertise was dismissed, on the basis that a national authority was better placed to weigh up the various interests involved in the question of regulation in such a space.[182] States have a greater margin of appreciation to regulate in the commercial sphere.[183]

The right to freedom of expression also extends to the artistic realm. The Court has noted that those who create works of art contribute to the exchange of ideas and opinions that forms an essential part of democratic society. However, the Court has sometimes not been prepared to overturn a judgment of a national body that a particular form of expression is so offensive to the morals of a society that it should be banned. The Court has taken the position that the national decision maker is in a better position to judge what a particular society's moral standards might require, and reiterated that there is no uniform European conception of morality.[184] This philosophy is apparent in the context of art[185] and books.[186] Here the form of the expression can be relevant. So, for instance, where a poem on one view contained some statements supportive of a Kurdish rebellion against Turkish rulers, the court took into account it was in the form of a poem, greatly restricting its audience, and not being likely to cause dissidents to take up arms.[187] Elsewhere the court has defended caricature in art, on the basis it is deliberately exaggerated, with a natural aim to provoke and agitate.[188]

It is also apparent in cases where freedom of expression might be thought to interfere with religious freedoms of others. The court has said in such cases that a wider margin of appreciation might be given to national legislators to properly balance these important freedoms.[189] So, for example, the Court rejected a challenge to United Kingdom blasphemy laws, applied to an individual who made a semi-pornographic movie depicting Jesus Christ and a nun involved in low-level intimate contact. The court dismissed an application seeking to declare the United Kingdom blasphemy law as being offensive to Article 10. The Court said the position had not yet been reached in member states where it could be said that laws forbidding blasphemy were unnecessary and incompatible with the Convention.[190] A greater margin of appreciation is applied to cases general questions of morality.[191]

Several cases have involved the question of the right of public servants to hold and express political views, and to participate in politics. One such case was *Kosiek v Germany*.[192] Relevant legislation stated that all candidates for public service posts were expected to uphold the free democratic system within the meaning of the Basic Law. Mr. Kosiek was a member of a political party which rejected the democratic order, wished to abolish parliamentary government and the multi-party system, and had an extreme nationalist and racist ideology. He was dismissed from a public service position when the government became aware of his views. The Court rejected his claim, finding there had been no breach of his Article 10 rights. The government had made a legitimate decision that Mr. Kosiek was not able to meet one of the requirements of the position. Similarly in *Rekvenyi v Hungary* it upheld a state requirement that members of the armed forces, police, and security services were prohibited from joining any political party and engaging in political activity.[193]

The Court had a different view in *Vogt v Germany*.[194] Vogt was a teacher employed by the state. Relevant legislation required Vogt, as a public servant, to uphold the free democratic constitutional system enshrined in the country's Basic Law. At the time she was employed by the state, she was a member of the German Communist Party. This party's policies included an adoption of the governance structures of the former East Germany, as opposed to the democratic structures of the former West Germany. Vogt held various positions within the Communist Party, and ran for office as one of its candidates. She was dismissed by the authorities due to her political activities, on the basis she did not meet the duty of loyalty towards German democratic governance. The European Court of Human Rights found that a breach of Article 10 had occurred.

The Court noted that states were entitled to enforce duties of loyalty on their employees. In particular, Germany's history explained and justified its insistence that employees be loyal to a democratic system of government.[195] However, here the duty of loyalty was owed by every public servant, regardless of rank.[196] It made no distinction between work and private life.[197] Other member states had not imposed similar duties of loyalty upon their employees.[198] There was no evidence that Vogt had made any anti-democratic statements or personally adopted an anti-democratic stance, or that she had sought to indoctrinate any students in these views.[199] The political party of which she was a member had not been banned by the government.[200] The Court concluded it was not necessary in a democratic society to dismiss her. Article 10 had been breached.

Similarly in *Grigoriades v Greece*,[201] the Court considered a provision of the Greek military criminal code which made it an offense for a member of the armed forces to insult the flag or the armed forces. This was punishable by a maximum six month jail term. The accused, while a member of the army reserve, sent a letter to his commanding officer suggesting the army was a criminal and terrorist apparatus with an intimidatory environment, which sought to transform people into instruments of oppression and fear. He was charged with a breach of the military criminal code provision. The Court found that the state had a legitimate interest in maintaining a system of military discipline, and to restrict speech that might threaten such a system. However, the speech concerned here was not likely to do so. It was not widely distributed. It did not directly insult individuals. As a result, it was not necessary in a democratic society to prohibit such speech.

The Court has accorded special deference to what it considers to be "value judgments." It has rejected national regimes which have sought to require those making value judgments to prove the veracity of their claims. So, for example, it dismissed an attempt to prosecute a journalist who had published facts about a charge against a sitting politician for allegedly inciting hatred and advocating doctrines espoused by Nazism. After the journalist published the fact of the charge, he went on to express an opinion that the politician's activities were probably in breach of the relevant prohibitions. The politician brought an action against the journalist for defamation. The Court rejected a suggestion from the national courts that the journalist should have to prove the truth of the implications he had drawn from the politician's public comments. They were in the realm of value judgments, which were of such a nature as could not be proven. A requirement that a person making a value judgment do so was itself a breach of the person's freedom of expression rights, in the opinion of the European Court.[202] In cases of value judgments, it will typically be sufficient for the person accused of wrongdoing to show their comments were fair in the sense that some evidence supported them.[203]

Even if a matter is categorized as a "fact" rather than a "value judgment," it will be sufficient if the author can show that their statements were made in good faith, rather than having to prove their truth, in order to avoid prosecution.[204] A national law requiring the maker of a statement to prove its truth in order to avoid conviction is not compatible with the Convention.[205] Similarly it has not supported a state provision which removed the truth defense with respect to events that occurred more than ten years before the comments were made.[206]

In terms of criticism of the government, the Court has said that the limits of permissible criticism are wider than in the case of a private citizen or politician.[207] Democracy required close scrutiny of government. Government enjoyed a powerful position, and must not abuse this powerful position to silence critical or dissenting voices. The Court noted this was particularly the case where there were other means available for government response to what had been said, other than punishment of the speaker.[208] In so saying, the Court apparently conceded the possible legitimacy of criminal laws against government criticism.[209] The facts involved an attempt to prosecute a politician who had commented on the deaths of Basque separatists, the apparent lack of government will to investigate the deaths, and suggestions that the government had been complicit in them. The politician was charged with a breach of the *Criminal Code*, which provided for long-term jail terms for those who "seriously insulted, falsely accused or threatened the government." The European Court found the national courts had not given the accused an opportunity to demonstrate that what he said either was true or was done in good faith, and there had been a breach of Article 10.

Similarly in Turkey, a national law criminalizing propaganda, meetings, and demonstrations aimed at undermining the territorial integrity of the state were challenged in *Baskaya and Okcuoglu v Turkey*.[210] There one of the applicants wrote a book about the Turkish government, published by the other applicant. The book criticized what it called the annexation and colonization of what it called "Kurdistan" by Turkish rulers. He was charged by the Turkish government with disseminating propaganda which undermined the territorial integrity of Turkey, by effectively suggesting some of the territory belonged to the Kurds. The penalty for such an offense was between two and five years' jail time. The accused were convicted and sentenced to jail terms of almost two years, and five months. They appealed, arguing the legislation infringed their freedom of expression.

The Court agreed. The realm of speech implicated here was political in nature. Democracy required the closest scrutiny of political actors and government. Government had to be careful in resorting to criminal sanctions against disfavored speech in such a realm, particularly where there were other avenues to respond to unjustified attacks and criticisms by opponents.[211] A greater margin of appreciation would be applied where the speech involved was likely to incite violence, including terrorism.[212] Here, although the political situation in the region remained volatile, it was unlikely that publication of this book would materially increase the likelihood of hostilities within the region. That risk did not outweigh the value of having different voices about a topic heard, unpalatable though it may be for the government and its supporters to hear.[213] The court was also influenced by the jail terms imposed on the author and publisher, concluding the punishments given were disproportionate to the government's legitimate aims and objectives.

A similar result occurred in *Ceylan v Turkey*.[214] There Ceylan was a trade union leader who wrote an article claiming that the Turkish government was involved in massacres and terrorism. He called for Turkish people to unite and oppose such government measures. He was charged with a breach of the *Criminal Code* which prohibited a person from inciting people to hatred or hostility on the basis of a distinction between social classes, races, religions, or regions, punishable by a jail term of between one and three years. Ceylan was convicted and sentenced to a jail term of one year and eight months and fined 100,000 Turkish liras. The European Court quashed the conviction, finding that the government had not met the high evidentiary bar required to justify limitation on political speech. It was true that the matter was highly politically charged, and the article appeared shortly after the Gulf War, but the material did not incite violence, armed resistance, or insurrection, in which case the government would have enjoyed a wider margin of appreciation for its legislation.[215] The court took into account the very serious penalty imposed on the applicant, the fact it cost him his position in the union, and had other consequences for his civil and political rights.[216]

The Court considered a case of a journalist insulting public servants in *Janowski v Poland*.[217] There a journalist came across public servant guards who were telling a street vendor they were not permitted to conduct trade in that area. In the course of telling the guards that they were incorrect, the journalist used insulting words to the guards, calling them ignorant oafs. The journalist was charged with an offense in the Polish criminal code concerning insulting a public servant in the course of carrying out their official duties. This offense was punishable by a maximum two year jail term. He was convicted, and sentenced to a suspended jail term and ordered to pay a fine of 1.5 million zlotys. He appealed, arguing his right to freedom of expression in Article 10 had been infringed.

The Court rejected this argument. Janowski got involved in the dispute as a private citizen, rather than as a journalist. Thus, the case did not concern the freedom of the press. He was not participating in an open discussion about matters of public concern.[218] The Court heard arguments that speech directed to public servants was entitled to more latitude than other kinds of speech; however the court distinguished between politicians, who should legitimately expect very close scrutiny and public debate and discussion about them, and public servants.[219] The Court accepted the legitimacy of laws protecting public servants from abuse while they were carrying out official duties. The Court concluded the actions of the guards "did not warrant resort to offensive and abusive personal attacks."[220]

In subsequent decisions the Court has apparently given more scope for individuals to criticize public servants. It has accepted broader freedom to criticize public servants than would apply to private citizens.[221] It has acknowledged the importance of public confidence in the public service, but indicated that this confidence must be earned, rather than absolutely ascribed.[222] Criticism of a public servant might be protected although it is expressed in an exaggerated, provocative, or sarcastic manner.[223]

The Court considered strict restrictions on political expenditure in *Bowman v United Kingdom*.[224] There legislation precluded any person or organization other than a candidate from spending more than five pounds to promote the election of a candidate. The maximum punishment for breach of the provision was one year jail time and/or a fine of five thousand pounds. Bowman was an anti-abortion campaigner who distributed pamphlets which highlighted the attitude of particular candidates to abortion issues. She was charged with a breach of the legislation. The government claimed its legitimate aim with the legislation was to promote fairness between competing electoral candidates by preventing wealthy third parties from influencing the outcomes of elections. The Court accepted this as a legitimate aim. On the other hand, free elections and freedom of expression, particularly freedom of political debate, was the bedrock of any democratic system.[225] This meant that, most critically during a pre-election period, there be a free flow of information. The Court noted that the threshold at which political expenditure by a third party became unlawful was very low.[226] While it only applied to the weeks leading up to an election, and the third party could lawfully spend money prior to that time, that would tend to defeat the third party's purpose in incurring the expenditure. Effectively, Bowman was precluded from publishing any information that might influence voters at the election. This went above and beyond what was necessary to secure the kind of equality the government claimed to be their legitimate objective. The legislation did not affect the ability of the press to support or not support any particular candidate. Nor did it preclude advertising, provided it was not intended to indicate support or otherwise for a particular candidate.[227] Thus, the legislation was disproportionate to the end sought, in the court's view.

In that light, and in the light of the earlier decision in *VgT v Switzerland* upholding a complaint about bans on political advertising, it was somewhat surprising that in *Animal Defenders International v United Kingdom* the European Court dismissed a challenge to United Kingdom legislation that banned political advertising. The decision accorded great deference to the considered decision of the jurisdiction to implement the ban in order to avoid effectively favoring wealthy individuals or organizations that wished to communicate a political message over those who similarly wanted to do so, but could not afford to run paid advertising.[228]

A major case involving freedom of expression is *Perincek v Switzerland*.[229] That case involved a Turkish political leader who made public comments in Switzerland denying that the Armenian genocide of 1915 by the Turks had occurred. He was charged with an offense under Article 261 of the Swiss *Criminal Code*. That section made it an offense for a person to:

- publicly stir up hatred or discrimination against a person or group of persons on the grounds of their race, ethnicity or religion;
- publicly disseminate an ideology aimed at systematic denigration or defamation of the members of a race, ethnic group or religion;
- encourage or participate in a propaganda campaign with the above aims; or
- publicly denigrate or discriminate against a person or group on the basis of their race, ethnic origin or religion in a manner which violates human dignity.

A breach of any of these provisions attracted a possible three year jail term.

The Court noted the provisions were prescribed by law and did impact freedom of expression. It noted that in terms of exceptions, Article 10(2) specifically permitted interferences with freedom of expression on the basis of preventing disorder. However, there was little evidence that the likely effect of the accused's speech was disorder.[230] The Court found this rationale did not apply, meaning the government would have to show the interference with freedom of expression here was necessary in a democratic society.

The Court noted that where freedom of expression was raised in the context of so-called hate speech or incitement to violence or intolerance, several factors were relevant in determining whether the legislation passed the proportionality requirement:

- whether the statements had been made against a tense political or social background;
- whether the statements could fairly be seen as a direct or indirect call for violence, or justification for violence, hatred or intolerance;
- the manner in which the comments had been made and their capacity, directly or indirectly, to lead to harmful consequences[231]; and
- where the statements dealt with historical matters, the likely impact of the statements and the length of time between the events and the statements would be relevant.

The Court noted that the current case also involved the Article 8 right to privacy. The Court recognized that the negative stereotyping of a particular ethnic group was capable, at a certain level, of impacting their sense of identity and members' feelings of self-worth and confidence. This could implicate their "private life" within the meaning of Article 8.[232]

The Court distinguished between expression on matters of public interest, and expression that promotes or justifies violence, hatred, xenophobia, or intolerance.[233] The former was entitled to protection; the latter typically would not.

The Court found that the relevant speech here was of the former type. The Court did not interpret the accused's statements as a form of incitement to hatred or intolerance. He did not express contempt or hatred for the victims of the 1915 events. He did not call the Armenians liars or attempt to stereotype them.[234] There was a lack of evidence that the accused had a racist agenda.[235]

The Court sought to distinguish decisions in which they had validated laws prohibiting Holocaust-denial, and the present situation. They said that Holocaust-denial "even if dressed up as impartial historical research, must invariably be seen as connoting an antidemocratic ideology and anti-Semitism."[236] Holocaust-denial was doubly dangerous in the court's view, particularly in states directly impacted by Nazism in the past. It was justified that governments in such states would take the position they had a special moral responsibility to distance themselves from the atrocities of the past by outlawing their denial. This was in contrast to the situation before the court in this case, where Switzerland had not enjoyed a special status in relation to the events surrounding Armenia in World War I.

In terms of the likely impact of the accused's comments, the Court concluded it was unlikely that it would cause serious friction in Switzerland between Turks and Armenians, or cause hatred between them.[237] This was partly because the speech related to events of a century ago. This weakened the argument of the state that bans on such speech were necessary to preserve the dignity of those who suffered harm as a result of the events of 1915, or their descendants.[238] Nor would the accused's comments likely have a substantial impact on the identity of Armenians as a group. It was also relevant to note that the reach of the accused's statements was relatively small, being confined to statements at three public events, as opposed to mass distribution of leaflets.[239]

Limits to the courts' tolerance of controversial race-based speech have been established. In *Balsyte-Lideikiene v Lithuania*[240] the Court considered the case of the accused, who distributed a Lithuanian nationalist calendar. Calendar entries claimed that the Polish had brutally murdered many Lithuanians during World War II. The calendar claimed that Jewish people were in control of the Lithuanian government, and that banquets were being held for Jews while Lithuanian beggars were ignored. She claimed execution of Lithuanians was caused by pro-Jewish politics, and concluded the only way that Lithuania could survive was by adopting nationalism. She had distributed the calendar for six years and was living largely from the proceeds of the book. She was alleged to have breached Article 214 of the Code on Administrative Law Offenses, in distributing information promoting ethnic, racial, or religious hatred. Her books were confiscated and she was fined. She claimed that such a proceeding infringed her Article 10 rights.

The Court found that Article 214, as applied to the accused, met a legitimate objective. Experts testified that one-sided portrayals of relations between nations could hinder the consolidation of civil society and promote racial hatred. Governments had a legitimate objective in seeking to stamp out such communication. The Court took into account the relatively light sanction on the accused, which did not include any jail time, in concluding that the legislature's response was legitimate and proportionate, so there was no breach of Article 10.

In *Hizb Ut—Tahrir and Ors v Germany*[241] the Court considered sanctions against those in German society who were preaching the need for jihad. The relevant individuals and organizations advocated the violent overthrow of Islamic governments around the world in order to establish a caliphate. The published statements of the individuals and organizations involved included that the Jewish state did not have a right to exist, and called for its destruction, and the killing of Jews. The authorities banned the relevant organization and ordered that its assets be confiscated. Affected individuals appealed on various human rights grounds. The court did not specifically deal with an Article 10 claim, but considered briefly a claim that the claimants' association rights under Article 11 were being infringed. It rejected such an argument on the basis of Article 17, which provides that an individual or organization cannot claim the human rights contained in the Convention where its evident purpose is the very destruction of those rights in others.

Another kind of hate speech was at issue in *Vejdeland and Others v Sweden*.[242] A Swedish criminal statute made it an offense to threaten or express contempt for a national, ethnic, or other group of persons with allusion to race, color, national or ethnic origin, religious beliefs, or sexual orientation. The offense was punishable by a maximum two year jail term. The alleged offenders had unlawfully entered school premises and distributed approximately 100 pamphlets entitled "Homosexual Propaganda." The pamphlet stated that society had now embraced "this deviant sexual proclivity." The pamphlet claimed that Swedish teachers knew that homosexuality had a morally destructive impact on the substance of society, but nevertheless would promote it as "normal and good." It blamed homosexuals for the spread of HIV/AIDS, and claimed that homosexual activists were trying to play down the evil of pedophilia and seek its legalization. They were charged with an offense against the Swedish statute. They argued Article 10 in their defense.

The Court stated that in order to commit an offense of inciting racial hatred, it was not necessary to show that the conduct incited or would tend to incite violence or other criminality.[243] Insult, ridicule or slander of particular groups was sufficient.[244] The court took into account that the offenders circulated their material to underage students, had trespassed upon premises to do so, and had been fined rather than jailed.[245] It found the government response proportionate in the circumstances, thus there was no Article 10 breach.

The Court has had to juggle in several cases the clash between religious freedom and freedom of expression. One leading example was *Otto-Preminger-Institut v Austria.*[246] The case involved an Austrian blasphemy law, criminalizing the insult of a religious figure or object of veneration within a religious community, or lawful custom or institution of such religious community. The offense was punishable by a maximum six month jail term. The appellant's manager was charged after the appellant screened a film which depicted God, Jesus Christ, and Mary in a negative light. Only those at least 17 years of age, and who paid an admission fee, could see the film. The film had attracted significant publicity, such that it was likely that only those who had some knowledge of the nature of the film would actually see it.

The Court found that although the applicant's freedom of expression rights had been breached, it was justified as being necessary in a democratic society. The Court held that the right to freedom of expression came with responsibilities, including avoiding expression that was gratuitously offensive to others, which infringed their rights, and which did not form part of public debate capable of advancing human affairs.[247] As there was no standard set of agreed morality in Europe, practically this meant states should be accorded significant freedom in determining the appropriate balance between freedom of expression and freedom of religion.[248] It could not be said that the measures here were disproportionate in seeking to achieve a legitimate objective. At times, this judgment seems inconsistent with statements elsewhere in the European case law to the effect that the Court is not a regulator of the manner in which individuals exercise their freedom of expression.[249]

The court shows a real tolerance for decisions that contracting states might make in relation to religion. The margin of appreciation in such a context is significantly broader.[250] This is typically on the basis that national authorities are said to be in a better position to judge the necessity or otherwise for the restriction, and the lack of a consistent standard about such matters across contracting states. Application of these principles resulted in the upholding of a provision of broadcasting legislation prohibiting radio and television broadcasters from carrying advertising directed towards, among other things, religious ends. The regulating authority banned the running of an advertisement for the running of a religious-themed documentary. The government argued that the regulation was necessary because of ongoing religious tensions in the country, such that advertising for one religion may offend or insult adherents of another religion. It claimed public order and safety as the justification for its regulation. The Court accepted these arguments, on the basis of the broader margin of appreciation in such cases, and that the ban related only to radio and television broadcasting, leaving the church group free to use other media to convey its message.

In relation to the Internet, a company recently unsuccessfully sought to avoid liability for posts on one of its discussion fora by reference to Article 10.[251] The applicant owned a news portal which featured large numbers of articles. The applicant encouraged readers to post their comments about featured stories. The site attracted large numbers of posts (about 10,000) each day. The site warned those who wished to post material that it would be monitored, and comments deleted if they contained threats or insults, incited hostility and violence, encouraged illegal activity, or contained vulgarity or obscenity. It employed software which automatically deleted posts which contained various offensive words. The company posted an article in which it accused the owner of a ferry company of scuttling plans to build an "ice road" between the mainland and various islands, forcing would-be commuters to use its ferries at a price. Many readers posted comments about the article in the online forum, abusing the owners of the ferry business with general abuse, including anti-religious abuse, and threats of or apparent incitements towards violence. The company's filtering system did not prevent these comments from being posted. Six weeks passed before the company removed the offensive posts. The company was charged with defamation. It denied it was responsible for the posts, and claimed the prosecution breached its right to freedom of expression.

The Court noted the company exercised substantial control over the posts. It provided a forum for them to be posted. There was an economic interest for the company in getting as many individuals to their forum as possible, in terms of advertising. In determining whether or not an online service provider could be liable for posts made, relevant factors included the context of the comments, the measures the provider took to prevent or remove defamatory material, whether the actual makers of the statements could be held to account, and consequences for the company of the proceedings.[252] Here potential victims could not do anything to prevent publication of the comments; in contrast the company was in a strong position to do so quite easily[253]; the company had taken far too long to respond to complaints[254]; and their business model would not need to change substantially to meet obligations regarding the content of posts.[255] As a result, an Article 10 challenge to the proceedings against the company failed.

Most recently the Court considered Article 10 rights in terms of an agitator for Chechnyan separatism against Russia. The applicant was both a journalist and civil activist. He published a newspaper entitled "Radical Politics." His articles contained several allegations:

- that its rulers had perpetuated an attack on a sovereign state and were killing innocent civilians there aimed at the physical extermination of the Chechnyan ethnic group;
- Russia's occupying forces were "maniacs, bloodthirsty sadists, murderers and degenerates";
- Russian "invaders" were intent on the "total genocide of the Chechnyan people."

He also referred to Russia's "colonial expansion" into Chechnya, referred to a President of the Chechnyan region, referred to Russia as a "scary black noisome abyss," referred to the immeasurable "scoundrelism and perfidy of Russia, the pathological falsity and criminality of Russia as a State" and claimed Russia had to be destroyed forever due to its "bloody cannibalistic atrocity" towards the tiny and helpless Chechnyan people.

He called for retribution against Russia for the genocide it had committed, and suggested that Chechnyans take up arms against the Russians. Referring to apparent terrorism in the Moscow underground, he called such acts natural, lawful, and justified given what the Russians had done to Chechnyans. He referred to the Russian President as a terrorist. The applicant was charged with offenses against the Russian Criminal Code on the basis that he had publicly appealed for extremist activities and had taken actions aimed at inciting hatred on the basis of race and ethnicity. He was convicted, and appealed on the basis his Article 10 rights had been infringed.

The Court found that many of his statements involved the incitement of hatred against Russian forces. He labeled all Russian soldiers as maniacs and murderers, and called for terrorism against them. He praised terrorist acts against the Russian state. Worse, these statements were uttered not long after the attacks, when the victims and their families were going through a grieving process. He rejected democratic principles and called for a violent uprising against an established government. The Court found these aspects of the accused's speech could be punished by the state. The laws were necessary to meet a pressing social need, and the reasons for it were relevant and sufficient. However other parts of the accused's speech, particularly his claims that Russia had committed genocide against Chechnyans could not be the subject of prosecution. Article 10 protected this speech, because it was part of an important debate about the cause of particular war crimes.

Reflections on the European Case Law

The first reflection is the fragility of democracy, inextricably connected with free speech rights, in Europe. While of course Europe has much older legal traditions than the other jurisdictions studied, it has a much more recent tradition of democracy. Many of its past governments involved unelected monarchies and reflected strictly hierarchical societies. Democracy as we know it today is of quite recent origins in Europe, with the obvious exception of the United Kingdom where the supremacy of the (elected) parliament over the monarchy was established in the Glorious Revolution of 1688, although parliament was hardly "democratic" in its representation until much later. It was only in the *European Convention on Human Rights* in 1950 that freedom of expression was formally enshrined as a human right, in sharp contrast to its appearance in the United States *Bill of Rights* in 1791. As part of this fragility, the European Court accepts the validity of legislation prohibiting criticism of existing democratic structures, in a way that no other jurisdiction studied would. Other countries would typically take the position that democracy is so strongly entrenched and embedded in the culture that there is no need to prohibit criticism of it. It is a confidence not (yet) apparent in the European experience.

There are other ways in which history continues to weigh on the free speech situation in Europe. Another is that European aristocracy were particularly sensitive to criticism from non-aristocrats, so that "insult" has traditionally been prohibited in Europe. While these systems have moved to extend their defamation laws to protect all citizens, there is a residual intolerance of speech that is "offensive" or "insulting." Laws that prohibit such speech are regularly upheld in Europe, in a way that is unlikely to occur in the United States, and which may not occur in Canada or Australia. This is also partly cultural. European culture seems more willing to suppress individual rights for a supposed greater good than American culture would tolerate. Notions of "equality" and "egalitarianism" pervade European legal culture. This provides support for laws outlawing speech seen to threaten these ideals, such as offensive speech. Where notions of "equality" and "egalitarianism" are threatened by free speech, European courts seem willing to readily cede the latter.

Further, the dark shadow of the events leading up to and during World War II remain over the European approach to free speech. There is understandable anxiety and consternation over so-called hate speech, particularly targeted against particular religions, but also at a more general level. Prohibitions on denial of "historical facts," including the Holocaust, have been upheld against challenge. The European Convention was clearly drafted as a response to World War II, and some of the relevant national constitutions were as well. As usual, the lessons of history may be ambivalent in this regard. Some might point to the role of oratory in the 1930s in whipping up hysteria against Jews and "others," using this example to justify suppression of hate speech. Others might say that anti-vilification laws existed in Germany in the 1930s, yet clearly did nothing to counter the dangerous rise of xenophobia. This will be discussed further in a subsequent book: *Freedom of Speech in Practice: Controversial Applications of Law and Theory*. The point here is that the European Court has readily accepted restrictions on hate speech. This may reflect an uneasiness that racial or other tensions are just below the surface and may re-surface at any time, thus justifying restrictions on speech that may precipitate this. It may reflect a lack of confidence that existing democratic or social structures can adequately deal with anti-social sentiment such as hate speech.

The second reflection is the somewhat fragile position of the European Court of Human Rights. That Court is acutely aware of the limits of its position. It is presiding over Europe, a continent with a vast array of different legal cultures and different legal histories, and different societies. The great difficulty in holding such an alliance together is fully acknowledged. This means that the European Court takes a somewhat deferential role at times in considering the law of a country, as being an expression of that country's culture, though without ignoring the requirements of the Convention. An example of this is the Court's preparedness to accept laws that depart from freedom of expression based on the judgment of a legislature in Europe as to the proper balance between, on the one hand, freedom of speech, and, on the other, rights such as religious freedom, or broader questions of morality. The Court is prepared to pay significant deference to the judgment of a sub-European legislature in these fields, in a way, and for reasons, that a court in any of the other jurisdictions studied would not. It is no doubt aware that a nation which has very serious reservations about decisions made by the Court about its laws might re-consider its recognition of the *European Convention*, and its place in the European Union. This is reflected in the attitude of deference and margin of appreciation accorded to national legislatures within Europe.

The third reflection is Article 17 of the *European Convention*, which specifically contemplates that free speech rights might have to yield in a situation where they conflict with other convention rights. The Court has used Article 17 regularly to validate laws which infringe free speech rights, because they do so for other legitimate ends within the Convention, such as anti-discrimination or equality, privacy, etc. While free speech is not absolute in any jurisdiction, and exceptions are recognized, no other jurisdiction has an express equivalent to Article 17. The existence of this article has broadened the scope of exceptional cases, where free speech has been required to yield to a broad range of other rights.

NOTES

1. *Reynolds v Times Newspapers Ltd* [2001] 2 AC 127, 207 (Lord Steyn).

2. James Weinstein, "Extreme Speech, Public Order and Democracy: Lessons from The Masses," in Ivan Hare and James Weinstein *Extreme Speech and Democracy* (Oxford University Press, New York, 2009), 26: "The commitment to popular sovereignty alone arguably creates a narrow but very powerful right of free speech. If the people are the ultimate source of political authority, they must be able to speak to each other about all matters within the scope of this authority; that is, on all matters of public concern. If, to the contrary, the government were able to prohibit speech on the ground that it will persuade the populace to formulate erroneous public policy, then the government, not the people, would be the ultimate sovereign. As James Madison argued over two centuries ago, a logical consequence of a commitment to popular sovereignty is that 'the censorial power is in the people over the Government, and not in the Government over the people.'"

3. *Reynolds v Times Newspapers Ltd* [2001] 2 AC 127, 207 (Lord Steyn), quoting *Broome v Cassell and Co Ltd* [1972] AC 1027, 1133 (Lord Kilbrandon).

4. *R v Secretary of State for the Home Department; Ex Parte Simms* [2000] 2 AC 115, 130 (Lord Steyn) (with whom Lord Browne-Wilkinson agreed), 131 (Lord Hoffmann); *Bank Mellat v HM Treasury* (No2)[2014] AC 700, 740 (Lord Neuberger, for Baroness Hale, Lord Clarke, Lord Sumption and Lord Carnwath).

5. *Associated Provincial Picture House Ltd v Wednesbury Corporation* [1948] 1 KB 223.

6. Eric Barendt, "Freedom of Expression in the United Kingdom Under the *Human Rights Act 1998*," *Indiana Law Journal* 84 (2009): 851.

7. *R v Secretary of State for the Home Department* [2000] 2 AC 115 (Lord Steyn); similar comments were made by Lord Keith for the House in *Derbyshire County Council v Times Newspapers Ltd* [1993] AC 534, 551: "in the field of freedom of speech there (is) no difference in principle between English law on the subject and Article 10 of the Convention"; and *Attorney-General v Guardian Newspapers Ltd* (No2)[1990] 1 AC 109, 283–284 (Lord Goff). Barendt suggests these views of Lord Steyn may have been "claiming for the common law an attachment to freedom of speech that earlier decisions did not strictly warrant," suggesting that the judges had sought to underplay the extent of change, and exaggerate the extent to which the prior United Kingdom had effectively protected speech rights: "Freedom of Expression in the United Kingdom Under the *Human Rights Act 1998*," *Indiana Law Journal* 84 (2009): 854. Elsewhere he said that "it is doubtful whether the change has so far been much more than cosmetic": *Freedom of Speech* (Clarendon Press, Oxford, Second Edition, 2005), 39.

8. *R (Daly) v Secretary of State for the Home Department* [2001] 2 AC 532, 547 (Lord Steyn, with whom Lord Cooke agreed). Lord Steyn there cited at least three important differences: proportionality required the reviewing court to assess the balance struck by the decision maker, not merely whether it was within a range of reasonable or rational decisions, proportionality analysis might invite review of the relative weight accorded to particular interests and considerations, and generally the intensity of the review would be greater; *R (Aguilar Quila) v Home Secretary* [2012] 1 AC 621, 643 (Lord Wilson, with whom Lord Phillips and Lord Clarke agreed); see Jeffrey Jowell, "Beyond the Rule of Law: Towards Constitutional Judicial Review" [2000] *Public Law* [2000]: 679.

9. Elena Yanchukova, "Criminal Defamation and Insult Laws: An Infringement on the Freedom of Expression in European and Post-Communist Jurisdictions," *Columbia Journal of Transnational Law* 41 (2003): 869. Whitman traces the European acceptance of the actionability of "insult" as being based on a desire to avoid self-help measures such as duelling. Regulators were trying to move the resolution of disputes from the individual one-on-one level to a more sophisticated plane where an independent third party would render a decision on the dispute: "Enforcing Civility and Respect: Three Societies," *Yale Law Journal* 109 (2000): 1315. This has parallels with early development of civil law, which by recognizing an early form of strict liability, sought to avoid resort to the "blood feud": Anthony Gray, *Vicarious Liability: Critique and Reform* (Hart Publishing, Oxford, 2018), 104.

10. Elena Yanchukova, "Criminal Defamation and Insult Laws: An Infringement on the Freedom of Expression in European and Post-Communist Jurisdictions," *Columbia Journal of Transnational Law* 41 (2003): 870.

11. Somewhat perversely, given their unspeakable evil and reign of terror, the Nazi regime is sometimes said to have ushered in the spread of rights against "insult" from the aristocracy to ordinary members of society, given their egalitarian view of society (at least, among those of the preferred race and religion): James Whitman, "Enforcing Civility and Respect: Three Societies," *Yale Law Journal* 109 (2000): 1328: "Nazi doctrinal analysis at last accepted the proposition that Germans of all social statuses participated in German honor . . . this 'nationalisation' of honor nicely paralleled a 'nationalisation' of honor that took place during the French Revolution."

12. James Whitman, "Enforcing Civility and Respect: Three Societies," *Yale Law Journal* 109 (2000): 1279.

13. The section states that a person who attacks the human dignity of others in a manner that disturbs the public peace by (a) goading to hatred against segments of the population; (b) demanding that violent or capricious measures be taken against them; or (c) verballing abusing them, maliciously exposing them to contempt, or slandering them, is punishable by said jail term.

14. Eric Heinze, "Viewpoint Absolutism and Hate Speech," *Modern Law Review* 69 (2006): 548.

15. 49.

16. Dieter Grimm, "Proportionality in Canadian and German Constitutional Jurisprudence," *University of Toronto Law Journal* 57 (2007): 385.

17. Alec Stone Sweet and Jud Matthews, "Proportionality Balancing and Global Constitutionalism," *Columbia Journal of Transnational Law* 47 (2008): 78.

18. The logistics of this have been more difficult than the line suggests. It has been observed that the British courts were somewhat slow to adapt their approach away from a *Wednesbury*-style standard of review in favour of a proportionality review. The European Court criticized British courts for this sluggishness in moving to proportionality analysis in applying Convention principles: *Smith and Grady v United Kingdom* [1999] ECHR 72, [138]; *Peck v United Kingdom* [2003] ECHR 44, [106]; *Hirst v United Kingdom No 2* [2005] ECHR 681, [80]; see for discussion Alec Stone Sweet and Jud Mathews, "Proportionality Balancing and Global Constitutionalism," *Columbia Journal of Transnational Law* 47 (2008): 147–151.

19. *R v Oakes* [1986] 1 S.C.R. 103.

20. *McCloy v New South Wales* (2015) 257 CLR 178.

21. *Case of Association Ekin v France* [2001](Application No.39288/88), [56].

22. Article 14 precludes interference with *Convention* rights without discrimination on the basis of sex, race, color, language, religion, political or other opinion, national or social origin, association with a national minority, property, birth, or other status.

23. Robert Kahn, "Flemming Rose, the Danish Cartoon Controversy and the New European Freedom of Speech," *California Western International Law Journal* 40 (2010): 255: "hate speech threatened the political order of unstable democracies and at worst opened the door to a Nazi resurgence."

24. See, for example, the *Framework Decision on Combating Certain Forms and Expressions of Racism and Xenophobia By Means of Criminal Law* (2008) stating that hate speech and Holocaust denial should be dealt with by proportionate penalties, whether criminal or civil.

Criminal penalties should carry a maximum jail term of at least one years' imprisonment. Civil penalties can include the denial of government benefits, refusal of permission to carry out a particular trade or business, being placed under "judicial supervision," or subject to a winding up order. The Framework Decision says that the fact that criminal activity was motivated by racism should be considered as a circumstance of aggravation.

25. Eva Brems, "State Regulation of Xenophobia Versus Individual Freedoms: The European View," *Journal of Human Rights* (2002): 495.

26. Robert Kahn, "Flemming Rose, the Danish Cartoon Controversy and the New European Freedom of Speech," *California Western International Law Journal* 40 (2010): 253.

27. Karen Bird, "Racist Speech or Free Speech? A Comparison of the Law in France and the United States," *Comparative Politics* 32(4) (2002): 399.

28. *Beauharnais v Illinois* 343 US 250 (1952).

29. For instance, the German Federal Constitutional Court has found that the nation's Constitution reflects notions of "Streitbare Demokratie" or militant democracy. This includes commitment to shared values, loyalty to the nation, and defense readiness. This allows Germany to ban political parties which have as part of their policy platform the destruction of German democracy, which has occurred. It is suggested that some current political parties are liable to be banned under this provision due to their far-right, nationalistic and xenophobic platforms: Eva Brems, "State Regulation of Xenophobia Versus Individual Freedoms: The European View," *Journal of Human Rights* 1(4) (2002): 487.

30. The United States derogated from Article 20 of the *International Covenant on Civil and Political Rights*, requiring signatory states to prohibit advocacy of national, racial, or religious hatred that constitutes incitement to discrimination, hostility, or violence, and Article 4 of the *International Convention on the Elimination of All Forms of Racial Discrimination*, requiring states to declare an offense punishable by law dissemination of all ideas based on racial superiority or hatred, incitement to racial discrimination, and acts of violence or incitement to such acts against any race or group of persons of another color or ethnic origin, as well as provision of assistance to racist activities. Signatory states are also required to declare illegal and prohibit organizations, and organized or other propaganda activities, which promote and incite racial discrimination, and recognize participation in such organizations or activities as an offense. The United States derogated from these articles, not accepting any obligation to restrict freedom of speech, assembly, or association in such space: Eva Brems, "State Regulation of Xenophobia Versus Individual Freedoms: The European View," *Journal of Human Rights* 1(4) (2002): 484.

31. 482–483: "under a model of substantive democracy, racist actions (discrimination in practice) are undemocratic because they deny the fundamental principle of equality. Racist views and proposals propagating discrimination or otherwise denying the fundamental rights of part of the population are liberticidal and therefore anti-democratic . . . to act or not to act? To take the risk of democracy leading to self-destruction or to take the risk of damaging it by protecting it too tightly? Europe is following the second road."

32. As Brems put it, "Hitler and his regime demonstrated the direct link between racist ideology and the destruction of democracy. In the USA, which experienced this regime only indirectly, racism is seen as a serious problem but not as something that could threaten the fundaments of democracy": 495.

33. *Perincek v Switzerland* [2015] ECHR 907, [196](Grand Chamber); *Faber v Hungary* [2012] ECHR 1648, [34].

34. [196].

35. [196].

36. *De Haes and Gijsels v Belgium* [1997] ECHR 7, [48]. On the other hand, the Court did take account of the form of the speech (poetry) in determining that material which on one view called for insurrection and rebellion by Kurds against Turkey could not be punished as criminal. The Court took into account that the material was in the form of poetry, in determining that they were unlikely to incite any uprising.

37. *Murat Vural v Turkey* [2014] ECHR 1113, [53].

38. *Annen v Germany* [2015] ECHR 1043, [64]; *Animal Defenders International v United Kingdom* [2013] ECHR 362, [102](Grand Chamber).

39. *Mondragon v Spain* [2011] ECHR 2426, [56].
40. *Stoll v Switzerland* [2007] ECHR 1060, [151].
41. *Stoll v Switzerland* [2007] ECHR 1060, [141].
42. *Appleby v United Kingdom* [2003] ECHR 222, [39]: "genuine effective exercise of this freedom (of expression) does not depend merely on the state's duty not to interfere, but may require positive measures of protection, even in the sphere of relations between individuals."
43. *The Sunday Times v United Kingdom* [1979] ECHR 1, [49].
44. *Rekvenyi v Hungary* [1999] ECHR 31, [34]. The concept of foreseeability will depend on matters such as the content of the text, its intended field, and the number and status of those to whom it is targeted: *Chauvy and Others v France* [2004] ECHR 295, [44].
45. *Chauvy and Others v France* [2004] ECHR 295, [45]–[48].
46. *Hashman and Harrup v United Kingdom* [1999] ECHR 133.
47. [40].
48. [35].
49. [32]. Prior restraints are not per se invalid under the Convention, but require careful scrutiny: *Case of Ekin v France* [2001](Application No.39288/88); *Chauvy and Others v France* [2004] ECHR 295, [66].
50. *North Cyprus Tourism Centre Ltd and Paradise Found Travel Company Ltd v Transport for London* [2005] EWHC 1698 (Admin).
51. *Perincek v Switzerland* [2015] ECHR 907, [196](Grand Chamber).
52. [196].
53. [208].
54. [197].
55. *Oberschlick v Austria* [1991] ECHR 30, [59].
56. Jean-Francois Flauss, "The European Court of Human Rights and the Freedom of Expression," *Indiana Law Journal* 84 (2009): 815: "the existence of a general interest debate leads ipso facto to a strengthening of European control . . . political controversy contributes by its very nature to general interest debates . . . (the Court) places general debates at the heart of democratic society (and has recognised that) general debate has the capacity to favour the progress of democratic society. The evolution of European jurisprudence is characterised by a manifest tendency to stretch the notion of what constitutes a general interest debate."
57. *Mamere v France* [2011] ECHR 2424, [20]; *Dupuis and Others v France* [2007] ECHR 5563, [40]: "Article 10(2) of the *Convention* leaves little scope for restrictions on freedom of expression in the area of political speech or in matters of public interest . . . very strong reasons are required to justify restrictions on political speech."
58. "ill feelings or even outrage, in the absence of intimidation, cannot represent a pressing social need for the purposes of Article 10(2)": *Faber v Hungary* [2012] ECHR 1648, [56].
59. *Stomakhin v Russia* [2018] ECHR 390, [113].
60. *Hrico v Slovakia* [2004] ECHR 365, [40]; *Stoll v Switzerland* [2007] ECHR 1060, [106]: "the most careful scrutiny on the part of the Court is called for when . . . the measures taken or sanctions imposed by the national authority are capable of discouraging the participation of the press in debates over matters of legitimate public concern."
61. *Faber v Hungary* [2012] ECHR 1648 (carrying a flag); *Vajnai v Hungary* [2014] ECHR 997 (red star); *Murat Vural v Turkey* [2014] ECHR 1113 (pouring paint over statues commemorating the founder of the nation).
62. *Nix v Germany* [2018] ECHR 298.
63. *Grigoriades v Greece* [1997] ECHR 93.
64. [196]; *Perincek v Switzerland* [2015] ECHR 907, [246], referring to a need to demonstrate "a rational connection between the measures taken by the authorities and the aim that they sought to realise through these measures, in the sense that the measures were reasonably capable of producing the desired result."
65. *Klein v Slovakia* [2006] ECHR 909, [47].
66. *Guerra and Others v Italy* [1998] ECHR 7, [53].
67. *Scharsach and Newes Verlagsgesellschaft v Austria* [2003] ECHR 596, [29]; in *Vereinigung Bildender Kunstler v Austria* [2007] ECHR 79 the Court was concerned with the very broad scope of an injunction against the alleged wrongdoer, not limited in time or space.

68. *Murat Vural v Turkey* [2014] ECHR 1113, [66](imposition of sentence of more than twenty-two years for repeatedly defacing statues commemorating the founder of the nation held to be grossly disproportionate to any legitimate objective and not necessary in a democratic society). In *Mondragon v Spain* [2011] ECHR 2426 the Court said that such measures could be justified if the speech impaired other fundamental legal rights: [59].

69. *Kyprianou v Cyprus* [2005] ECHR 873, [171].

70. *Stomakhin v Russia* [2018] ECHR 390, [131]; in contrast, a novel has relatively narrow reach, making it harder to justify restrictions on its content: *Lindon and Others v France* [2007] ECHR 836, [47].

71. *Stomakhin v Russia* [2018] ECHR 390, [131].

72. *Animal Defenders International v United Kingdom* [2013] ECHR 362, [124]: "access to alternative media is key to the proportionality of a restriction on access to other potentially useful media"; *Appleby and Others v United Kingdom* [2003] ECHR 222, [48].

73. *Lingens v Austria* [1986] ECHR 7, [42]: "freedom of the press furthermore affords the public one of the best means of discovering and forming an opinion of the ideas and attitudes of political leaders."

74. *Cumpana and Mazare v Romania* [2004] ECHR 692, [114].

75. *Cumpana and Mazare v Romania* [2004] ECHR 692, [115].

76. *Cumpana and Mazare v Romania* [2004] ECHR 692, [118].

77. *Von Hannover v Germany* [2004] ECHR 294, [65]–[66].

78. In *Kyprianou v Cyprus* [2005] ECHR 873 the Court was concerned with the chilling effect on speech by lawyers if a legal representative could be imprisoned due to remarks they had made in court directed at the judges, rude though the comments may have been: [175].

79. *Balsyte-Lideikiene v Lithuania* [2008] ECHR 1195, [81].

80. *Lindon and Others v France* [2007] ECHR 836, [59].

81. *Animal Defenders International v United Kingdom* [2013] ECHR 362, [111](Grand Chamber).

82. "By reason of their direct and continuous contact with the vital forces of their countries, their societies and their needs, the legislative and judicial authorities are best placed to assess the particular difficulties in safeguarding the democratic order in their state . . . the state must therefore be accorded some discretion as regards with country-specific and complex assessment": *Animal Defenders International v United Kingdom* [2013] ECHR 362, [111](Grand Chamber).

83. *Stoll v Switzerland* [2007] ECHR 1060, [155].

84. *Muller and Others v Switzerland* [1988] ECHR 5.

85. *Animal Defenders International v United Kingdom* [2013] ECHR 362, [123](Grand Chamber).

86. *Zdanoka v Latvia* [2006] ECHR 994, [115]: "the court has stressed the need to assess any electoral legislation in light of the political evolution of the country concerned, with the result that features unacceptable in the context of one system may be justified in the context of another."

87. *Faber v Hungary* [2012] ECHR 1648, [28].

88. *Faber v Hungary* [2012] ECHR 1648, [42].

89. *Zana v Turkey* [1997] ECHR 94 (speaker expressing support for the PKK national liberation movement in southeast Turkey, but expressly not condoning violence, but at a time when the PKK was engaged in active combat with Turkish forces).

90. *Lehideux and Isorni v France* [1998] ECHR 90, [55].

91. *Stomakhin v Russia* [2018] ECHR 390.

92. *Garaudy v France* [2003](Application No.65831/01). Various European jurisdictions have criminalized Holocaust denial: see, for example, the *Gayssot Act 1990* (France); Article 130 Criminal Code (Germany) which prohibits "agitation of the people," incitement to hatred and violence, attacking human dignity, publication of materials inciting to national, racial, religious, or ethnic hatred, or statements approving, denying, or minimizing the Holocaust. Alternatively, s185 enshrines an offense of insult, and s189 punishes defamation of the memory of the dead. See Robert Kahn, *Holocaust Denial and the Law: A Comparative Study* (Palgrave Macmillan, New York, 2004).

93. *Jersild v Denmark* [1994] ECHR 33, [35], though on the facts the prosecution of the journalist who interviewed those who expressed abhorrently racist views was struck out. This was because the journalistic program "could not objectively have appeared to have as its purpose the propagation of racist views and ideas": [33]; *Norwood v United Kingdom* [2004] ECHR 730 (prosecution for breach of the *Public Order Act 1986* (UK) upheld for displaying a poster on his premises with a photograph of the Twin Towers, an epithet "Islam out of Britain—Protect the British People," and a symbol of a crescent and star in a prohibition sign. The Court found it was a "public attack on all Muslims in the United Kingdom. Such a general, vehement attack against a religious group, linking the group as a whole with a grave act of terrorism, is incompatible with the values proclaimed and guaranteed by the Convention, namely tolerance, social peace and non-discrimination"); *Delfi As v Estonia* [2015] ECHR 586. The Committee of Ministers of the Council of Europe defines hate speech as "all forms of expression which spread, incite, promote or justify racial hatred, xenophobia, anti-Semitism or other forms of hatred based on intolerance, including intolerance expressed by aggressive nationalism and ethnocentrism, discrimination and hostility against minorities, migrants, and people of immigrant origin" (1997). In 2008 the Council of the European Union resolved that all member states must punish incitement to racial hatred. Some possible selectivity is noted here, with Jean-Francois Flauss, "The European Court of Human Rights and the Freedom of Expression," *Indiana Law Journal* 84 (2009): 849 concluding that "whether for historical reasons or in order to conform to current trends, the court endeavours above all to combat far-right extremism, which it correctly views as presenting the biggest threat to values protected by the Convention. Nevertheless, bad-intentioned or disgruntled minds might be tempted to link the court's relative moderation with respect to far-left extremism to old political sympathies of some judges."

94. *Stomakhin v Russia* [2018] ECHR 390, [92].

95. *Lehideux and Isornia v France* [1998] ECHR 90, [53].

96. Specifically, it recommended that member states: (a) ensure the offenses are clearly defined and take due account of the need for criminal sanction to be applied; (b) ensure the offenses are defined in such a way as to allow them to develop in line with changes in technology; (c) ensure prosecutions for such offenses are brought on a non-discriminatory basis and are not used as cover to suppress criticism of government policy, political opposition, or political beliefs; (d) ensure the effective participation of targets of hate speech in the proceedings; (e) provide penalties for hate speech that take account of the serious consequences of such speech and the need for a proportionate response; (f) monitor how effective the investigation and prosecution of complaints is; and (g) ensure effective co-operation between police and prosecuting authorities.

97. Explanatory Memorandum accompanying General Policy Recommendation No.15, Council of Europe European Commission Against Racism and Intolerance. These materials were cited by the European Court of Human Rights in *Stomakhin v Russia* [2018] ECHR 390, [71]–[72].

98. Eric Heinze, "Viewpoint Absolutism and Hate Speech," *Modern Law Review* 69 (2006): 544.

99. *Lehideux and Isorni v France* [1998] ECHR 90, [47].

100. Article 20(2) of the *International Covenant on Civil and Political Rights*: "any advocacy of national, racial or religious hatred that constitutes incitement to discrimination, hostility or violence shall be prohibited by law"; Article 4 of the *International Convention on the Elimination of All Forms of Racial Discrimination* (1965), which requires signatory nations to condemn all propaganda and all organizations based on ideas or theories of the superiority of one race over another or which attempt to justify or promote racial hatred or discrimination; various offenses in the *Racial and Religious Hatred Act 2006* (UK) in relation to actions intended to stir up racial hatred, and s26 of the *Equality Act 2010* (UK) regarding harassment in relation to, among other things, a person's race, religion, or belief which has the purpose or effect of violating the person's dignity.

101. *Faber v Hungary* [2012] ECHR 1648, [37].

102. *Faber v Hungary* [2012] ECHR 1648, [58].

103. "Democracy constitutes a fundamental element of the European public order . . . the Preamble to the Convention . . . establishes a very clear connection between the Convention

and democracy by stating that the maintenance and further realisation of human rights and fundamental freedoms are best ensured on the one hand by an effective political democracy and on the other by a common understanding and observance of human rights. The Preamble . . . affirm(s) that European countries have a common heritage of political traditions, ideals, freedom and the rule of law . . . the Convention was . . . designed to maintain and promote the ideals and values of a democratic society . . . democracy is the only political model contemplated by the Convention and . . . the only one compatible with it . . . in order to guarantee the stability and effectiveness of a democratic system, the state may be required to take specific measures to protect itself": *Zdanoka v Latvia* [2006] ECHR 994, [98]–[100].

104. *Zdanoka v Latvia* [2006] ECHR 994; see similarly *Van Wambeke v Belgium* (No.16692/90, 12 April 1991); *Volkmer and Petersen v Germany* (Nos.39799/98 and 39793/92, 22 November 2001) and *Sidabras and Dziautas v Lithuania* (No.55480/00 and 59330/00).

105. *Attorney-General v Observer and Times Newspapers Ltd* [1990] 1 AC 109, 283 (Lord Goff).

106. *Derbyshire County Council v Times Newspapers Ltd* [1993] AC 534, 551 (Lord Keith for the Court); *Attorney-General v Guardian Newspapers Ltd* (No2)[1990] 1 AC 109, 283–284 (Lord Goff).

107. Eric Barendt, "Freedom of Expression in the United Kingdom Under the *Human Rights Act 1998*," *Indiana Law Journal* 84 (2009): 851.

108. Compare the decision in *Attorney-General v Guardian Newspapers Ltd and Others* [1987] 1 W.L.R. 1248 with the result on appeal in Strasbourg: *The Sunday Times v United Kingdom* (No2)[1991] ECHR 26.

109. *R v Secretary of State for the Home Department; Ex Parte Simms* [2000] 2 AC 115, 126 (Lord Steyn, with whom Lord Browne-Wilkinson and Lord Hoffmann agreed); *R (Animal Defenders) v Culture Secretary* [2008] 1 AC 1312, 1346 (Lord Bingham).

110. For similar reasons the High Court overturned a decision of the Secretary of State which had prevented the BBC from conducting an interview with a person who had been detained without charge in a British jail for seven years. The Court found the Secretary's refusal was an unjustified interference with the claimant's right to freedom of expression: *R (BBC) v Justice Secretary* [2013] 1 WLR 964.

111. *R v Central Independent Television PLC* [1994] 3 W.L.R. 20, 30: "a freedom which is restricted to what judges think to be responsible or in the public interest is not freedom. Freedom means the right to publish things which government and judges, however well motivated, think should not be published. It means the right to say things which 'right-thinking people' regard as dangerous or irresponsible" (Hoffmann LJ, as he then was).

112. *R (BBC) v Justice Secretary* [2013] 1 WLR 964, 972 (Singh J for the Court) (QBD).

113. *R (BBC) v Justice Secretary* [2013] 1 WLR 964, 973 (Singh J for the Court) (QBD).

114. *R (BBC) v Justice Secretary* [2013] 1 WLR 964, 983 (Singh J for the Court) (QBD).

115. *R (BBC) v Justice Secretary* [2013] 1 WLR 964, 984 (Singh J for the Court) (QBD).

116. "The approach to proportionality adopted in our domestic case law under the *Human Rights Act 1998* (UK) has not generally mirrored that of the Strasbourg court. In accordance with the analytical approach to legal reasoning characteristic of the common law, a more clearly structured approach has generally been adopted, derived from case law under Commonwealth Constitutions and Bills of Rights, including in particular the *Canadian Charter of Rights and Freedoms*": *Bank Mellat v HM Treasury* (No2)[2014] AC 700, 790 (Lord Reed, dissenting in the result). He then acknowledged the criteria used by the United Kingdom courts had an "affinity" with those formulated by the Strasbourg court in relation to Articles 8–11 (Article 10 being protection for freedom of expression): 790.

117. *De Freitas v Permanent Secretary of Ministry of Agriculture, Fisheries, Lands and Housing* [1999] 1 AC 69 (Lord Clyde), adopted in *R v Shayler* [2003] 1 AC 247, 281.

118. Lord Reed in *Bank Mellat v HM Treasury* (No2)[2014] AC 700, 791 observed a margin of appreciation was to be applied here. It was not for the judge to substitute their decision as to where the line should be drawn for that of the decision maker. A court could often find a less drastic or less restrictive way in which the legislature might have crafted its legislation. Further, he noted that in federal structures, a margin of appreciation was clearly appropriate, since the existence of different legislation on the same topic in different jurisdictions within the federa-

tion would often demonstrate the possibility of many feasible alternatives in drafting legislative solutions to an identified issue.

119. *Huang v Secretary of State for the Home Department* [2007] 2 AC 167, [19](Lord Bingham for the House); *R (Aguilar Quila) v Home Secretary* [2012] 1 AC 621, 643 (Lord Wilson, with whom Lord Phillips and Lord Clarke agreed). Bank Mellat v HM Treasury (No2)[2014] AC 700, 771 (Lord Sumption, with whom Baroness Hale, Lord Kerr, and Lord Clarke agreed).

120. [1986] 1 SCR 103; this point was made by Lord Bingham for the House in *Huang v Secretary of State for the Home Department* [2007] 2 AC 167, 187.

121. *R (BBC) v Justice Secretary* [2013] 1 WLR 964, 975 (Singh J for the Court) (QBD).

122. *Bank Mellat v HM Treasury* (No2)[2014] AC 700, 790 (Lord Reed).

123. T R S Allan, "Human Rights and Judicial Review: A Critique of Due Deference," *Cambridge Law Journal* 65 (2006): 671; Jeffrey Jowell, "Judicial Deference and Human Rights: A Question of Competence," in Paul Craig and Richard Rawlings ed *Law and Administration in Europe* (Oxford University Press, Oxford, 2003); "Judicial Deference: Servility, Civility or Institutional Capacity," *Public Law* [2003}: 592; *R v Secretary of State for the Home Department* [2015] AC 945, 1007–1009 (Lord Kerr, dissenting).

124. [2001] 2 AC 127, 210–211: "a test expressed in terms of a category of cases, such as political speech, is at variance with the jurisprudence of the European Court of Human Rights which in cases of competing rights and interests requires a balancing exercise in the light of the concrete facts . . . (I am) sceptical of the value of a rule dependent on general categorisation, with the attendant sacrifice of individual justice in particular cases."

125. *Mayor Commonalty and Citizens of London v Tammy Samede* [2012] EWCA Civ 160, [41](Sir Terence Etherton MR, for Stanley Burnton and McFarlane LJJ).

126. *R (Animal Defenders) v Culture Secretary* [2008] 1 AC 1312. A challenge to the European Court was dismissed: *Animal Defenders International v United Kingdom* [2013] ECHR 362.

127. *VgT Vereingegen Tierfabriken v Switzerland* [2001] ECHR 412.

128. 1346.

129. *Animal Defenders International v United Kingdom* [2013] ECHR 362.

130. *Regina (ProLife Alliance) v British Broadcasting Corporation* [2004] 1 AC 185.

131. "The primary right protected by Article 10 is the right of every citizen not to be prevented from expressing his opinions. (They have) the right to receive and impart information and ideas without interference by public authority" (Lord Hoffmann, 236).

132. 236.

133. 244–245: "We are fortunate enough to live in . . . a mature democracy. In a mature democracy political parties are entitled, and expected, to place their policies before the public so that the public can express its opinion on them at the polls. The constitutional importance of this entitlement and expectation is enhanced at election time. If . . . a political party's desired election broadcast is factually accurate . . . and relevant to a lawful policy on which its candidates are standing for election, I find it difficult to understand on what possible basis it could properly be rejected as being offensive to public feeling. Voters in a mature democracy may strongly disagree with a policy being promoted by a televised party political broadcast but ought not to be offended by the fact that the policy is being promoted . . . indeed . . . the public in a mature democracy are not entitled to be offender by the broadcasting of such a programme . . . refusal to transmit such a program based upon the belief that the programme would be offensive . . . (is not) necessary in a democratic society . . . such a refusal would, on the contrary be positively inimical to the values of a democratic society, to which values it must be assumed that the public adhere . . . (the rejection of the ads) denigrates the voting public, treats them like children who need to be protected from the unpleasant realities of life, seriously undervalues their political maturity and can only promote voter apathy." Julian Rivers also criticises the decision: "Proportionality and Variable Intensity of Review," *Cambridge Law Journal* 65 (2006): 206.

134. *A v British Broadcasting Corporation* [2015] AC 588, 607 (Lord Reed, for the Court).

135. *Core Issues Trust v Transport for London* [2013] EWHC 651 (Admin).

136. [131].

137. [140]–[141].
138. [142].
139. [144].
140. [132].
141. [2002] QB 1391.
142. 1401 (Lord Phillips, for the Court). These are the only express references to Mr. Farrakhan's expressed views that appear in the judgment.
143. 1418 (Lord Phillips, for the Court).
144. 994.
145. 1007–1009.
146. *Belfast City Council v Miss Behavin' Ltd* [2007] 1 WLR 1420.
147. 1442 (Lord Neuberger), 1426 (Lord Hoffmann) and 1433 (Lord Mance).
148. 1442: "when it comes to restrictions on the dissemination of pornographic material, the margin of appreciation afforded to member states must, it appears to me, be wide" (Lord Neuberger, with whom Lord Mance agreed).
149. *Campbell v MGN Ltd* [2004] 2 AC 457, 499: "there are undoubtedly different types of speech . . . some of which are more deserving of protection in a democratic society than others. Top of the list is political speech" (Baroness Hale).
150. *Campbell v MGN Ltd* [2004] 2 AC 457, 499: "Intellectual and educational speech and expression are also important in a democracy, not least because they enable the development of individuals' potential to play a full part in society and in our democratic life. Artistic speech and expression is important for similar reasons, in fostering both individual originality and creativity and the free-thinking and dynamic society we so much value" (Baroness Hale).
151. *R (British American Tobacco UK Ltd and Others) v Secretary of State for Health* [2004] EWHC 2493, [37](McCombe J); *Boehringer Ingelheim Ltd and Others v VetPlus Ltd* [2007] Bus LR 1456.
152. *R (Animal Defenders) v Culture Secretary* [2008] 1 AC 1312, 1348 (Lord Bingham, with whom Lords Carswell and Neuberger agreed).
153. *R (Farrakhan) v Home Secretary* [2002] QB 1391, 1418 (Lord Phillips, for the Court).
154. For example, the action for breach of confidence: *Campbell v MGN Ltd* [2004] 2 AC 457, 465 (Lord Nicholls)
155. *In Re S* (*A Child*)[2005] 1 AC 593.
156. *Regina v Humza Ali* [2018] EWCA Crim 547, [17](Treacy LJ, for Calvert-Smith and Munro J).
157. *Sheffield City Council v Fairhall and Others* [2017] EWHC 2121, [88](Males J).
158. *City of London Corporation v Samede* [2012] EWCA Civ 160, [39](Lord Neuberger).
159. *City of London Corporation v Samede* [2012] EWCA Civ 160, [39](Lord Neuberger).
160. *Sheffield City Council v Fairhall and Others* [2017] EWHC 2121, [89](Males J).
161. Examples here include *Hammond v DPP* where the Court upheld the prosecution of a preacher who held up placards with the messages "stop immorality" and "stop homosexuality." Hammond was successfully prosecuted for a breach of then s5 of the *Public Order Act 1986*, which made it an offense to use "threatening, abusive or insulting words or behaviour or display any sign which is threatening, abusive or insulting." His challenge to his conviction was dismissed: [2004] EWHC 69 (Admin). Similarly in *Norwood* [2003] EWHC 1564 (Admin) the offender was successfully prosecuted under the same provision for posting signs in his flat in the aftermath of 9/11 to the effect "Islam out of Britain" and "Protect the British People." An appeal to the European Court of Human Rights was unsuccessful: *Norwood v United Kingdom* [2004] ECHR 730. For criticism see James Weinstein, "Extreme Speech, Public Order and Democracy: Lessons from The Masses," in Ivan Hare and James Weinstein *Extreme Speech and Democracy* (Oxford University Press, New York, 2009), 37–40, 46–47; Andrew Geddis, "Free Speech Martyrs or Unreasonable Threats to Social Peace—'Insulting' Expression and Section 5 of the *Public Order Act 1986*," *Public Law* [2004]: 867.
162. [2017] EWHC 2669 (Admin).
163. [2019] EWCA Civ 1127.
164. [105](Irwin and Haddon-Cave LLJ, Sir Jack Beatson).
165. [127].

166. *A v British Broadcasting Corporation* [2015] AC 588, 600 (Lord Reed, for the Court).
167. *Bank Mellat v HM Treasury* (No2)[2014] AC 700, 730 (Lord Neuberger, with whom Baroness Hale, Lord Clarke, Lord Sumption and Lord Carnwath agreed).
168. *A v British Broadcasting Corporation* [2015] AC 588, 607 (Lord Reed, for the Court).
169. [2015] AC 588, 614–615 (Lord Reed, for the Court).
170. *Arrowsmith v United Kingdom* [1978] ECHR 7.
171. *The Sunday Times v United Kingdom* [1979] ECHR 1. On the other hand, in *Worm v Austria* [1997] ECHR 52 where the journalist wrote about pending legal proceedings, where there was evidence that the journalist intended to influence the outcome of a pending trial, potentially compromising the right of an accused to a fair trial, the Court found that the interference with the journalist's freedom of speech was justified.
172. *Thorgeir Thorgeirson v Iceland* [1992] ECHR 51.
173. *Roemen v Luxembourg* [2003] ECHR 102; *Goodwin v United Kingdom* [1996] ECHR 16, [45]; *Cumpana and Mazare v Romania* [2004] ECHR 692, [106]; *Tillack v Belgium* [2008] ECHR 1901, [53].
174. *Stoll v Switzerland* [2007] ECHR 1060, [131].
175. [1995] ECHR 12.
176. [34].
177. [34].
178. A similar view is evident in *De Haes and Gijsels v Belgium* [1997] ECHR 7, where the Court emphasized the limited extent to which members of the judiciary could respond to attacks, justifying protection of them from unfounded attacks: [37]. There the Court found Article 10 had been breached. There was some factual basis for the statements made; similarly *Hrico v Slovakia* [2004] ECHR 365.
179. [37].
180. *Kyprianou v Cyprus* [2005] ECHR 873, [174].
181. *Barthold v Germany* [1985] ECHR 3; *Markt Intern Verlag GmbH and Klaus Beermann v Germany* [1989] ECHR 21.
182. *Casado Coca v Spain* [1994] ECHR 8.
183. *Case of Sekmadienis Ltd v Lithuania* [2018] ECHR 112, [73].
184. *Muller and Others v Switzerland* [1988] ECHR 5. There has been criticism. David Pannick, citing the *Handyside* and *Muller* decisions, concludes that "these decisions indicate a fundamental failure to understand that freedom of expression in relation to art and literature cannot properly be impeded because the contents of the material may offend others": "Article 10 of the *European Convention on Human Rights' King's College Law Journal* 4 (1994): 49.
185. *Muller and Others v Switzerland* [1988] ECHR 5.
186. *Handyside v United Kingdom* [1990] ECHR 32.
187. *Karatas v Turkey* [1999] ECHR 47. Presumably, the same sentiments expressed at a large public rally, through mass produced flyers, or online to a large audience could have legitimately attracted government sanction.
188. *Vereinigung Bildender Kunstler v Austria* [2007] ECHR 79, [33].
189. *Wingrove v United Kingdom* [1996] ECHR 60.
190. [57]; contrast *Case of Sekmadienis Ltd v Lithuania* [2018] ECHR 112, [81]: "in a pluralist democratic society those who choose to exercise the freedom to manifest their religion cannot reasonably expect to be exempt from all criticism. They must tolerate and accept the denial by others of their religious beliefs and even the propagation by others of doctrines hostile to their faith."
191. *Case of Sekmadienis Ltd v Lithuania* [2018] ECHR 112, [73].
192. [1986] ECHR 10.
193. *Rekvenyi v Hungary* [1999] ECHR 31.
194. [1996] ECHR 106.
195. [59].
196. [59].
197. [59].
198. [59].
199. [60].

200. [60].
201. [1997] ECHR 93.
202. *Oberschlick v Austria* [1991] ECHR 30, [63]; similarly *Lingens v Austria* [1986] ECHR 7, [46].
203. *Scharsach and News Verlagsgesellschaft v Austria* [2003] ECHR 596, [39]; "sufficient factual basis": *Shabanov and Tren v Russia* [2006] ECHR 1093, [41].
204. *Schwabe v Austria* [1992] ECHR 56, [34]; Jean-Francois Flauss, "The European Court of Human Rights and the Freedom of Expression," *Indiana Law Journal* 84 (2009): 817.
205. *Colombani et al v France* [2002] ECHR 521, [66]; cf *Mamere v France* [2011] ECHR 2424, [23]: "people prosecuted as a result of comments they make about a topic of general interest must have an opportunity to absolve themselves of liability by establishing that they acted in good faith and, in the case of factual allegations, by proving they are true."
206. *Mamere v France* [2011] ECHR 2424, [24].
207. *Castells v Spain* [1992] ECHR 48; *Oberschlick v Austria* (No2)[1997] ECHR 38, [29].
208. [46].
209. "it remains open to the competent state authorities to adopt, in their capacity as guarantors of public order, measures, even of a criminal law nature, intended to react appropriately and without excess to defamatory accusations devoid of foundation or formulated in bad faith": [46].
210. [1999] ECHR 42.
211. [62].
212. [62]–[63].
213. [65].
214. [1999] ECHR 44.
215. [36].
216. [37].
217. [1999] ECHR 3.
218. [32].
219. [33].
220. [34].
221. *Case of Mamere v France* [2011] ECHR 2424, [27].
222. [28].
223. [25].
224. [1998] ECHR 4.
225. [42].
226. [45].
227. [47].
228. [2013] ECHR 362, [115]–[119].
229. [2015] ECHR 907.
230. [154].
231. [204]–[207].
232. [200].
233. [230].
234. [233].
235. [238].
236. [243].
237. [244].
238. [252].
239. [254].
240. [2008] ECHR 1195.
241. [2012] ECHR 1045.
242. [2012] ECHR 242.
243. [55].
244. [55].
245. [56]–[59].

246. [1994] ECHR 26. See for discussion Robert Kahn, "A Margin of Appreciation for Muslims—Viewing the Defamation of Religions Debate through *Otto-Preminger Institut v Austria*," *Charleston Law Review* 5 (2011): 401.
247. [49]; and a claim that the state could regulate "the manner in which religious beliefs . . . are opposed or denied": [47].
248. [50].
249. For example, *Hrico v Slovakia* [2004] ECHR 365, [40].
250. *Murphy v Ireland* [2003] ECHR 352. On one view this is quite ironic, since it was the push for greater religious tolerance in Europe in the Middle Ages that gave birth to freedom of expression in Europe: Kevin Boyle, "The Danish Cartoons," *Netherlands Quarterly of Human Rights* 24 (2006): 188.
251. *Delfi As v Estonia* [2015] ECHR 586.
252. [142].
253. [158].
254. [159]
255. [161].

Chapter Six

Comparison

Having succinctly described the relevant case law in each of the chosen jurisdictions, it is now possible to make some comparison of the extent and the way in which freedom of speech is protected in each of them. There are some obvious points of similarity, and obvious points of difference. Perhaps the general view that is taken when comparing the protection of freedom of speech in the United States with elsewhere is that the United States protects that freedom to a much larger extent than elsewhere. While that observation was generally borne out by my consideration of the cases, in some cases to my surprise the law of other countries seemed to provide greater protection for speech than the United States. I will explain this in more detail later in this chapter.

PRELIMINARY POINTS

Before any meaningful comparison can be made between the extent to which freedom of speech is protected in the United States, Canada, United Kingdom/Europe, and Australia, some preliminary points must be made. The first is that the (relevant) legal history of each must be borne in mind, as well as structural characteristics of each jurisdiction's legal process. The first historical point is the past commonplace regulation of an individual's speech. Government concern with the possible dangers of unbridled speech and its threat to existing power structures, and therefore attempts to censor undesired speech, has been a feature of legal structures for millennia, including ancient Greek times. This is reflected in the early law in England, where speech deemed to be threatening to the government was dealt with using a range of powerful legal tools, and for many years the government actively pursued a policy of prior restraint. Similarly in mainland Europe, calls for restrictions on speech came at least originally from concern with protecting members of the aristocracy and society elite from insult by others.

The other essential feature of the English legal system is acceptance of parliamentary supremacy, that whatever law passed by parliament is valid, and no courts have the power to declare a law to be invalid. This principle was accepted to some extent in Canada and Australia. Thus, it is not surprising that at least in the early years of the legal system of those jurisdictions, very limited protection is given to common law rights such as freedom of speech. It exists only to the extent that legislatures do not see fit to take it away or abrogate it.

This background contrasts quite sharply with that pertaining to the United States. Individuals living in colonies that would become the United States had heightened concern about protection of rights, since the distant United Kingdom government would constantly ignore the rights that individuals claimed to have. Their concern with rights was heightened. The United States was keenly aware of the kind of religious persecution that had been occurring in Europe, some of which pertained to speech. Political thought had also moved away from a Hobbesian-infused view of individuals as lawless aggressors who required a strong government to bring them into line and towards a Lockean social contract approach, emphasizing the limited nature of government and the natural rights of individuals. In this environment, it is not surprising that the United States decided on a written *Bill of Rights* shortly after their *Constitution* was ratified, and that it would expressly protect freedom of speech, freedom of assembly and the right to petition for the redress of grievances. This is correct, although it is conceded there remain a range of views as to the precise intent of Madison and others who advocated for the express protection of free speech, and whether they intended it merely to prohibit the kind of prior restraint that stained the English legal system until 1694, or whether it was intended to be broader than that. The other thing was the adoption of the United States *Constitution* as a written document, with carefully defined powers of the legislature. This perhaps implies a kind of limit to legislative power conspicuously absent from the United Kingdom model, and not surprisingly the early United States Supreme Court expressly adopted a system of judicial review under which the Court could declare laws to be invalid if they were inconsistent with the *Constitution*. While this was not inevitable with a written *Constitution*, it was likely. This development significantly enhanced at least the potential of the United States *Bill of Rights* to protect speech in ways that the parliamentary supremacy-infused models never could, a potential that would take time to be realized but which was always inherently likely to occur given the express protection of free speech, together with the impact of *Marbury v Madison*.

The United States also seemed to accept a democratic culture from the start, a fact scholars like de Tocqueville acknowledged and admired. This emphasized significant public participation in government, reflecting the government of the people, by the people and for the people in a way that was foreign to much of mainland Europe, with its system of hereditary monarchies and aristocracies in many states. The way that the American people felt isolated and removed from power during the end stages of British rule fired them with a determination that structures must be enshrined to preserve the role of the people in government. Democracy would come much more slowly to Europe than its early embrace in the United States. Given the obvious links between democracy and freedom of speech, this also crimped notions that freedom of speech needed to be expressly enshrined in mainland Europe.

It is interesting that it is often only after terrible oppression that the wish to enshrine and protect human rights gains traction. This may be said of the 1789 *Declaration of the Rights of Man and of the Citizen* of 1789 in the shadows of the French revolution, and the United States *Bill of Rights* 1791 shortly after fighting and winning a war of independence. For Europe as a whole, that pivotal time was World War II. Within five years the *Universal Declaration of Human Rights* would be written, as would the *International Covenant on Civil and Political Rights* and the *European Convention on Human Rights*. This is not so in the case of Canada, which adopted its *Charter* in 1982 as an evolutionary process rather than a reaction to terrible oppression, nor in Australia, which has not adopted a general express human rights instrument at all. It has never experienced the kind of general oppression of its citizens such as would feed sentiment for rights protection. Of course it was involved in World War II, but did not have "front row seats" to the kind of violence that occurred in that war, as much of Europe did.

The fact that much of the human rights apparatus applicable in Europe was developed in the shadows of World War II is important to understanding the differences between human rights protection in that jurisdiction, as compared with the United States. It helps to explain why, as will be discussed further below, European legislatures have criminalized speech such as Holocaust denial and/or pro-Nazi speech, in a way that no American legislature has done. Furthermore, the European court has validated such laws against freedom of speech challenges, in a way that would not likely occur in the United States. This must be explained in terms of the memory of the horrors of World War II, societies that were invaded or threatened by the Nazi regime, and a determination that such must never be allowed to happen again. Given that the Americans never lived through such horrors, that country's courts would likely have a very different attitude to laws prohibiting Nazi propaganda, or attempted so-called banning of hate speech.

Further, the rights contained in documents such as the *European Convention* and the *International Covenant* are expressed in limited terms. Now different views will be expressed regarding the importance of the express terms of human rights instruments. It is considered that, while perhaps not determinative in all cases, the text of the human rights provision remains very important. Thus, it is noteworthy that the rights to free speech in Europe are expressly limited. They can be limited as considered necessary in a democratic society. Article 10(2) specifically contemplates that they can be limited during times of national security or public safety concern, to prevent "disorder," reputation, confidentiality, and maintenance of the authority of the judiciary. This approach is also taken in the text of the Canadian *Charter*. It sharply contrasts with the text of the American *First Amendment*, which appears to confirm freedom of speech, the right to peacefully associate and the right to petition for the address of grievances in absolute terms. These rights are not expressed to be limited at all.

In other words, in making the observation that the United States *Constitution* protects freedom of speech more significantly than Europe, it must be borne in mind that the two jurisdictions have very different historical experiences which help color their perception of the importance of unbridled speech, and further that there are significant textual differences in the comparable documents, with one expressly contemplating limits on speech, and the other apparently absolute in nature.

The other point by way of preliminaries is the delicate position of the European Court of Human Rights, and the *European Convention on Human Rights*. Again this is a product of World War II. The very idea of a united Europe, with common institutions, is a reaction to the horrors of past wars, and an attempt to bind nations together, to limit the prospects of a repeat of the kinds of conflicts and upheavals seen in the first part of the 20th century. It was obviously a very difficult challenge to try to meld together the countries of Europe, with their own distinctive societies, cultures, and legal systems, to accept a set of common human rights, and a common court to enforce and apply them. It is somewhat remarkable that this structure has held. We continue to see the challenges of such a structure, partly witnessed by the so-called Brexit vote of 2016, with the United Kingdom voting to leave the European Union. One of the reasons given for the success of the vote to "leave" was the loss of sovereignty that some United Kingdom citizens felt given the extent of decision making in Europe, and the fact that court decisions made in Europe were sometimes in conflict with how British courts had dealt with matters. At the time of writing it remains unclear the extent to which European precedents will continue to influence British law, though it seems that the United Kingdom will continue to recognize the *European Convention on Human Rights*. The main point for present purposes is the great difficulty in melding together such a series of diverse communities and societies, and having them agree to abide by decisions of a common human rights court. The risk is always that a jurisdiction will leave the European Union, if it is dissatisfied with the ways in which its laws are considered by the *European Court of Human Rights*, or that it will ignore the court's rulings if it strongly objects to them, though there may be consequences for that. It means that while the European Court has great power in terms of interpreting the *Convention* and applying it to the laws of numerous nations, this position that it holds is precarious, and fragile. This fragile agreement is also seen in the liberal express exceptions to human rights recognition contained in the *European Convention* itself, expressly contemplating a broad range of circumstances in which departure from the stated rights might be warranted.[1]

It seems the Court itself has been sensitive to these challenges. This partly explains the concept of the "margin of appreciation." This is the freedom that the courts grant to national legislatures in Europe in terms of legislating in ways that abrogate rights. It implies that human rights are not absolute in nature, and that legislatures sometimes have good reason to abrogate rights, and that in some cases their (reasonable) decisions to do so must be respected. It is not surprising in this climate that the European court should have adopted (from German law) the concept of proportionality, under which the consistency of national laws with the *European Convention* is tested. It suggests a balancing of different rights, with due deference being accorded to the national legislature, and its decision to regulate in a certain way, which presumably reflects its balancing of rights. Thus, the European Court can appear somewhat loathe to interfere in the legislature's assessment of the right balance to be struck between conflicting rights. As will be noted below, this deference can sometimes seem to be at its greatest in relation to cases involving morality and religion. In such contexts, it appears to be consistently very deferential to decisions of national legislatures in relation to such matters, reasoning that there is no such thing as a common morality across Europe, and that national legislatures are usually the best judges of what standard community morality requires. Thus it has validated national laws punishing "blasphemy"[2] and validated national laws forbidding advertising about religious issue.[3] In the United States, courts eventually permitted legislatures to infringe freedom of religion consistent with the *First Amendment*, provided the laws were of general application and did not single out religious practice for special regulation.[4]

The other thing that the European Court will do as evidence of its sensitivity to its place when considering national laws is to consider whether other countries in Europe have similar laws to the ones being challenged in the case at hand. The more widespread is a particular kind of law, the less likely the Court will strike it down; conversely where laws are unique or unusual, the Court seems more comfortable with finding the law fails proportionality analysis.[5] Simply, such a factor would not occur in free speech cases in any of the other jurisdictions studied. It reflects the unique position of the European Court, asked to interpret a human rights instrument applicable to a broad range of countries with different legal traditions and cultures.

This kind of deference is seen less in the case of the *First Amendment.* While there is some degree of respect and recognition for the position of state legislatures, this is much more muted than in Europe. The American court does not generally need to concern itself that a state which is unhappy with decisions of the Supreme Court might leave the Union, or to refuse to enforce the decision. Here I leave aside the historical secessions of the 1860s and the reaction to Supreme Court decisions like *Brown v Board of Education*, where some Southern governors did refuse to enforce the court's decision. While America is also a federation as is Europe, obviously the regional differences are less pronounced in the former jurisdiction. The most notable aspect of *First Amendment* case law where recognition of regional differences has been noted has been in the regulation of pornography, where the Court has been concerned again not to impose a kind of national morality, accepting that what people in New York might regard as objectionable might be very different from what those in Mississippi might think. Thus, in both Europe and the United States there is some recognition in freedom of speech cases (or human rights overall) of the challenges of federalism. This concern is not as evident in the human rights case law of Canada or Australia.

The other cultural difference between the United States, on the one hand, and Europe on the other (at the risk of generalizing) might be the great emphasis in the United States on the individual. The United States is essentially a very strongly liberal state, envisaging small government, partly in order to maximize the liberty of the individual. This affects how Americans perceive rights. Rights are usually seen as "trumps." Someone who perceives rights in this way may not be comfortable with an approach whereby rights can be balanced away in favor of other objectives. In that way, it may not be surprising that American courts would eventually abandon the "ad hoc" balancing process described in Chapter 2.

Pildes notes that the American *Constitution* reflects a "fragmentation of authority" in a way that is not apparent in European equivalents. He writes that prior to the American Revolution, society was generally conceived as an organic whole. The boundaries that we regard as axiomatic today, for instance, between the public and private realm, between the state and religion, between different types of government power (i.e., legislative versus judicial) did not exist to the same extent. Pildes describes it thus:

> Social order required harmony and consensus; this entailed a unified hierarchy of authority and values. Authority flowed from the top down and horizontally across all domains; authority was continuous and identical between what we would now regard as different domains. This was a world of unity, not diversity. It was a world of tightly structured and all-encompassing values, not pluralistic values. It was a world organized around a sense of organic connection, not differentiation and separate spheres of authority.[6]

Pildes states that a central achievement of the republican model adopted by the United States post-revolution was a move away from this type of model to a more pluralistic model involving the (deliberate) fragmentation of authority. This is clearly evident in aspects of United States constitutional governance, such as the separation of powers principle, and the idea of a federal structure. He says that the new American constitutional arrangements was a "response to the increasing inability to conceive society as a whole as a tightly integrated, unified whole."[7] He says the founding fathers embraced that reality, responding with a new system of government that permitted different spheres to operate semi-independently, rather than in the coherent sense which was a feature of pre-revolutionary times.

In Europe there is a much stronger sense of the individual as a member of a collective community. We see this in recent debates in Europe regarding the banning of the face veil in France, for example. The French Government sought to justify the ban on the basis that the exercise of the individual's right would damage the social fabric and integration of the community. This argument was accepted by the European Court of Human Rights. In other words, individual rights can be sacrificed for the greater good.[8] In this view of the world, limitation of the rights of one individual in favor of the broader public good are much more easily justified. The idea is that a constitution reflects values and principles. These values and principles must be maximized to the greatest extent possible.[9] The rights of an individual may be sacrificed if sufficient justification exists, in terms of what Kumm calls a "collective judgment of reason about what justice and good policy require."[10] This fits nicely with proportionality analysis. At the risk of simplification, in the United States we see an exemplar of the liberal philosophical view; in Europe, we see an exemplar of the utilitarian philosophical view.[11]

There are also major differences in how the role of the court is perceived in the various jurisdictions. Classically, an American court would typically see its role in giving effect to the contents of the *Bill of Rights* in a counter-majoritarian way in terms of protecting the rights of vulnerable individual minorities in a system whereby the legislature reflects (broadly) the will of the majority. The Court is there to defend the rights of an individual against the will and might of the powerful legislature. This reflects the historical distrust of government and authority which permeates American political culture and reflects the history and experience of its citizens. Rights are a way of limiting government power. Rights are trumps. It also reflects a strong separation of powers between the non-judicial and judicial arms of government, in particular.

This culture can raise difficulties with a balancing or proportionality approach, on the basis that it grants "too much" power to those with already substantial power (judges) determine the ambit of rights. There is fear that a court might be too willing to trade away rights in pursuit of broader community goals. The suspicion of government is not limited to those in the legislature; it extends to those in the judiciary. Proportionality analysis may be seen to conflict with the social contract into which individuals notionally entered and through which the government was conceived. It might be argued that the terms of this social contract are laid down in the text of the *Constitution*. As a result, the contents, including those rights articulated in the *Bill of Rights*, cannot and should not be subject to balancing or proportionality analysis, because this undercuts the social contract. These notions contrast sharply with the way in which a European would typically view her or his government. The starting premise of distrust of government is not evident in European political culture.

As indicated, democracy has always been a feature of American constitutionalism, in a way in which it has not been in mainland Europe. American democracy is centered on representative government, with the people as sovereign, delegating limited powers to a government for the broader good. European nations do not generally share this history of representative government; they typically experienced a monarchical system of government, supplemented by some form of legislature. In a system of representative government, involving the ceding of limited powers by the sovereign body to a delegated body, concern that fundamental rights of members of the sovereign not be traded away by the delegated body is understandable.[12] One way that this system seeks to limit governmental power and reflects its distrust of government is by dividing such power, reflected by the strong separation of powers principle and federal structure.

Many see the role of courts in Europe very differently. This is demonstrated by the writing of Cohen-Eliya and Iddo Porat. They use the example of Germany, but in terms that can be applied more broadly given the links between the theory and proportionality, which has been applied across Europe. They describe the role of the German court "as a political organ that constitutes an integral part of the state and shares with the task of elaborating and shaping social values and norms."[13] They say that proportionality is applied in Germany "to harmonize and integrate the various state organs around shared values."[14] Proportionality seeks to "optimize values in conflict . . . both legal values need to be limited so that each can attain its optimal effect."[15] It reflects the idea of rights as principles,[16] not trumps. Thus conceived, they are not designed as limits on power, but as general values by which a society has agreed to be governed. The role of the court is to optimize these values in a given case. This is very different to how the United States Supreme Court typically sees its role. In a jurisdiction with a strong separation of powers philosophy, entrenched in its written Constitution, judges would not typically see their role as "sharing" with the legislature a common goal of elaborating and shaping social values and norms. They are often in conflict. It may not be a coincidence that the common law tradition of dispute resolution is an adversarial one, pitting parties against one another. In contrast, the inquisitorial model, commonly used in Europe, adopts a more conciliatory style, involving both parties working together to a common goal. There are thus substantially different conceptions of the role of the judiciary, and how disputes are resolved, between the American model and the European model. Complicating that explanation somewhat, it must be conceded that the Canadian court, a country with (at least primarily) a common law tradition, has taken on board the European concepts, and particularly proportionality.[17] It is too early to tell what the direction of Australian law will be, given it only embraced proportionality in this space in 2015.

One concrete example of the difference that these models suggest is that while an American court might be very focused on the extent to which a challenged law impacts on the human right, a European court might focus more on the extent to which there are justifiable reasons for the intrusion.[18]

Category Approach v Proportionality

A major point of distinction between freedom of speech as protected in the United States and freedom of speech as protected in Europe, Canada, and Australia is the categorization of speech in the former, as opposed to the use of proportionality in the other jurisdictions.[19] In this way, American law is something of an exception. Some have called proportionality analysis "the most dominant doctrine in constitutional adjudication worldwide."[20]

As shown in Chapter 2, the United States case law has embraced a categories-based approach to freedom of speech issues. In some ways this may be seen as almost inevitable, given the very broad terms in which freedom of speech is expressed in the *First Amendment*, and the lack of express restrictions or qualifications to that *Amendment.* Intuitively, it seems that some speech should be regarded as more important than other speech.[21] It is hard to argue, for example, against the view that political speech should be given more free speech protection than, for example, pornography.

The categories-based approach really crystallized in the 1940s decision of *Chaplinsky v New Hampshire*, where the Court articulated several categories of speech that were said to merit little or no *First Amendment* protection, such as fighting words, obscenity, and pornography. Over time, a few extra categories have been added to the list, but the Supreme Court now appears disinclined to add further categories to the list, and has narrowed the meaning of some of the categories over the years. Another way in which categories are used in *First Amendment* case law is that different tests are applied according to the speech involved—thus a compelling justification will be needed to justify restrictions on political speech,[22] but restrictions on commercial speech will be permitted if they are reasonably based and narrowly tailored. Further, the cases draw a distinction based on where the speech occurs, in terms of whether the speech is a public forum, limited public forum, or private forum, and these may also be seen as part of the categorizations process.[23]

It should be noted that the United States did use a so-called ad hoc balancing approach to the *First Amendment* for a time. This is probably the closest that the United States approach came to the approach in the other jurisdictions studied. Under this approach, freedom of speech was balanced against the legitimate interests the government might have had in passing the challenged law. Ad hoc balancing came to be associated with the now-discredited decision in *Dennis v United States*, and the result in that case and others came to signify the deficiencies of a so-called ad hoc balancing approach, in that it accorded too little weight to the constitutional protection.[24] Free speech absolutists Black and Douglas JJ consistently railed against ad hoc balancing on this basis, and eventually succeeded in overturning that approach. Ad hoc balancing was analogous to proportionality, but current proportionality doctrine is more sophisticated and structured than ad hoc balancing was, with specific questions asked as part of the proportionality analysis.[25] This at least partly overcomes the criticisms of ad hoc balancing that there were essentially no principles involved, apart from a judge's personal views about how the balance lay.[26]

Of course, there is a paradox in the fact that the United States law draws a strong distinction between content-based and content-neutral laws. Given the application of the strict scrutiny test to content-based laws, it is very difficult for a government to have these types of laws validated.[27] However, the very use of categories of speech itself involves the use of distinctions based on the content of speech. This paradox has been frequently criticized.[28]

The proportionality approach applicable in the other jurisdictions differs substantially from the categories of speech approach. In a proportionality-based approach, the same principles and standards are applied regardless of the category of speech involved. The law does not particularly distinguish between categories of speech in terms of identifying the relevant law or the principles to be applied. The concept of proportionality was apparently derived from German constitutional law, before forming the basis for the approach taken to the *European Convention on Human Rights*.[29]

In discussing the "proportionality approach," it should not be assumed that this approach is uniform across Europe, Canada, and Australia.[30] It has been observed, for instance, that Canadian courts are more likely to find that laws do not pass the requirement of "necessity" than are European courts.[31] It is sometimes argued that in jurisdictions where proportionality is less established, courts apply the test of "necessity" with more rigor.[32]

In Europe, once a measure has been found to have infringed the freedom of expression, the court considers whether the measure is "prescribed by law," and whether it is "necessary" in a democratic society. The notion of "prescribed by law" is similar to the United States void for vagueness principle. Under it, occasionally the European court has struck out a law on the basis that it is so uncertain that individuals could not know what the law expected of them. While the principles are somewhat analogous, there are many more examples of United States laws that have been found void for vagueness, than there have been European measures found not to be prescribed by law.

European law also considers whether the measure is "necessary." Here the Court considers the legislature's justification for the legislation, whether it is legitimate and relates to a pressing social need, and whether the law is carefully tailored and proportionate to meeting the objective. It must be minimally invasive of the relevant right, although this is subject to the margin of appreciation. There is no distinction between content-based and content-neutral measures, or between viewpoint-based and viewpoint-neutral measures. There is no equivalence to strict scrutiny, as indicated generally applicable to content-based restrictions, intermediate scrutiny, as indicated generally applicable to content-neutral restrictions, or rational basis review. All measures regardless of content are evaluated in the same manner. That having been said, the context of the measure does have an impact on the proportionality review, through the concept of the margin of appreciation. Through the margin of appreciation, the court takes into account, for instance, that it is dealing with a law prohibiting political speech, as compared with other kinds of speech. It will have less tolerance for laws prohibiting political speech than it would a law prohibiting pornography. Thus, in this way, the European law also considers, indirectly, the subject matter of the relevant law.

Canada applies proportionality analysis in a similar, but not identical, way to that in Europe. It must first find that a breach of the s2 freedom of expression has occurred, before it applies proportionality analysis under s1. Not all speech is protected. Speech involving the urging of violence is not protected by s2. Laws regulating speech that have the effect of infringing speech will breach s2 only if the relevant speech relates to at least one of the purposes of free speech. Proportionality analysis under s1 involves similar considerations as in Europe, with consideration of whether the legislation is aimed at a legitimate objective, is carefully tailored to meeting that objective, minimally impairs the right, and there is proportionality between the effects of the measures on speech and the state's legitimate objective.

Proportionality is slightly different again in Australia, with a consideration of whether the measures are compatible with representative government, considering the purpose of the law and the means adopted to achieve it. If this test is passed, the court considers proportionality, which in that country involves three issues: whether the law is suitable, being rationally connected to its purpose, whether the law is necessary, in that there is no obvious other way to achieve the objective in a manner less invasive of the right, and whether the law is adequate in its balance, if it was reasonable given the importance of the purpose of the measure compared with the extent to which it impacted on the freedom. The High Court of Australia has specifically held that it will not necessarily be influenced by how proportionality has been applied elsewhere, but the essential principles appear to be very similar to what occurs in Europe and Canada.

The next issue to consider is the relevant merits of the category-based approach as opposed to a proportionality, standards-based approach.

Merits of a Category-Based Approach

The first advantage of a category-based approach taken in the United States is that is follows what is considered to be an intuitive path. It is considered that intuitively, people would generally believe that some kinds of speech are more important than others. As indicated above, most people understand that freedom of speech has its most significant application in the political context. It is much less important in other applications. A category-based approach allows us to take different approaches to different kinds of speech. We test whether pornography is protected by the *First Amendment* in a different way than we determine whether a public protest is protected. Many would support this. Given that it permits a greater level of specificity, since it applies to a category of cases rather than all speech, it is considered that this approach is likely to better reflect that category of speech. The hope is that there will be greater consistency in deciding cases involving that category of speech, because there is a common test that has been tailored for that type of situation, rather than a supposedly all-encompassing rule. It may provide more certainty, by reducing judicial discretion.[33]

In this light, it is interesting that some proponents laud the flexibility of the alternative approach, involving proportionality, on the basis of "its being an empty concept that allows the courts to do whatever they want."[34] Of course, as they say beauty is in the eyes of the beholder. While some laud a category-based approach on the basis that it might reduce the ability of courts to do "whatever they want,"[35] others who favor proportionality laud this as an advantage of the alternative proportionality test.

It has also been argued that given the range of speech possible, it is so broad that it is simply impossible to reduce freedom of speech to one underlying principle or approach;[36] in other words, that a category-based approach is basically inevitable. A category-based approach might also be lauded on the basis that it reflects ideas of formal equality, with "like" cases being subject to the same rule and presumably, decided in a consistent manner. Of course, consistency in decision making leads to predictability and certainty in the result, a desirable end in itself.[37]

The claimed disadvantage of a balancing approach, also known by some as an ad hoc balancing approach or proportionality approach, and thus a positive of a categories approach, is that such an approach might better reflect the importance that most place on freedom of speech. It is the very first amendment to the United States *Constitution* (even though it only attained that status because two other amendments failed to pass), which gives it special status in the minds of some. It has been said before that freedom of speech is the ultimate human right, in that if it does not exist, none of the other freedoms can exist either. Some argue that ad hoc balancing does not accord freedom of speech its rightful place in the pantheon of rights.[38] It too readily assumes the ability of legislatures to take away freedom of speech when they have a legitimate objective and draft the law carefully. Many argue that in terms of results, a category-based system generally has protected *First Amendment* freedoms to a greater extent than a proportionality type approach.[39] Naturally then, those who favor stronger *First Amendment* protection might advocate a category approach. Certainly, most commentators would suggest that the United States protects freedom of speech more than do the other jurisdictions studied here. As indicated, the United States is the only one of these jurisdictions which takes a category-based approach. This raises an interesting chicken-and-egg problem. Is freedom of speech more strongly protected in the United States because it adopts a category-based approach? Or is it the other way, that a category-based approach is more appropriate in the United States than elsewhere, because its commitment to freedom of speech is stronger, and its cultural and political make-up suggests (or demands) stronger free speech protection?

Some argue that the founding fathers already conducted the balancing exercise between freedom of speech and other possibly competing rights. It is said that their resolution of that debate was the *First Amendment*. In other words, it is argued that the founding fathers have already conducted the kind of balancing/proportionality testing, clearly siding with freedom of speech, such that it is not appropriate to conduct any further balancing of *First Amendment* rights.[40]

Accepting that content-based speech is a category, it can be argued that there is strong merit in treating content or viewpoint-based restrictions on speech in a more serious manner than content-neutral speech. It is consistent, if not mandatory, with adopting a category-based approach that we make this distinction.[41] Such a distinction reflects the absolute abhorrence of a totalitarian state of government where the government could control or censor speech. This distinction is also supported by various theories of freedom of speech, most particularly Meiklejohn's democratic self-government rationale, and the distrust of government rationale offered by Schauer. Both Canada and Australian case law considers as being relevant to proportionality analysis whether the law is or is not content-based.[42] European law does not evidently take this into account as a specific relevant factor.

Another observation about the American categories is the distinction based on the status of the geographical area affected by the regulation. United States law draws a sharp distinction between cases whether the relevant forum is a public one, limited public one, or a private forum. We see this aspect being considered in Canadian law as well; however it has not generally featured in European case law or Australian case law. It makes intuitive sense when considering whether a law is compatible with freedom of speech to consider the context in which the regulation appears. It seems right that the government *should* have to justify curbs on speech in public areas traditionally used for speech much more significantly than restrictions applicable to private property.

It should be noted by way of finality that categories of speech may overlap. Commercial speech may be obscene, or it may also amount to political speech. This complicates an attempt to apply rules to a particular category of speech, which perhaps implicitly suggests that the categories are watertight compartments, logically discrete and separate from one another.

Merits of a Proportionality Approach

Those who favor the proportionality approach favored in Europe, Canada, and Australia,[43] and by Breyer J on the United States Supreme Court,[44] laud its flexibility.[45] The argument is that the courts are well-equipped to make decisions about resolution of conflict between different values. They regularly do this. Further, it is argued that the proportionality approach recognizes the non-absoluteness of freedom of speech, and that sometimes government interests override an individual's freedom of speech. The proportionality approach would typically permit the government greater latitude in terms of interfering with freedom of speech, where it has good reason. Certainly, it would be easier for a legislature to pass proportionality analysis than the kind of strict scrutiny applicable to different kinds of regulation of speech in the United States, such as content-based restrictions or restrictions on political speech. The argument is that proportionality better balances the individual's human rights with the collective rights of the society, said to be reflected in the legislature's decision about how rights should be balanced in a particular way. The court thus has a residual role in defending rights, but accords legislatures as democratically elected bodies a margin of appreciation with its legislation, permitting the legislature to deal with social issues in the manner it sees fit, subject to judicial review where exceptionally, the court might find that the legislature has exceeded its margin of appreciation and interfered with freedom of speech in an unjustified way.

Weaknesses of a category-based approach are indirectly strengths of a proportionality approach. Critics of a category-based system argue that such a system can only work where the meaning of particular concepts is clear.[46] They argue that key concepts are in fact far from clear. The Supreme Court has struggled to articulate what obscenity is, for example. It has struggled to articulate what pornography is. It has struggled to define a "true threat." The argument is that the category-based system does not deliver the kind of certainty that it promises, since it is often not clear whether particular speech belongs to a particular category or not. Speech may well belong to more than one category, which becomes problematic when different rules apply to the different categories.

It can also be argued that the category-based approach becomes inflexible and distinctions become difficult to justify.[47] So, for instance, the categories to which *First Amendment* protection is apparently not accorded are, according to the Supreme Court, effectively closed. The justices appear to be very reluctant to open new categories, even when they seem quite analogous to some of the existing categories. For instance, if child pornography can be banned consistently with the *First Amendment*,[48] a position with which the author does not quibble, it becomes difficult to justify the court's refusal to permit the banning of depictions of animal cruelty, as it did in *Stevens*. It justified child pornography being banned consistently with the *First Amendment* on the basis of the great harm that creation and distribution of such material would likely cause to children. No argument there. However, one might that thought that depictions of animal cruelty might be analogous. Surely, if such material can be lawfully made and distributed, this is likely to cause harm to animals because individuals know they can do so with impunity. One would have thought that the same rationale for permitting the effective banning of child pornography material might also have justified the effective banning of depictions of animal cruelty. Yet the Supreme Court says one is entitled to *First Amendment* protection, and one is not. Obviously, under a proportionality analysis, it is not necessary for the Court to resort to such fine distinctions.

Some have lauded structured proportionality of the kind practiced in Europe and Canada on the basis that it is more certain than ad hoc balancing was, asking specific questions in a logical, ordered fashion.[49] It thus leads to decisions that are defensible and transparent.[50] It appropriately constrains judicial discretion.[51] Others laud its "combined flexibility and structure."[52] It can also improve the quality of lawmaking,[53] focusing legislatures on means and ends, requiring it to think through its objectives and ensuring its legislation meets those objectives, is minimally invasive of rights, etc.[54]

Leading proponents of proportionality analysis Cohen-Eliya and Porat claim that proportionality is based on a movement away from a culture of authority to one of justification.[55] They state that a culture of authority is concerned with whether the decision maker has the appropriate authority or not to act as they have. In contrast, a culture of justification is based on the idea that it is not sufficient that governments have power to act. They must also show to an independent third party that their actions were rational, reasonable and justified. Relatedly, others have pointed out to pathologies of legislative decision making that make proportionality-based judicial review attractive. These pathologies are said to include legislative thoughtlessness based on tradition, convention or preference, illegitimate reasons for decision making, decision making based on hyperbole or ideology, and decisions caused by capture of the legislature by special interest lobby groups. For these reasons, Kumm argues that a court must apply a robust proportionality analysis, to weed out laws that are illegitimate exercises of power and not reflecting a reasonable, considered judgment as to the collective good.[56]

There is likely to be little practical point in determining whether a European-style proportionality analysis or an American-style category analysis is "better." The debate between fixed rules and generalized standards, between supposed certainty and supposed flexibility, is as old as the law itself, and is never going to be settled one way or the other. Different jurisdictions will choose different methods, and legal taxonomy will flick across this spectrum over time. There are clear cultural differences that explain European attachment to a proportionality analysis and American attachment to a categories approach. The choice of these approaches can also be said to logically fit the differing constitutional structures. A natural question is whether there is likely to be convergence or divergence of approaches, or the extreme suggestion that either of the current systems might take on the approach taken by the other. This is considered very unlikely. Just as proportionality is now well entrenched in Europe and Canada, a categories approach is well entrenched in the United States. It must be considered very unlikely, if not impossible, that the Europeans will adopt a category approach, or that the Americans will adopt proportionality analysis. Proportionality is ingrained in the very structure of the *European Convention*, and arguably the *Canadian Charter*. The weight of American precedents that have taken the category-based approach similarly count against any move to adopt proportionality analysis. Given that neither side is likely to adopt the process used by the other, it is rather pointless to mount an argument as to which is the "better" approach. Of course, this is a loaded question, the answer to which depends on any number of variables. I must respectfully reject the suggestion that is sometimes made that the proportionality approach is somehow a temporary step along the way to a category-based system. There is nothing temporary about the use of proportionality in European constitutional law, or for that matter its use in Canada. The position is more contested in Australia, which has come to the proportionality principle very late in the day.

Regarding the argument that neither the American category system nor the European proportionality is likely to be abandoned due to deep cultural differences, political contexts, in the case of Europe, the text of the human rights convention and, in the case of the United States, precedent, some may take the example of Canada. This is a country whose approach has morphed, from a British-infused parliamentary supremacy model involving a light-touch *Wednesbury*-unreasonableness standard of review, to a full-throated proportionality approach. This is conceded. However, the radical shift was heralded by the passage of the *Canadian Charter of Rights and Freedoms* itself, rather than any kind of "judicial revolution." It is hard to see any equivalent occurring in Europe or the United States which might herald such a change. Others may take the example of Australia. To some extent it too has morphed. Some formerly believed that parliamentary supremacy principles should be applied in Australia, even in a country which accepted judicial review many years ago. It embraced *Wednesbury*-unreasonableness as a basis for review of decisions. It has never embraced a bill of rights at federal level. However, in 2015, it moved to a proportionality analysis in terms at least of the implied freedom of political communication it discerned from the text and structure of the *Constitution*. It remains to be seen whether it will apply the same approach in the context of other human rights. Though the High Court of Australia decries comparisons with proportionality elsewhere, its approach is clearly very similar to the use of that doctrine in Europe, which has been adopted in Canada. Thus the point must be accepted that jurisdictions do switch approaches, with both Canada and Australia switching to proportionality analysis (in the case of Australia, at least in the context of political communication; in the case of Canada, at a more general *Charter* level). And the United Kingdom has (eventually) also moved to the proportionality table, away from its deferential "irrationality" approach, well after its supposed accession to the *European Convention*, but no doubt because of it. That having been acknowledged, it is not considered likely that the European approach or the United States will switch to the other. It is too late in the day, it is counter-cultural, in the case of Europe it is counter-textual, and in the case of the United States, contrary to precedent.

PRIOR RESTRAINT

As indicated earlier in the book, England practiced a system of prior restraint, requiring that publications be submitted for approval prior to publication. This system did not lapse until 1694. That experience features heavily in the approach to free speech taken by most of the jurisdictions considered in this book. Generally a prior restraint system, requiring speech or communication to be approved by the government or government body first, would not be permissible in the United States,[57] Europe,[58] or Canada.[59] The Australian position is more equivocal. The High Court validated legislation which person from either (i) distributing any printed matter on a public thoroughfare or (ii) preaching, haranguing, canvassing, touting for business, or conducting a survey on such a thoroughfare, unless they obtained Council permission.[60] The Court dismissed a free speech challenge to the provision.

WHETHER THE AFFECTED SPEECH WILL FURTHER FREE SPEECH GOALS

It is interesting to consider the extent to which the law of the jurisdictions studied seek to connect freedom of speech principles with rationales for the freedom. It has already been pointed out that the courts generally do not just favor one of the theories of freedom of speech, in recognition of the likelihood that no one theory can adequately explain the state of free speech principle.[61] The Canadian jurisprudence most clearly does this. It specifically will and has taken into account in undertaking its proportionality analysis whether the relevant speech will further free speech aims.[62] If it will not, it will be accorded slighter protection than if it would be likely to further such aims.[63] This is part of a broader debate about whether the court should assess the value of speech in determining whether, and to what extent, the law should protect it. This kind of debate, and the reasonable differences of opinion that it might involve, is also noteworthy in cases like *United States v Alvarez*, involving the question of whether the *First Amendment* protected speech that was demonstrably factually false.

It is understandable that the Canadian court might wish to connect the protection of speech with its perceived worth in terms of the objectives of free speech. The United States Supreme Court seemed to do a similar thing when in *Chaplinsky* it nominated categories of speech than did not warrant *First Amendment* protection. It will be recalled that these categories were nominated for non-protection by the Court in that case on the basis that they were not part of the essential exposition of ideas and of very slight social value as a step to truth. However, subsequently in cases like *Stevens* the court moved away from this position, declaring that courts were not and could not arbiters of the value of speech. This led a majority to accord *First Amendment* protection to demonstrably false statements of fact.

The logic in connecting the extent of a right with its purposes is acknowledged.[64] Having said that, it must also be acknowledged that none of the current purposes espoused for the freedom of speech principle can explain existing American *First Amendment* case law.[65] This might mean that an attempt to only extend freedom of expression to the extent that it furthers legitimate ends of free speech is an attempt in effect to corral free speech doctrine so that it is more limited in nature than the protection available in American law.

On the other hand, of course the danger of the slippery slope in this area is very real. If we start to permit legislatures to prevent "false views" (or fake news) from being presented, we risk a slippery slope by permitting content-based restrictions on speech, and risking the development of government censorship, with the government being able to criminalize the spreading of "false views," and danger that it will use this kind of legislation to stamp out or discourage dissenting views or criticism. This is far from an idle fear; history has taught us that governments have and will constantly seek to suppress critics and naysayers. Courts are typically very wary of such possibilities.[66]

Given that the dangers of government censorship are most particularly acute in the realm of opinion rather than fact, I have considered whether the government might be permitted some leeway to prohibit the dissemination of statements about factual matters that are clearly not true, while denying their ability to prohibit the dissemination of opinions that the government believes to be untrue or dangerous. Frederick Schauer suggests that *First Amendment* doctrine should make this distinction.[67] Having considered it, I am not convinced that a line can be neatly maintained between matters of fact and matters of opinion, such as would make such a distinction viable. It is acknowledged here that the European case law attempts to do so, while acknowledging that the boundaries between them can be fuzzy.[68]

There is, in any event, a lively debate about whether false statements or in the mind of most unreasonable opinions contribute anything in terms of the objectives of free speech. The argument I find most compelling is that even the expression of totally unreasonable opinions contributes something to the purposes of free speech. It educates others, by sharpening their thoughts against the outrageous idea. It encourages public debate about the topic raised. Thus, I am somewhat loath in any event to conclude that the expression of a totally outrageous opinion will contribute nothing to the purposes of free speech, including search for truth, marketplace for ideas, etc. Further, there is an argument that statements that are factually false also get people talking about an issue, and a belief that society itself will generally deal with those spreading false facts. So, though I do have some sympathy with arguments that the spreading of demonstrably false facts contributes nothing to public debate and thus could and should conceivably be banned, in distinction from the expression of opinion, in the mind my skepticism about the use of such a law, and the contribution to debates of material that may in fact be false, convinces me that government regulators should not generally venture into this area. I would make an exception for false statements of fact that are clearly damaging and cause "harm" to others in the community. For example, there should be no free speech objection to prohibitions of false and misleading statements in the commercial realm, or false and misleading statements to government regulators, to the stock market, or to government taxation officials. Such speech has absolutely zero value.

WHERE FREE SPEECH CONFLICTS WITH OTHER HUMAN RIGHTS

Article 17 of the European Convention is unique in relation to the other human rights instruments studied in this book, by expressly confining rights, including freedom of expression, where they are aimed at destroying other rights in the Convention. None of the other jurisdictions have specific provisions regarding this, although the Canadian and Australian courts may take this account in terms of proportionality analysis, and it may be part of the government's attempted justification in relation to a law in the United States. For example, a "reasonable time, place and manner" restriction may take into account how the exercise of one person's right to free speech may impact on the rights of others to go about their lawful business. However, the European context is the only one in which this trade-off is specific.

Perhaps partly for this reason, and partly for historical reasons alluded to above, the European Court takes a different attitude towards so-called hate speech and Holocaust denial than would be the case in the United States. Canada has narrowly upheld hate speech laws. The position in Australia is not currently known, as anti-hate speech laws have not been subject to constitutional challenge as yet. I will consider the position of so-called hate speech in more detail in the later book.

Thus, Europe has validated provisions making it a criminal offense to deny the Holocaust.[69] It has recognized a category of "historical facts," denial of which can be criminalized. It has validated hate speech laws.[70] It has validated laws forbidding the expression of Nazi or neo-Nazi views. The Court has also validated laws forbidding speech which is said to "deny the foundations of a democratic society." Through this means legislatures have successfully denied members of the Communist Party the right to run for office.[71] It has also successfully regulated speech deemed to be offensive,[72] though paradoxically at other times it has denied that speech can be banned based on the fact that it may be offensive to some, or that it could have been expressed in more temperate tones.[73]

It is very likely that none of these laws would be constitutionally valid in the United States. Of course, that jurisdiction has invalidated laws seeking to prohibit the wearing of swastikas in a street march, and laws seeking to criminalize the burning of crosses.[74] These are obvious examples of hate speech. Though for a time the United States validated anti-communist statutes,[75] it turned against that kind of law,[76] and today would be most unlikely to hold valid a law preventing the expression of political views of this nature. The United States Supreme Court has repeatedly denied the right of legislatures to ban speech on the basis that it might be deemed to be "offensive."[77]

The position in Canada is more equivocal. While it narrowly validated hate speech legislation in *R v Keegstra*[78] in the context of Holocaust-denial, it is questionable whether it would invalidate legislation prohibiting the expression of Nazi or neo-Nazi views. While on one view this would inevitably be hate speech, and therefore subject to the *Keegstra* ruling, on another view it might be seen as speech that was more political in nature, and thus worthy of greater protection in proportionality analysis that pure hate speech would. A law prohibiting it would be content-based, which is frowned upon. It is possible the Court would find that such speech does not further free speech objectives, but it would be undesirable for the court to enter into the political fray to apparently uphold the validity of some political views, whether they be liberalism, conservatism, or environmentalism, and not others, such as communism or nationalism, as distasteful as some may find the views of others.

The position in Australia is also not known. While there have been successful prosecutions of individuals for expressing views favoring communism,[79] these were during the Cold War, and at a time well before the High Court recognized the implied freedom of political communication in 1992. Australia does have anti-hate speech laws currently in operation.[80] These have never been constitutionally challenged. A law dissolving the Communist Party was held invalid, but this was because of constitutional aspects unrelated to freedom of communication or association principles.[81] The court has not developed freedom of association as a standalone right. Thus, it is not currently clear whether the High Court would invalidate a law prohibiting the expression of some kinds of political views, for example, views about Nazism or extreme nationalism.

As indicated above, the harsh European position on hate speech and vilification is very likely to be a product of the experience of World War II, where propaganda and hate were used to such deadly and disastrous effect. Similarly, prohibition on Holocaust denial can be seen in that light. While it is understood why the horrific historical experience leads Europe to its current legal stand, this does not necessarily justify such impositions on free speech. More detailed consideration of the regulation of so-called hate speech is reserved for *Freedom of Speech in Practice: Controversial Applications of Law and Theory*.

WHERE EUROPEAN LAW PROTECTS FREEDOM OF SPEECH MORE THAN THE AMERICAN LAW DOES

The orthodox view is that the United States protects free speech more completely than does Europe. This is generally true, shown by the category-based approach and the use of the difficult to satisfy compelling justification test to determine whether restrictions on speech are valid. However, in at least a couple of areas, it appears that European law protects freedom of speech to a greater extent than the United States.

Firstly, there is the situation of the free speech rights of members of the military. It is instructive to compare the decision of the European Court of Human Rights in *Grigoriades v Greece*[82] with the United States Supreme Court decision in *Parker v Levy.*[83] In the former case a member of the army reserve sent a letter to his commanding officer suggesting the army was a criminal and terrorist organization with an intimidatory environment which sought to condition soldiers inappropriately. He was charged with a breach of the military criminal code. The Court agreed that the state had an interest in restricting speech that might threaten military discipline, but the speech here was unlikely to achieve that effect. The Court found it was not necessary in a democratic society to restrict such speech.

Compare this decision with *Parker v Levy*. There an army officer was court-martialled for public comments he made accusing the military of discrimination, and some military officers of being liars, thieves, and murderers of women and children. He was prosecuted for conduct unbecoming of an officer and gentleman, likely to disrupt good order and discipline and the good name of the military. He was jailed for three years with hard labor. His *First Amendment* challenge to the sanction applied to him was dismissed. The Court claimed that strong sanction for misconduct was valid in the military context in order to preserve discipline. While one must be careful about drawing broad conclusions from just one or two cases, it seems that at least in relation to members of the military, European courts may be more willing to uphold an officer's free speech rights than in the United States.

In another way, the United States position is less favorable to government employees. Firstly, it has validated legislation by which those employed by government are forbidden from, among other things, run for political office or actively participate in partisan political activity. This was held valid, although it could apply to a vast array of employees, even those whose personal political views could have no bearing on the manner in which they did their job.[84]

This outcome should be contrasted with the European Court of Human Rights decision in *Vogt v Germany.*[85] In that case Vogt, a teacher, was dismissed when her employer discovered she was a member of a political party, held various roles within it, and had run for office as a political candidate. The Court found her dismissal infringed her freedom of expression. The restriction was overbroad, applicable to employees regardless of rank. There was no evidence that Vogt's political views made her unable to discharge her duties, or had compromised her ability to do so.

The other area in which Europe appears to be noticeably more willing to protect freedom of speech is in relation to protection of the media. The first context is the confidentiality of journalists' sources. In several cases the European Court has protected such confidentiality when the state has sought to know the source/s from which a publication was derived.[86] In *Roemen* the Court found that a raid on a journalist's premises in order to discover the source of information used by the journalist in an article critical of a government minister breached the journalist's freedom of expression rights, and was not justified. The Court noted that protecting the confidentiality of journalists' sources protected a cornerstone of a free press. It noted that without such protection, people may not be willing to assist the press. As a result, the ability of the press to perform its watchdog role could be compromised.[87] The Court agreed in *Tillack*, noting that the confidentiality of journalists' sources must be treated with "utmost caution." Further, it was irrelevant whether the journalist obtained the information in question through lawful or unlawful means.[88] In Canada, even in pre-*Charter* days, the Court was also very protective of the media, including in relation to the confidentiality of journalists' sources.[89]

In sharp contrast is the decision of the United States Supreme Court in *Branzburg v Hayes*.[90] In that case journalists argued that the *First Amendment* protected the confidentiality of their sources, and refused to comply with a grand jury request to testify as to the sources of information they had used to write articles about drug taking within a community. A majority said that journalists were required to comply with such a subpoena, because government had an important interest in law enforcement to protect the community. It rejected an argument that if journalists were required to divulge confidential sources, their ability to do their job would be compromised. The majority found that such a claim was, at best speculative,[91] and they cast doubt on the extent to which the flow of information from informants to reporters would in fact be chilled by the fact that reporters may be called to answer questions before a grand jury.[92] Strongly worded dissents by Douglas Stewart Brennan and Marshall JJ were extremely concerned that the press would be hampered in fulfilling its essential role within a democracy if the confidentiality of sources could not be guaranteed.

The other somewhat surprising instance of this relates to reporting about prisons. In *Houchins v KQED Inc*[93] a majority denied the press a right to access a prison facility in order to take footage and to report on conditions in the jail. A majority of the Court found that the *First Amendment* was not implicated, on the basis that it did not found a right to access sources of information within government control. Similarly in the Australian High Court decision in *Wotton v Queensland*,[94] the Court validated a legislative provision under which a prisoner was granted parole on various conditions, including that he would not speak with the media. The Court found this measure was not inconsistent with the implied freedom of political communication.

In sharp contrast is the decision of the House of Lords in *R v Secretary of State for the Home Department; Ex Parte Simms* where the Court ordered that the media have access to prisoners.[95] There the Court emphasized the important role the media could have in such a context, for example, by bringing to light human rights abuses or abuses of power.[96]

CONCLUSION

A comparison among the chosen jurisdictions have revealed a shared commitment to free speech. However, it was not a total surprise that the jurisdictions "draw the line" between legally defensible speech and legally indefensible speech in a different way. It is evident that, of all the jurisdictions studied, the United States protects freedom of speech the most. This is particularly evident in areas such as so-called hate speech, where the other jurisdictions studied have upheld bans on such speech that would not be upheld in the United States. These differences in outcomes are explained by important differences in the history of each of the different nations, and different cultures. There is an interesting difference in how the jurisdictions determine whether laws that impinge on free speech are valid or not. Most jurisdictions have adopted proportionality analysis, though they differ to some extent in how they go about this. The closest the United States came to this approach was when it adopted the so-called ad hoc balancing approach, but it has since re-asserted its category-based approach, where different rules are applied to different categories of speech. While this system certainly has its advantages, it is difficult to counter the inconsistency at the heart of *First Amendment* jurisprudence, where the Supreme Court consistently frowns upon content-based restrictions on speech, but then adopts an approach to considering validity which focuses on the content of the speech. However, both approaches have their merits and weaknesses. It is considered unlikely we will see a convergence of these approaches.

It has proven to be difficult for courts to resist the temptation to embark on the dangerous analysis of determining whether particular speech is "valuable" and protecting it in accordance with its perceived value. This tends to undercut democratic arguments about speech, that it is for all members of society to determine what is valuable to discuss. The risk is that judges might be influenced by their personal perception of what is valuable to discuss, which runs counter to majoritarian democratic arguments to support free speech, which most will defend, if not as an exclusive explicator of the scope of the right.

The United States, its *Bill of Rights* architect James Madison, and its Supreme Court decisions and academic jurisprudence, has provided brilliant intellectual leadership to the democratic world in terms of the *First Amendment*. That great democracy created the beacon of free society and freedom of thought which most jurisdictions recognized and sought to emulate only centuries later. That having been said, there were some contexts where, surprisingly, freedom of speech was protected to a greater extent in Europe than in the United States, specifically in relation to journalists and the confidentiality of their sources, and in the context of public sector employees, including the military.

Having set out the history and philosophical bases of free speech protection as succinctly as I can, having summarized the law of four jurisdictions as succinctly as I can, offered some reflection on the present law and compared across state lines, I turn now to consider freedom of speech in particularly difficult areas. These include regulation of so-called hate speech, the speech of government employees, speech in the University sector, and regulation of technology. My discussion of these appears in *Freedom of Speech in Practice: Controversial Applications of Law and Theory*. If history has taught us anything, it is that we must be eternally vigilant against those who would deny individuals the right to speak freely. While the context has changed over the centuries, this theme has never really gone away, and we consistently today hear calls for further regulation of speech that is argued to be "harmful." Mill may not recognize the Internet, but he surely would be acutely aware of the kinds of arguments about free speech versus harm that it sharpens. He would surely be disquieted by the growing use of "safe spaces" on University campuses. It is to a consideration of these very challenging issues, on which reasonable people have and will continue to disagree, that my attention now turns.

NOTES

1. Moshe Cohen-Eliya and Iddo Porat, "Proportionality and the Culture of Justification," *American Journal of Comparative Law* 59 (2011): 484.
2. *Otto-Preminger-Institut v Austria* [1994] ECHR 352.
3. *Murphy v Ireland* [2003] ECHR 352.
4. *Employment Division, Department of Human Resources of Oregon v Smith* 494 US 872 (1990). This case overturned a previous requirement that a law impacting religion had to be justified by a "compelling interest" (i.e., strict scrutiny): *Sherbert v Verner* 374 US 398 (1963). Some states subsequently legislated to re-introduce the compelling justification test for laws impacting freedom of religion. A federal attempt to do so was ruled constitutionally invalid: *City of Boerne v Flores, Archbishop of San Antonio* 521 US 507 (1997).
5. *Stoll v Switzerland* [2007] ECHR 1060, [155].

6. Richard Pildes, "Avoiding Balancing: The Role of Exclusionary Reasons in Constitutional Law," *Hastings Law Journal* 45 (1994): 719.

7. 722.

8. *SAS v France* [2014] ECHR 341.

9. Robert Alexy *A Theory of Constitutional Rights* (Oxford University Press, Oxford, 2002).

10. Mattias Kumm, "The Idea of Socratic Contestation and the Right to Justification: The Point of Rights-Based Proportionality Review," *Law and Ethics of Human Rights* 4 (2010): 157.

11. Moshe Cohen-Eliya and Iddo Porat, "Proportionality and the Culture of Justification," *American Journal of Comparative Law* 59 (2011): 485 refers to a "European organic and perfectionist conception of rights and of the state, which is different from the classic American belief in state neutrality. Europeans, especially Germans, do not regard the state as merely an aggregation of individuals who live in given territory and coordinate their activities by means of the state, but instead as a union of people who have a shared system of values and endeavour to promote them. Rather than subscribing to the atomized conception of the self, European political theory generally rejects the notion of the separateness of the person and emphasizes the role of the person within the community that shares common values and that expresses solidarity towards all members. This organic conception of the state is based on a premise of reciprocal cooperation among all state organs. Rather than operating as side constraints on government power, which is based on the view that government is antagonistic to the individual, such conception views rights as standing for shared values which need be optimized."

12. Moshe Cohen-Eliya and Iddo Porat, "The Hidden Foreign Law Debate in Heller: The Proportionality Approach in American Constitutional Law," *San Diego Law Review* 46 (2009): 395–398.

13. 390.

14. 392.

15. Konrad Hesse, *Grandzuge Des Verfassungsrechts Der Bundesrepublik Deutchland* (Legal Verl, Mueller, 1988) 851.

16. Robert Alexy, *A Theory of Constitutional Rights* (Oxford University Press, Oxford, 2002) 66.

17. *Reference re Secession of Quebec* [1988] 2 S.C.R. 217, 292: "the constitution is more than a written text. It embraces the entire global system of rules and principles which govern the exercise of constitutional authority," and "no single principle can be defined in isolation from the others, nor does anyone principle trump or exclude the operation of any other" (248).

18. Richard Pildes, "Avoiding Balancing: The Role of Exclusionary Reasons in Constitutional Law," *Hastings Law Journal* 45 (1994): 744.

19. It should also be noted that American constitutional law embraces concepts of proportionality in contexts other than the *First Amendment*: Vicki Jackson, "Constitutional Law in an Age of Proportionality," *Yale Law Journal* 124 (2015): 3104–3110.

20. Moshe Cohen-Eliya and Iddo Porat, "The Hidden Foreign Law Debate in *Heller*: The Proportionality Approach in American Constitutional Law," *San Diego Law Review* 46 (2009): 369; and at 380: "this proportionality model has been embraced by judges in almost every Western jurisdiction outside of the Unites States, becoming one of the clearest features of global constitutionalism."

21. Frederick Schauer, "Categories and the *First Amendment*: A Play in Three Acts," *Vanderbilt Law Review* 34 (1981): 287: "the refusal to categorise is frightfully counter-intuitive."

22. *Snyder v Phelps* 562 US 443 (2011) (the Court noted that political speech was entitled to the highest protection); *McIntyre v Ohio Elections Commission* 514 US 334, 347 (1995): "when a law burdens core political speech, we apply 'exacting scrutiny,' and we uphold the restriction only if it is narrowly tailored to serve an overriding state interest."

23. Canadian case law also considers the forum in which the relevant speech occurred: *The Queen in Right of Canada v Committee for the Commonwealth of Canada and Others* [1991] 1 S.C.R. 139, 198. Apart from a couple of isolated judgments (e.g., *Australian Capital Television Pty Ltd v Commonwealth* (1992) 177 CLR 106, 235 (McHugh J)), the Australian law does not

typically view the question of the nature of the forum used to be relevant to its free speech analysis.

24. Frederick Schauer, "Categories and the *First Amendment*: A Play in Three Acts," *Vanderbilt Law Review* 34 (1981): 304: "discretion-limiting rules have traditionally provided far more in the way of *First Amendment* protection than has particularized balancing."

25. Vicki Jackson, "Constitutional Law in an Age of Balancing," *Yale Law Journal* 124 (2015): 3099–3100: "structured proportionality in . . . Canada, Germany (or elsewhere) includes an additional stage—proportionality as such—asking whether the intrusion on the challenger's rights can be justified by the benefits towards achieving the important public goal. This step calls for an independent judicial evaluation of whether the reasons offered by the government, relative to the limitation on rights, are sufficient to justify the intrusion. While this step is sometimes referred to as involving 'balancing,' the proportionality as such question in structured proportionality differs from balancing tests that tend to focus primarily on quantification of net social good, as in Dennis v United States . . . proportionality as such is a part of a doctrine that . . . prioritizes the right, putting the burden of justification on the government. In this respect structured proportionality differs from . . . United States striking a balance case law." She also points out that with proportionality analysis in Canada and Europe, laws will have been already knocked out prior to any balancing if the government interest in the type of law passed is insufficient, or if the rationale or means chosen are insufficient (3100).

26. *Communist Party v Subversive Activities Control Board* 367 US 1, 164–166 (1961) (Black J, dissenting); *Beauharnais v Illinois* 343 US 250, 275 (1952) (Douglas J, dissenting).

27. However, as Frederick Schauer points out, American law contains vast swarthes of content-based regulation of speech, including securities legislation, antitrust legislation, labor relations legislation, Uniform Commercial Code, the law of fraud, conspiracy, and the law of evidence, none of which have been found to raise serious *First Amendment* issues: "The Boundaries of the *First Amendment*: A Preliminary Exploration of Constitutional Salience," *Harvard Law Review* 117 (2004): 1768.

28. Wayne Batchis, "On the Categorical Approach to Free Speech—And the Protracted Failure to Delimit the True Threats Exception to the *First Amendment*," *Pace Law Review* 37 (2016): 14.

29. Mosie Cohen-Eliya and Iddo Porat, "Proportionality and the Culture of Justification," *American Journal of Comparative Law* 59 (2011): 463. Those authors trace proportionality to the bitter experience of World War II, where fledgling democracies fell victim to ruthless dictatorships who subverted the popular will. They say that proportionality is a natural response to the kind of dangerous populism whipped up by demagoguery in the 1930s (483). While this might explain why proportionality was adopted as part of the structure of the European Convention on Human Rights, obviously it does not explain the concept of proportionality itself, which was apparently developed in the 19th century in (then) Prussian administrative law.

30. This was explicitly noted by the Australian High Court in *McCloy v New South Wales* (2015) 257 CLR 178, 195–196 (French CJ Kiefel Bell and Keane JJ).

31. Dieter Grimm, "Proportionality in Canadian and German Constitutional Jurisprudence," *University of Toronto Law Journal* 57 (2007): 384.

32. Alec Stone Sweet and Jud Mathews, "Proportionality Balancing and Global Constitutionalism," *Columbia Journal of Transnational Law* 47 (2008): 163.

33. Kathleen Sullivan, "Post-Liberal Judging: The Roles of Categorisation and Balancing," *University of Colorado Law Review* 63 (1992): 306; Kathleen Sullivan, "Foreword: The Justices of Rules and Standards," *Harvard Law Review* 106 (1992): 22.

34. Moshe Cohen-Eliya and Iddo Porat, "Proportionality and the Culture of Justification," *American Journal of Comparative Law* 59 (2011): 466.

35. Daniel Farber, "The Categorical Approach to Protecting Speech in American Constitutional Law," *Indiana Law Journal* 84 (2009): 932: "rules have the advantage of providing clearer guidance for both lower courts and the public. Because they leave less room for discretion, they also provide less of a toehold for subjective biases. These advantages may be particularly important in *First Amendment* litigation. In cases involving free expression, we have particular reason to want to avoid having the judges' ideological biases enter the decision, lest those biases then have a distorting effect on public discourse."

36. Frederick Schauer, "Categories and the *First Amendment*: A Play in Three Acts," *Vanderbilt Law Review* 34 (1981): 277: "freedom of speech need not have any one "essential" feature. It is much more likely a bundle of interrelated principles sharing no common set of necessary and sufficient defining characteristics. It is quite possible that the protection of political discussion and criticism, the aversion to censorship of art, and the desire to retain open inquiry in science and other academic disciplines for example are principles not reducible to any one common core."

37. Justice Scalia identified six advantages of what he called "rules" (equivalent to a categories approach) over "standards" (equivalent to a proportionality approach): consistency and the perception of consistency, uniformity, predictability, judicial restraint, judicial protection from popular disapproval, and separation of law from facts: "The Rule of Law as a Law of Rules," *University of Chicago Law Review* 56 (1989): 1175.

38. John Ely, "Flag Desecration: A Case Study in the Roles of Categorisation and Balancing in *First Amendment* Analysis," *Harvard Law Review* 88 (1975): 1501: "where messages are proscribed because they are dangerous, balancing tests inevitably become intertwined with the ideological dispositions of those doing the balancing—or if not that, at least with the relative confidence or paranoia of the age in which they are doing it."

39. Daniel Farber, "The Categorical Approach to Protecting Speech in American Constitutional Law," *Indiana Law Journal* 84 (2009): 921 uses the example of allegedly subversive speech. He says that while at one time balancing was used, when the court in *Brandenburg v Ohio* set up the categorical rule that such speech could only be punished if it were likely to incite imminent lawless action, and to have this effect, speech was much more protected than it had been, and prosecutions in this area practically ceased. He concludes that "this is one area where the categorical approach has been highly successful as a method for protecting speech . . . from the first Adams administration through the early Cold War period, political dissidents faced considerable risk of prosecution for criticizing the government during crisis periods . . . by announcing a clear, rule-based test, the Court decisively shut the door on a historic pattern of abusive government regulation."

40. T Alexander Aleinikoff, "Constitutional Law in the Age of Balancing," *Yale Law Journal* 96 (1987): 991–992: "balancing undermines the checking and validating functions of constitutional law . . . ultimately the notion of constitutional supremacy hangs in the balance. For under a regime of balancing, a constitutional judgment no longer looks like a trump. It seems merely to be a card of a higher value in same suit."

41. Further, it is possible that a jurisdiction which adopts proportionality analysis also makes the distinction between content-based and content-neutral laws. This distinction is made in Australian law, but that country also applies proportionality analysis.

42. *Irwin Toy Ltd v Quebec* [1989] 1 S.C.R. 927, 976; *Hogan v Hinch* (2011) 243 CLR 506, 555.

43. Clay Calvert, "Beyond Headlines and Holdings: Exploring Some Less Obvious Ramifications of the Supreme Court's 2017 Free-Speech Rulings," *William and Mary Bill of Rights Journal* 26 (2018): 916: "proportionality is embraced by courts in other nations, but not by the United States Supreme Court."

44. Benjamin Pomerance, "An Elastic Amendment: Justice Stephen G Breyer's Fluid Conceptions of Freedom of Speech," *Albany Law Review* 79 (2016): 506.

45. Moshe Cohen-Eliya and Iddo Porat, "Proportionality and the Culture of Justification," *American Journal of Comparative Law* 59 (2011): 466.

46. Wayne Batchis, "On the Categorical Approach to Free Speech—And the Protracted Failure to Delimit the True Threats Exception to the *First Amendment*," *Pace Law Review* 37 (2016): 54.

47. "Absolute rules would inevitably lead to absolute exceptions, and such exceptions would inevitably corrode the rules. The demands of free speech in a democratic society as well as the interest in national security are better served by candid and informed weighing of the competing interests, within the confines of the judicial process, than by announcing dogmas too inflexible for the non-Euclidean problems to be solved": *Dennis v United States* 341 US 494, 505 (1951) (Frankfurter J).

48. *New York v Ferber* 458 US 747 (1982).

49. Vicki Jackson, "Constitutional Law in an Age of Proportionality," *Yale Law Journal* 124 (2015): 3142; Alec Stone Sweet and Jud Mathews, "Proportionality Balancing and Global Constitutionalism," *Columbia Journal of Transnational Law* 47 (2008): 72.

50. Wallace Mendelson, "On the Meaning of the *First Amendment*: Absolutes in the Balance," *California Law Review* 50 (1962): 825–826: "open balancing compels a judge to take full responsibility for (their) decisions and promises a particularized, rational account of how (they) arrives at them—more particularized and more rational at least than the familiar parade of hallowed abstractions, elastic absolutes and selective history. Moreover, this approach should make it more difficult for judges to rest on their predispositions without ever subjecting them to the test of reason. It should also make their accounts more rationally auditable."

51. Aharon Barak, "Proportionality and Principled Balancing," *Law and Ethics of Human Rights* 4 (2010): 15.

52. Moshie Cohen-Eliya and Iddo Porat, "The Hidden Foreign Law Debate in *Heller*: The Proportionality Approach in American Constitutional Law," *San Diego Law Review* 46 (2009): 380.

53. Mattias Kumm, "The Idea of Socratic Contestation and the Right to Justification: The Point of Rights-Based Proportionality Review," *Law and Ethics of Human Rights* 4 (2010): 163.

54. Janet Hiebert, "New Constitutional Ideas: Can New Parliamentary Models Resist Judicial Dominance When Interpreting Rights?" *Texas Law Review* 82 (2004): 1970; Janet Hiebert, "Parliamentary Bills of Rights: An Alternative Model?" *Modern Law Review* 69 (2006): 7; Janet Hiebert, *Charter Conflicts: What is Parliament's Role?* (McGill-Queen's University Press, Montreal, 2002). The European Court of Human Rights noted with disapproval the lack of evidence that the United Kingdom Parliament had undertaken any proportionality analysis in its prisoner voting ban struck out in *Hirst v United Kingdom* (No2)[2005] ECHR 681, [79].

55. Moshe Cohen-Eliya and Iddo Porat, "Proportionality and the Culture of Justification," *American Journal of Comparative Law* 59 (2011): 474–476.

56. Mattias Kumm, "The Idea of Socratic Contestation and the Right to Justification: The Point of Rights-Based Proportionality Review," *Law and Ethics of Human Rights* 4 (2010): 163.

57. *Near v Minnesota* 283 US 697 (1971) found that while generally such a system would not be permissible, it might be acceptable during a time of war, to enforce decency standards, or to preserve public safety.

58. *Chauvy and Others v France* [2004] ECHR 295, [66].

59. *Saumur v City of Quebec* [1953] 2 SCR 299.

60. *Attorney-General (SA) v Corporation of the City of Adelaide* (2013) 249 CLR 1.

61. Frederick Schauer, "The Boundaries of the *First Amendment*: A Preliminary Explanation of Constitutional Salience," *Harvard Law Review* 117 (2004): 1786: "if there exists a single theory that can explain the *First Amendment*'s coverage, it has not yet been found."

62. *Irwin Toy Ltd v Quebec* [1989] 1 S.C.R. 927, 976.

63. *Edmonton Journal v Attorney-General of Alberta and Canada* [1989] 2 S.C.R. 1326. The Australian High Court has not articulated which, of any, of the purposes of free speech underpin the Australian version of the freedom.

64. Frederick Schauer appears to support doing so: "Categories and the *First Amendment*: A Play in Three Acts," *Vanderbilt Law Review* 34 (1981): 293: "a subcategory must have some relationship to a permissible first amendment purpose . . . it should be apparent here that offensiveness simpliciter as a category is hardly consistent with most of the antimajoritarian premises of the *First Amendment*."

65. Frederick Schauer, "The Boundaries of the *First Amendment*: A Preliminary Exploration of Constitutional Salience," *Harvard Law Review* 117 (2004): 1785–1786: "none of the existing normative accounts appears to explain descriptively much of, let alone most of, the *First Amendment*'s existing inclusions and exclusions . . . if there exists a single theory that can explain the *First Amendment*'s coverage, it has not yet been found."

66. Frederick Schauer, "Categories and the *First Amendment*: A Play in Three Acts," *Vanderbilt Law Review* 34 (1981): 283 refers to the "extreme reluctance to assign differing values to the speech that is covered by the *First Amendment*. The works of Shakespeare have the same

First Amendment value as Playboy, which in turn has the same First Amendment value as wearing a black armband or arguing for the virtues of Nazism"; and at 295–296: "we must guard against the pressure to create subcategories that will leave to judges in a particular case the determination of either the truth or the social utility of a covered communicative act." Daniel Farber, "The Categorical Approach to Protecting Speech in American Constitutional Law," *Indiana Law Journal* 84 (2009): 935 refers to the "scepticism about the ability of anyone other than the individual listener to assess the value of speech."

67. "Categories and the *First Amendment*: A Play in Three Acts," *Vanderbilt Law Review* 34 (1981): 287: "when statements of fact are concerned . . . many of the sceptical presuppositions of the *First Amendment* are either irrelevant or highly attenuated . . . it may be that appropriate categories could recognize the differences in the extent to which *First Amendment* principles are applicable to the variety of speech acts, of which advocacy and factual description are but two."

68. European case law protects "value judgments" more strongly, not requiring someone making such a judgment to prove the veracity of their claims. It is sufficient in such cases for the person to show there was some reasonable basis for their judgment. In the realm of fact, it will be sufficient if the statements were made in good faith: *Schwabe v Austria* [1992] ECHR 56, [34].

69. *Garaudy v France* [2003](Application No. 65831/01).

70. *Jersild v Denmark* [1994] ECHR 33, [35].

71. *Zdanoka v Latvia* [2006] ECHR 994.

72. *Farrakhan v Secretary of State for the Home Department* [2002] QB 1391; *R (Ngole) v University of Sheffield* [2017] EWHC 2669 (Admin).

73. *R (BBC) v Justice Secretary* [2013] 1 WLR 964, 983.

74. *R.A.V. v St Paul* 505 US 377 (1992); *Virginia v Black* 538 US 343 (2003).

75. *Dennis v United States* 341 US 494 (1951).

76. *Brandenburg v Ohio* 395 US 444 (1969).

77. *FCC v Pacifica Foundation et al* 438 US 726, 745 (1978).

78. [1990] 3 S.C.R. 697.

79. *R v Sharkey* (1949) 79 CLR 121; *Burns v Ransley* (1949) 79 CLR 101.

80. Eg s18C *Racial Discrimination Act 1991* (Cth).

81. *Australian Communist Party v Commonwealth* (1951) 83 CLR 1.

82. [1997] ECHR 93.

83. 417 US 733 (1974).

84. *United Public Workers v Mitchell* 330 US 75 (1947); *United States v National Treasury Employees Union* 513 US 454 (1995).

85. [1996] ECHR 106.

86. *Roemen v Luxembourg* [2003] ECHR 102; *Goodwin v United Kingdom* [1996] ECHR 16, [45]; *Cumpana and Mazare v Romania* [2004] ECHR 692, [106]; *Tillack v Belgium* [2008] ECHR 1901, [53].

87. [46].

88. *Tillack v Belgium* [2008] ECHR 1901, [65].

89. *In the Matter of Three Bills Passed by the Legislative Assembly of Alberta* [1938] S.C.R. 100. The matter has not been considered by the Australian High Court to date.

90. 408 US 665 (1972).

91. 694 (Burger CJ White Blackmun Powell and Rehnquist JJ).

92. 695 (Burger CJ White Blackmun Powell and Rehnquist JJ).

93. 438 US 1 (1978).

94. (2012) 246 CLR 1.

95. [2000] 2 AC 115.

96. 126 (Lord Steyn, with whom Lord Browne-Wilkinson and Lord Hoffmann agreed).

References

Aleinikoff, T Alexander, "Constitutional Law in the Age of Balancing," *Yale Law Journal* 96 (1987): 943–1005.

Alexander, Lawrence, and Horton, Paul, "The Impossibility of a Free Speech Principle," *Northwestern University Law Review* 78 (1984): 1319–1358.

Alexy, Robert, *A Theory of Constitutional Rights* (Oxford University Press, Oxford, 2002).

Allan, TRS, "Human Rights and Judicial Review: A Critique of Due Deference," *Cambridge Law Journal* 65 (2006): 671–695.

Aroney, Nicholas, "Towards the Best Explanation of the Constitution: Text, Structure, History and Principle in *Roach v Electoral Commissioner*," *University of Queensland Law Journal* 30 (2011): 145–164.

Aroney, Nicholas, "A Seductive Plausibility: Freedom of Speech in the Constitution," *University of Queensland Law Journal* 18 (1995): 249–274.

Baker, Edwin, "Freedom of Speech," *UCLA Law Review* 25: 964–1040.

Baker, Edwin, "Autonomy and Free Speech," *Constitutional Commentary* 27 (2011): 251–282.

Barendt, Eric, *Freedom of Speech* (Clarendon Press, Oxford, 2nd ed, 2005).

Barendt, Eric, "Freedom of Expression in the United Kingdom Under the *Human Rights Act 1998*," *Indiana Law Journal* 84 (2009): 851–866.

Batchis, Wayne, "On the Categorical Approach to Free Speech—And the Protracted Failure to Delimit the True Threats Exception to the *First Amendment*," *Pace Law Review* 37 (2016): 1–54.

Bentham, Jeremy, *A Fragment on Government* (Cambridge University Press, Cambridge, 1988).

Berlin, Isaiah, *Four Essays on Liberty* (Oxford University Press, London, 1969).

BeVier, Lillian, "The First Amendment and Political Speech: An Inquiry into the Substance and Limits of Principle," *Stanford Law Review* 30 (1978): 299–358.

Bharak, Aharaon, "Proportionality and Principled Balancing," *Law and Ethics of Human Rights* 4 (2010): 1–18.

Bickel, Alexander, *The Morality of Consent* (Yale University Press, New Haven, 1975).

Bird, Wendell, "Liberties of Press and Speech: 'Evidence Does not Exist to Contradict' the . . . Blackstonian Sense in Late 18th Century England," *Oxford Journal of Legal Studies* 36(1) (2016): 1–25.

Bird, Karen, "Racist Speech or Free Speech? A Comparison of the Law in France and the United States," *Comparative Politics* 32(4) (2000): 399–418.

Blackstone, William, *Commentaries on the Laws of England 1765–1769* (Clarendon Press, Oxford, 1768).

Blasi, Vincent, "Milton's Areopagitica and the Modern *First Amendment*" (*Yale Law School Occasional Papers*, Paper No. 6, 1995).

Blasi, Vincent, "Reading Abrams Through the Lens of Schauer," *Notre Dame Law Review* 72 (1997): 1343–1360.

Blocher, Joseph, "Institutions in the Marketplace of Ideas," *Duke Law Journal* 57 (2008): 821–890.

Bogen, David, "The Origins of Freedom of Speech and Press," *Maryland Law Review* 42 (1983): 429–465.

Bollinger, Lee, "Free Speech and Intellectual Values," *Yale Law Journal* 92 (1983): 438–474.

Bork, Robert, "Neutral Principles and Some *First Amendment* Problems," *Indiana Law Journal* 47 (1971): 1–35.

Boyle, Kevin, "The Danish Cartoons," *Netherlands Quarterly of Human Rights* 24 (2006): 185–192.

Brant, Irving, "Seditious Libel: Myth and Reality," *New York University Law Review* 39 (1964): 1–19.

Brems, Eva, "State Regulation of Xenophobia Versus Individual Freedoms: The European View," *Journal of Human Rights* 1(4) (2002): 481–500.

Brietzke, Paul, "How and Why the Marketplace of Ideas Fails," *Valparaiso University Law Review* 31 (1997): 951–970.

Bush, Darren, "The 'Marketplace of Ideas': Is Judge Posner Chasing Don Quixote's Windmills?" *Arizona State Law Journal* 32 (2000): 1107–1148.

Buss, William, "Constitutional Words About Words: Protected Speech and Fighting Words Under the Australian and American Constitutions," *Transnational Law and Contemporary Problems* 15 (2006): 489–514.

Calvert, Clay, "Beyond Headlines and Holdings: Exploring Some Less Obvious Ramifications of the Supreme Court's 2017 Free Speech Rulings," *William and Mary Bill of Rights Journal* 26: 899–938.

Calvert, Clay, and Bunker, Matthew, "Fissures, Fractures and Doctrinal Shifts: Paying the Price in First Amendment Jurisprudence for a Half Decade of Avoidance, Minimalism and Partisanship," *William and Mary Bill of Rights Journal* 24 (2016): 943–994.

Cameron, Jamie, "The Original Conception of Section 1 and its Demise: A Comment on *Irwin Toy Ltd v Attorney-General of Quebec*," *McGill Law Journal* 35 (1990): 253–277.

Cameron, Jamie, "The Past, Present and Future of Expressive Freedom Under the *Charter*," *Osgoode Hall Law Journal* 35 (1997): 1–74.

Campbell, Tom, and Sadurski, Wojciech, ed., *Freedom of Communication* (Aldershot, England, 1994).

Campbell, Tom, and Crilly, Stephen, "The Implied Freedom of Political Communication: Twenty Years On," *University of Queensland Law Journal* 30 (2011): 59–78.

Campbell, Tom, "Democracy, Human Rights and Positive Law," *Sydney Law Review* 16 (1994): 195–212.

Cass, Deborah, "Through the Looking Glass: The High Court and the Right to Speech," *Public Law Review* 4 (1993): 229–247.

Chafee, Zechariah, "Freedom of Speech in War Time," *Harvard Law Review* 32 (1919): 932–973.

Chesterman, Michael, *Freedom of Speech: A Delicate Plant* (Aldershot, Ashgate, 2000).

Chomsky, Noam, *Necessary Illusions: Thought Control in Democratic Societies* (CBC Enterprises, Montreal, 1989).

Coase, Ronald, "The Nature of the Firm," *Economica* 16(4) (1937): 386–405.

Cohen-Eliya, Moshe, and Porat, Iddo, "Proportionality and the Culture of Justification," *American Journal of Comparative Law* 59 (2011): 463–490.

Cohen-Eliya, Moshe, and Porat, Iddo, "The Hidden Foreign Law Debate in Heller: The Proportionality Approach in American Constitutional Law," *San Diego Law Review* 46 (2009): 367–414.

Colclough, David, *Freedom of Speech in Early Stuart England* (Cambridge University Press, Cambridge, 2005).

Collins, Anthony, *Discourse of Free Thinking* (Garland Publishing, New York, 1713).

Craig, Paul, *Public Law and Democracy in the United Kingdom and the USA* (Clarendon Press, Oxford, 1990).
Craig, Paul, and Rawlings, Richard, *Law and Administration in Europe* (Oxford University Press, Oxford, 2003).
Cramer, Frederick, "Bookburning and Censorship in Ancient Rome: A Chapter from the History of Freedom of Speech," *Journal of the History of Ideas* 6(2) 1945: 157–196.
Craven, Greg, "Original Intent and the Australian *Constitution*—Coming Soon to a Court Near You?" *Public Law Review* 1 (1990): 166–185.
Delgado, Richard, "Words That Wound: A Tort Action for Racial Insults, Epithets and Name Calling," *Harvard Civil Rights-Civil Liberties Law Review* 17 (1982): 133–182.
Dicey, Albert Vere, *An Introduction to the Study of the Law of the Constitution* (Macmillan, London, 1959).
Donaghue, Stephen, "The Clamour of Silent Constitutional Principles," *Federal Law Review* 24 (1996): 133–172.
DuVal, Benjamin, "Free Communication of Ideas and the Quest for Truth: Towards a Teleological Approach to *First Amendment* Adjudication," *George Washington Law Review* 41 (1972): 161.
Ely, John Hart, *Democracy and Distrust: A Theory of Judicial Review* (Harvard University Press, Cambridge, 1980).
Ely, John, "Flag Desecration: A Case Study in the Roles of Categorisation and Balancing in First Amendment Analysis," *Harvard Law Review* 88 (1975): 1482–1509.
Emerson, Thomas, "Towards a General Theory of the *First Amendment*," *Yale Law Journal* 72 (1963): 877–956.
Emerton, Patrick, "Political Freedoms and Entitlements in the Australian Constitution—An Example of Referential Intentions Yielding Unintended Legal Consequences," *Federal Law Review* 38 (2010): 169.
Estlund, Cynthia, "Speech on Matters of Public Concern: The Perils of an Emerging *First Amendment* Category," *George Washington Law Review* 59 (1990): 1.
Eule, Julian, and Varat, Jonathan, "Transporting *First Amendment* Norms to the Private Sector: With Every Wish There Comes a Curse," *UCLA Law Review* 45 (1998): 1537–1634.
Evans, Carolyn Maree, *Legal Protection of Religious Freedoms in Australia* (Federation Press, Sydney, 2012).
Farber, Daniel, "The Categorical Approach to Protecting Speech in American Constitutional Law," *Indiana Law Journal* 84 (2009): 917–938.
Finley, Moses, *Democracy Ancient and Modern* (Rutgers University Press, New Jersey, 1985).
Flauss, Jean-Francois, "The European Court of Human Rights and the Freedom of Expression," *Indiana Law Journal* 84 (2008): 809–850.
Fraser, Andrew, "False Hopes, Implied Rights and Popular Sovereignty in the Australian Constitution," *Sydney Law Review* 16 (1994): 213–227.
Freund, Paul, *On Understanding the Supreme Court* (Greenwood Press, Connecticut, 1950).
Geddis, Andrew, "Free Speech Martyrs or Unreasonable Threats to Social Peace—'Insulting' Expression and Section 5 of the *Public Order Act 1986*," *Public Law* [2004]: 853.
Goldsworthy, Jeffrey, "Originalism in Constitutional Interpretation," *Federal Law Review* 25 (1997): 1–50.
Goldsworthy, Jeffrey, "Constitutional Implications and Freedom of Speech: A Reply to Stephen Donaghue," *Monash University Law Review* 23 (1997): 362–374.
Goldsworthy, Jeffrey, "Constitutional Implications Revisited," *University of Queensland Law Journal* 30 (2011): 9–34.
Gray, Anthony, *Criminal Due Process and Chapter III of the Australian Constitution* (Federation Press, Sydney, 2016).
Gray, Anthony, "The First Amendment to the United States Constitution and the Implied Freedom of Political Communication in Australia," *Common Law World Review* 47(3)(2019): forthcoming.
Gray, Anthony, "Freedom of Association in the Australian Constitution and the Crime of Consorting," *University of Tasmania Law Review* 32(2) (2013): 149–183.

Gray, Anthony, "The Protection of Voting Equality in Australia," *Federal Law Review* 44(3)(2016): 557–585.
Gray, Anthony, *Vicarious Liability: Critique and Reform* (Hart Publishing, Oxford, 2018).
Greenawalt, Kent, "Free Speech Justifications," *Columbia Law Review* 89 (1989): 119–155.
Greenawalt, Kent, *Speech, Crime and the Use of Language* (Oxford University Press, New York, 1989).
Greenawalt, Kent, "Free Speech in the United States and Canada," *Law and Contemporary Problems* 55 (1992): 5–34.
Grimm, Dieter, "Proportionality in Canadian and German Constitutional Jurisprudence," *University of Toronto Law Journal* 57 (2007): 383–397.
Gunther, Gerald, "Learned Hand and the Origins of Modern *First Amendment* Doctrine: Some Fragments of History," *Stanford Law Review* 27 (1975): 719–774.
Hamburger, Phillip, "The Development of the Law of Seditious Libel and the Control of the Press," *Stanford Law Review* 37 (1985): 661–766.
Hamill, Sarah, "Of Malls and Campuses: The Regulation of University Campuses and Section 2(b) of the *Charter*," *Dalhousie Law Journal* 40 (2017): 157–188.
Hare, Ivan, and Weinstein, James, *Extreme Speech and Democracy* (Oxford University Press, New York, 2009).
Hay, David, "Contempt by Scandalising the Court: A Political History of the First Hundred Years," *Osgoode Hall Law Journal* 25 (1987): 431–484.
Heinze, Eric, "Viewpoint Absolutism and Hate Speech," *Modern Law Review* 69 (2006): 543–582.
Held, David, *Models of Democracy* (Stanford University Press, Stanford, 3rd ed 2006).
Helle, Steven, "Whither the Public's Right (Not) to Know—Milton, Malls and Multicultural Speech," *University of Illinois Law Review* (1991): 1077–1100.
Hesse, Konrad, *Grandzuge Des Verfassungsrechts Der Bundesrepublik Deutchland* (Mueller, Legal Verl., 1988).
Heyman, Steven, "Righting the Balance: An Inquiry into the Foundations and Limits of Freedom of Expression," *Boston University Law Review* 78 (1998): 1275–1392.
Hiebert, Janet, "New Constitutional Ideas: Can Parliamentary Models Resist Judicial Dominance When Interpreting Rights?" *Texas Law Review* 82 (2004): 1963–1988.
Hiebert, Janet, *Charter Conflicts: What is Parliament's Role?* (McGill-Queen's University Press, Montreal, 2002).
Hiebert, Janet, "Parliamentary Bills of Rights: An Alternative Model?" *Modern Law Review* 69 (2006): 7–28.
Hobbes, Thomas, *Leviathan* (Broadview Press, Ontario, 2005).
Hogg, Peter, *Constitutional Law in Canada* (Carswell, Ontario, Fifth Edition 2007).
Holdsworth, William, *A History of English Law* (Methuen, London, 1922).
Holmes, Oliver Wendel Jr., "The Path of the Law," *Harvard Law Review* 10 (1897): 457–478.
Huscroft, Grant, "The Constitutional and Cultural Underpinnings of Freedom of Expression: Lessons from the United States and Canada," *University of Queensland Law Journal* 25 (2001): 181–202.
Huscroft, Grant, "Romance, Realism and the Legitimacy of Implied Rights," *University of Queensland Law Journal* 30 (2011): 35–52.
Ingber, Stanley, "The Marketplace of Ideas: A Legitimizing Myth," *Duke Law Journal* (1984): 1–91.
Jackson, Vicki, "Constitutional Law in an Age of Proportionality," *Yale Law Journal* 124 (2015): 3094–3197.
Jackson, Thomas, and Jeffries, John, "Commercial Speech: Economic Due Process and the *First Amendment*," *Virginia Law Review* 65 (1979): 1–42.
Jay, Stewart, "The Creation of the *First Amendment* Right to Free Expression: From the Eighteenth Century to the Mid-Twentieth Century," *William Mitchell Law Review* 34 (2008): 773–1020.
Jowell, Jeffrey, "Judicial Deference: Servility, Civility or Institutional Capacity," *Public Law* [2003]: 592–601.

Kagan, Elena, "Private Speech, Public Purpose: The Role of Government Motive in *First Amendment* Doctrine," *University of Chicago Law Review* 63 (1996): 413–518.

Kahn, Robert, "Flemming Rose, the Danish Cartoon Controversy and the New European Freedom of Speech," *California Western International Law Journal* 40 (2010): 253–290.

Kahn, Robert, *Holocaust Denial and the Law: A Comparative Study* (Palgrave Macmillan, New York, 2004).

Kahn, Robert, "A Margin of Appreciation for Muslims—Viewing the Defamation of Religions Through *Otto-Preminger Institut v Austria*," *Charleston Law Review* 5 (2011): 401–456.

Kennett, Geoffrey, "Individual Rights, the High Court and the Constitution," *Melbourne University Law Review* 19 (1994): 581–614.

Kenyon, John, *The Stuart Constitution 1603–1688 Documents and Commentary* (Cambridge University Press, Cambridge, 1986).

Kirk, Jeremy, "Constitutional Implications from Representative Democracy," *Federal Law Review* 23 (1995): 37–76.

Kirk, Jeremy, "Constitutional Implications II: Doctrines of Equality and Democracy," *Melbourne University Law Review* 25 (2001): 24–57.

Koppelman, Andrew, "Veil of Ignorance: Tunnel Constructivism Free Speech Theory," *Northwestern University Law Review* 107: 647–730.

Kumm, Mattias, "The Idea of Socratic Contestation and the Right to Justification: The Point of Rights-Based Proportionality Review," *Law and Ethics of Human Rights* 4 (2010): 140–175.

Lee, HP, "The Australian High Court and Implied Fundamental Guarantees," *Public Law* [1993]: 606–624.

Lee, Cynthia, "Freedom of Speech in the Public Workforce: A Comment on the Public Concern Requirement," *California Law Review* 76 (1988): 1109–1146.

Levy, Leonard, *A Legacy of Suppression* (Harvard University Press, Cambridge, 1960).

Levy, Leonard, *Emergence of a Free Press* (Oxford University Press, New York, 1985).

Lindell, Geoffrey, *Future Directions in Australian Constitutional Law* (Federation Press, Sydney, 1994).

Locke, John, *An Essay Concerning Human Understanding* (Dent, London, 1959).

Locke, John, *Two Treatises of Government* (Cambridge University Press, Cambridge, 1960).

Londono, Patricia, Smith, ATH, and Eady, Justice, *Arlidge, Eady and Smith on Contempt* (Sweet and Maxwell, London, 5th ed., 2017).

McChesney, Fred, "A Positive Regulatory Theory of the *First Amendment*," *Connecticut Law Review* 20 (1988): 355–382.

McHugh, Michael, "The Law-Making Function of the Judicial Process—Part I," *Australian Law Journal* 62 (1988): 15–31.

Macpherson, C, *The Life and Times of Liberal Democracy* (Oxford University Press, Oxford, 1977).

Mackinnon, Catherine, *Only Words* (Harper Collins, London, 1993).

Madison, James, *The Writings of James Madison 1790–1802.*

Maitland, Frederic, *A Constitutional History of England* (Cambridge University Press, Cambridge, 1908).

Manchester, Colin, "A History of the Crime of Obscene Libel," *Journal of Legal History* 12 (1991): 36–57.

Massaro, Toni, "Significant Silences: Freedom of Speech in the Public Sector Workplace," *Southern California Law Review* 61 (1987): 1–78.

Matsuda, Mari, "Public Response to Hate Speech: Considering the Victim's Story," *Michigan Law Review* 87 (1989): 2320–2381.

Mayton, William, "Seditious Libel and the Lost Guarantee of a Freedom of Expression," *Columbia Law Review* 84 (1984): 91–142.

Meagher, Dan, "What is Political Communication? The Rationale and Scope of the Implied Freedom of Political Communication," *Melbourne University Law Review* 28 (2004): 438–473.

Meagher, Dan, "The Brennan Conception of the Implied Freedom: Theory, Proportionality and Deference," *University of Queensland Law Journal* 30 (2011): 119–134.

Meiklejohn, Alexander, "The *First Amendment* is an Absolute," *Supreme Court Review* (1961): 245–266.

Meiklejohn, Alexander, *Political Freedom: The Constitutional Powers of the People* (Oxford University Press, New York, 1960).

Meiklejohn, Alexander, *Free Speech and its Relation to Self-Government* (Harper Bros, New York, 1948).

Mendelson, Wallace, "On the Meaning of the *First Amendment*: Absolutes in the Balance," *California Law Review* 50 (1962): 821–828.

Meyerson, Denise, "The Legitimate Extent of Freedom of Expression," *University of Toronto Law Journal* 52 (2002): 331–348.

Mill, John Stuart, *Utilitarianism, On Liberty, Considerations on Representative Government* (Geraint Williams, ed., Everyman, London, 1910).

Milton, John, *Areopagitica* (Holland and Co, London, 1906).

Milton, John, *A Treatise of Civil Power in Ecclesiastical Causes* (London, 1659).

Milton, John, *True Religion, Heresie, Schism and Toleration* (London, 1673).

Montesquieu, Charles, *The Spirit of Laws* (Duncan, Robertson and Shaw, Glasgow, 1793).

Moon, Richard, *The Constitutional Protection of Freedom of Expression* (University of Toronto Press, Buffalo, 2000).

Moon, Richard, "Justified Limits on Free Expression: The Collapse of the General Approach to Limits on *Charter* Rights," *Osgoode Hall Law Journal* 40 (2002): 337–368.

Pannick, David, "Article 10 of the *European Convention on Human Rights*," *King's College Law Journal* 4 (1994): 44–51.

Patmore, Glenn, "Making Sense of Representative Democracy and the Implied Freedom of Political Communication in the High Court of Australia," *Griffith Law Review* 7 (1998): 97–123.

Pildes, Richard, "Avoiding Balancing: The Role of Exclusionary Reasons in Constitutional Law," *Hastings Law Journal* 45 (1994): 711–752.

Plato, *The Republic* (Benjamin Jowett trans, The Modern Library, New York, 1941).

Pomerance, Benjamin, "An Elastic Amendment: Justice Stephen G Breyer's Fluid Conceptions of Freedom of Speech," *Albany Law Review* 79 (2016): 403–508.

Popper, Karl, *Conjectures and Refutations: The Growth of Scientific Knowledge* (Routledge, London, 1989).

Post, Robert, "Meiklejohn's Mistake: Individual Autonomy and the Reform of Public Discourse," *University of Colorado Law Review* 64 (1993): 1109–1138.

Post, Robert, "Reconciling Theory and Doctrine in *First Amendment* Jurisprudence," *California Law Review* 88 (2000): 2353–2374.

Pound, Roscoe, "Interests of Personality Parts I and II," *Harvard Law Review* 28 (1915): 343–365, 445–456.

Pound, Roscoe, "The Scope and Purpose of Sociological Jurisprudence," *Harvard Law Review* 25 (1912): 489–516.

Quick, John, and Garran, Robert, *An Annotated Constitution of the Australian Commonwealth* (Angus and Robertson, Sydney, 1901).

Redish, Martin, "Value of Free Speech," *University of Pennsylvania Law Review* 130 (1982): 591–645.

Reed, O Lee, "A Free Speech Metavalue for the Next Millennium: Autonomy of Consciousness in First Amendment Theory and Practice," *American Business Law Journal* 35 (1997): 1–46.

Reid, Lord, "The Judge as Lawmaker," *Journal of the Society of Public Teachers* of Law 12 (1972): 22–29.

Rivers, Julian, "Proportionality and Variable Intensity of Review," *Cambridge Law Journal* 65 (2006): 174–207.

Roach, Kent, *The Supreme Court on Trial* (Irwin Law, Toronto, 2001).

Roach, Kent, "American Constitutional Theory for Canadians (And the Rest of the World)," *University of Toronto Law Journal* 52 (2002): 503–522.

Rosenberg, Norman, *Protecting the Best Men: An Interpretive History of the Law of Libel* (University of North Carolina Press, Chapel Hill, 1986).

Rude, George, *Paris and London in the Eighteenth Century* (Viking Press, New York, 1970).
Sadurski, Wojciech, *Freedom of Speech and its Limits* (Kluwer International Publishers, Boston, 1999).
Sadurski, Wojciech, "Offending With Impunity: Racial Vilification and Freedom of Speech," *Sydney Law Review* 14 (1992): 163–195.
Saxonhouse, Arlene, *Free Speech and Democracy in Ancient Athens* (Cambridge University Press, New York, 2006).
Scalia, Antonin, "The Rule of Law as a Law of Rules," *University of Chicago Law Review* 56 (1989): 1175–1188.
Scanlon, Thomas, "A Theory of Freedom of Expression," *Philosophy and Public Affairs* 1 (1972): 204–226.
Schauer, Frederick, "Uncoupling Free Speech," *Columbia Law Review* 92 (1992): 1321–1357.
Schauer, Frederick, *Free Speech: A Philosophical Enquiry* (Cambridge University Press, Cambridge, 1981).
Schauer, Frederick, "Is There a Right to Academic Freedom?" *University of Colorado Law Review* 77 (2006): 907–928.
Schauer, Frederick, "Categories and the *First Amendment*: A Play in Three Acts," *Vanderbilt Law Review* 34 (1981): 265–307.
Schauer, Frederick, "The Boundaries of the First Amendment: A Preliminary Exploration of Constitutional Salience," *Harvard Law Review* 117 (2004): 1765–1809.
Schofield, Henry, "Freedom of the Press in the United States," *Publications of the American Sociological Society* 9 (1914): 67.
Shientag, Bernard, "From Seditious Libel to Freedom of the Press," *Brooklyn Law Review* 11 (1942): 125–154.
Smith, Steven, "Skepticism, Tolerance and Truth in the Theory of Free Expression," *Southern California Law Review* 60: 651–730.
Smith, D Gordon, "Beyond 'Public Concern': New Free Speech Standards for Public Employees," *University of Chicago Law Review* 57 (1990): 249–278.
Solum, Lawrence, "Freedom of Communicative Action: A Theory of the *First Amendment* Freedom of Speech," *Northwestern University Law Review* 83 (1989): 54–135.
Stephen, James Fitzjames, *A Digest of the Criminal Law* (Macmillan, London, 1904).
Stokes, Michael, "Constitutional Commitments Not Original Intentions: Interpretation in the Freedom of Speech Cases," *Sydney Law Review* 16 (1994): 250–273.
Stone, Geoffrey, "Restrictions on Speech Because of its Content: The Peculiar Case of Subject-Matter Restrictions," *University of Chicago Law Review* 46 (1978): 81–115.
Stone, Adrienne, "The Limits of Constitutional Text and Structure: Standards of Review and the Freedom of Political Communication," *Melbourne University Law Review* 23 (1999): 668–708.
Stone, Adrienne, "Rights, Personal Rights and Freedoms: The Nature of the Freedom of Political Communication," *Melbourne University Law Review* 25 (2001): 374–417.
Stone, Adrienne, "Freedom of Political Communication, the *Constitution* and the Common Law," *Federal Law Review* 26 (1998): 219–258.
Sullivan, Kathleen, "Two Concepts of Freedom of Speech," *Harvard Law Review* 124 (2010): 143–177.
Sullivan, Kathleen, "Post-Liberal Judging: The Roles of Categorisation and Balancing," *University of Colorado Law Review* 63 (1992): 293–318.
Sullivan, Kathleen, "Foreword: the Justices of Rules and Standards," *American Journal of Comparative Law* 59 (2011): 463–490.
Sweet, Alec Stone, and Matthews, Jud, "Proportionality Balancing and Global Constitutionalism," *Columbia Journal of Transnational Law* 47 (2008): 72–164.
Taylor, Julie, "Human Rights Protection in Australia: Interpretive Provisions and Parliamentary Supremacy," *Federal Law Review* 32 (2004): 57–78.
Tham, Joo-Cheong, "Possible Constitutional Objections to the Powers to Ban Terrorist Organisations," *University of New South Wales Law Journal* 27 (2004): 482–523.
Tingley, Charles, "Reputation, Freedom of Expression and the Tort of Defamation in the United States and Canada: A Deceptive Polarity," *Alberta Law Review* 37 (1999): 620–647.

Trenchard, John, and Gordon, *Thomas Cato's Letters: Essays on Liberty, Civil and Religious* (Wilkins et al, London, 1733).

Tribe, Laurence, "Towards a Metatheory of Free Speech," *Southwestern University Law Review* 10 (1978): 237–246.

Tribe, Laurence, *American Constitutional Law* (Foundation Press, New York, 2nd edition 1988).

Tsesis, Alexander, "Free Speech Constitutionalism," *University of Illinois Law Review* (2015): 1015–1068.

Vance, Willis R, "Freedom of Speech and of the Press," *Minnesota Law Review* 2 (1918): 239–260.

Walker, Jack, "A Critique of the Elitist Theory of Democracy," *American Political Science Review* 60 (1966): 285–295.

Walker, Jeffrey, "A Poison in Ye Commonwealthe: Seditious Libel in Hanoverian London," *Anglo-American Law Review* 25 (1996): 341–366.

Weinberg, Jonathan, "Constitutional Protection of Commercial Speech," *Columbia Law Review* 82 (1982): 720–750.

Wellington, Harry, "On Freedom of Expression," *Yale Law Journal* 88 (1979): 1105–1142.

Wells, Michael, "Section 1983, the *First Amendment* and Public Employee Speech: Shaping the Right to Fit the Remedy (and Vice Versa)," *Georgia Law Review* 35 (2001): 939–1020.

Whitman, James, "Enforcing Civility and Respect: Three Societies," *Yale Law Journal* 109 (2000): 1279–1398.

Williams, George, *Human Rights under the Australian Constitution* (Oxford University Press, Melbourne, 2002).

Williams, George, "Sounding the Core of Representative Democracy: Implied Freedoms and Electoral Reform," *Melbourne University Law Review* 20 (1996): 848–870.

Williams, John, "Race, Citizenship and the Formation of the Australian *Constitution*: Andrew Inglis Clark and the *Fourteenth Amendment*," *Australian Journal of Politics and History* 42 (1996): 10–23.

Wolfson, Nicholas, "Free Speech Theory and Hateful Words," *University of Cincinnati Law Review* 60 (1991): 1–42.

Yanchukova, Elena, "Criminal Defamation and Insult Laws: An Infringement on the Freedom of Expression in European and Post-Communistic Jurisdictions," *Columbia Journal of Transnational Law* 41 (2003): 861–894.

Yassky, David, "Eras of the *First Amendment*," *Columbia Law Review* 91 (1991): 1699–1755.

Index

About the Author

Anthony Gray is a professor of law at the University of Southern Queensland, Australia. He has published approximately 130 refereed journal articles, including in leading Australian law journals, and journals in the United Kingdom, Canada, and the United States. He is primarily a constitutional lawyer, with a particular interest in human rights. This is the sixth academic book he has authored.

www.ingramcontent.com/pod-product-compliance
Ingram Content Group UK Ltd.
Pitfield, Milton Keynes, MK11 3LW, UK
UKHW041126071026
15587UKWH00009B/258

9 781498 581981